AMERICANS

AMERICANS

A Collision of Histories

*

EDWARD
COUNTRYMAN

HILL AND WANG

A DIVISION OF FARRAR, STRAUS AND GIROUX

NEW YORK

The maps on pages 24 and 25, from David J. Weber,
The Spanish Frontier in North America, published by
Yale University Press in 1992, are used by permission of
David J. Weber.

LIBRARY OF CONGRESS CATALOGING-IN-PUBLICATION DATA
Countryman, Edward.
Americans, a collision of histories / Edward Countryman.—1st
ed.
p.   cm.
Includes bibliographical references and index.
1. National characteristics, American. 2. United States—
Civilization—To 1783. 3. United States—Civilization—19th
century. 4. Group identity—United States—History. I. Title.
E169.1.C792   1996   306'.0973—dc20   95–47728 CIP

CONTENTS

MAPS

In history there are no control groups. There is no one to tell us what might have been. We weep over the might have been, but there is no might have been. There never was.

—CORMAC MCCARTHY

The joy of history lies in its telling, and in its relevance to current times and relationships.

—KATE BORNSTEIN

PREFACE

This book began with a chance encounter. On a summer evening late in the 1980s a young black man stopped me to ask for directions in the English town where I used to live. That was no surprise. Asian, African, Afro-Caribbean, black British, and white people all live in the neighborhood. His speech, however, was American, and I was delighted to hear it. I speak American too, despite my long time overseas, and he was just as glad to hear me. I walked him to the pub he was seeking and we talked a while before going our ways. Neither learned the other's name.

Our differences were great. He was from Texas; I still called myself a New Yorker. He was a serviceman from the nearby air base; I was a peace campaigner. He was African-American and I am white. In the poisoned racial atmosphere of the United States, that difference often cannot be overcome. Had we met in his native San Antonio or my native Albany or in Dallas, where I live now, we might have been polite, at best. We might have felt mutual suspicion, each representing danger to the other, especially on an open street at night. But in Royal Leamington Spa, Warwickshire, we felt what we had in common.

By then it was on my mind to attempt the theme of "being American" in historical terms. Writers have proposed many answers to that problem. There have been a distinctive "American character" and an "American political tradition." We have been "characteristically American" and a "people of plenty." One distinguished Cornell scholar when I was studying there in the late 1960s still thought he could trace an "American quest." But another was coming to see his conflicted, Janus-faced subjects as a "people of paradox."[1]

Beginning to address these large issues, I had been wondering for some time about the significance of the American Revolution in defining our

society and in releasing the nineteenth century's enormous burst of creative energy. I had been wondering as well what the price of that creativity was, and who paid it. My generation of historians had redefined
the Revolution, seeing it as profoundly disruptive and transforming. Our
goal had been to understand the complexities of how the United States
became a separate power and Americans a separate people in the world.[2]

The Revolution turned subjects of the British monarchy into citizens
of the American Republic. It fundamentally changed relationships of
power, authority, obligation, and subordination. The Revolution altered
how every person and every group of the time lived their lives. All sorts
of people affected the Revolution, and it affected them. The rising republic of George Washington was very different from the troubled colonies of George III. The Revolution was genuinely revolutionary.[3]

I began wanting to see where all these changes led. Using a teacher's
prerogative, I organized my courses around that problem, perhaps to my
students' puzzlement. I was trying to bring together current thinking
about the Revolution and the larger enterprise of American social historians who have worked on the seventeenth, eighteenth, and nineteenth
centuries. Students at Warwick, Cambridge, Yale, and now Southern
Methodist University all have endured my efforts.

Like lemmings, historians often rush toward the same cliff, and many
others were thinking along the same lines. My own first published attempt asked whether the Revolution made a difference in how people
with money to invest used it.[4] Shortly afterward Pauline Maier addressed
that same problem in "The Revolutionary Origins of the American Corporation."[5] Alfred Young was putting together an anthology to follow
the influential volume that he had edited in 1976. That earlier collection
is called *The American Revolution: Explorations in the History of American
Radicalism*. Its theme is internal struggle during the Revolution, and
Young's intent was to continue along that line.[6] His writers, however,
cared more about consequences than process in the new volume, *Beyond
the American Revolution*.[7] About the same time, Gordon Wood published
a book that promised to show "how a revolution transformed a monarchical society into a democratic one unlike any that had ever existed."[8]
He stretched the Revolution well into the nineteenth century, made
Andrew Jackson and Martin Van Buren actors in it, and turned Alexis
de Tocqueville into its most astute observer. Clearly, my own interest in
the Revolution's larger significance was one eddy in a powerful current.
The young republic's achievements had turned into a major problem of
historical understanding.

But something is missing from the current round of studies, with their stress on republicanism's American success. It is missing from accounts that would see us in terms of a single tradition or character, or in terms of a material abundance that many Americans never have enjoyed. For all my own willingness to employ Marxian ideas, it would be missing from an account framed solely in terms of social class.[9] Ideas derived from European experience do make sense in the American context, whether we speak of the Protestant east coast heritage, Catholicism in Louisiana and New Spain or Irish immigrant Boston, the republican political tradition, or Marx's attempt to understand how capitalist society emerged and works. Nonetheless, America is not just a "neo-Europe." It cannot be understood solely in terms of its white people and their own particular heritage. My encounter with that Texas airman has helped me (I believe) to identify why that is so and what its significance is.

The achievements of the young American Republic are undeniable. Fascinated intellectuals went to America during the early nineteenth century to see and report. Alexis de Tocqueville, Michel Chevalier, Frances Wright, Frances Kemble, Frances Trollope, Harriet Martineau, and Charles Dickens all did it and there were many others. Thinkers who never made the journey also addressed the problem of America. After the French Revolution collapsed into terror and tyranny, Friedrich von Gentz asked about the difference between it and the successful American Revolution. Half a century later Marx considered the meaning of the Civil War, wrote with admiration about Abraham Lincoln, and thought about going to America. Richard Wagner thought about it too. Neither went, though José Martí, Leon Trotsky, and Ho Chi Minh did go. Franz Kafka made the journey within his own wild and wonderful mind, aided only by travel brochures. So, horrified and fascinated, did the Spanish-Mexican-East German artist Josep Renau. To the present day, America never has ceased to compel the attention of foreign observers.

Americans got into the act too, most notably James Fenimore Cooper in his nonfictional *The American Democrat*.[10] What is perhaps the greatest achievement of mid-nineteenth-century American letters, Herman Melville's *Moby-Dick* may represent its author's attempt to come to terms with his own culture after a long time abroad. For all its literary merit, Melville's novel went almost unnoticed at its publication in 1851. One key to that epoch's other unnoticed triumph, Henry David Thoreau's *Walden*, is that it begins with its author's parody upon the theme of wandering and return. Foreign or American, traveler or stay-at-home, the more astute observers realized that Americans knew tragedy and loss as well as rising glory. That returns me to my chance encounter on an English summer night.

That black airman came from Texas. In all probability his ancestors had gone there as slaves in the mid-nineteenth century, torn from places they knew and people they loved. In cotton-growing East Texas they settled on land that had been a province of Mexico not long before and that Caddo Indians regarded as their own. To borrow the astute comment of an African-American student whom I taught in Dallas,[11] that airman *was* Texas. He *was* the South. To extend the point, he *was* America in all of the country's capacity to confuse and disrupt. So were the Lone Star State's Indians, Hispanics, and Anglos among whom he had grown up and among whom I now live.

On their way west, the ancestors of both that airman and my student probably passed through Mississippi. Counties there bear such names as Washington, Adams, Hancock, Jefferson, Lafayette, Madison, Warren, and, for that matter, Bolivar. The white people who founded those communities came from New England as well as from Virginia and the Carolinas. They intended those history-laden names to honor the revolutionaries, whose heirs they were. They honored another history too, with county names like Issaquena, Tunica, Pontotoc, Choctaw, and Yalobusha. We need not doubt their sincerity, in either case.

But all of those counties "became southern."[12] They turned into places of intense suffering for the people who transformed their wooded, often swampy soil into productive plantations. The Revolution, with its assertions about the equal unalienable rights of all men, may have thrown into sharp relief the contradiction between American slavery and American freedom. It may have been—it was—among the events that transformed slavery from a simple fact of life into a perceived moral abomination. It may have contributed—it did—to slavery's ultimate extinction. But the same American Revolution that set free the creative, expansive, liberating energy of the Republic's white people led to slavery's expansion and intensification for black ones. The same forces that freed my maternal ancestors to travel from overcrowded New England to the open prairies of Illinois and then back to New York State sent that airman's forebears on a very different journey.

Nor is that all. Both his ancestors and mine moved west onto soil that other people already had made their own. For the Illinois prairie to become the land of Abraham Lincoln, for the Black Belt, the Mississippi/ Yazoo Delta, and East Texas to become the Cotton Kingdom, required

that Indian people no longer use it their way. In 1830 it became government policy to force all Indians who lived east of the Mississippi to
go west of that river, whether or not they had taken to white ways,
whatever treaties had been made, whether they had fought for or against
the young republic in its wars. In practice, that policy was underway
well before the law was passed. Not all did go, but most were forced at
gunpoint into "Indian Territory," now Oklahoma.

Among their descendants the bitterness is not forgotten. Yet today
when Native American nations gather at Grand Prairie, Texas, for the
National Pow Wow Championships, dancers bear a Stars and Stripes into
the central arena, claiming the Republic for their own. Then Congressman and now United States Senator Ben Nighthorse Campbell made the
same point in 1992, when he officiated in full Plains chief regalia as co-
grand marshal of the 1992 Tournament of Roses parade in Pasadena,
California.

Pasadena occupies ground that Spanish-speaking Europeans and their
mixed-race progeny had claimed while English speakers were just beginning their westward push. Once it was called the Rancho San Pascual.
Practically every event and process that pitted Europeans, Africans, and
Natives against one another in the East has its southwestern counterpart.
The great Pueblo Indian rebellion of 1680 far outstrips both the scope
and the significance of eastern uprisings. British and Spanish alike encountered Indians on the same bloody, disease-ridden, alcohol-soaked
terms. By the second quarter of the nineteenth century, Mexican communities and missions defined a line from Texas to Arizona and up the
California coast. To the advancing Anglos, their people were semi-
savages, whatever their color or language. By 1850 all those people,
Indian, mestizo, and Hispanic alike, had become Americans, not by migration but by military conquest.

The expulsion of the Indian nations was at the hands of the President
Andrew Jackson, who operated Tennessee and Mississippi plantations
throughout his presidency. The conquest of the Far Southwest was at
the hands of Jacksonians, particularly Jackson's self-proclaimed heir, the
slave-owning President James K. Polk. These are the same Jackson and
Polk whose version of democracy is now being offered as the American
Revolution's final achievement.[13] That interpretation of Jacksonian
democracy—that it completed the Revolution's political promise—has
much to commend it. Jackson himself eloquently articulated the ideology
of "equal rights" that the Revolution had begun to shape, most notably
in his message to Congress vetoing renewal of the Second Bank of the

United States. "There are no necessary evils in government," Jackson wrote. "Its evils are only in its abuses. If it would confine itself to equal protection and, as Heaven does its rains, shower its favors alike on the high and the low, the rich and the poor, it would be an unqualified blessing."[14] Jackson and his followers helped make the Revolution's language of equal citizenship into a powerful defense against the erosion of individual freedoms. But the link that joins romantic American democracy, slavery's expansion, the eastern Indians' stark choice to be expelled or destroyed, and the conquest of northern Mexico is not happenstance. The connection among the four is fundamental to nineteenth-century American social history.

We have our political tradition; we have a long history of people rejecting its hypocrisies; we also have a tradition of people claiming it even though it might seem to mean nothing to them. We are a people of plenty; we are also a people of want and poverty. We are a people of paradox; we also like to think we are innocent (or used to be innocent sometime in our past). I seek to explore all these matters and to offer a social history of many kinds of American people before full modernity.[15]

Each of the founding American peoples has its own story. For the people who were here first, it is one of catastrophic defeat, near-destruction, and difficult survival. For Africans who became American, it is one of being enslaved and then painfully forging their own freedom. For English-speaking white migrants, it is a triumphant tale of colonization, independence, expansion, republicanism, and capitalist development, tempered by a tragic and bloody civil war. For Tejanos, Nuevomejicanos, and Californios, it is a story of lost possibilities. None of these stories reveals its full sense unless we see it in reference to the others. Each of these stories is different.

Nonetheless, all the stories circle around the mixture of hope and disappointment of Thomas Jefferson's proclamation that "all men are created equal." All the people in all the stories have found themselves living in a world of disruption and transformation. All of them have tried to form meaningful ties with other people in the same plight so they could establish patterns that would give their lives sense and cohesion. They have not always succeeded. Indian treaties and African-American families were broken by forces too powerful to withstand. Prairie land refused to flower, or turned out to be owned by a distant speculator. The streets of Manhattan and Lowell and San Francisco were not paved with gold. Nineteenth-century immigrants lived their lives without ever escaping the tenements to which migration first took them.

Nonetheless, people kept trying to make sense of their lives, to organize the world around them, and to claim American freedom for themselves. In the sense that we all have faced those problems, we have far more in common than most of us may realize. That may be what the airman and I implicitly understood. Had he chanced to be Native American or Hispanic instead of black (or I any of those instead of white), we still might have shared the recognition.

I study American history to understand the people of whom I am a part. One result of my long stay among the British was to learn that I never would be one of them, however great my taste for "real ale" and fish and chips doused in salt and vinegar, however adept I am at driving on the left. That encounter in Leamington helped me see why. As a white American, rather than a European, I am the product of a society that many kinds of people have produced, not just the children of Europeans. Fundamentally, this book is about how we have produced categories to separate ourselves from one another but have nonetheless shared enough to call ourselves a people. The categories blur if we look at them closely, dissolving into what is shared, despite all enmity and difference.

If I, a white American, would understand what shaped me, if I would not be a stranger to myself, I must understand people who may not look like me but whose history is fundamentally, inextricably, and forever intertwined with my own. Indeed, that history is my own, just as all American history in its terrible and exciting complexity belongs to all of the American people. *Americans* offers some ideas about how that became so.

A NOTE ON METHOD AND CITATION

This book is unashamedly interpretive and eclectic. The preface gives my personal reasons for writing it. My academic justification is the existence of a huge body of fine work on American social history during the period it covers, more, in fact, than any sane person can really master. Without doubt, there is good material that I have missed. That's my fault, and I am sure that reviewers will let me know where the omissions weaken my argument, or actually discredit it. My own sense, from random readings and conference sessions, is that I am on the right track.

Clearly, there are important debates among the scholars who have produced this work, but for the most part I do not attempt to be historiographical. Instead, I have sought to take their work "as read." I try here to fit it together into a coherent picture of how Americans became a distinctive people, allowing for all their differences. One way or another, this scholarship has centered on the central problems that I pose here: the establishment and continuation of "race" followed by nationality as primal American social categories; the emergence of such other important categories as class, gender, ethnicity, party, community, and section; the social significance of the American Revolution; and the common experiences of many different groups as they faced the single reality of developing America.

My title, *Americans: A Collision of Histories*, speaks to the point. I have not sought a spurious "inclusivity" or "multiculturalism" that merely mentions names. Nor have I sought to write *the* whole history of my subjects. That would be incredibly arrogant, given how little we can really know about the people with whom we live closely, even intimately, let alone the dead who leave only traces behind. I have sought only to address the terms on which many kinds of people shared a place and experiences over a long period of time despite their differences, and how they ultimately came to share an identity as well.

In some places dealing with these problems has meant abandoning traditional chronology and looking instead at how the same problem has provoked similar answers in different places and times. My model for working that way while still attempting a narrative that shows process and makes sense across time is the title essay in the late Herbert G. Gutman's influential collection *Work, Culture, and Society in Industrializing America* (1976). As I wrote, I found myself listening over and over and over to Richard Wagner's *Ring of the Nibelungen*. I found myself reading William Faulkner's novels and stories too. Eventually I realized why. Like Gutman, those two majestic artists address the problem of telling many different stories at the same time, within a single account that makes sense of them all. Compared to what a musician or a novelist can accomplish, written history can seem a poor, thin thing, nailed to the earth with notes and bibliographies. But there is merit to being limited by what the evidence permits us to say. It is that we are talking about people who once lived lives as uncertain as our own, not simply about figments that our imaginations conjure up. We can try to know those people, both in the ways that they were like us and in the ways that they were not.

Back to earth. I don't give citations for "classical" quotes from sources like Walt Whitman. In most places where I do provide notes, I simply cite the immediate scholarship on which I am drawing. As I was working toward this book I tested some of my ideas with heavily researched essays, which are cited in the appropriate places with their masses of bibliography and direct evidence. In some places I draw on primary material or complex debates. In those cases my citations are heavier. Nonetheless, my central concern is not "what can we prove?" but rather "what if it should be true that these things do hang together?" I borrowed that formulation from Daniel Calhoun's *The Intelligence of a People* (1973) once before, and I am happy to acknowledge my debt to him again.

THANKS

When I started to create this file my word processor refused the file name "acknowledgments." It's too long. So I called it "thanks" instead, and that seems good enough a heading too. I owe many thanks indeed.

Southern Methodist University made this book possible in a number of ways. I began thinking about it long before my move to Dallas, but SMU's fine library system, excellent support for faculty productivity, and exciting intellectual atmosphere all have made a difference to me. I started to name individuals among my colleagues in the Clements Department of History, but quickly realized that I owe something to practically everybody with whom I have worked here over the last four years. Enough, perhaps, to let Daniel T. Orlovsky ("Dr. Dan, the Chairman man"), who has presided over this remarkable group with a leprechaun-like wit, stand for all the rest.

I owe a lot to the SMU history majors and graduate students who have pushed me, challenged me, and given me good suggestions after reading parts and drafts of the manuscript. Among them are Corey Capers, Lonnie Dean, Mark Easley, Jane Lenz Elder, Kenneth Larisch, Kate Haulman, James McMillan, Guy Nelson, Elizabeth Stearns, Cameron Taylor, Ondria Weinberg, Anne-Elizabeth Wynn, and Amanda Wright. Corey, in particular, took real interest and offered many good ideas over a long period of discussion. There are quite a few others and I apologize for not naming them all. I owe a great debt to the adult students who took my evening courses in the Master of Liberal Arts program. The pay was good, but the interchange with nonacademic people who just wanted to *know* was terrific. I should note my debt to the people of Texas too. This Yankee who lived overseas for a long time found himself really challenged by the shift in perspective that moving to the Lone Star State required. Thanks, y'all.

Outside SMU I owe debts to my Yale graduate students when I visited there, particularly David Waldstreicher. Too many undergraduates to name joined willingly as I tried out ideas in classes there, at Warwick, and (years ago, when the book first began to gestate) at Cambridge. I owe institutional debts to New York University and the American Antiquarian Society (for research facilities and support) and to the American Historical Association, the American History Seminar of the University of Cologne, the Dallas Social History Group, the Institute of Early American History and Culture, the John Carter Brown Library, the Milan Group in Early United States History, the Organization of American Historians, the Philadelphia Center for Early American Studies, and the faculties/departments of history at Cambridge, Oxford, and Warwick for chances to talk to informed audiences. I want particularly to thank James Axtell, Susan Branson, David Brion Davis, Richard Dunn, William Dusinberre, Drew Gilpin Faust, Eric Foner, Robert A. Gross, Woody Holton, Rhys Isaac, Charles Joyner, Christopher Morris, David Narrett, J. R. Pole, Carroll Smith-Rosenberg, Fredrika Teute, Loretta Valtz-Mannucci, and Marion Winship for helpful and sometimes pointed comments at those presentations. At the very last moment Charles E. Curran helped me track down some elusive biblical citations. Again, I'm sure that I am leaving people out and I apologize.

Philip De Loria, Sylvia Frey, June Namias, Gordon S. Wood, and Michael Zuckerman gave formal commentaries on preliminary pieces. Michael McGiffert saw two of those pieces through the press at the *William and Mary Quarterly*. Carol Berkin gave me the chance to spend an incredibly stimulating week with a summer seminar of high school teachers at Princeton, thinking together about some of the issues I consider here. In addition to people I have already named, Joyce Appleby, James Baird, Alan Conway, John Mack Faragher, Steven Hackel, James A. Henretta, Allan Kulikoff, Neil Salisbury, Luke Trainor, and Richard White gave me written commentaries at one point or another. John Cumbler and Ronald Hoffman have talked many an idea through with me. Neil Evans has too, both formally in a number of sessions at the remarkable Coleg Harlech, Wales, and informally while we climbed Cadair Idris, Cnicht, and Rhinog Fawr and strolled on Traeth Harlech. He read the whole manuscript and made boundless good suggestions as well. Lizbeth Cohen also read the final manuscript, to good effect. My sister and brother-in-law, Judith and Leo Fournier, stepped in at a vital moment. So did Lyn Mitchell, the incomparable "Mum."

Alfred Young has encouraged me more than he can know ever since

I first began to play with these themes. He gave me both a well-placed caveat and a happily received cheer as I approached the end. Arthur Wang understood what I wanted to do in this book and has given me his fine editing skills. It is a privilege to publish with him, and I feel very honored that I have had the privilege twice. Ollie and friends helped too.

It's conventional to thank an author's spouse/partner/significant other at the very end, but my thanks to Evonne go way beyond convention. She saw me through a very bad time and she has done much more than just watch as I saw this book through, in a much better time. The dedication tries, at least, to convey how very much I owe to her. But, like most words, all it can do is hint.

E.C.

PART ONE

SLAVERY AND FREEDOM,
LOSS AND GAIN

{T}o observe the character of a particular people we must examine the objects of its love. And yet, whatever those objects, if it is the association of a multitude not of animals but of rational beings, and is united by a common agreement about the objects of its love, then there is no absurdity in applying to it the title of a "people."

—ST. AUGUSTINE

CHAPTER I

A COLLISION OF HISTORIES

THREE separate histories collided in the Western Hemisphere half a millennium ago, and American history began. The European navigators of the fifteenth and sixteenth centuries drew upon an energy that set people in motion across every sea and every great landmass save Australia. Knowing already about Africa and Asia, Europeans went to them in this "age of reconnaissance" to trade. Whether it was for spices, silk, gold, or slaves made little difference. Knowing little if anything about what the navigators found to the west, Europeans set out to make these "new islands" their own.

In numbers that swelled to the hundreds of thousands, Europe's willing people and Africans under great duress started to cross the Atlantic. They carried their worlds with them in their heads (memory, skills, language, knowledge, and beliefs), in the holds of the ships (implements, goods for trade, sacred objects, clothing, food, seeds, and animals), and in their own bodies (microbes and antibodies). What the Europeans and the Africans brought intersected immediately with the knowledge, the objects, and the other living species that the Western Hemisphere's people already had. The coming of the Old World made the Americas truly new to everyone involved: the Europeans, the Africans, and the tens of millions of people already there.

Discovery, settlement, colonization, conquest, contact, encounter, a "moving frontier," the taming of "virgin land," civilizing the "wilderness": all these terms have been proposed to explain what began in 1492. Some, like "discovery" and "settlement" and "peopling," presume that only the Europeans made American history. Others, like "encounter" and "contact," try to deal in neutral terms with the meeting of groups. To use the word "multiracial" is to assume that the concept of race had the meaning then that the modern world associates with it now, which is not true.[1] To speak about "conquest" or "invasion" is to understand that what some gained, others lost. Each set of terms has its merits, even the outmoded language of "discovery," which appreciates at least that Europeans posed a problem for everyone else.

A different approach will be attempted here. What happened after Columbus was a collision of histories. The people involved began as complete strangers. But in America all three groups, red, white, and black, became inextricably intertwined. All became different from their forebears, living in a different world. In most historical confrontations the parties agree about the questions, even as they quarrel and kill about the answers. Protestants challenged Catholics during the Reformation about the meaning of Christianity. Both royalists and republicans understood that the great problem of the American and French revolutions was political society. For the West and the Soviets during the Cold War, the defining issue was how to organize industrial production and large-scale trade. In these epochs, each side has had more in common with its opponent than either has had with anyone from another time. But during the "invasion of America" there were no shared terms or shared questions. Europeans and sub-Saharan Africans knew one another slightly, especially along the Mediterranean rim. It was not as equals: the institution of slavery already existed. But the people of the Old World and the people of the New were utter strangers.

Even the name deceives. Before the invasion there was no "America." The hemisphere's people had names for the places that were theirs, but they had no idea of being Americans or "Indians." The modern names that we associate with them—Iroquois, Catawba, Seminole, Creek, Cherokee—were not what they called themselves. Becoming "Indians" was a change that the invasion forced upon them. Becoming Catawbas rather than Sugarees or Shuterees, becoming Creeks and Seminoles rather than Muscogulges, was forced upon them as well.

Captured Africans were in no position to name the places where they were taken or the communities they belonged to, not, at least, with names that historians can recover. It was struggle enough to name themselves and their children, rather than have someone who claimed to own them say what they would be called. No more than the Natives, or the white tribes called English, Welsh, Scottish, Irish, Dutch, German, French, and Spanish, were Africans a single people. They left Africa as Ovimbundu, BaKango, Mbundu, Mayombe, Limba, Lokko, Gizzi, and many more. Many whites knew that. They valued different Africans for their different abilities and knowledge and for what the whites thought was their tribal character. In time, however, the captives and their American-born descendants became just "Negroes"—or some term like it—in the captors' minds. Most eventually became "Negroes"—or some term like it—in their own minds as well. It marked the beginning of a long search for a Western Hemisphere identity that did not reek of what had happened to them.

The Europeans thought that they alone brought change. They would teach Christianity and save heathen souls. They would build cities with cathedrals and churches, palaces and markets, universities and colleges. They would bring law. They would make this "New" World into an image of the "Old," improved perhaps, but recognizable: *Nueva* España, *Nouvelle* France, *Nieuw* Amsterdam, *New* England. New Englanders especially believed that they were chosen by God to build a "citty upon a hill" that would show humanity how to live. Yet the Natives and the Africans changed the Europeans even as the Europeans were changing them. All became "Americans," and they did it because of their entanglement with all the others.

By the end of the colonial years, whites throughout the hemisphere were Europeans no more and they knew it. Both the North American and Spanish American movements for national independence demonstrated so. The white English speakers of the northern continent's Atlantic seaboard declared themselves a people in 1776 and assumed their equal station among the powers of the earth. They changed "American" from a term of geography to a badge of identity. They would extend that badge, perhaps, to other white settlers who spoke French and Spanish. But "Indians not taxed" and the "persons" whom they "held to service" were among them, not of them. The Declaration of Independence caught their mood and perspective. The miscreant George III had "excited domestic insurrections" by promising freedom to slaves who would support the royal cause. He had "endeavoured to bring on the inhabitants of our frontiers, the merciless Indian savages, whose known rule of warfare, is an undistinguished destruction of all ages, sexes and conditions." Slaves and Natives were not part of the "one people" that was separating its "political bands" to another. They figured among the reasons for the separation.

As they moved somewhat later toward their own separate peoplehood, the *Criollo* descendants of the Spanish *Conquistadores* knew better. They realized that *Indios*, *Mestizos*, *Negros*, *Zambos*, and *Mulatos* were necessarily a part of their American world. Those peoples' very presence helped distinguish American Spaniards from *Peninsulares*. The English speakers misunderstood both themselves and their world. The effects of their mistake are with us still.

In the beginning, there was death. Even Europeans who emigrated freely encountered a new environment and climate and suffered from it. Life expectancy for a "seasoned" white Virginia male was as low as forty-eight years in the mid-seventeenth century, about what it was in England. For newcomers, unused to hot summers or to malaria and yellow fever, it was lower. Virginians spent the seventeenth century "living with death."[2] In the Carolinas and the Caribbean it was far worse for everybody concerned.

The worst danger the colonizers faced was themselves. From Virginia to Barbados, young white men with no bonds to one another arrived to conquer, pillage, and make someone else work for their benefit. Where nobody else could be found, those who enjoyed power forced the rest to labor. The tobacco boom of early Virginia illustrated what could happen. The crop began to be grown about 1616. Three years later "the best grade sold for export at three shillings a pound," thirty-six times as much as it would bring in 1630, when the boom collapsed. Would-be planters and indentured English servants "poured . . . into Virginia," worked a while, and died. Perhaps 3,500 persons migrated during the very first years of the boom. With these added to the number already there, Virginians should have totaled roughly 4,200 by the early 1620s but only 1,240 were actually alive at the end of 1622. "It Consequentlie followes . . . that we had then lost 3000 persons," noted Samuel Wrote, "a disgruntled and disillusioned investor."[3] Perhaps 15,000 more people came by 1640, but Virginia's white population rose to no more than 8,000.

Disease, mistreatment, and actual starvation lay behind the carnage-like death rates. So did the sheer disorder of a society where people had no purpose beyond getting rich and getting out. The servants who grew the tobacco were young, poor men from the streets of London or from shire counties that offered no future. As servants in England, they might have enjoyed some protection from the church, the law, the nearness of their families, or the chance to change master or mistress at year's end. Even now the English town of Warwick celebrates an annual Mop Fair, commemorating the day servants moved. If necessary, a servant could disappear into England's swollen cities, especially London. In Virginia none of these safeguards existed in more than bare outline. Servants were at their masters' mercy, and mercy was in short supply. The dying was of some Englishmen at the hands of others, but they at least had brought it upon themselves by going. For Natives and Africans what happened was far worse and they had no choice at all.

The demographic disaster that struck the hemisphere's aborigines after 1492 has no equal in history, not even the Black Death. Historical demographers debate the size of the Native population in 1492; the highest estimates suggest as many as 100,000,000. Whatever the actual figures, there is general agreement that the falling-off after contact was in the range of 90 percent. Tiny Block Island near Narragansett Bay had about 1,200 Native inhabitants on its eleven square miles as late as 1662, but virtually all disappeared by the seventeenth century's end.[4]

An absence of resistance among people who had never been exposed to Old World microbes was one reason for the disaster. "Wildfire" or "green field" or "virgin soil" epidemics of plague, measles, smallpox, diphtheria, chicken pox, and influenza took a terrible toll. One disease or strain might follow upon another, perhaps quickly over one generation, perhaps more slowly, over four or five or six. Europeans and Africans brought the diseases, but once started an epidemic could leap from village to village without a white or African getting near. Even contact with the infected crew of a fishing boat could start death spreading. That happened in Massachusetts in 1616. Puritans arriving there a few years later thought it was God's way of clearing the land for them, the new Israel entering their Land of Canaan.

The epidemics struck the young, the adolescent, the adult, and the old. They could destroy the whole social fabric that might have enabled some who survived to tend others and help them survive too. William Bradford, governor of the *Mayflower* Pilgrims' Plymouth Colony, wrote of Indians who were "not able to help one another, no not to make a fire nor to fetch a little water to drink, nor any to bury the dead."[5] Traditional ideas about medicine were no help and might even increase the danger. The great death struck as well at the Natives' self-awareness and self-esteem. Their historical memories and sacred knowledge were oral or hidden within objects, rather than written. If the wise man or woman who knew the stories and understood the objects' meaning died before the knowledge could be passed on, the knowledge would die too. If the holy rituals failed to cure, they might cease to be holy and just be forgotten.

The migrants' alcohol seemed to offer a quick way to see visions of the spirit world. But the result might be mayhem as self-restraint disappeared. Under alcohol's influence a Native might sign a legal document without realizing that it gave away all that the village had, or created debt that never could be paid off. Behind the death, drink, desecration, and dispossession lurked the danger of enslavement, particularly by the English. Algonquian speakers along the Connecticut River, Rappahannocks and Pamunkeys in the lower Chesapeake, Choctaws near the Tombigbee and Pearl rivers, and Pawnees on the western tributaries of the Mississippi all faced raiders from the English colonies who wanted to use them as forced labor.

A Dutch boat brought twenty black people to Jamestown, Virginia, in 1619. It was the middle of the tobacco boom, and there is no reason to think that they fared any better than did the English servants who were complaining of being treated "like damn'd slaves."[6] By this time the Atlantic slave trade was more than a century old. Tens of thousands of its victims had already been taken to the Mediterranean, Iberia, São Tomé, the Canaries, Madeira, the Spaniards' New World kingdoms, and Brazil. Slavery was already everywhere and these first Africans to enter British North America were most likely slaves when they boarded ship. But there is no reason to think that they remained slaves in Virginia. The law of England, which governed Virginia if any law did, contained no provision that recognized the legality of enslavement. By the middle of the century there was a free black community a few hundred strong on Virginia's Eastern Shore, the tongue of land between Chesapeake Bay and the open Atlantic.

We know some of those people's names, what they did, and what they owned. Anthony Johnson, as he came to call himself, arrived in 1621. He came from nobody knows where, but it was probably the West Indies. In 1625 he was a servant growing tobacco. If ill luck brought him to Virginia, it did not last. He married "Mary, a Negro Woman," and they spent four decades together, surviving their servitude, and acquiring hundreds of acres. When "an unfortunate fire" destroyed their buildings in 1653 the "county justices viewed the damage," decided the Johnsons needed help "in the 'obtayneing of their Livelyhood," and freed them of taxes. Anthony Johnson gave legal testimony, raised tobacco, sought redress against whites who aggrieved him, argued with officials, and had servants of his own. At his death he was farming a three-hundred-acre leasehold in Maryland. His widow renegotiated the leasehold in her own name, receiving a tenure of ninety-nine years.[7]

If all arriving black people had fared like Anthony and Mary Johnson, African-American history would have been far different. But during the Johnsons' lifetimes Virginia was loosening its bonds upon white servants and imposing new burdens upon black ones. In 1676 there was open rebellion. Named for the English adventurer who led it, Bacon's Rebellion was an inchoate, ugly affair, but it demonstrated the fragility of Virginia's social order. Most especially, it posed the problem of servants who survived their time and wanted land as well as freedom. The problem would disappear if neither land nor freedom ever could be claimed. Slaves could be had whenever white colonists decided to spend the higher price that slavers charged. After 1660 it "probably . . . became more advantageous for Virginians to buy slaves" than servants. Making the decision did not arouse moral qualms.[8]

During the next four decades white Virginians broke with their English heritage of personal freedom and created their own New World law of slavery. By 1700 black Virginians could not bear arms, testify against any white, or be punished with longer terms for running away. They already were serving for life. Husbands and wives, parents and children enjoyed no protection from the law. They had no hope of escape, other than fleeing into the forests or swamps. Some did flee, establishing independent "Maroon" communities in the Dismal Swamp south of the James River. Some found a welcome among Indians. Others did not. In the eighteenth century the Catawbas accepted the role of catching and returning slaves who were trying to free themselves. It was the price they had to pay for their own survival.[9]

Black men and women made up a tiny fraction of Virginians in 1640. They comprised 15 percent in 1690, and by the middle of the eighteenth century they accounted for two Virginians in every five. Some 54,000 slaves entered the province between 1700 and 1740, all but 5,000 of them imported from Africa rather than the West Indies. They came to Virginia from Senegambia, Sierra Leone, the Windward and Gold Coasts, the Bight of Biafra, Angola, Mozambique, and Madagascar, but to Virginians it made little difference. Complicit now in direct enslavement rather than simply buying people who were slaves anyway, eighteenth-century planters wanted young, strong men. The tobacco boom was long since over, so the planters had less incentive to drive their slaves to the absolute limit, as Virginia's first masters had driven the servants. Nonetheless, the Africans experienced all the shock and disruption and stress of being ripped out of their communities, transported under horrific conditions, prodded, inspected and sold, brought to a country where they knew neither language nor custom, and subjected to a new regimen of work unlike any they had known, in a new climate, colder in winter than they ever could have imagined.

Traders and masters understood that the first year was most risky. It was the most trying for whites as well, and they learned to arrive in the autumn, avoiding the first summer's heat and disease. However, Africans were generally imported in the spring, as the tidewater heat was beginning to build. The odds were that one out of every four would die from respiratory disease before the first year was out. Virginia's slave population did become self-sustaining by roughly 1740, and at mid-century the total number of its slaves was twice the total number who had been imported. By the eve of American independence, most black Virginians probably had been born there. The roughly 12,500 Africans who died during their first year after their arrival in Virginia were the price that had been paid.[10]

In other places that price was far higher. The heaviest slave concentrations of all were in the West Indies sugar islands. Throughout Caribbean slavery's history until it declined in the nineteenth century, it was sustained by the African trade rather than natural growth. Jamaica imported about 750,000 slaves before the trade was closed at the end of the eighteenth century. Yet its reported slave population in 1808 was only 324,000.[11] In the midst of such enormous losses only one consolation remained: the island's population became almost entirely black and a distinctive Jamaican culture could emerge, with only a veneer of English influence.[12]

The other great mainland black community took shape in South Carolina. That province's first black people came from Barbados with their white masters during the late seventeenth century. From the start, slavery defined the legal condition of black Carolinians, but for perhaps half a century after its founding South Carolina had no plantations. Like the lower Mississippi Valley somewhat later, it began as a "frontier exchange economy" based upon forestry, small farming, open-range herding, and the trade in animal skins.[13] A slave in earliest South Carolina might well be a cowboy, herding cattle without the master's supervision on an interior savanna much as his West African forebears had done.

Early in the new century South Carolina changed, and the reason was rice. Who taught whites that the grain could grow in the Carolina lowlands remains an open question. Some have said the knowledge came from Italy. Some even have said China. Most likely, the knowledge came from West Africans, to whom rice cultivation was perfectly familiar. The actual strain of rice grown in South Carolina was not the same as in Africa, but Carolina rice cultivation used many West African techniques. These planters imported skills as well as labor, preferring "above all to have slaves from the Senegambia, which meant principally Bambara and Malinké." They wanted Africa's rice-growing people, rather than just any slaves. Many whom they brought were Muslims, building their lives in America as they had in Africa around the Koran. Some were literate in Arabic.[14]

Once the ability to grow the grain was shown, white Carolinians moved rapidly into rice production. At first it was on "dry, upland soil, using rainfall to water their crop," but "most rice production" shifted "to marshy areas along the coast."[15] The whites knew that the swamps were deadly in the summer, thanks to what they called "fever and ague," which they attributed to miasma and "bad air." We know now that it was an African strain of malaria known as *falciparum*. The disease was carried to America in the bodies of slaves and then transmitted through the bites of *Anopheles* mosquitoes. Whites also believed that Africans could survive where they themselves could not. The belief was correct; the genetic sickle-cell trait that many Africans carried created an environment in a carrier's bloodstream where the parasite that causes *falciparum* malaria could not survive. The trait is not "racial," restricted to Africans. It flourishes genetically among Europeans and Asians where malaria is endemic as well, and in principle they could have survived the rice swamps. The trait does not offer protection against the nonfatal forms of the disease that were native to America. Carriers of the sickle-cell trait might not die from *falciparum* malaria. But malaria's American varieties could leave their bodies fevered and pain-wracked, too weakened to resist other diseases or the sheer stress of their lives.

No one, black or white, connected the Africans' ability to survive in the swamps with the short, difficult lives of many of their children. These children were victims of sickle-cell anemia, which can result when two carriers of the trait conceive a child together. The red blood cells of a person who has it may not carry adequate oxygen to the body. Collapsing into the sickle shape that gives the disease its name, they can clump together in a sticky mass that blocks blood vessels, causing terrible pain and destroying vital organs. Sickle-cell anemia would not receive clinical recognition until the twentieth century. We still have no cure.[16]

However well the Africans could survive malaria, they did not survive the conditions of rice cultivation during the early decades. As in Virginia or the West Indies, cheap land, cheap labor, and high profit on what the land and labor could produce meant disaster. When Carolina's rice boom began just after 1700, the African trade was in full force and there was no question of using servants. Black people formed Carolina's majority by 1708 and the slave trade went unabated until about 1740, when a major rebellion prompted whites to cut it off for a time. Still South Carolina wanted slaves. Twice more, just before the Revolution and early in the nineteenth century, it opened its ports to the ships from Africa. Carolina slaves generated wealth beyond any to be found elsewhere on the mainland. A careful and rigorous sampling of probate records filed in 1774 showed that nine of the ten richest colonials who died that year were Carolinians.[17]

Carolinians, like Virginians, wanted young, single men. For a time in the eighteenth century the Carolina lowlands became "more like a Negro country," with an overwhelming black majority. Between 1720 and 1740, while rice was being established as South Carolina's major cash crop, the province's black population doubled. By the end of those two decades the province had almost 40,000 black people, but the growth was driven by the slave trade, not natural increase. Conditions in the emerging rice country were fierce. Shocked by enslavement, the Africans were ill shod or barefoot, ill clothed, and poorly housed and fed. They drained swamps, dug ditches, built dams, and planted and harvested rice while their immune systems tried to cope with American diseases. A man who survived might spend his whole life without the possibility of a woman's love, because planters generally imported male and female slaves at a ratio of two to one. For women who did come, the disruption of menstrual cycles and the capacity to bear and nurse a child can only be imagined. Planters did not care. They knew that it would be cheaper to work their slaves to the limits of endurance and replace them when they died. During the first great burst of the Carolina slave trade, from roughly 1720 to 1740, the rate of death was so great and the rates of childbirth and infant survival were so low that the slave population could not sustain itself. The population grew, but only because fresh Africans were entering even faster than other Africans could die.

Slaves were brought to every colony, northern or southern, British, Dutch, French, Spanish, or Portuguese. By the middle of the eighteenth century perhaps a fifth of the people of New York City were black and their number was several thousand strong. Twice, in 1712 and 1741, rumors circulated in New York City that slaves were plotting revolt. Each time, white New Yorkers met the rumors with mass arrests. "Thirteen slaves" whom they arrested "were hanged, one [was] left to die in chains without sustenance, three [were] burned, one [was] burned over slow fire for eight to ten hours, and one [was] broken on the wheel."[18] There was no place in early-eighteenth-century America where being black did not also mean being enslaved, stripped of all honor, and subjected to some European's absolute, total power.

[II]

A society driven by death cannot sustain itself. One of the central problems in early America turns on the fact that places where illness and early death were the norm became societies where people could expect to live. By the middle of the eighteenth century the change had happened among both Europeans and Africans. It was starting to happen among Indians as well.

The *Mayflower* Pilgrims of Plymouth Colony experienced a brief "starving time" when they arrived in 1621. It was brought on by their own poor planning, not by the structural causes that brought mass death to Native people, early Virginia white servants, or incoming Africans. The main New England group that settled Massachusetts Bay after 1630 did not have a starving time at all. In the Massachusetts town of Andover, the first generation had a life expectancy higher than seventy years, men and women alike. An Andover couple could expect at least five children. Almost nine of every ten children born during the first generation would survive to age twenty.[19]

Andover's low mortality and high infant survival were not identical to other towns'. But seventeenth-century New Englanders survived astonishingly well into adulthood and old age, in comparison both to the other colonies and to the Old World. Perhaps 20,000 people migrated to New Hampshire, Massachusetts, Plymouth, Rhode Island, New Haven, and Connecticut during the two decades that followed the voyage of the *Mayflower* in 1621. Then civil war broke out in the home country between Parliament and the monarchy of Charles I and migration virtually stopped. When the English began to emigrate again after the monarchy was restored in 1660, they did not find the Puritan provinces attractive. Nor did most other Europeans. Nonetheless, the population grew rapidly, thanks to the health of New England's own settlers.

This was due to ecological and social factors rather than medical. New England's topography and its colder climate do not lend themselves to tropical and subtropical diseases. Its forests offered vast amounts of wood

for housing and winter fuel. But more important is what New Englanders did with these resources. From the beginning, they were going to
America to stay. A man in Massachusetts was not rootless, young, and
socially isolated. Nor was he bent on enriching himself and returning
"home" to become a landed gentleman or to flaunt his wealth in London.
Nor would he be a servant in the Virginia sense. Massachusetts settlers
represented the whole spectrum from the newborn to the elderly and
they came primarily from the middle ranks. Though founding governor
John Winthrop advised his fellow voyagers in the first fleet that "God
. . . hath so disposed . . . of mankinde, as in all times some must be
rich some poore, some highe and eminent in power and dignitie; others
meane and in subjeccion," neither the genuinely rich nor the really poor
joined the venture.[20] Even if they went out alone, most New England
male settlers were married, and they expected their wives and children
to follow. They sold what they had and made the proceeds a basis for
starting again. The sex ratio evened out rapidly and a society of families
took shape within the first decade.

As family life emerged in Virginia, the individual farm or plantation
remained the most important unit of society. In New England the basic
social unit became the town. Our modern image of white clapboard
houses, a meetinghouse with its spire, all surrounding a village green, is
nothing like what the Puritans actually created. There was no typical
town. Boston and Salem both became centers of commerce. Marblehead
was a largely male fishing port, as rough as any place in Virginia. Springfield, in the Connecticut Valley, began as a fur-trading outpost under
the father and son William and John Pynchon. Andover and Dedham
were communities of farmers whose plan was to create static perfection
for themselves and their families.

John Winthrop called the sermon that he preached to the first voyagers "A Modell of Christian Charitie." Likening his people to a new
Israel, he called upon them to build a "citty upon a hill" that would
show the Lord's way to the "eies of all People." He did not exaggerate
the Puritans' audience. English Protestants and Catholic observers in
France, Spain, and the Vatican all watched with interest what the Puritans were doing. Winthrop's call was for a hierarchical social order.
That was God's desire. But all within that order should be "knitt more
nearly together in the Bond of brotherly affeccion."[21]

Some Puritan towns made serious attempts to live out what Winthrop
had sketched. The town founders of Dedham started with a covenant to
establish their terms for living together, including old "English ways"

that they wanted to transfer intact.[22] The next step was to petition for land, which the provincial authorities granted to the town as a whole. Then either the whole town meeting or selectmen whom the meeting chose divided the land. Some towns experimented with open-field agricultural patterns, with the land cut into strips and worked communally rather than fenced into farms and worked separately. Towns did not divide their land equally. One man's prestige brought from England, another's large family, the need to attract a minister or a miller or a blacksmith: these factors could make a difference in deciding how much land a man got, where it lay, and how fertile it was.

Dedham seems like a neo-peasant utopia, what medieval "bond men" might have established should the lord's castle be toppled and themselves "made free."[23] That, perhaps, is what the founders intended. Not all towns adopted open-field farming, and not all towns sought to create perfection. But in farming, commercial, fur-trading, and fishing villages alike, New Englanders built enduring social structures. Town meetings; gathered Congregational churches whose members were "Visible Saints"; powerful families in which parental control lasted well into the younger generation's adulthood: these created a strong though undoubtedly constricting sense of belonging. Epidemic illnesses appeared among Puritan New Englanders just as they did among Indians who had no immunity, Africans in the aftershock of enslavement, and white Virginians and Carolinians who had developed no more than the most basic forms of social organization. But when illness struck in New England there was someone who had an obligation to give care. That is one reason why New Englanders survived so well in a world that surrounded them with suffering and death.

Closing his shipboard sermon, Winthrop admonished his listeners to "choose life, that wee, and our Seede, may live." The transition to a demography of life that the Puritans achieved so quickly took others much longer. "Virginia was founded in 1607," a historian has written, "but it was not settled until nearly a century later."[24] For most of the seventeenth century it remained a ramshackle place, torn by conflict. The tidewater finally began to evolve a distinctive and permanent social order after Bacon's Rebellion in 1676 and that order was not fully in place until the 1730s. Unlike New Englanders, who started off with a vision of community, white Virginians created community slowly. The first step was to even the sex ratio. Women first came to Virginia as servants, and, like male servants, some survived their terms and gained freedom. A female servant had little recourse against a master who approached her with sex on his mind; pregnancy during servitude would merely prolong her service, whoever the father was. But once free she might marry well, within the possibilities Virginia offered. For women as well as men, Virginia's less healthy climate and more demanding economy than New England's meant the probability of a short life. The hazards of childbirth were bad enough in New England, where death from its complications terminated perhaps one marriage in four during the woman's fertile years. In Virginia the danger was worse, by far. But a white woman who outlived her husband might inherit much of his property and become a highly desirable partner. An ambitious Virginian would seek the widow rather than the daughter of a man who had left a good estate. George Washington's choice of Martha Custis offers a perfect example.

As the sex ratio evened out and more families were formed, the outlines of a larger society began to take shape. By the early eighteenth century successful planters were building the elegant mansions that still line the estuaries and rivers feeding into Chesapeake Bay. These were more than dwellings. They were public statements about wealth and community. Most Virginians lived at a much cruder level and a planter could easily dominate his lesser neighbors. Nonetheless, he and they had two things in common: growing the province's single staple crop and controlling the slave population. A great planter might be a member of the provincial House of Burgesses, a vestryman of the state-established Anglican Church, a militia colonel, and a judge of the county court. Such marks of distinction set him apart. So did his costume, the horse he rode, the carriage he maintained, his diet, the books he read, the distant people he wrote to and heard from, and the good wine that he drank. But in Virginia's emerging synthesis a planter was also bound to lesser whites. He represented them, prayed with them, commanded them, and judged them. He also entertained them at the annual barbecue, drank and gambled with them at the tavern, and raced his horses and pitted his gamecocks against theirs. Most of the adult males among his neighbors had the sixty acres of freehold land required to vote. If the planter had political ambitions he would stand to receive his fellows' votes at open-air elections, ceremoniously thanking each "gentleman freeholder" who voted for him. Eighteenth-century Virginia became a far more stratified place than New England. In no sense did it proclaim or value human equality. But it did create a social order that freed its white people from the squalor the founders had wrought.

[III]

For enslaved Africans and their first African-American descendants, community and the conditions of survival came more slowly and with much greater difficulty. While the slave trade remained, southern planters continued to need young men, and the young men continued to arrive, work, and die. Women also began to come. Africans of both sexes survived the shock, the work, and the disease and the survivors began to form families. The first New England-born Puritan generation had enormous difficulties with its English-born parents because they did not share the parents' English experiences.[25] We have no way of knowing how enslaved Africans and their African-American children dealt with one another, if the parents lived long enough to know their children as adults. But America was the only world the children knew. Their America was a harsh, demanding place, where families could be disrupted by sale, inheritance, or movement. If a wife and husband belonged to different masters the probability of disruption was even higher. Nonetheless, family and community life did take shape and a demography of life rather than of death began to emerge. By the middle of the eighteenth century Virginia's black population was increasing naturally, just as New Englanders and white Virginians were. The province no longer needed the slave trade and white Virginians could afford to feel moral qualms about it. The slave population began to grow of its own accord in South Carolina too, but whites there still wanted all the slaves they could buy.

Slaves who worked alone for a poor farmer or artisan knew that the master shared their labors. But finding a wife or husband, teaching and protecting their children, or joining with others to celebrate or mourn could be difficult. It was not impossible. By the early eighteenth century New York City's black population was creating its own life in hidden places that whites could not see. It was from this that the attempted rebellions of 1712 and 1741 emerged. Where the number of slaves was larger, the master might not realize what he forced the slaves to endure and he might push them all the harder. But on the plantation a slave community was easier to form. The whites of Middlesex County, Virginia, knew about the "negro road" that wound through the woods on their farms and plantations. But they knew very little about what went on along it, and because they were the ones who kept the records it is difficult for modern observers to know much more.[26]

Nonetheless, we can get glimpses. On the James River plantation called Carter's Grove careful archeological work sponsored by the Colonial Williamsburg Foundation has re-created the slave quarter as it looked around the year 1770. The houses are made of wood and brick from the plantation itself, and they were built with tools and techniques that the slaves would have used. The slave village stands only a few hundred yards from the elegant brick great house. But it belongs to another world. Built around a central square, intensely communal and inward-looking, open through many cracks to the cold Chesapeake winter winds, the buildings that comprise the quarter are a tiny part of Africa washed up on the shores of the New World. Carter's Grove bespeaks the aspirations and achievements of its master. The quarter bespeaks the slaves' yearning, their memories, and their means of survival.

The strongest African-American communities emerged in South Carolina, where physical conditions were most harsh. Though the death rate during the rice boom was appalling, the continuing arrival of the slave ships created a largely black world. During the summer malaria months every white left who could. In 1739 that world exploded in the uprising called the Stono Rebellion. Slaves who aimed to free themselves and escape to Spanish Florida slew some sixty whites before armed militia crushed them. Nonetheless, the enduring monument of that time is not the memory of rebellion. It is the beginning of Gullah culture, which still survives on the Carolina and Georgia Sea Islands. The people of the low country and the islands developed a distinctive speech, part African and part English. They transferred folktales, foods, work patterns, marriage customs, and religious beliefs to this new world that they could not escape. They Americanized themselves while they Africanized America. Gullah culture shares much with what black majorities created elsewhere. British West Indies patois offers one example; so does the French-African creole of Louisiana. All are distinctively American.[27]

Despite its fierce demands, rice culture lent itself to a regimen different from the gang labor of tobacco and sugar and later of cotton. South Carolina evolved a "task system" that gave slaves considerable control over their lives. They developed customs that even governed their relations with their masters. Nothing they could do would alter Carolina's environment of heat and disease or its economy of rice. The place where they found themselves remained hungry for new Africans long after Virginia had imported enough and closed its ports. Nonetheless, on the rice plantations the slaves opened a sizable zone of autonomy.[28]

[IV]

By the mid-eighteenth century the Natives had lost the coastal wood-lands. In the Chesapeake, the Carolina lowlands, southern New England, and the Hudson Valley, the tribes were virtually gone. Indians farther inland survived, but in ways that were drastically changed. When Europeans first came to the Carolina piedmont or the Mississippi hill country in the late seventeenth century to trade for deerskins, Indians set the terms on which they met. By the eighteenth century the balance of power and the formal ceremonies that signified it were shifting. Remnants of old villages were forming into tribes, such as the Carolina Catawbas. It was necessary; otherwise they would simply have disappeared. As Catawbas they became secure on their own land, thanks to a treaty with the provincial government. But less and less did they set the terms of a meeting. Less and less did their customs determine a meeting's etiquette. They had become totally dependent upon European goods and they protected themselves from whites by catching escaped slaves.[29]

The Iroquois nations of the Mohawk Valley and the Lake Ontario plain fared better. They too traded in furs, but astute diplomacy and their reputation as a warrior people served them well. They created a "Covenant Chain" that bound them to the government of New York and that made them, in the English view, suzerains over lesser tribes like the Delawares and the remnants of the Susquehannas. Although the Iroquois established a special relationship with New York, they understood that their interest would best be served if they could play that province off against others, British and non-British alike. Dealing with Pennsylvania, they happily signed away land that actually belonged to other Indians. Among the Iroquois nations the easternmost Mohawks were most closely linked to the English. The Senecas, "keepers of the western gate," kept links open to the French. Both nations kept their own counsel during the imperial wars. Even if they did fight on different sides in the Europeans' wars, they remained Iroquois and maintained their league of peace with one another.

After 1750 Iroquois dealt with the English most often at Johnson Hall, the frontier mansion of Britain's northern Indian superintendent, Colonel William Johnson. Johnson set out to make himself a lord in almost medieval style, staking out his estate on one people's turbulent border with another and peopling it with tenants whom he would treat well and who would be loyal to him. He meant his estate to be a quasi-feudal buffer between Iroquois and land-hungry whites. The British government agreed. It rewarded Johnson by making him a hereditary baronet, one step down from nobility. It gave his son a knighthood at the same time, even though Sir John would someday inherit his father's new title. In 1763 the British established a "proclamation line" down the crest of the Appalachian Mountains from Maine to Georgia. It was to set a western limit to white settlement. It was hopeless as a means of penning up the whites, but it represented an attempt to preserve the western Indians in their own ways.[30]

Nonetheless, the Iroquois nations and the tribes farther west had large grievances. Their Tuscarora relatives had been driven out of North Carolina in 1714, settling in Iroquoia proper as a junior sixth member of the Confederacy. The Mohawks, "keepers of the eastern gate," remembered losing the 800,000-acre Kayaderosseras Patent. In 1753 the Mohawk council speaker whom whites knew as Hendrick declared his people's absolute independence to New York's governor, George Clinton:

> Brother when we came here to relate our Grievances about our lands, we expected to have something done [and] we have told you that the Covenant Chain of our Forefathers was like to be broken. . . . [nothing had been done and] Brother we desire to hear no more of you.[31]

The Mohawks did hear a great deal more of the whites. Even by the time Hendrick spoke, Virginia and Pennsylvania were encroaching on the upper Ohio Valley and challenging Iroquois dominion over Delawares, Mingoes, and Shawnees. The Iroquois image was still one of great power. But the Six Nations were surrounded and they knew it.[32]

So too were all the Indians between the Atlantic and the Mississippi. Webs of war, diplomacy, sexuality, and commerce spread all over the eastern half of the continent by the mid-eighteenth century. French traders, soldiers, missionaries, settlers, and the mixed-race trappers called *coureurs de bois* mingled with Indians until France's historic withdrawal from North America in 1763. A world of agricultural and hunting villages covered what we call the Midwest, which the French knew as the *pays d'en haut*. For nearly two centuries, roughly from 1640 to 1815, the people of that world lived in balance, even if they were enemies. When Indians and whites first met they were mutually ignorant. Now the people of the *pays d'en haut* dwelt together, fully aware of one another and appreciative of each other's ways.[33]

In what we now call Mississippi, the Choctaws worked out much the same strategy as the Iroquois. They had English, Spanish, and French neighbors, and they used war, trade, and diplomacy to play their neighbors off against each other while the Europeans struggled for mastery of America. The English were to their east, in South Carolina and Georgia. The French were to their west, the whole length of the Mississippi. The Spanish were to their southeast along a line from St. Augustine to Pensacola. Like the Iroquois, the Choctaws controlled a vast land that whites thought was "howling wilderness." Like the Iroquois, they dominated lesser tribes. Unlike Indians farther north, they avoided direct involvement in the great Anglo-French wars. Nonetheless, when the French withdrew from the lower Mississippi Valley in 1763, the Choctaws' land then belonged to England, as far as European claims to sovereignty went. Another consequence was that the Choctaws' tactic for survival was reaching the end of its time.[34]

The evidence is skimpy, but it seems that, like coastal whites and blacks, Indians west of the mountains were negotiating the transition from a demography of death to one of life. Their eighteenth-century populations were not high. The Cherokees apparently dropped from about 32,000 in 1675 to only 8,500 in 1775. Creek numbers bottomed out at 9,000 in 1700 and rose to 14,000 in 1775. By the time of American independence the Choctaws and Chickasaws were rebounding too, reaching roughly the same level, as were the Algonquians of the western Great Lakes, in a "village world" in which the boundaries of race had partially dissolved.[35] Among the Muscogulge people of the Gulf coast "destruction" was giving way to "regeneration." In the Ohio country the Miami nation "fell dramatically in number" early in the eighteenth century, "their total warrior strength" dropping from about 1,500 in 1781 "to about 550 in 1736." By 1750, however, a combined community of Iroquois refugees, Shawnees, Wyandots, Delawares, and Miamis had 1,000 to 1,500 warriors available.[36]

Whether we speak of Iroquois, Cherokees, Choctaws, Shawnees, or anybody else west of the mountains, we are talking about people who were coping with their new world. The West had become stable, as a zone where cultures met and traded and warred without absolute destruction. There was no moving "frontier" that marked an expanding culture off from a retreating one. Compared with Europeans and Africans the Indian numbers are small. But they suggest recovery from what had begun when the Indians, Europeans, and Africans first collided. The worst could have been over. But that was not to be.

CHAPTER 2

BRAUDEL'S AMERICAN MOSAIC

WRITING from "the perspective of the world," the great French historian Fernand Braudel once pictured colonized America as "a mosaic." Within it glittered "a hundred different colours: modern, archaic, primitive, or curious mixtures of all these."[1] The "modern" was commercial capitalism. The "archaic" was a mélange of European, African, and Native customs that fit ill with capitalist development or imperial needs. The "primitive" was how Europeans organized other people's lives for their own benefit, without regard to the others' goals or interests.

Eighteenth-century colonial society included all the pieces of Braudel's mosaic, fitted into a pattern that was uniquely their own. The shocks of collision had mostly passed and a way of life without historical precedent had taken shape. America partook of both the European *ancien régime* and the American situation at the edge of empire. It was a place that Europeans were remaking in their own images, not just along the east coast but well into the interior. Already it was profoundly shaped by its Africans. Yet most of it remained firmly possessed by Native Americans, on terms that they negotiated with the invaders or that they simply imposed. This mosaic society was entirely American, but it was not what the Indians had made when they still ruled the continent. Nor was it what triumphant white people would shape when they became a separate nation and began driving toward complete mastery of that same continent.

[I]

A hundred years ago, another historian coined another image for American history. "Stand at Cumberland Gap," wrote Frederick Jackson Turner, "and watch the procession of civilization, marching single file —the buffalo following the trail to the salt springs, the Indian, the fur-trader and hunter, the cattle raiser, the pioneer farmer—and the frontier has passed by."[2] Turner located his observer at the mountain pass where Virginia tumbles into Kentucky about the year 1763, just as large numbers of would-be settlers were starting west. Nonetheless, the image of a westward-moving line does no justice to American reality as it was then. Let us imagine instead a perspective above where the Mississippi and Missouri rivers join, with an unimpeded view in all directions.

We would see the marks of invasion any way we looked. Along the Gulf Coast a great arc of French towns stretched from Mobile through Biloxi and New Orleans. It terminated inland at Natchitoches, on the Red River in western Louisiana. Another French arc ran up the Mississippi and along the Great Lakes and St. Lawrence all the way to Quebec. A traveler ascending it from New Orleans might stop at Natchez (which the French called Fort Rosalie for a time), Arkansas Post, Kaskaskia, Ste. Genevieve, and St. Louis before turning east toward Fort Pontchartrain (Detroit) and Montreal. Along the way the traveler might encounter both worldly-wise merchants reading Voltaire and Catholic priests.[3]

Beyond these arcs Spaniards were inscribing another across the mostly dry lands between East Texas and the Pacific coast. It began at the presidio of Los Adaes, not many miles west of Natchitoches. Nagodoches, San Antonio, El Paso, Albuquerque, Santa Fe, Tucson, and the Sonora Desert mission of Tubac marked its westward course. By the end of the war of United States independence, the Spanish arc reached to San Francisco. This was the northermost of the California missions, presidios, and towns that Spaniards established between 1769 and 1782. The others included San Diego, San Juan Capistrano, Los Angeles, San Gabriel, Santa Barbara, San Luis Obispo, San Antonio de Padua, Monterey, and San Jose.

Settlement in these places did not begin with the Europeans. The French Mississippi Valley emplacements at Baton Rouge, Natchez, Kaskaskia, and Cahokia all stood on Indian sites. While medieval Europeans were constructing their castles, southwestern Indians were building on almost the same scale. Zunis, Acomas, Hopis, and Navajos constructed some 13,000 rooms between 1250 and 1400, as well as irrigation canals

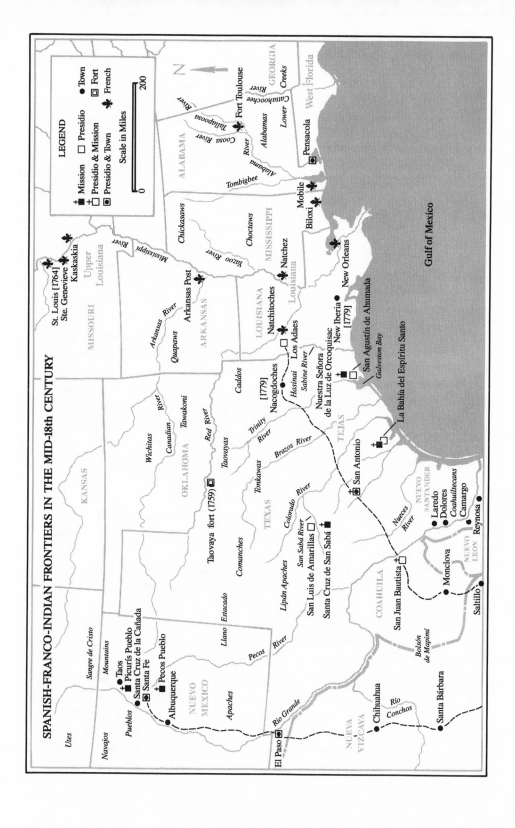

SPANISH-FRANCO-INDIAN FRONTIERS IN THE MID-18th CENTURY

LEGEND

✚ Mission ☐ Presidio ● Town
☐ Presidio & Mission ☐ Fort
◉ Presidio & Town ❋ French

Scale in Miles
0   200

N

Gulf of Mexico

GEORGIA

Creeks

Fort Toulouse

Catahoochee River
Tallapoosa River
Coosa River

Lower
Alabamas

WEST FLORIDA

Pensacola

ALABAMA

Alabama River

Tombigbee

Mobile

Biloxi

Chickasaws

Choctaws

MISSISSIPPI

Yazoo River

Natchez

LOUISIANA

New Orleans

MISSOURI

St. Louis [1764]
Ste. Genevieve
Kaskaskia

Upper Louisiana

Mississippi River

Arkansas River

Quapaws

Arkansas Post

ARKANSAS

Caddos

Natchitoches

Los Adaes

Hasinai

Nacogdoches [1779]

Sabine River

Nuestra Señora
de la Luz de Orcoquisac

New Iberia

San Agustín de Ahumada [1779]

Galveston Bay

La Bahía del Espíritu Santo

KANSAS

Wichitas

Canadian River

Tawakoni

Red River

Taovayas

Taovaya fort (1759)

OKLAHOMA

Comanches

TEXAS

Tonkawas

Trinity River

Brazos River

Colorado River

San Antonio

TEXAS

Nueces River

NUEVO SANTANDER

Laredo
Dolores
Coahuiltecans
Camargo
Reynosa

Llano Estacado

Lipán Apaches

San Sabá River

San Luis de Amarillas

Santa Cruz de San Sabá

COAHUILA

San Juan Bautista

Monclova

NUEVO LEÓN

Saltillo

Sangre de Cristo Mountains

Utes

Navajos

Pueblos

Taos
Picurís Pueblo
Santa Cruz de la Cañada
Santa Fe
Pecos Pueblo

NUEVO MEXICO

Albuquerque

Apaches

Pecos River

Rio Grande

El Paso

NUEVA VIZCAYA

Chihuahua

Río Conchos

Santa Bárbara

Bolsón de Mapimí

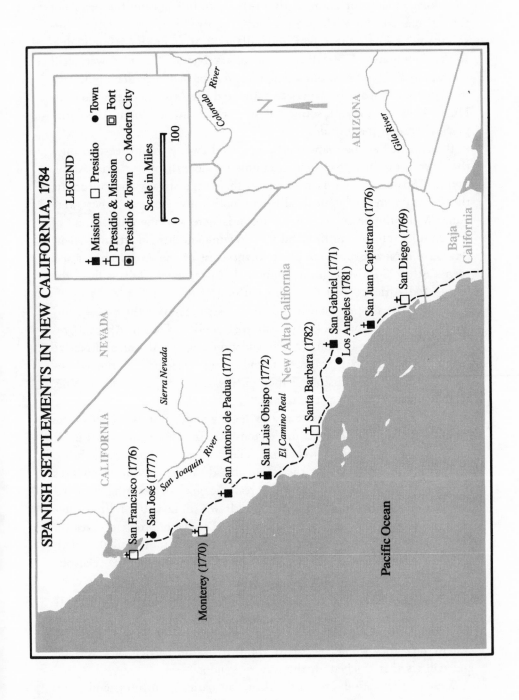

SPANISH SETTLEMENTS IN NEW CALIFORNIA, 1784

LEGEND

Mission ◼   Presidio ☐
Presidio & Mission ◼‡
Presidio & Town ◉   Town ●
                          Fort ▣
                          Modern City ○

Scale in Miles

0   100

CALIFORNIA

NEVADA

ARIZONA

Colorado River

Gila River

Sierra Nevada

San Joaquin River

New (Alta) California

El Camino Real

Baja California

Pacific Ocean

San Francisco (1776)
San José (1777)
Monterey (1770)
San Antonio de Padua (1771)
San Luis Obispo (1772)
Santa Barbara (1782)
San Gabriel (1771)
Los Angeles (1781)
San Juan Capistrano (1776)
San Diego (1769)

N

and storage places for grain. Early in the sixteenth century the people of the Arizona and New Mexico pueblos numbered perhaps 248,000, "residing in 134 or more towns and villages." Most of the High Plains, Rocky Mountains, Great Basin, and Sierra Nevada/Cascades were still "unexplored" by whites, but these, too, were or had been densely inhabited. In 1620 a Spanish Franciscan estimated the Apaches of the southern High Plains at "400,000 souls."[4] However accurate his count, the figure gives a sense of magnitude.

If we looked at the maps the Europeans drew we would see two lines that were new in 1763. One, running the length of the Mississippi, divided "Spanish" territory from "English." Linguistically and culturally, the French remained. Juridically and politically, however, they were gone. While the peace negotiators in Paris were working out the end of French rule, someone in England was drawing another line from Chaleur Bay on the New Brunswick coast to the crest of the Appalachians and then south to Spanish Florida. Supposedly, it separated Indians from the whites and Africans. In fact, it did nothing of the sort.

At the Mississippi's mouth and well upstream was a three-race community, whose people spoke Spanish, metropolitan French, African Creole French, Acadian (Cajun) French, and a mélange of African and Native tongues. They hunted, trapped, farmed, traded, slept, and cooked together. Among their historical monuments is the region's rich cuisine, "creole" in every sense of the term.[5]

South of the Great Lakes, was a "village world," just as mixed as the lower Mississippi and just as full of tensions. In 1763 conflict within it came to war, as Pontiac's Rebellion. The war was an attempt to bring all Indians together, not for the impossible dream of driving the whites completely back, but for the more realistic goal of securing regional Indian control against English pressure. It was linked to a religious revival inspired by Pontiac's brother, the "Delaware Prophet" Neolin. None of its goals was achieved. Projects for tribal unity failed to jell. Despite being besieged, the English at Fort Pitt (Pittsburgh), Detroit, and Niagara held fast. Defeat left the northwestern Indians only one more card to play, the possibility of an alliance with the British against the colonists. From the Iroquois to the Kickapoos, most Indians came to understand that fact. Many had long been part of the French imperial system; now they would be part of the British, full participants in trade and politics that reached all the way to London.[6]

West of the coastal provinces, then, lay nations, cultures, and races that were rubbing against each other and sliding into each other's ways.

Turning east, and raising our perspective across the Atlantic, we would see still more of the mid-eighteenth century's continent- and ocean-spanning turmoil.

The peace of 1763 ended half a century of war among the European powers. Merchant vessels were safe against capture, and the Western Hemisphere wanted slaves. Among Britain's possessions, the southern mainland colonies wanted them most. Between 1761 and 1770, Georgia, the Carolinas, Virginia, and Maryland imported more than 69,000 slaves, compared with Jamaica's 62,300, the 33,000 who went to Barbados, and the 68,000 who were taken to all the other British provinces combined.[7]

These enslaved people were the product of another enormous world of tension and violence, where Europeans met Africans and Africans met one another. Within Africa, Muslims confronted "infidel" animists. Members of various speech groups and nations faced one another down. Just as different Native Americans responded to the Europeans in terms of their own needs, so did Africans. A Gola from Upper Guinea who was dragged onto a ship for Charleston might have been captured by Muslim Mandingos, who regarded war against pagans as a holy war, a *jihad*. That slave might also have been sold by an African ruler who wanted "the best cloth . . . the most alcohol and . . . the widest collection of durable goods for prestige purposes." If alcohol was the price, it might have been New England rum distilled from West Indies molasses that other enslaved Africans had produced. If the price was cloth, it might have been dyed with South Carolina indigo. Should such a great man be enslaved, "Europeans made every effort" to "rectify the situation [both from] fear of retaliation . . . and a desire to protect trading interests."[8] African involvement in no sense excuses the European and white American shipmasters and merchants who took and sold the slaves, or the colonial planters, farmers, artisans, preachers, and politicians who presumed to buy other people's whole lives and progeny. Nonetheless, African cooperation happened.

Looking straight east, our perspective would show emigrant ships setting sail from Germany, Britain, and Ireland. Even when relations between colonies and metropolis were in tatters and war looked imminent, they kept coming. September 1775 was the last month when emigration was possible, and 1,115 people departed from British ports. The vast majority of them were Scots.[9]

The numbers arriving in Philadelphia give a sense of the migration's scale. During the Seven Years' War, migrants numbered only in the hundreds and in 1756 there were only 85 altogether. After the peace there were only two years, 1764 and 1768, when Philadelphia received fewer than 1,000 British migrants. In 1771 there were nearly 2,000. Migrants from Germany had fallen to almost nil during the Seven Years' War, after a period that had seen one annual migration of 8,778 (1749) and three others higher than 4,000. After 1763 there were two years when German migration approached 2,000; in all the rest it continued to number in the hundreds.[10]

Migrants leave one place because of reasons that "push." They go elsewhere for reasons that "pull." Different people's reasons for doing the same thing can vary, and within this westward flow there were many variations. From London and the south of England came single young men. Many were indentured servants, though not in the seventeenth-century Virginia sense. Servants came to work in Philadelphia's shops, in the iron foundries of New Jersey, Pennsylvania, Maryland, and Virginia, and on farms in the wheat-growing hinterland. Migrants from the north of England, Scotland, and Ireland were different. They traveled in whole families, leaving places that they could bear no longer. Highland Scots, particularly, were refugees, fleeing drastic changes as Anglicized lairds evicted smallholding crofters and substituted herding for agriculture on their huge estates. In America these people went inland, settling in an arc from Nova Scotia and Newfoundland, through the interior of New York, Pennsylvania, and Virginia, as far south as the Carolinas. Most north country people were Evangelical Protestants but some Highland Scots were Catholics. The "Irish" were the Protestant descendants of Lowland Scots whom the English had resettled in northern Ireland. All these had learned to regard others—any others—as enemies, almost automatically. It was with people of this sort that the land between the settled English provinces and the mixed-race, mixed-culture interior now began to fill.[11]

Along the southern Atlantic coast planters liked to pretend that they were simply English gentlemen who happened to live across the Atlantic. They read English books and journals, copied English fashions, imported English goods. They imitated the practices of Britain's House of Commons in Virginia's House of Burgesses and South Carolina's Commons House of Assembly. Nonetheless, a southern plantation never was an American version of an English manor. Enslaved labor and staple-crop production made the tobacco plantations of Virginia and the rice and indigo plantations of South Carolina wholly American institutions.

Consider the South Carolina plantation known as Mulberry, built in 1714 near Charleston. From the front, Mulberry is a superb example of provincial elegance, a sign of its builder's cultural debt to the British metropolis and his commitment to South Carolina. Eventually it would be the home of Mary Boykin Chesnut, the Confederacy's great diarist. A view survives, however, that shows Mulberry as it looked in 1770 from the rear. Between the house and where artist Thomas Coram placed himself stood eight slave dwellings in African style. These and the great house vie to define the plantation's human space. Such clashes, rather than mere provincial mimesis, shaped the world that planters and slaves alike inhabited.[12]

North of the Chesapeake, both society and the economy were more complex. By 1700, Boston's 7,000 inhabitants lived in a miniature London. Its artisans ranged from Benjamin Franklin's candlemaker father to shipwrights and goldsmiths. Harvard College linked both clergymen and the worldly elite to European learning. Printing presses spread the good news of Christian salvation, Puritan style. After 1707 newspapers brought worldly information that Bostonians needed. Boston vessels cruised the whole Atlantic Ocean. The need to finance voyages and insure ships and cargoes was creating a money market. Boston had become an entrepôt, a complex node of information, production, and exchange within the broad Atlantic web. By 1760 the same was true of New York and Philadelphia.[13]

Early northern commerce had begun with furs, linking the Indians directly to Europe. By the eighteenth century, commerce linked all three American races to one another and to Europe as well. To this day the cuisines of New England, the West Indies, and southern France bear the mark of colonial trade in the form of salt cod. Yankees enjoy it as codfish cakes; Jamaicans like it fried with onions, tomatoes, and the tropical fruit called ackee; Provence knows it as *morue*. Until overfishing exhausted St. George's Bank and the Grand Banks, almost all of it came from American waters. By 1700 much of it was caught and salted by New England fishermen, packed in barrels made by New England coopers, and shipped in New England-built vessels with New England crews. Those ships carried New England rum to Africa, slaves from Africa to the plantations, and plantation products to market, including the molasses that New Englanders distilled into more rum. Ships needed sails and rope, so a shipyard would generate sail lofts and rope walks. They needed metalware, despite the fact that in 1750 Parliament forbade the manufacture of colonial iron beyond the crudest stage of smelting. The southern colonies were economically and socially simple. The northern ones were complex.

Consider Benjamin Franklin, spending his youth in Boston. Harvard was not for him, but his father showed him each of the town's trades. Franklin had choices. When he became an apprentice in his brother James's printshop, he entered a world whose chief commodity was information, just as surely as for privileged students at the college across the Charles River. For Harvard students and apprentice printers alike, that world already spanned the Atlantic. However, Franklin found both James's printshop and the town of Boston stifling. Otherwise he would not have left for Philadelphia in 1723.

When Franklin arrived in Philadelphia, it was not much more than a shipping point, where the products of forests and fields changed hands. Franklin's career there was not a sign of what any American boy might do, because he was not any American boy. It does show what an emerging commercial center made possible. Philadelphia offered opportunities and for Franklin the biggest was the opportunity to create himself. Although he had not finished his apprenticeship, he began his new life at the higher level of journeyman printer. He formed connections that reached to the provincial governor. He tried his lot in London in 1725 and 1726, not with the idea of migrating permanently but to see the world. When he returned to Pennsylvania and became a master printer, his *Pennsylvania Gazette* and *Poor Richard's Almanack*, his job printing business, and his government contracts made him rich. He retired at forty-two.

While still an active printer Franklin organized a "junto" of rising men like himself, to share what they knew. After retiring he could afford to call himself a gentleman and live in cultured leisure. His electrical experiments won him world fame. He helped found Philadelphia's Library Company, the American Philosophical Society, and the city's hospital and college. He organized a militia and became its colonel. He challenged the Penn family, seeking to have the province's government transferred from them to the Crown. His honorary degrees from St. Andrews, Oxford, and eventually Harvard and his political success on the world stage all stem from leaving active business behind. Nonetheless, a deep continuity binds Franklin the printer, Franklin the civic builder, and the Franklin of world repute together: his own ability to use and distribute information for the world's benefit and for his own. Knowledge could be increased, exchanged, and used, rather than simply preserved and passed on. Franklin had begun to appreciate that point in his Boston youth, but Philadelphia offered a spectacular site for putting it to work.

Had Franklin gone farther south, settling, perhaps, in Charleston,

South Carolina, he might have found far less chance to use his talents and far less reason for others to notice him. Charleston became rich and elegant in the eighteenth century, but its economy remained simple. It shipped rice and indigo to a market that was virtually guaranteed and it imported goods and slaves. Pennsylvanians faced greater challenges. Franklin's readers were farmers, millers, and bakers marketing grain, flour, and bread, shippers seeking cargoes, and craftsmen fending off competition. Franklin's self-appointed job as a printer and publisher was to give them information they needed. The gentleman Franklin of later years did much the same, but now philosophy, politics, high policy, and speculation in western land replaced prices current as the subjects of his interest.

[II]

By the third quarter of the eighteenth century parts of the east coast could have passed for Britain. Boston's lanes resembled London's Cheapside. Philadelphia's broad streets, Georgian buildings, and open squares looked much like London's newer areas, Bloomsbury, and the West End. The De Lancey family's rural Manhattan retreat included a stone monument. Lanes were cut through the woods to show the monument off, just as on a rich Englishman's lands. Philipse Manor in the lower Hudson Valley included a deer park. The lord of the manor ate beneath an ornate ceiling crafted by an English plasterer. George Washington had the wooden beams of Mount Vernon beveled to resemble the stone blocks of an English manor house.

Washington failed to enter the large transatlantic world. As a brash young militia colonel he found that his advice was rebuffed and that he ranked below the most junior British regular captain. He never got over it. But other colonials made themselves at home in the big world. Staats Long Morris of New York rose to lieutenant general in the regular army, entered Parliament, and married a widowed duchess. Susannah De Lancey became Lady Susannah Warren and the mother-in-law of three peers. Benjamin Franklin returned to London as a major figure in culture and politics. A colonial sailor could feel just as at home on Liverpool's waterfront as on New York's.[14]

Yet the colonies and their people were not really English at all. Though Indians went to London on business, Philadelphia and Charleston saw them far more often. England had roughly 10,000 black people in 1770, but these were only one sixtieth the number in the colonies. Most of the American blacks were growing crops that British soil would never yield. The hills of Britain stood largely bare, stripped by centuries of tree cutting and sheep raising, their soil held in place by moorland and tussock. The Appalachians, about as tall as the British peaks, were still thickly forested. In England hunting was a gentleman's privilege or a poacher's crime. For the most part, it still is. In America it became virtually any man's right.[15] Mount Vernon was built of Virginia wood, not English stone.

In terms of race and class, freedom and slavery, religion and culture, gender and region, colonial people differed enormously. Yet they faced one contradiction running through their lives. Every colonial learned about a social ideal that put enormous stress upon personal autonomy. All of them lived, however, within a social reality of subordination to someone else. All were *subject* in some way to the will and purposes of another.

Natives came closest to living out the ideal that every single person should stand free. Woodland Indian children learned about respecting their community and conforming to its customs; they did not learn to submit to restraint or accept subordination. What the ancestors taught or the community required, an Indian might feel compelled to do. But nobody, not a chief or war leader or shaman or parent or spouse, could force the Indian to do it. European notions of political or even parental power are virtually useless for understanding how woodland Native communities worked. Both sides adopted the image of fatherhood to convey the relationship between European monarchies that were moving toward continental dominance and the Indian communities that filled most of the continent, but the image conveyed misunderstanding as much as it did agreement. To the Europeans, fatherhood, patriarchy, and power went together. It seemed to them that by accepting the imagery Indians were also accepting subordination. To Indians, however, a biological father was a kind and loving figure who exercised no power over his children. If that had to be done, their mother's brother was the appropriate person. European and white colonial generals and politicians misunderstood time after time what Indians would do, and why. Nonetheless, the meanings fused in a creative process based as much on mutual misunderstanding as on actual agreement. Within this "process of mutual invention" each side acquired means for dealing with the other.[16]

To Indians, personal autonomy was not an absolute human right, incapable of alienation. It went with belonging to a family, village, and clan. Belonging was one thing, however. Subjection in the sense that Europeans understood it was another. For Indians, only captives in war were truly subject, and even captives might be adopted into the community and restored to control of their lives. Yet once the invasion of America was complete the power of the great European monarchies did loom over them all.

Whites agreed that autonomy was good and that a person found it within society. The great majority could read the Bible, learning about the freedom of individuals from sin and the freedom of ancient Israel from its captivity in Egypt and Babylon. They could "know the truth" that would make them free; they were "called unto liberty" by no less a Summoner than the Lord.[17] Nonetheless, their Christian freedom was tempered by commandments and injunctions: "servants, obey your masters . . . render unto Caesar that which is Caesar's . . . the Powers that be are ordained of God."[18] Only Quakers carried the notion of equality among all souls to its logical conclusion, regardless of worldly condition. In mid-century they were caught between their teaching, which pointed toward pacifism and hostility to slavery, and their situation, which pointed toward submission to authority and retreat from the world, as a peculiar people.[19]

A would-be lawyer or magistrate who studied the English common law learned how its arcane procedures protected individuals and communities against the power of a ruler. For the male elite, there was college education: at Harvard, William and Mary, and Yale by the end of the seventeenth century, joined by the College of Rhode Island (Brown), King's College (Columbia), the College of New Jersey (Princeton), and the College of Philadelphia (the University of Pennsylvania) in the mid-eighteenth. Anyone who went to college learned about "civic humanism," a tradition of political thought that ran back to the seventeenth-century English Commonwealth, the city-states of Renaissance Italy, and classical antiquity.[20] History books, dramas such as Joseph Addison's *Cato*, political pamphleteering by both British and colonial authors, more abstract commentary by respected European thinkers: all these drove the same point home. In the good life a man stood free. He stood free, however, as the head of a family, not as an individual on his own, and the good life was easily lost.[21]

For anyone who was black, or for a white who was born female, autonomy was visible, but it was also almost beyond reach. By the mid-eighteenth century virtually every black person in America was a slave, for life. This was as true in Boston, Albany, and Philadelphia as in

Williamsburg, Norfolk, and Charleston. In 1776 there were perhaps 6,000 black people in the whole Chesapeake whom no one claimed to own, a bare 2 percent of the area's black population.[22] Their example offered virtually no hope. Slaves who heard talk about liberty might have raged among themselves against what the whites had done to their lives. But slavery's realm was everywhere and the North Star did not yet point toward freedom. Dishonored outsiders, captives of society rather than members of it, they had little basis for claiming the liberty that the masters enjoyed.[23]

For single white women the situation was significantly better. They could hold property, make contracts, bring lawsuits, bear witness in court, administer estates, or run businesses. Unlike a black woman, a white's body enjoyed the law's protection; a man who raped her could hang for it. But full autonomy was almost as impossible a dream as for slaves. Being young and female meant being someone's daughter, or dependent sister, or niece. Adulthood meant becoming a wife. Only a few women had any sense that they could control their own sexuality or fertility.[24] Married adulthood meant submerging legal personhood into one's husband's. If a woman wanted to protect or control the property she brought to her marriage, male "trustees" had to do it for her. A white woman did count as a person at law, but when she married and became a *femme couverte*, her personhood could virtually disappear.[25]

Even white males experienced subordination, as dependent sons, apprentices, indentured servants, common sailors, or militia privates. Only when a man reached mastery—over land as a freeholder or over a trade as an independent craftsman—did he approach autonomy. Then he was ready to control someone else, as husband, father, master of apprentices, purchaser of indentured labor, or owner of slaves. Such a man valued what he enjoyed. It had cost him a high price and taken him over a long road. The course of his life and the visible example of black men and women, white females, and younger or poorer white men showed him daily what liberty was not.

The colonial world's understanding of its key term—liberty—differed radically from ours. Its white men organized their sense of what was right as much around subjection as around liberty or autonomy. A precursor of Thomas Jefferson, formulating the colonial social creed, might have affirmed the self-evident truths that no person is equal to any other, that the rights people enjoy vary with their social stations, and that the foremost right of any person is to the protection that a more powerful person can offer. The distant British Crown offered a metaphor for the entire social order.[26] Every wife, son, daughter, apprentice, and slave stood in subjection to the father of the household just as all subjects from servants to royal princes stood below the king. Their liberties sprang directly from their subjection. A subject in need could claim the king's protection. The use of the same word—court—to describe the place in Westminster where the king encountered his subjects and the places throughout the realm and dominions where his subjects encountered the law is not accidental. Even in the distant colonies, people seeking justice approached a Court "of King's Bench."

In this sense, a slave's situation was different in degree, not in kind, from that of anyone else. A slave's "liberty" under the Crown was little more than the formal right to life. Deliberately killing a slave was murder, and the king's justice could punish the guilty. In reality, punishment was nearly impossible, even if the murder was rumored to be particularly brutal, since slaves and free black people could not bear witness against whites. But just as "loyal" subjects could invoke the king's protection by "humble petition," slaves who accepted their situation could invoke their masters against virtually anybody else. So, at least, the half-articulated theory ran. Whether slaves actually accepted their situation and whether masters actually extended protection was another matter.

Whatever value Indians placed on autonomy, they understood that the weak needed the strong. The power of the six Iroquois nations was derived from the claim that their "Covenant Chain" could protect lesser tribes. They understood that the chain reached beyond them to the governor in New York City and the British Crown. For the Delawares, Iroquois protection meant becoming symbolic "women" and losing the right to conduct diplomacy and make war. The Delawares even had to submit when the Iroquois gave away their land at the fraudulent Pennsylvania "Walking Treaty" of 1736. The Delawares discarded their symbolic womanhood as soon as they were able.[27]

In Indian-white relations womanhood was a metaphor as well as a biological fact. Mastery was a metaphor too. It had different meanings between owner and slaves on a Carolina plantation, between proprietor and apprentices in a New York City printshop, and between fathers and dependent sons on rock-strewn New England farms. But the meanings were close enough so that any person involved in any of those situations could understand what the metaphor meant in the others. Mastery was good, even if most people would never enjoy it. Red, black, and white, male and female, rich and poor, "highe and eminent in power and dignitie . . . meane and in subjeccion," all the people of colonial America understood that within their common situation, mastery of some sort offered the only road to freedom. The time for an Abraham Lincoln to meditate that "as I would not be a slave, so I would not be a master" was still far off.[28]

The colonials lived in a tough, unequal, violent world which is not to be romanticized. But given the realities of conflict and power and the premise of fundamental human inequality, that world did make sense. When the Massachusetts woman Mary Rowlandson fell into the hands of warring Indians in 1676, she turned without difficulty to the language of mastery and enslavement to describe her plight. She and her minister husband may well have held a slave or two of their own. If so, the tables had been turned. She did not like what had happened—who would?— but she submitted to it, as the will of an inscrutable God.[29] The wonder, perhaps, is that the notion of equal human rights under the laws of nature and nature's comprehensible God could have emerged from a world so remote from any such idea as this.

[III]

For coastal white males, social conditions did reinforce the ideal of a person standing on his own. Yeoman farmers from New England to the deepest South wanted their own land, and they wanted to be certain that nobody could dispossess them. A man might endure tenancy, but most saw it only as a way station between poverty and possessions. The Hudson Valley was lined by the middle of the eighteenth century with great tenanted estates. George Washington was beginning to replace slavery with tenancy, thanks to his decision about 1761 to shift his main crop from tobacco to wheat. In old England tenancy could mean real prosperity. The tenant would hold a sizable tract under a titled aristocrat or county gentleman and could hire the "strolling poor" to labor when the need arose.[30]

In America, however, the idea developed that farming someone else's land, erecting fences around someone else's fields, planting fruit trees and building houses and barns that someone else would inherit, should hardly be a permanent situation. Where the landlord was benevolent, cohesive estate communities did develop. Tenants on Philipse Manor in the Hudson Valley or Sir William Johnson's Kingsborough straddling the Mohawk knew their leases would run for three lives, or ninety-nine years.

Following occasional English practice, some leases ran for 999 years. Both Frederick Philipse and Sir William conscientiously played the good landlord. Nonetheless, any American farmer wanted "his own vine and fig tree," in an image from the Book of Micah that they often invoked.[31]

Many white men did achieve that goal, particularly in New England and on the rich wheat-producing soil of eastern Pennsylvania. The latter became known as "the best poor man's country" in the world. But a young Yankee coming of age in eastern Massachusetts around 1760 might remain under his father's dominion well into adulthood if he wanted to stay in the village. When he finally acquired his patrimony it might not be enough to support a family. Almost certainly, it would not provide in turn for the next generation.[32]

Nor was this problem unique to New England. Since the discovery that Chesapeake Bay area soil could produce fine tobacco, Virginia and southern Maryland had thrived under a land system that required constant expansion. Tobacco exhausts the soil that grows it. The Chesapeake coastal plain is broad, and the rich piedmont that stretches behind the fall line where rivers tumble down to sea level was not hard to enter. Plantation culture spread across that whole huge area, both because of soil exhaustion and because prosperous Virginians wanted all their children to benefit by inheritance, not just the eldest son who would maintain the home estate. By the time New England's eastern towns were growing overcrowded, however, the Blue Ridge loomed in the way of Chesapeake society's further expansion. The limit was not absolute in either place; fertile, open land did remain. Nonetheless, both societies had to expand in order to continue to prosper. Their other choice was to change how they lived. With his large investments west of the Blue Ridge and his decision about 1761 to shift Mount Vernon from tobacco to grain, George Washington demonstrated that he understood the dilemma his society faced.[33]

To any white male in the countryside, independence meant land, whether the man was a Yankee villager, a Pennsylvania wheat farmer, a Chesapeake "cropmaster" who took great pride in the leaf his plantation produced, or a Carolina rice planter who, when the sickly season came each summer, fled the swamps and the slaves that made him wealthy. For townsmen, the road to personal independence was different. Though the merchant sector dominated urban economic life, few could hope to enter it, even at its lower levels. On the eve of independence Philadelphia's merchant community comprised barely more than 300 men, out of an urban population that was approaching 30,000.[34] If a townsman was to stand upon his own feet, it would be as an artisan or mechanic, the master not of a freehold farm but rather of a craft.

Except for a few trades, colonial cities did not develop the rigid, exclusionary guilds of their European counterparts. Nonetheless, to enter urban apprenticeship was to become both a student of one's chosen craft and a legally bound unpaid laborer.[35] It was also to enter the master's household, subordinate just like a natural son to whatever the master required. After apprenticeship and acquiring skills came the status of journeyman, which meant being an employee. Only when an artisan acquired his own shop was he truly a master in his own right. Now he controlled the skills of his trade, his tools, raw materials on their way to being finished goods, his family, and the apprentices who joined his household in turn. Like a freehold farmer, a master artisan would be a workingman producing goods, a businessman in the world of exchange, and a patriarch, dominating others because of their youth or their sex or because he had purchased them.

Master artisans varied enormously in their wealth, their sophistication, and their emplacement in the larger world. Benjamin Franklin's rise from runaway apprentice to master printer to scientist, gentleman, and politician became famous. Few could expect to follow that course, no matter how well they read his *Autobiography* or *Poor Richard's Almanack*. But a successful practitioner of a luxury trade—a painter like Boston's John Singleton Copley or a silversmith like the same town's Paul Revere—could hope to do well and live comfortably. Most artisans lived below that level: bakers, bricklayers, weavers, candlemakers, butchers, and carpenters. For these, even mastery of a trade and a shop might offer only a lifelong struggle to hold on in good times and survive during bad ones. Careful quantitative studies of the distribution of urban property have shown it becoming considerably more skewed toward the rich. In 1687 the top 5 percent of Bostonians controlled 30 percent of the town's taxable wealth. By 1771 they held almost half.[36]

For men who entered some trades—shipbuilding, sail or rope making, iron work, or seafaring—mastery was unlikely to be achieved. Even in the eighteenth century these trades required more capital than most men would ever see. Moreover, almost anyone with maritime skills—a merchant seaman, a harbor boatman, a fisherman—had to face the real danger of being impressed into the royal navy during wartime. Going to sea voluntarily during times of peace was bad enough, since a merchant captain could have a sailor flogged. The navy meant conditions of legalized violence, danger, and squalor that rivaled slavery. Yet seamen valued

their independence as much as did any Paul Revere or Benjamin Franklin. They too were "freeborn Englishmen."[37] American seafarers knew
that within the boundaries of a colonial port a naval officer could order
an impressment only with the permission of the local government. Even
then, a press was likely to provoke a riot. It happened in Boston in 1747
and again in New York City in 1764.

White colonials claimed the historic liberties that went with being
English. In the words of one common-law dictionary, a liberty was a
particular "privilege held by grant of prescription, whereby men enjoy
some benefit or favour beyond the ordinary subject." In these terms, the
city of New York enjoyed the liberty of the "benefit of ye market" or
"privileges of market and fairs" that gave it control over its own commerce. The College of William and Mary enjoyed the liberty of being
directly represented in Virginia's House of Burgesses, just as the universities of Oxford and Cambridge were represented in the unreformed
House of Commons. Britons and colonials had the liberty of being taxed
only by their own representatives. In some ways, colonials enjoyed
broader liberties than the English. White males had wider access to
property in America and through property they enjoyed far more political
participation. The three New York manors that sent their own representatives to the provincial assembly offered an analogy to the "rotten bor-
oughs" whose owners possessed what amounted to personal seats in
Parliament. But most colonial political practices were far more open than
those in England. In other ways, most notably the automatic condemnation of an entire race to slavery, colonial liberties were far more narrow.
Colonial liberties were like those of England, not the same as those in
England. There lay a huge problem.

[IV]

The emergence of merchants whose home and commitment lay in the
northern ports distinguished those towns from Charleston, South Carolina, or Kingston, Jamaica. Northern ports contained the seeds of self-
driving capitalist development; the South did not. The distinction is not
absolute. Northern colonial merchants did not form a coherent group.
One line among them separated transatlantic operators from intra-
American traders; often the former either were immigrants or had close
ties of family and friendship with British merchant houses. Like a British
trader who went to the West Indies or a Spaniard who sojourned a while

in Cartagena, these served the metropolis, not the colony. Another line separated general "sedentary" merchants who brought manufactured goods in and shipped agricultural products out from traders who dealt in provincial manufactures, particularly iron. A third line distinguished the well-connected traders who could expect lucrative military contracts from the rest who did not have the government's favor.

Nonetheless, the northern merchants created the economic web that emerged by the mid-eighteenth century. Some merchant fortunes were truly huge; claims for upward of £100,000 were filed in London by New York loyalists who lost their estates during the Revolution. One common theme in the genesis of truly great colonial merchant fortunes is how wartime gains could turn modest beginnings into monumental wealth. The intermarried De Lancey, Watts, and Franks families of New York City established a consortium that won large supply contracts during the Seven Years' War, when the city was the main funnel for British troops and supplies. They realized total profits of about £1,700,000.[38]

These greatest winners in American commerce were not getting their wealth from production. In the sociologist Max Weber's terms, they were "capitalistic adventurers" who aimed at "the acquisition of booty, whether directly in war or" by using "slaves, or directly or indirectly forced labour."[39] They invested their money safely, in notes of hand, bonds, and land, including massive speculations in land taken from the Indians. Hardly any put what they had into projects that led to future American development. Only one of New York's great loyalist traders was involved in the province's flourishing iron sector. As in the southern plantation economy, the great northern merchants' use of their investment capital demonstrated the limits of the colonial world in which they lived.

[V]

Early merchant capitalism arrived in the New World in the first English ships, of course, but it was not all that the Europeans brought. The settlers rewove as much as they could of the strands of European society that they had broken when they left, and their web proved thick and strong. Trying to escape from the modern world, Puritan villagers imported "English local law and custom," however archaic. Anxious about their place in that same world, colonial assemblymen mimicked the House of Commons. The imagined cosmos of English witchcraft reappeared in many instances besides the famous outbreak at Salem. Remnants of feudalism flourished in the Hudson Valley and appeared in many other places. There were echoes of European charivari (or "rough music" or "skimmington") whenever crowds harassed violators of community norms.[40]

Consider just two instances, the neo-feudal estates of the Hudson Valley and the quasi-legitimate crowd uprisings that might appear anywhere from New Hampshire to Georgia. New York's land system was not unique in early America. Tenanted estates appeared as far south as Virginia and the Carolinas. Two provinces, Pennsylvania and Maryland, were granted on feudal terms to single families, the Penns and the Calverts, respectively. Until the end of the colonial period both the vast bulk of Pennsylvania's land and its powerful governorship passed from Penn father to Penn son, much like an earldom or a duchy. Though the Penns were never ennobled, they enjoyed a great deal more political power in their American province than any British peer who sat in the House of Lords.

Nonetheless, the Hudson Valley seems most reminiscent of the European old order. The first of its great estates began with a grant by the Dutch West India Company to Kiliaen Van Rensselaer of a tract forty miles on a side surrounding modern Albany. With the grant went the hereditary title of patroon. The English conquered Holland's colony in 1664. After a briefly renewed period of Dutch rule a decade later, they made their possession permanent. During their first decades, well-placed men acquired tracts of land on a similar grand scale, with formal titles and rights. Some lordly rights, such as judicial power over the tenants in a medieval-style "court leet" and a "court baron," were never exercised despite being granted on paper. Others, such as direct representation for their manors in the provincial assembly, were valued and used.[41]

Such rights were empty unless tenants gave value to the land. During the eighteenth century New York was a less attractive destination than Pennsylvania, partly because its frontiers were less peaceful, partly because of its considerable population of conquered Dutch, and partly because of its land system. Landlords did offer free rent to beginners and aid in setting up farms. In return, tenants built fences and roads, cleared forests to create fields and orchards, and erected barns and houses. What they built, cleared, planted, and erected would never be theirs. They could sell their "improvements." But the landowner had first option to buy and could claim some of the sale price in any case.

On some estates this produced friction and outright rebellion. By the mid-eighteenth century Rensselaerswyck and neighboring Livingston Manor were alive with unrest. The Livingston family used its rights aggressively and was not inclined to grant long leases. Livingston Manor's eastern reaches were disputed land, claimed both by New York and the family and by Massachusetts and its westernmost towns. A map of 1774 showed both sets of claims, including a line that extended the manor into both Massachusetts and Connecticut. The boundary uncertainty was one reason for unrest, but the issue ran deeper. In mid-century tenants began pulling down the landlord's fences, cutting his forests, and disrupting his ironworks. Once they kidnapped the sheriff of Albany County. The conflict that was beginning would not cease until the 1840s. But although the third lord of Philipse Manor raised the rents when he succeeded to his seat in 1750, he also announced that he would never do it again. His estate went untroubled. He chose loyalism when the Revolution came and so did most of his tenants.[42]

Uprisings in colonial cities enjoyed a legitimacy that no modern rioting could have. In good part this was because colonial cities took on the legal privileges and responsibilities of their English counterparts. The royal charters of Philadelphia, New York, and Albany made them corporate entities, enjoined to control the local economy. Though legally it was only a town, Boston did the same. Local economic needs came first, including affordable necessities and an avoidance of monopolizing. Violating market customs was a criminal offense. An "assize of bread" regulated the price, size, and quality of ordinary brown loaves. But there was no police force or bureaucracy to enforce the authorities' will. Raising the "hue and cry" in London or a posse in New York amounted to little more than drawing a crowd into ranks and giving it official sanction. In a crisis crowds might set and enforce a "just price" for what the populace needed. The Massachusetts politician Thomas Hutchinson said in 1768 that "mobs, a sort of them at least, are constitutional." Custom, not law, made them so.[43]

Red, black, or white, colonial Americans lived in a world where local custom and the interplay of racially defined groups provided much of the texture of life. Whites who wanted to deal with Indians learned Indian customs, until the balance of power shifted and Indians had to learn white ways. The Natives became a symbol of what was most American. When Bostonians disguised themselves before they dumped tea into Boston Harbor in 1773, they were invoking a deep European heritage. But by donning "Mohawk" costumes they were proclaiming their own

Americanness. By the eighteenth century any white enjoyed privileges denied to every black. But from the Chesapeake to Georgia whites and blacks lived within a shared southernness that expressed itself in speech, food, dance, and a profound sense of place and family.

Among whites, custom often enjoyed a status in law and public affairs that it does not have today. Notions of "positive" enacted law were only beginning to take form. Parliament and the colonial assemblies did legislate in the modern sense, declaring the will of the highest authority. But their major purpose was to decide and announce what had "always" been right. Parliament itself existed because of custom that reached back to the Middle Ages. So did the English "liberties, privileges, franchises, and immunities" which the colonists claimed for themselves.

Custom was often intensely local. "Constitutional" mobs in both America and England operated in the belief that small communities ought to regulate themselves, as the primary units of both production and consumption. There were times when long-distance trade was legitimate; there also were times when the community should cut itself off, whether because of a government embargo or by the action of a crowd. Such "persistent localism" could spill into formal legal practice. Courts acted in terms of the local community's interests and perceptions, not in terms of a "supreme law of the land." Even long-distance trade proceeded according to the informal *lex mercatoria*, which meant the law and customs of the merchant community. English common law rested on custom and precedent. As late as 1786 "A Citizen" in Albany, New York, felt free to protest a rise in local mill tolls in the name of "immemorial custom . . . a law not written, established by long usage and consent." "Particular customs," he wrote, "are always to be taken for law" even if they were "against the general custom of the Kingdom and the maxims of [written] law."[44]

In these terms custom could be profoundly static, particularly regarding the legitimate use of property. Nonetheless, for prerevolutionary white Americans the most privileged form of property was productive land, and its ideal use was "quiet enjoyment" without disturbance to the rights of heirs or neighbors. Owning land meant having a badge of community membership, not possessing a commodity for trade. Trade itself often meant exchange among neighbors, carried on to satisfy mutual needs. Community meant local networks of obligation. The "public good" meant keeping those networks in repair. This was the white version. For Indians, community meant keeping alive all that was possible of their world despite the irrevocable changes that began when the first

Europeans arrived. For slaves it meant protecting themselves against a situation that tried to deny them any form of self-protection at all, beyond a master's goodwill. For the three races, it meant the presence of the others, in their streets, stores, houses, beds, and lives, whether they liked it or not.[45]

[VI]

This was the complex world into which British policymakers blundered after 1763 with their attempts to tax, their writs of assistance, their juryless courts, their petty functionaries, their assertions that they were supreme. Colonial subjects were hardly a united people, and John Adams once likened their response to thirteen clocks striking as one. His metaphor meant more in an age of crude mechanical clockwork than it does in an age that tells time by the vibrations of crystals and atoms. Adams was thinking of whites. For Indians and Africans, the metaphor fails, not because it is too complex but because it is not complex enough. Yet if we would understand the American Revolution and how it ended the colonial order, we must see it in terms of the different peoples involved, not just the whites who began it with their grievances and resolved it in their own interests.

CHAPTER 3

COLONIAL REVOLTS, AMERICAN REVOLUTION

THE American Revolution began because Britain's rulers decided to reform their empire. In 1763 Britain stood supreme from Bengal to Mexico, but it also stood exhausted. For both administrative and financial reasons, the ministry proposed to make white colonials pay for their protection and governance, on terms that ministers, not colonials, would set.

They laid bare the empire's ambiguities instead, as the colonials began thinking about their situations, rights, identities, and relationships. The Revolution began as no more than revolt against unwanted change. British history is full of such events, from the peasant rising of 1385 to the Scottish Jacobite rebellion of 1745. But what began with protest became the first modern revolution. It spread from white men to many other peoples. It abolished what had made its own development possible. It created a society without precedent, whether we speak of that society's achievements or dwell upon what it failed to do.

[I]

The narrative need only be sketched. A series of parliamentary acts tried to secure a permanent revenue for North American defense and government. These were the Sugar (or Revenue) Act of 1764, the Stamp Act of 1765, and the Townshend taxes of 1767. All shared the premise that Parliament could tax the colonists for revenue, despite never having done so. The colonists protested against the Sugar Act but they accepted it in practice. They defeated the Stamp Act by hard argument, direct resistance, and support from sympathetic Britons, including many in Parliament. The Townshend taxes brought further protest, both in print and

45

in the streets. In 1770 four of the five Townshend taxes were repealed.

Each time it retreated, Parliament insisted that it could tax the colonials if it chose. In 1773 it tried to combine taxing them with rescuing the bankrupt East India Company, by giving the company direct access to America. Company tea would undercut colonial merchants' prices, despite the one remaining Townshend tax, even if the colonials' tea was "honestly smuggled." Instead, most ports refused to admit the tea vessels. Tea ships entered Boston Harbor before the town could refuse them and Governor Thomas Hutchinson would not let them depart without unloading. So in the middle of December townspeople dumped the tea into the harbor. Parliament responded by punishing both Boston and Massachusetts. Resistance to the punishment brought the collapse of royal government throughout Massachusetts, support for Massachusetts from other colonies, and escalating tension between British forces that now occupied Boston and armed colonials in the surrounding countryside. War broke out on April 19, 1775, at Lexington and Concord. Independence followed fourteen months later.[1]

Britain, not the colonies, was on the advancing edge of political development. It was becoming a modern unitary state that ruled over a complex, clashing society, where the government declares whose particular good will be called public. Bringing the colonies under control was part of that process. As Sir William Blackstone wrote in 1765, "there is and must be . . . a supreme, irresistible, uncontrolled authority, in which . . . the rights of sovereignty reside."[2] On mainland Europe such thinking had led to absolute monarchy. In Britain it produced the King-in-Parliament. *"L'état, c'est moi,"* said Louis XIV, but the First Gentleman of England gloried in his limits. "The pride, the glory of Britain, and the direct end of its Constitution is political liberty," George III wrote when he was Prince of Wales, and he held to that position all his life.[3] Nonetheless, his government was as supreme, irresistible, and uncontrolled as any Bourbon king's. In this sense, "British liberty" amounted to the conditions of absolute British power.

The modern British state was only beginning. In many ways the country remained a "composite monarchy," organized around a single monarch who ruled many separate polities. Britons distinguished the "realm" of England, Scotland, and Wales from the outlying "dominions." Within the realm, Scotland and Wales retained their identities. Ireland, the Isle of Man, and the Channel Islands were not part of the realm at all. The "best of kings" ruled over each of these separate places on its own terms. Colonists believed that though they were British subjects they were not part of the central "realm" either. As the Stamp Act Congress put it in 1765, "the People of these Colonies are not, and . . . cannot be Represented in the House of Commons in *Great-Britain*."[4] Therefore, it could not tax them.

Such arrangements had been normal not long before. Medieval monarchies joined many polities together, each continuing in its ways. Sicily and Aragon came under one crown in 1282, Poland and Lithuania in 1386, and the Dutch provinces joined with one another in 1463. France joined with Burgundy and Brittany. Spain (*Castilla y Aragón*) joined with the Netherlands, Portugal, and its separate American kingdoms, each under its own viceroy. The Swedish monarch ruled Estonia, Livonia, and Pomerania. Even in the nineteenth century the Austro-Hungarian monarch was emperor in Vienna but only king in Budapest.[5]

In all these places, notables had a gathering to protect the ancient liberties and their own interests: a Parliament, a *Parlement* or *Etats Généraux*, a *Cortes*, a *Sjem*, a *Rat*, a House of Burgesses. If that failed, a revolt might follow and notables would lead it: Owain Glyndwr in fifteenth-century Wales; the Duke of Monmouth in the seventeenth-century Welsh Marches; Prince Charles Stuart in eighteenth-century Scotland. So too in America after 1765, as rulers led their fellows into resistance to preserve traditional rights. Owain Glyndwr bears more than a passing resemblance to George Washington. Each was an ambitious man of rank from the distant periphery. Each felt a provincial's yearning for metropolitan respect. Had Glyndwr entered the English court or Washington won the respect of British army officers, as they desired, each probably would have risen. But neither would have become a hero to his people.

To the colonials, Lord Bute, George Grenville, Charles Townshend, Lord Hillsborough, Lord North, Lord Chief Justice Mansfield, Lord George Germain, and George III became the villains of the piece. By independence many were sure there was a monstrous plot to destroy liberty. "Every spot of the old world is overrun with oppression," wrote Thomas Paine in *Common Sense*, his great pamphlet of January 1776 that argued it was time to part. "Freedom hath been hunted round the globe. Asia and Africa have long expelled her. Europe regards her as a stranger, and England hath given her warning to depart." Jefferson made the same point in the Declaration of Independence: "The history of the present King of Great Britain is a history of repeated injuries and usurpations, all having in direct object the establishment of an absolute tyranny over these states."

Yet the king and his ministers thought themselves friends to liberty. The problem began because even in 1765 British rulers and white colonials understood liberty differently. To colonials, it meant neither the supremacy of Parliament nor (yet) that all men were created equal. They just wanted to protect the specific liberties that went with being who they were. "The People here, as every where else, retain a great Fondness for their old Customs and Usages," said the Stamp Act Congress of 1765.[6] That was the whole matter.

Taxes were the driving material issue, but Parliament portended more. Beyond the seacoast provinces all French claims in America were gone. The West was crisscrossed by lines drawn under the terms of colonial charters, royal and provincial grants, and Indian purchases. Lines intersected and claims overlapped. Some land titles belonged to the Natives, some to the British Crown and its agencies, and some were inherited by treaty from France. It was as tangled a landscape as any that feudalism had imposed upon Europe. The lines that defined it protected Indian rights, extended provinces westward, promised wealth, and offered solutions to east coast problems. Those lines also posed a huge problem to British administrators.

In 1763, the administrators proclaimed their western line to limit white expansion. It was almost completely ineffective, but it did show Britain's intent to nullify the morass of chartered confusion. Speculators got the point. In 1774, as the crisis with the east coast provinces verged on war, the Quebec Act removed the Ohio and Illinois country from the jurisdiction of the east coast provinces and placed them under the appointed government in Montreal. If that reform had held, it would have radically simplified affairs west of the mountains. A radical simplification in fact was about to take place, but not at British hands and not to Indians' benefit.[7]

In those years the British were also starting to consider the problem of slavery. The interests and power of British slaveholders in the Caribbean and the mainland colonies were enormous. Nonetheless, the same Sir William Blackstone who extolled Westminster's unlimited power wrote in the first edition (1765) of his *Commentaries* that "a slave or negro, the moment he lands in England, falls under the protection of the laws and with regard to all natural rights becomes *eo instanti* a freeman." This was the scholarship of an Oxford professor, not a binding judicial opinion, and Blackstone himself backed off from it. But when the Virginia-born slave James Somerset sued in 1771 against being shipped from England to Jamaica, his attorneys drew on Blackstone and advanced a powerful argument against slavery. It was "a state which the English Mind revolts at." Lord Mansfield's decision in *Somerset's Case* is often cited as abolishing slavery in England. In fact, it fell short. Not until 1778, and then only in Scotland, was slavery formally abolished anywhere in Britain. But Mansfield did save Somerset from being sent to Jamaica, condemning "so high an act of dominion" as "forcibly confining a slave aboard a ship in order to be sold overseas." "Even courts soon confused" the arguments and the rhetoric "with the decision itself," reinforcing "Britain's reputation as a free country."

Mansfield and his fellow judges were very careful not to extend any condemnation of slavery to the colonies. As late as 1823, Lord Justice Stowell insisted that a slave who gained freedom by entering England could be reenslaved in Antigua.[8] White colonials protesting for their own freedom would not have dared to mention *Somerset's Case* as a grievance, but they knew about it. Slaves knew it as well. As early as 1772 "the first black refugees began arriving in London . . . following the Somerset decision."[9]

The British government had no plot in mind, not a malevolent one to crush American liberty, not a progressive one to rationalize and modernize its own power, not a benevolent one to protect Indians or free slaves. It was merely responding to its own predicament, ruling in near-bankruptcy over a vast, complex empire. The men in charge in London believed in hierarchy and subordination as well as in British liberty. They saw no contradiction between these positions, and neither did colonials. Ministers understood, however, that they faced problems that their predecessors never had to confront. What they undertook after 1763 began unraveling a world that they and white colonials alike believed worth conserving. The colonials' responses rendered that world's survival impossible.

[II]

It started as a notables' revolt. It led to "the mob" beginning "to think and to reason," as a privileged young New Yorker, Gouverneur Morris, wrote "with fear and with trembling" while a mass meeting was electing a committee in 1774. "Poor reptiles," he called them, " 'ere noon they will bite."[10] Revolt began to turn into revolution as gentry like Morris and "the mob" learned that their interests differed. Yet Morris chose revolution. He and others who feared revolt within America made it their project to yield "to the torrent" in order to "direct its course." To an astonishing extent, they succeeded.[11] They emerged from the Revolution conscious of themselves as a distinctive group with their own separate interests. For a time they made themselves "an American ruling class." They never felt the wrath of a populace that saw them as the Revolution's enemies.[12] Yet by the Revolution's end they and their fellows dwelt in a drastically altered social landscape.

Harvard graduates, Boston merchants, and Connecticut Valley "River Gods" in Massachusetts; Yale men in Connecticut; New York City and Albany merchants and great landlords in New York; Quakers and Anglicans, traders and lawyers in Pennsylvania; the planters of the South: these groups never formed a single colonial "ruling class." Until the crisis they hardly knew one another. Within their own provinces they were divided against one another. The only exception was Virginia, where a small confident group of planters led their society into revolution, created open political institutions in which any white male could challenge their rule, and continued to rule in the new order.

Nonetheless, even the Virginians were troubled. Practically everything that propped them up also threatened them. Tobacco brought them prosperity and it immersed them in debt. The Anglican Church gave them moral order but its clergy challenged their power and threatened their values. Some whites were abandoning decorous Anglicanism for Evangelical enthusiasm. That meant addressing even slaves as brethren and sisters. The gentry thought they were akin to the virtuous patricians of the ancient Roman republic. Yet the corruption that they believed was devouring English virtue seemed to be nibbling at them as well. Finally, the Stamp Act was the clearest sign of all that they did not really rule their world. Their treasured image was of self-control; their clear reality in English eyes was colonial subordination. Virginia gentlemen provided a stirring lead, and they meant every word of protest, written or spoken.

Leadership and a certain legitimacy came from the old colonial rulers, who realized they had a lot to lose. The energy that turned the taxes into dead letters, fought the battles, and turned colonies into states and subjects into citizens came from other sorts as well. Initially these were the white workingmen of the port cities. They saw themselves at first simply as members of threatened communities, but they and others began to understand that their interests and the leaders' interests were not necessarily the same.

Britain's reforms threatened to smother the developing American economies, especially where the economies showed most promise. The old "Navigation System" had guaranteed markets for such colonial goods as tobacco and naval stores. These were "enumerated," which meant they could be shipped only to Britain. Colonial shipping was protected both by treaties and by the royal navy. Britain stimulated colonial shipbuilding. It provided connections and credit across the sea. The system was not entirely closed. After 1741 rice could be marketed directly in Southern Europe. So could colonial wheat and flour.

But Britain also constrained and directed colonial growth. After 1732 colonials could not manufacture their own hats for sale in other provinces. After 1750 they could not refine iron ore beyond the first crude stage. It had to be shipped to England to be turned into finished goods. After 1764 colonials could not make their paper currencies a legal tender, despite a near-absence of hard coin. Colonial boundaries became thickets of bureaucratic complexity if one wanted to buy or sell. Failure to comply with the rules meant risking that goods and vessel would be confiscated. A legion of functionaries and informers aided by the royal navy descended to see that the law was enforced. All would be paid by a percentage of whatever they caused to be condemned, on the same terms that applied to enemy "prizes" in war.

After 1763 new taxes required payment in coin, although coin was not available. They would be enforced in vice-admiralty courts without juries, outside the rules of common law. The judge would hold his post "at pleasure," and he could lose it if he displeased higher authority. The Stamp Act of 1765 imposed a tax on virtually every business transaction in the colonies. Unless the tax was paid by buying a stamp the transaction would be invalid and the people involved could be prosecuted. The main trend of northern development was toward a society as complex as Britain's. The thrust of British policy was precisely to block that trend and choke colonial development. The new taxes were passed in the midst of a severe depression. The number of people who were genuinely poor was rising. At the peak of Britain's historic world triumph, being a British colonial was turning into a major problem.

For established local rulers to rouse their fellows was perfectly within the tradition of legitimate risings and revolts. It was not within that tradition for a self-appointed leadership to claim that it spoke for ordinary people rather than to them. The plotters who organized Boston's Stamp Act resistance in 1765 were braziers and brewers and printers, not gentlemen. They called themselves the "Loyal Nine." They understood that direct resistance was necessary, not just words. They realized that poverty, unemployment, and outright fear were as much at stake as the colonies' historic practice and "liberty" of taxing themselves.[13]

When colonials nullified the Stamp Act in 1765 and 1766 they saw themselves simply as "brave colonists" or "free men and Englishmen." By 1770, people's language and consciousness were changing. When nonimportation against the Townshend Acts collapsed in 1770, a fierce debate raged over who should have a say in ending it. Merchants' business had suffered and they maintained that the decision was theirs to make, alone. A New York writer who called himself Brutus responded that nothing was "more flagrantly wrong than the assertion . . . that the Mechanics have no right to give their Sentiments." His choice of pen name recalled the assassins of Julius Caesar, but the target of his own verbal knife was "our mercantile dons." By 1774 artisans in New York had bought a meeting place, named it Mechanics' Hall, and were forming a "general committee." The committee became their forum for working out their vision of the American future.

The events that culminated in the "Boston Massacre" on March 5, 1770, show how domestic and imperial issues intersected as the Revolution was taking form. In 1767 Boston became headquarters for the newly created American Board of Customs Commissioners. The commissioners were most unwelcome and Bostonians showed it. In 1768 the ministry sent two regiments of troops to protect the commissioners and their minions. The troops acted like an army of occupation, parading in the streets, seizing public buildings for barracks, and challenging Bostonians as they went about their lawful affairs. Off-duty soldiers competed with Bostonians for scarce jobs.

Customs informer Ebenezer Richardson was the sort of man whom the troops were there to protect. In February 1770, Richardson tried to stop a crowd that was setting up a finger sign reading "importer" that pointed toward a loyalist merchant's business. The crowd's next step might have been to bedeck the business with "Hillsborough paint." Named for Lord Hillsborough, the Colonial Secretary, this was human waste dredged from outdoor "necessary houses." The crowd turned on Richardson and he retreated into his own house, pointed a gun out a window, and fired, killing eleven-year-old Christopher Sneider. The patriot leader William Molineux saved Richardson from the crowd's rage.[14] At the boy's funeral thousands of Bostonians walked behind the cortege.

On March 2, an off-duty soldier from the 29th Regiment came to John Gray's rope walk for work. When a rope worker offered a job cleaning his necessary house the soldier fetched comrades and a brawl broke out. Three nights later soldiers from the same regiment were guarding the customs house. A crowd gathered and advanced on the sentries, throwing brickbats and hard-packed snowballs. The guards opened fire. They killed five people, including Samuel Gray, who had been at the rope-walk fight. Another of the dead was Crispus Attucks, whose ancestry was black and Indian. The five were the first martyrs to American liberty and Bostonians kept March 5 as a day of mourning for many years.[15]

The revolutionary movement makes no sense unless we see how great events, grand rhetoric, and individual lives intersected, as they did in Boston that February and March. But until after the Boston Tea Party something was missing. Colonial leaders and urban workingmen alone could not have confronted Britain successfully when it finally committed its full power against the American rebellion. The overwhelming majority of white colonial males were small farmers, and it was these who precipitated the fall of the old order.

Mere revolt turned into outright revolution in central and western Massachusetts during the summer of 1774. The immediate issue was Parliament's punishments for the Tea Party, particularly the Massachusetts Government Act. The act abolished the old provincial charter and created a new council under royal authority; it forbade towns to meet more than once a year; courts of justice had to do their business under its terms. The fundamental political issue lay absolutely exposed. For the British, Parliament was sovereign and could do as it chose, including altering a charter that a previous king, acting without Parliament, had granted. For the colonials, their own institutions existed as a matter of right, like Parliament itself.

Toward the end of the summer the county courts were preparing for a new term. Townsmen throughout Massachusetts agreed that the courts should not convene. The closing would be orderly, by the vote of town meetings. Militia officers would direct the resistance: there would be no disorderly mobs. But town meetings themselves were now illegal if they tried to do more than elect local officials. Where the captain or colonel refused to take the lead he found himself deposed, with another taking his place. There was no actual violence. But in Springfield, Worcester, Concord, and every other county seat outside occupied Boston the judges resigned their posts and doffed their ceremonial wigs and robes. Royal government died throughout Massachusetts, except where the king's troops could march.

Until then New England farmers had virtually ignored what was going on, except for passing a few resolutions and not reelecting overt
governor's men to the assembly. To them the fracas was Boston's problem. Some even suspected that it was a Boston plot, so merchants could
clear their overstocked shelves while patriotic colonials boycotted Britain.
As early as 1772 the Boston town meeting appointed a committee of
correspondence to rouse the lethargic interior. The committee met only
limited success until 1774.

Nonetheless, the farmers had long memories. They knew that almost
a century earlier the British had forced another change in government
upon their ancestors, abolishing their provinces and creating a single
Dominion of New England under a governor and an appointed council.
The governor, Sir Edmund Andros, realized that legally New England
towns had never enjoyed the right to hold land in common or make
grants to individual townsmen. That meant that New Englanders did
not really own their land at all. The governor was free to make grants
to himself and his friends and to extort outrageous fees from farmers if
they wanted their titles reconfirmed. The very first grant that Andros
made was the town common that the people of Cambridge had thought
was theirs. When news arrived from England in 1689 that Andros's
master, James II, had been overthrown, Andros himself was clapped in
the Boston jail. People still told the story eight decades later.

New Englanders knew the story of Oliver Cromwell, leader of the
Puritan Revolution that had overthrown and executed King Charles I.
After 1765 they began naming baby boys Oliver in Cromwell's memory.
When Britain imposed the Massachusetts Government Act in 1774 as
punishment for the Boston Tea Party, militia commissions, seats on the
provincial council, and judgeships all became available. To more and
more people in the interior a man who accepted those posts was selling
out his community. He might even have an eye on his neighbors' land,
should unpaid taxes lead to a sheriff's sale. Thoughts, memories, and
fears all came together as the farmers realized during the summer of
1774 that they had to close the courts, confining the old provincial
government and its army to Boston. During the autumn and winter that
followed townsmen and townswomen collected supplies while militiamen
drilled. In the spring they went to war.[16]

The Revolution was more than a confrontation between the colonials
and Britain, but it was not a simple confrontation of one class with
another. Colonial America was far too variegated, even where two local
situations seem much the same. In Maryland as in Virginia, tobacco was

the cash crop. In both provinces, planters, smaller white farmers, and slaves comprised most of society. In Virginia, whites cohered during the Revolution. In Maryland, they fought among themselves. Some of Maryland's gentry families, such as the Carrolls, were Catholics, excluded by colonial law from public office. Perhaps long exclusion rendered them unable to bind lesser whites to themselves with the ties of culture and dependency that formed white Virginians into one people. Perhaps the problem stemmed from Maryland's being farther north, straddling the line where tobacco cultivation yielded to wheat. Perhaps it stemmed from Maryland's having Baltimore while Virginia had no towns of note at all. Perhaps it was a matter of geography, the Chesapeake's separation of Maryland into two parts. Whatever the reason, Maryland's divisiveness, like New York's or South Carolina's, was as much rooted in its own situation as was the cohesion of Virginia and Massachusetts. There was no single path that colonials followed as they turned into revolutionaries.

[III]

Throughout American history, war and social change have gone together. So too with the War of Independence, the longest the United States fought before Vietnam. The war raised two great immediate problems, fighting it and supporting it. Immediately after Lexington and Concord, outraged Americans thought they would defeat the "ministerial army" without trouble. First events seemed to justify that belief. The British forces that went to Concord on the night of April 18, 1775, to seize arms retreated to Boston under severe fire, suffering heavy losses. An impromptu force that was not yet an army assembled around the occupied capital and laid siege. Early in June the Americans fortified Breed's (Bunker) Hill, across the mouth of the Charles River. Had they placed artillery there it would have made Boston untenable. British troops assaulted their position and finally captured it, but not before colonial fire had decimated wave after wave of them. Outside New England, men paraded and seized public arsenals. Committees of safety, provincial congresses, and the Continental Congress in Philadelphia started turning themselves into an alternative government.

New people pushed into public affairs. Even in Virginia, yeoman farmers insisted on "an important role in making public policy." In Albany County, New York, committeemen bearing famous colonial names like Van Rensselaer or Gansevoort gave way to men of obscurity, some so poor that they had paid no land taxes at all. New York City tradesmen debated the shape of the new society and addressed the provincial congress as just their "elected delegates." Philadelphia committee elections produced a "revolution of the elite" followed by a "revolution of the middle classes." Militia privates there elected their own committee, demanded that a plain hunting shirt be the American uniform, and proposed to elect all officers, even at the highest ranks.[17]

Ideas, language, and experience came together in Thomas Paine's pamphlet *Common Sense*, published in January 1776. An Englishman of Quaker background, Paine had been a corset maker, a customs man, and a dabbler in political writing. He met Benjamin Franklin in London and at Franklin's suggestion he came to Philadelphia in 1774 with the vague idea of opening an academy for young ladies. Franklin's sponsorship gave him entry to Philadelphia's community of artisans and self-taught intellectuals. He made friends among the radical leadership, such people as the physicians Benjamin Rush (who had studied at Edinburgh) and Thomas Young (who had only an informal apprenticeship despite claiming a Yale degree), the painter Charles Willson Peale, and the instrument maker David Rittenhouse. Paine became this world's political voice. To him the problem was not a particular king, not even George III, "the royal brute of England." It was kingship itself. "Of more worth is one honest man to society and in the sight of God," he wrote, "than all the crowned ruffians that ever lived." Paine turned a quarrel about the terms of being British into "the cause of all mankind." *Common Sense* sold over 100,000 copies within months, in a day when 5,000 copies marked an excellent sale of a book.[18]

One of Britain's responses in 1774 to the Boston Tea Party had been to name General Thomas Gage, its American commander in chief, as governor of Massachusetts, but Gage found that he simply could not enforce his will. When he sent his secretary to dissolve the Massachusetts Assembly it barred the door and declared the governorship vacant. New York's governor, William Tryon, fled to a British warship. In December 1775, Tryon dissolved the old assembly and called an election in the hope of shoring up his own power. By then most actual power was in the hands of a provincial congress, which called an election of its own, lest the new official assembly interfere in "political subjects." In Virginia the House of Burgesses simply reconvened as a congress after Lord Dunmore dissolved them for the last time. Like Tryon, Dunmore fled to a British naval vessel.

By early 1776 there was continuity of the old order in only three provinces. Two, Rhode Island and Connecticut, already had complete self-government under their seventeenth-century royal charters. In Pennsylvania outright loyalism died early, but the patriot wing of the old elite remained cautious. They controlled the provincial assembly and they used its power to stall while the question of independence grew ever more pressing. Finally, in May 1776, radicals in Congress who wanted independence joined with radicals in Philadelphia who wanted internal change and overthrew them. The old assembly collapsed. It had been the last institution that still acknowledged royal authority. For the moment, Britain had no way to enforce its will anywhere between New Hampshire and Georgia.

In rejecting the Crown, the colonials were rejecting the idea of human inequality that kingship symbolized. They also were rejecting the social order that had bound them together and given them coherence across the lines of race, gender, and class. They needed coherence just as much after independence, but it would have to be on different terms. The difference meant that a whole new set of questions about human society was about to be raised. There would be no coherence at all until those questions began to be resolved. The terms of their resolving provided a new agenda for conflict as much as they provided domestic tranquillity.

[IV]

Indians had most to lose from the fall of the old order. The thirteen years between the end of the Seven Years' War and independence gave them one last moment to resist the terrible pressure from the east. With numbers that were beginning to recover from demographic disaster, with considerable military strength and an even more considerable military reputation, and with the support of British administrators, the woodland Indians had enough to keep the whites at bay. The English king had taken over the role of father to Indians that the French king had abandoned. In Sir William Johnson, the British had (until his death in 1774) a Superintendent of Indian Affairs who knew his people and lived intimately with them, at least partly on their terms. Administrators in provincial capitals and in London grumbled about costs and tried to cut budgets. General Sir Jeffrey Amherst went further during Pontiac's Rebellion in 1763, committing the atrocity of using smallpox-infected blankets as a weapon of war. There were Britons as well as Americans who coveted Indian lands. Nonetheless, the tribes who lived in and beyond the Appalachians had a place in the empire's social order and a claim on its rulers' protection. It offered them at least a standpoint for protecting what was theirs. They understood that point. Most acted accordingly.

In 1768 Iroquois and British negotiators met at Fort Stanwix (now Rome) in western New York to work out a land treaty. The Iroquois were there to sell a huge tract of land that they claimed south of the Ohio River, covering most of modern Kentucky. Sir William Johnson, who led the British team, was happy enough to buy it, despite his responsibility to enforce the proclamation line that had been issued five years before. Speculators were equally pleased. Nothing but fear of Indians could stop would-be settlers from crossing the line, but the treaty promised a renewal of legal land acquisition on a large scale. Settlers who went west to farm in quasi-isolation were one thing. Turning the land into potential capital recognized by English law and waiting for large-scale development was another.

But other Indians rejected the idea that the Iroquois had the right to sell the land. Late in September the following year "Shawanese Chiefs with some Chiefs of the Ottawas, Potowatomies, Chippewas, and Hurons" met to consider the problem. Women of those tribes took part in the deliberations. Messages recorded in wampum and remembered from speeches were on hand from more distant tribes like the Cherokees and "the Quabach." The immediate concern was how the Quabach and the Six Nations had "insulted" Indians farther westward by their "concessions of lands" that did "not belong to them." There was only one possible answer: "Have only the same mind all of you who inhabit the same continent and are of the same colour." Even Cherokees, who were represented by belts of wampum, agreed on the need for "Peace with the Shawanese, and all the other Nations of Indians upon this Continent that they should be united." With that agreement the tribes involved reconstituted themselves as a political force and became active participants in Virginia's revolution. That ultimately they lost is important, of course, but they were far more than passive observers of a revolution waged only by whites.[19]

Symbolically and perhaps militarily the two Indian nations that counted most were the Mohawks and the Cherokees. They were closest geographically to the whites. Each controlled rich land. Each had a long record of cooperation with the English, though the two tribes were not friends. Each enjoyed powerful connections. The Mohawk Thayendanagea (Joseph Brant) was related to the Johnson family. Like many another

Indian of part-white ancestry, he was a "man of two worlds." Inducted
into white culture at the Reverend Eleazar Wheelock's Connecticut
school, he was confident enough to deal with high British officials. He
met George III during a trip to London. Distinguished artists competed
to paint his portrait. Thayendanagea became a major British commander
on the New York frontier and most Mohawks followed him.

The other Iroquois nations split, but they might as well have followed
the Mohawk lead. In 1779 the American generals John Sullivan and
James Clinton led a major expedition westward in response to Mohawk
and loyalist guerrilla war. They met virtually no resistance, and they
swept across Iroquoia, ruining towns and crops as far as the Genesee
River, regardless of the tribe they belonged to. Worse for the Indians,
the soldiers saw the richness of the Iroquois domain. In the war's aftermath, with no British allies, the Iroquois would lose almost all of what
had been theirs. Merely to survive would be a victory.[20] For Cherokees,
Creeks, Chickasaws, Choctaws, and the Algonquian-speaking nations of
the "middle ground" of the western Great Lakes the large story was
much the same, although it took decades rather than years to work itself
through. For all Indians east of the Mississippi River, the Revolution
turned into a war about their own land and existence. Its large effect for
them was to transform their contact with whites from trade and interchange across a frontier zone into constant retreat west behind a moving
frontier line.[21]

Some Indians did serve their interests and protect their existence by
choosing the American side. By the outbreak of war the Catawbas of
South Carolina were a beaten, surrounded people. But they still were a
people, living on their own land, and for them supporting the British
made no sense. So they entered the war on the American side. Already
used to serving South Carolina by catching slaves, they turned to catching loyalists. They joined Carolina's war against the Cherokees in 1779
and 1780. They fought in the terrible guerrilla strife that followed the
British invasion in 1780. They evicted white tenants on their lands who
chose the Crown. Politically, they adopted a republican identity under
elected leaders. Carolina whites let the Catawbas keep what they had.
They had earned it. But what they had amounted to very little and they
offered no refuge for slaves seeking freedom.[22]

By 1776 black Americans had a long history of resisting enslavement.
Their "fondness for freedom" had drawn many rebukes from whites who
simply could not understand it. If they took direct efforts to secure
freedom, they got more than rebukes. Mass executions of rebellious slaves

in New York City in 1712 and 1741 and in South Carolina in 1739 were evidence of how serious whites were about keeping black people down.[23] A black colonial seeking freedom had almost nowhere to go. Communities of escaped slaves, called Maroons, took form in Virginia's Dismal Swamp, but, unlike similar communities in Jamaica or Brazil, they were too close to the whites to survive for long. Some Indian tribes were hospitable to slaves claiming freedom; others, like the Catawbas, knew that their own survival depended on returning escapees. Slaves who rebelled in South Carolina in 1739 had started out for Spanish Florida, on the principle that the enemy of one's enemy is one's friend. They might have found refuge there, but the Spaniards practiced black slavery too. African culture itself understood the idea of slavery, although on different terms from white America.

"For these reasons," writes one historian, "most slaves resorted to self-reliance and survival strategies and to flight" rather than challenge the institution of slavery. They loathed their situation. But they could understand it as "a natural institution, practiced by the ancestors, sanctioned by the gods."[24] Ending the sense that slavery was part of how things are and raising the possibility of its complete abolition was one of the major changes the Revolution wrought. In part, the change was the work of the British. In part, it was the work of conscience-stricken whites. In largest part, it was the work of blacks who found their chance either to reject America or to claim their own version of American freedom.

John Murray, Earl of Dunmore and last royal governor of Virginia, was a most unlikely social revolutionary. A titled adventurer, he came to America to make money and he took his chances as they came. In 1774 he provoked a brief war with Pennsylvania over land along the upper Ohio. His moment against slavery came after he fled to a ship in Chesapeake Bay. Dunmore knew where the great weakness of white Virginians lay. In November 1775, he proclaimed freedom for "all . . . servants, Negroes, or others" who belonged to rebels and were "able and willing to bear Arms" for the king. Some eight hundred people reached Dunmore's ship "within a week" and perhaps as many as five hundred enrolled in his "Ethiopian Regiment," wearing the motto "Liberty to Slaves" on their uniform buckles. John Adams reported that twenty thousand more would rise "if one thousand regular troops should land and their commander is provided with arms and clothes enough, and proclaim freedom to all the negroes, who would join his camp."[25] Adams chose his words carefully: "with arms and clothes enough." Slaves had "a wonderful art of communicating intelligence among themselves" and they appreciated Dunmore's weakness. Most Virginia slaves by this time were native-born and they understood how an adult man's departure would affect the woman and children he loved. They chose not to pay that price. The number who enrolled is not much more than twice what Washington held. But Dunmore did force the issue in a way that could not be ignored.

Writing for the Virginia committee of safety, Patrick Henry called for "an early and unremitting Attention to the government of the SLAVES" against Lord Dunmore's "dangerous Attempt." The Continental Congress accused Dunmore of "tearing up the foundations of civil authority" and forbade any black, free or slave, to serve on the American side. It needed Washington's urging to lift the prohibition for free people who wanted to serve. Washington was making a gesture of respect toward black men and a statement that they might gain the honors of war. Dunmore was a slaveholding British governor and Washington was a slaveholding American general; the slavery question cut across all other political lines. As they calculated their own best interests, slaves rallied to both sides and tried to stay neutral. For their own reasons, whites and Indians were doing the same.

When the British invaded South Carolina early in 1780, Sir Henry Clinton issued a proclamation much like Dunmore's. He promised the slaves of rebels "full security" behind his lines, but he did not call on all slaves to rise.[26] Black loyalists aided the British sieges of Savannah in 1779 and Charleston in 1780. They guided British troops through coastal Carolina's low, wet terrain. At war's end, upward of three thousand black people evacuated Savannah with the British. Perhaps ten thousand departed from Charleston. Thousands more left from New York City. They scattered widely, going to Canada, Britain, and even returning to Africa, where they helped found Sierra Leone.

Black people fought on the patriots' side where whites would let them. They dared the whites to live up to their own words, petitioning for an end to all slavery and bringing lawsuits to end the slavery they labored under themselves. A slave named Quok Walker brought a freedom suit in Massachusetts in 1783 and Chief Justice William Cushing decided it in his favor. Within Massachusetts, Cushing ruled, slavery was "as effectively abolished as it can be." Vermont had already abolished slavery outright, when it cut free of New York in 1777. In 1780 Pennsylvania had begun gradual abolition. A pattern was emerging: being black in America did not have to mean being enslaved. The North Star was starting to point to freedom.

Southerners felt the issue's moral urgency as well. In 1767 Arthur Lee attacked slavery in the *Virginia Gazette*. Jefferson tried in the Declaration of Independence to blame both slavery and slave uprisings on the king. What Jefferson wrote revealed his troubled conscience, but historically it was obvious nonsense and Congress cut it from the final version. Robert Carter, whose slave force numbered 509, freed them all. Jefferson's teacher in the law, George Wythe, freed his slaves as well and as a high judge he tried to end slavery altogether from the bench, as Cushing did in Massachusetts. He failed, but a free black community that would come to number in the tens of thousands began to take shape in the Chesapeake. Even in the North the destruction of slavery would encounter strong resistance. There would be slaves in Connecticut in the 1830s. A few hundred would remain in New Jersey as late as 1850. But both the institution and the idea of human slavery were beginning to break up.

White women found that a republic which proclaimed human equality raised questions about themselves. Women had a long tradition of taking part in rebellions. Like men, they could be brutal: in 1676 fishwives in Marblehead, Massachusetts, murdered helpless Indian captives from King Philip's War. They could be ribald: Boston women dumped chamber pots on defeated soldiers, calling out, "Is your piss-pot charged, neighbour? So-ho, souse the cowards."[27] Women helped to sabotage an unpopular plan to institute a Boston town market in 1736. But men also cast frivolous girls who would not give up their fashions as symbols of antipatriot selfishness. In 1783 one wrote what he thought was a humorous piece for a newspaper. He described a "female legislature" as it debated "bewitching kisses . . . pouting lips . . . and . . . the Currency of Rapture."[28] Like Jefferson trying to blame the king for slavery, the author revealed his own anxieties. Significantly, his anxiety turned not on mere "luxury" and "corruption," which had long traditions of being associated with "effeminacy," but on the idea that women might actually come to power.

During the 1760s men called on women to be "Daughters of Liberty." Women who answered "commenced perfect citizens" (as one put it). During the inflation of the late 1770s, women helped to set "just" prices on the goods in "monopolizers'" stores.[29] A very few disguised themselves and took up arms as soldiers. Many more became "women of the army," receiving half pay, cooking and laundering, and being subject to military discipline. Some found they had to deal with the world on their own. Mary Bartlett of New Hampshire was writing to her congressman husband about "your farming business" in 1776, but it was "our farming business" by 1778. Esther De Berdt Reed's Philadelphia broadside of 1780, *The Sentiments of an American Woman*, led to a Ladies' Association to ease the plight of Continental soldiers. Women who answered her call formed committees and collected funds door to door until they had a considerable sum. Reed argued with Washington about what to do with the money. She wanted to make a direct gift; he wanted the women to make shirts. He won, and the soldiers got shirts. Women had raised wartime supplies before. They had argued with men before. But the independent action of the Ladies' Association had no precedent.[30]

Indians, slaves, and women all had taken part in the colonial wars, but those were wars of the old order. Even France's defeat in 1763 made no great difference to the pattern of North American society. The war of the Revolution did make a difference. Partly it was because of the rhetoric that the white males who began the war chose to use. Partly it was because the revolutionaries had to organize the whole war on their own. Partly it was because the British understood what both slaves and Indians could do for their own side.

[V]

While the crisis was moving toward war, the revolutionaries wanted every possible person to join them. Many, however, did not. Guesses about how many loyalists there were have varied widely. At the least we can cite the roughly 60,000 who emigrated to Canada and England. Even that number represents five times as many emigrating per thousand as would flee revolutionary France.[31] Sheer numbers, however, are not the issue. What counted was influencing the course of events.

One reason loyalists chose to side with the Crown was that it had been good to them. Royal councillors, militia generals, judges of the highest courts, lieutenant governors and full governors of provinces: all these had been well rewarded by London. Salaries, fees, land grants, and high-level transatlantic connections defined their lives. Benjamin Franklin's son William acquired the governorship of New Jersey and chose his king rather than his father. New York's De Lancey politicians joined the outcry against the Stamp Act in 1765. But with the friendship of an Archbishop of Canterbury and the marriage of one of their daughters into the British aristocracy, there was little chance that they would join in rebellion, and they did not. The state of New York confiscated loyalist property in 1779 and it took more than £200,000 from this one family. Even in Virginia almost 60 percent of the men high on the colonial political ladder, the provincial councillors and highest judges and most senior militia officers, chose the Crown. In only five states did fewer than half of such men become loyalists.[32]

What loyalists could do varied with their absolute numbers, their own situation, and the course of the war. The prosperous farmers around New York City simply welcomed the British army when it invaded in August 1776. In the Hudson Valley and on Maryland's Eastern Shore loyalism brought resistance and banditry. Along the Mohawk it meant civil war from 1775 to 1782. In the Carolina backcountry it meant sullen disaffection at first. After the British invaded in 1780 disaffection turned into the worst bloodshed the Revolution saw.

British strategists counted on loyalists giving them support and on winning neutrals back. But both loyalists and neutrals proved to be too ill organized and too scattered to become an effective force. They frustrated and confounded the Revolutionaries' politics. They roused patriots' wrath. They suffered severe punishments. Their land was confiscated. They were forced into exile. They endured punitive taxation. They lost their legal and political rights. But, like the patriots, the loyalists were too complex a group to fit into any single category, beyond agreeing that somehow they remained British. The claims that more than three thousand filed for compensation from the British government have been analyzed. But the claimants fit no discernible pattern. Their reasons were as complex as the Revolution that they rejected.[33]

Loyalists and patriots struggled hard to make up their minds. Families and communities came apart. Neighbors became enemies. There were midnight arrests, arbitrary imprisonments, and atrocities. The many who finally did choose exile ceased to be American, though they often found that they were not as British as they had thought. There is now a Delancey Street in London's Camden Town as well as the more famous one on the Lower East Side of New York. Both are named for the same family.[34]

Loyalists had their own vision of "the liberty we seek" and from all social levels they risked or lost their lives. The "ideological division" between patriots and loyalists "was deep," writes one scholar of their thought.[35] " 'I believe,' 'I obey,' these were part of the Loyalist code," writes another.[36] Isaac Low was one of thirty-five thousand New York

State people who chose the British side. He had been rich and powerful and until war broke out he had been part of the Revolution. But then he rejected the Revolution and the Revolution's triumph broke his life. He did not regret his choice. Writing to his patriot brother from his exile in London in 1788, he expressed no envy for "the Happiness of others, who are advocates for republican Government. The height of my Ambition was and is to live and die a British subject."[37] Low defined the issues: subjection or citizenship; a known place within an ordered world or the possibilities for failure and success in a society that claimed it prized both equality and opportunity. What the Revolution created was no heaven on earth. Any Indian, any slave, any loyalist exile knew better. But what it created was very different from what it had destroyed.

White Americans backed into revolution to protect what they feared they were about to lose. There were indeed losers among them on both the patriot and loyalist sides, but as a people they gained enormously from it. For Indians the Revolution promised no good and brought less. For black people it half opened a window to freedom. Some climbed through and began to make their own freedom all around the Atlantic; most found they could not. But if the window proved too narrow it still opened on possibilities that had never been available before. Some white women did much the same. Again, most did not. But for women and for slaves, a beginning had been made.

CHAPTER 4

THE REVOLUTION AND
THE REPUBLIC

IN 1783 the United States and Britain ended their war. The peace-makers met in Paris, where the Anglo-French struggle for empire had ended two decades before. The new republic would have the same southern and western boundaries that Britain had won then. Its northern border would run along the Great Lakes and the St. Lawrence. As of 1763, everybody within those lines had been considered British in some sense. Now they all would be "American." The problem was what the new description would mean.

[I]

As peace returned, there were people on the move throughout the continent's eastern half. At least sixty thousand white colonials were accepting exile rather than submit to the Revolution. Many went to Nova Scotia and Ontario, where the term "empire loyalist" is still used for their descendants. Others became "British Americans," forced to live their lives out in England but knowing they never really would belong there.[1] Former slaves departed by the thousands to those same places and to Africa. For them, exile meant not heartrending loss but freedom and the chance to form communities on nobody's terms but their own.[2]

The number of Natives who left was not large, partly because many had no idea that they had suffered defeat. The Iroquois, however, were ruined as a power. The easy route westward that they long had been able to block lay open. Albany had been a trading center where Indians and whites met. Now it became a way station for New Englanders migrating west along the Mohawk or north up the Hudson. By 1790 a thousand whites had settled in the Genesee country of western New York; two years later that figure had risen sixfold.[3] As New Englanders occupied Iroquoia, people from farther south were crossing the Alleghenies, Cumberlands, and Great Smokies. Before independence coastal Americans had crept westward; now they would surge.

But American society did not "expand" at all. Between the Treaty of Paris of 1763 and the Louisiana Purchase four decades later, the space that it occupied remained the same. So, fundamentally, did the makeup of its people. What did change, profoundly, was how those people dealt with one another.

The Revolution transferred final power over land and human relationships from the British Crown to the American people, now sovereign over themselves. In every colony there had been men with an expansive vision looking for good western land open to speculation and settlement. Benjamin Franklin and George Washington offer striking examples.[4] Indians understood that point. "But Brothers, do you remember that the difference is about our land?" said the Cherokee chief Old Tassel to white patriot negotiators in 1777. He and his audience understood one another. They were heirs to more than a century of common history. But that history might be about to end. Not long before Old Tassel spoke, South Carolina militiamen were getting orders to "cut up every Indian cornfield, and burn every Indian town and every Indian taken shall be the slave and property of the taker and . . . the nation be extirpated and the lands become the property of the public."[5]

The Revolutionary War did not bring movement. It changed where people moved and accelerated their speed. White immigration ended in 1775, not to resume in large numbers until about 1820, after the whole age of republican revolutions was over. The slave trade to North America stopped in 1775 as well, as part of the boycott of all external commerce that the First Continental Congress adopted in response to Britain's coercive or "intolerable" acts the year before. Above South Carolina it never would resume. Nonetheless, 90,000 more enslaved Africans entered the United States through Charleston and Savannah before the trade reached its legal end in 1808. These were a quarter of all who came after 1700.[6] Admittedly, their number is dwarfed by the 439,000 who after American independence went to the British Caribbean, the 356,000 to Haiti and the other French possessions, and the 605,000 to Brazil. But the Republic remained as hungry for slaves as the colonies had been.

White colonials had traded with one another before the war, northern ships carrying southern produce, Pennsylvania and Chesapeake wheat feeding New Englanders, New York staves made into barrels to hold

Carolina rice. Most economic life, however, had been either imperial or local. If it was imperial, it was protected and controlled by the Acts of Trade and Navigation. If it was local, it was subject to the powerful constraints of colonial communities. Never before the late 1770s did the people of the Atlantic provinces have to work together under their own direction toward a single common purpose. The war changed this permanently, melding politics, production, and exchange together into the beginning of the American national economy.

That economy began with revolutionary politics. Rebellious Massachusetts could not have survived in 1774 and 1775 if it had had to survive alone. The whole project of the First Continental Congress was to define what had begun in Boston as the business of everybody in the future nation, and it roused support from Georgia to New Hampshire. Cooperation against an armed enemy was the immediate issue, not economics for its own sake. Cooperation was the issue as well when Congress appointed the Virginian George Washington to command an army of New Englanders. Cooperation was on John Adams's mind when he told Thomas Jefferson, "You are a Virginian, and a Virginian ought to be at the head of this business," as they prepared the Declaration of Independence.[7]

But political cooperation did not clothe, feed, or house soldiers. It did not put weapons on their shoulders, ammunition in their packs, or pay in their pockets. When war first broke out, that did not seem to matter. Militant colonials expected swift British defeat. Their genuine successes along the road back from Concord and at Bunker Hill in 1775 promised it. So did the capture of Fort Ticonderoga, guarding the Lake Champlain corridor between Albany and Montreal. So did the British evacuation from Boston in March 1776. But as Congress published the Declaration of Independence, the largest seaborne expedition the modern world had seen was pushing into New York Harbor and disgorging 30,000 troops on Staten Island. Crossing to Long Island and then Manhattan, the redcoats and hired German "Hessians" drove the Continental army ever back, until New York's whole southern district was lost. It would not be recovered until 1783.

The war became a struggle of endurance. "Summer soldiers" (in Thomas Paine's phrase) departed the American ranks. So did farmers and artisans who knew that only their labor would keep their families from starvation. The Continental army ceased to be a force of virtuous patriots in arms for a season. Its ranks filled with young men whose futures were bleak, serving for long terms under tough discipline, commanded by gentleman officers. A long war fought by such an army was bound to generate huge costs.[8]

Those costs had to be met. So too did the costs of militia units on short-term service. Congress cost money, as did diplomats. There was only paper currency with which to pay, and as the war persisted and the costs rose, the currency lost value. The "disaffected" refused to accept American paper. Cautious traders would take it only at a discount. Even committed revolutionaries realized that nothing would protect the Continental dollar. By 1779 it was virtually without value. Within three years after independence the United States was deep in its first national economic crisis.

Necessities like flour and salt fell into short supply. Crowds of frustrated consumers, often women, seized "hoarded" goods, paying only "just" prices. Conventions and committees assembled to set prices for both wages and goods. State governments imposed embargoes on exports in order to safeguard what people had to have. It was perfectly legitimate under both long-standing custom and the terms of the emerging new order. Five separate state constitutions allowed such embargoes in time of need.[9] It also was completely futile, because the problem was national and the solution had to be national too. In the final analysis, it was unpatriotic. It was bound to harm the army and if the army failed, the Revolution was lost.

Congress, the army, the quartermaster service, and the beginnings of a diplomatic corps were all novelties. The men who filled these emerging national institutions varied widely, but almost all came from the "better sort." Some were paragons, like Washington. Already he was aware of his world reputation and place in history. He had never been a man who took his reputation lightly and after 1775 he calculated everything he did with an eye on what the world and the future would think of him. Some leaders became corrupt, most notoriously Silas Deane of Connecticut, whose dealings as American agent in France led to great scandal.[10] The records of others were mixed. Robert Morris of Philadelphia performed one enormous public service by assembling necessities for the army. He performed another by stabilizing the currency. But he never hesitated to profit by giving public contracts to businesses he owned.

The significance of these men does not lie in the virtue of some or the corruption of others. It is that in virtue and corruption alike they were becoming a national elite. They were learning each other's characters and qualities, strengths and weaknesses. They were learning to think of themselves as a group, and to identify their perspective and interests with the Republic and its Glorious Cause.[11] Their perspective, experience, and knowledge of one another were central to the creation of the United States.

Nonetheless, the Revolution did not belong exclusively to them. With the disruption of war, with the necessity to keep the army in the field, people who were becoming Americans disputed over what their Revolution was about and where it should lead. These included people whom white revolutionaries would not have recognized as American at all, but who would be as much a part of American national society as they had been part of the British colonial mosaic "of a hundred colours."

[II]

Whatever their politics, condition, place, race, or gender, the people of the Revolution had to face questions more fundamental than most people ever face in their lives. Deciding whether to be British or American was difficult enough. Diaries, correspondence, and the records of political police like New York's "Commissioners for Detecting and Defeating Conspiracies" show people making the choice in great hesitancy and enormous pain. "Those who thought Congress were in the right," said the moderator of one clandestine meeting in 1776, "should go and those who thought the King was right should stay." But he "did not know who was right."[12]

Choosing independence meant rejecting monarchy and all that it signified. Before independence, colonials liked to invoke the image of England's Glorious Revolution of 1688, which is why they called themselves Whigs. Led by Parliament, Whig Britons had dismissed King James II for his crypto-Catholicism and invited his Protestant daughter Mary and her Dutch husband, William of Orange, to reign instead. Together with Parliament, William and Mary would rule on new terms, but they still would be king and queen. In 1776, however, the British memory that loomed largest was of the Puritan Revolution of the 1640s. That not only dethroned a king but also killed him, turning Parliament into the centerpiece of a short-lived republic.[13] "Great Cromwell," a Massachusetts farmer, Asa Douglass, called Washington in 1776, thinking of the Puritan Revolution's leader.[14] Symbolically at least, King George III died at his American subjects' hands. The idea of kingship did die among them.[15] There would be no American William of Orange, called as a new king to replace one who had forfeited the crown. The crown itself was shattered.

With the king symbolically dead and monarchy genuinely destroyed, Americans entered new ground. How Thomas Jefferson came to define that ground with the not at all self-evident truth that "all men are created equal" remains an enduring mystery. What he actually meant remains an open question too. But he wrote it and Congress accepted it. With the exception of ancient Israel, no people have argued more than Americans about the terms of their own existence. No other people at all have made the argument a major reason for their being. The quarrel begins with the contradiction between what Jefferson wrote and the continuing realities of American life.

In 1776, the Declaration signified the equality of Americans among other peoples. That, however, begged the question of who Americans were. The former colonials rejected both monarchy and the principle of subjection, working toward the notion of citizenship in its stead. They were relocating sovereignty, the supreme social and political power, from a position above society to a position within it. During eleven years of debate, innovation, and conflict after 1776, they resolved the fundamental problems of political society among whites that their break with Britain and with monarchy raised. They invented a way for what they were creating to extend itself across space without having to confront the problems that Britain's expansion into America had caused. How they did it, however, required that Natives either get out of the way or lose what was distinctive about themselves. It presumed as well that black Americans would remain subordinate, whether they were free or slave, whatever the Declaration said about equality and the pursuit of happiness.

The narrative of the American Republic's creation need only be summarized. Among whites, the most fundamental difficulty was how to give the notion of a sovereign people some workable meaning. In 1780, after four years of experiment in the states, Massachusetts solved that problem through the device of a special convention to "ordain and establish" the highest law and a popular vote to accept it. That same device was used again to write and ratify the United States Constitution. It has been employed time after time since in America and many countries abroad.

The first state constitutions were more than abstract statements about "the people" being their own sovereigns. They were groping attempts to reshape society. So was the enduring document that was produced at

Philadelphia in 1787, except that the federal Constitution did not grope. All attempted to distribute power among the new citizenry. New Jersey's constitution used the word "inhabitants" rather than "men" to set the qualifications for voting.[16] William Livingston, who wrote it, had no intention of extending the vote beyond white men. But for a time his language let both white women and a growing population of blacks who were not slaves claim the vote. Black men began to vote elsewhere as well. One ran for the Maryland Assembly in 1792.

The white male revolutionaries' fundamental, unspoken, unconsidered, bedrock assumption, however, was that full citizenship and political liberty meant being white and male.[17] Whatever the ambiguities of their language, they did not even think they had to say so. In the poetic words of a distinguished sociologist dealing with the historical problem of freedom, it seems hard to avoid such limits:

> We, the citizens, the people, the free—those whom we "hold dear," those whom we marry, kith, kin, "not in bondage, noble, glad, illustrious," "beloved"—we the politically free body of men always, it would seem, tragically require the them who do not belong: the ignoble, the nonkith, the nonkin, the people we do not marry, the alien within—the serf, the Jew, the Slav, the slave, the Negro, the people who cannot vote—who demarcate what *we* are, the domestic enemy who defines whom *we* love.[18]

In this sense, the "we" of the new United States yielded to no simple definition. It was the ideologically defined "we," who "held these truths." It was the military "we," who confronted and defeated British arms. It was the producing and buying and selling "we," who created the national economy. It was the elite "we," who learned to work nationally. There was nothing within the Republic's rhetoric to stop the "we" from referring to every single person within its bounds. But a great deal of experience said otherwise.

The American Revolution's enduring glory was to proclaim itself in universal terms. The American Republic's enduring problem was that experience, not ideology, would determine what "American" should mean for purposes of citizenship, belonging, and honor. A paradox was coming into focus that never had been posed before. The British liberty that colonials had set out to protect had no problem with subjection, specificity, and exclusion. The American liberty that white citizens proclaimed posed large problems about these that could be ignored but ultimately not avoided. What the revolutionaries declared implied citizenship, not subjection, generality rather than specificity, and inclusion rather than exclusion. The subjection, specificity, and exclusion remained, of course. But these had to be justified, not just accepted as how things naturally were. The contrast between the "self-evident truths" that the United States proclaimed at its origin and its determination to remain a society of unequal men and women set the terms of the enduring contradiction that would bedevil its public life. After two centuries the contradiction remains not completely resolved.

[III]

Between the Declaration and the writing of the federal Constitution, the revolutionary generation produced many great documents of state. These included the original constitutions of the separate states, the Articles of Confederation, and the Treaty of Paris of 1783. They also included the three Northwest Ordinances that the Confederation Congress passed between 1784 and 1787, and the treaties that the United States began to make with Indian tribes. These founding documents of the American polity varied greatly. Some canceled out others. Yet all shared a solemnity that stemmed from a revolutionary people's awareness of the unique nature of what was being done and from their understanding, or at least hope, that the results of their acts would last. This was a moment of rewriting society's most fundamental rules. The rewriting took place in the name of the abstraction that Americans called "the people" and it was done by "the people's" representatives. But necessarily it affected many real flesh-and-blood people who had no say in shaping the new order at all.

As we have seen, many whites chose independence with the firmly fixed idea that a good society must be small, simple, and able, if necessary, to close out the world. The strongest evidence of this is in the clauses in the constitutions of South Carolina, North Carolina, Maryland, Pennsylvania, and Vermont permitting "embargoes, to prevent . . . the exportation of any commodities." Yet clearly this was an impossible project. Both the immediate needs of the military and the complexity of American society made it so.

One way to read what followed is to see it in terms of people adjusting their laws and ruling institutions to the realities of economics and race. The first casualty was the notion of a coherent, virtuous public. Many of the states lodged enormous power in their representative assemblies, on the assumption that a public-spirited citizenry need only express its will and all would be well. But it did not work. After six years of experience with Virginia's powerful legislature, Thomas Jefferson came to the decision that the "173 despots" in its assembly and senate could "surely be as oppressive as one."[19]

The problem that revolutionary Pennsylvania faced applied everywhere. In 1776 Pennsylvania adopted the most radically democratic constitution of any state. Its legislature had only one house, elected annually. Members could serve for no more than three terms in a row, so that they would not become a permanent ruling elite. No state had broader suffrage, and any voter could also hold office. Major bills were supposed to be printed in the newspapers for general public discussion before they passed into law. There was no governor, just the president of an executive council whose job was to administer the laws. The assumption was that Pennsylvanians of goodwill could put their differences aside and work together. With its major city of Philadelphia, its lesser towns, its openness to religious experiment, its manufactures, and its commercial farming, Pennsylvania "had never been a single-interest society, and neither the Revolution nor the new constitution could make it one." However, the men who took control at independence wanted a single-interest society. They thought institutions could make it so, and they nearly came to civil war when the vision faltered during the economic crisis of 1779. These men were the Revolution's "angry, frustrated outsiders rushing through the doorways to . . . power and . . . status," its "idealistic patriots who sacrificed gladly for a bright new vision," its "fearful patriots who saw enemies . . . all around them." As their most sensitive historian notes, "such men are seldom a revolution's winners. . . . they are, however, among a revolution's most characteristic and creative actors."[20] Their project lost its popular appeal by the mid-1780s and the project's enemies succeeded in destroying it with a new constitution that the commonwealth adopted in 1790.

The belief that white Americans could act as a virtuous people seemed justified by the flush of excited patriotism in 1775 and 1776. By the mid-1780s, the belief was almost gone, as people struggled to accept that their public life should express their differences as well as their shared American identity. In Pennsylvania the struggle was ongoing between the enemies and the friends of the Constitution of 1776. In New York, legislative and electoral politics abandoned early pretenses of serving only the public good and began to organize openly along party lines.[21]

In the towns of rural western Massachusetts notions of a single good and a simple economy lasted longest. It took Shays's Rebellion in 1786 to show what was at stake. Coastal merchants, Harvard graduates, and Boston professional men put themselves in charge of the commonwealth. To these men the public good meant the credibility of Massachusetts in the world of Atlantic commerce, not the self-protection of small communities. In the midst of a severe economic crunch following the war, they imposed a stiff policy of hard money and no protection for debtors. To many people in the interior the policy raised the specter of losing their land for taxes and debts. To people in small towns that valued cohesion, it raised the need to act together.

They tried resolutions in town meetings and conventions "for redress of grievances." They tried petitions. None worked, and in 1786 they rose in armed revolt to close the courts and stave off the effects they feared from the commonwealth's policies. The rebellion took its name from Daniel Shays of the hilly farming town of Pelham, a former captain in the Continental army who emerged as the rebels' military leader. Governor James Bowdoin sent militia under the vastly more experienced General Benjamin Lincoln to crush the rebels, which the troops did easily. Shaysites begged humbly for forgiveness. Chief Justice William Cushing condemned a few to death and they were deliberately taken to the gallows before carefully timed reprieves from the governor arrived. Some people among the elite began to think that American republicanism had no future. It would end in civil strife and military takeover, just as every other attempt at republicanism from ancient Rome to Cromwellian England had done. Others turned to national politics to redefine American life under a new constitution.

If the rebellion shocked eastern Massachusetts, the way that the government put it down with armed force and terror shocked the west. People realized that the new political order would brook no direct opposition. "Revolutionary time" had perished and only two choices remained. One was to go west, which many New Englanders began to do. Daniel Shays joined the migration and spent the rest of his days in western New York. The other way was to organize themselves to participate in a society that was necessarily complex.[22]

The "state" did not suddenly become a "neutral umpire" that could mediate between conflicting interests and side permanently with none. States never are. But the old ideology which held that people of goodwill could arrive at a single public interest had passed its time. The rulers of Massachusetts had to learn that fact in 1786 as much as did the ruled.

Each side, in a sense, was teaching it to the other, the rulers recognizing that commerce could not be escaped, and the ruled with their insistence that suffering people had to be heard. The former perspective played a considerable role during the next two years in shaping the institutions and long-term future of the United States. People of the latter sort were "present" at the federal convention in Philadelphia too, not in the flesh but as ghosts and specters, reminding the Framers of limits beyond which they ought not dare to go.[23]

[IV]

White Americans were accepting their complexity and admitting that there were different interests among them. To Native Americans the whites had only one interest: Indian land. In the colonial period acquiring land had been a constant goal. But the realities of colonial politics had tempered it, including the Indians' capacity to make war and the continuing need for frontier trade. Now those realities and needs began to die. The new terms of engagement were set by a series of treaties in central and western New York.

The first was held in 1784 at Fort Stanwix, where the Proclamation Line had been breached sixteen years before. "Representatives of the Six Nations and United States commissioners for Indian affairs" met, with "agents for both Pennsylvania and New York in attendance." The fundamental American claim was that Iroquoia was theirs by "rights of conquest." If Indians remained, it would be a matter of favor. Though the Iroquois "League refused to confirm the treaty," the United States, not the League, was in control. The following year Oneidas and Tuscaroras ceded much of what is now New York State's southern tier of counties to the state, so that it would not be taken by "private parties." In July 1788 a meeting brought the sale of all the Seneca lands east of the Genesee River. Two months later Onondagas "ceded all the nation's land, but specified a reserve for their people." Cayugas gave up their lands in the Finger Lakes region in June 1790. Finally, in the autumn of 1794, the Six Nations and the United States negotiated a general "treaty of peace and friendship" that included "quitclaims to lands previously ceded." Except for small reservations, all New York stood open.[24]

If whites needed the land Indians would have to give it up, assuming whites could muster the necessary force. New lines would be inscribed on maps of "the West," separating towns and counties, territories and states. These lines would replace lines previously drawn or understood in terms of villages and tribes. The Confederation Congress and its agents addressed this problem in a series of great policy innovations. The first came during the war, even preceding adoption of the Articles of Confederation. The eastern states ceded their colonial-era claims north of the Ohio River, where a welter of conflicts defied easy resolution. To white Americans, what is now Ohio, Indiana, Michigan, Illinois, and Wisconsin belonged to the United States as a whole. The American negotiators in Paris got the British to confirm the point, to the wrath of undefeated Indians who thought the land was theirs and who denied that the British could give it away. Meanwhile, Congress recognized the claims of Virginia to Kentucky, North Carolina to Tennessee, and Georgia to Alabama and Mississippi. An enormous treasure had passed into white Americans' hands, to be administered by white institutions under white rules.

Between 1784 and 1787 Congress reorganized its western treasure and started transferring it to private hands. Two of its Northwest Ordinances dealt with politics and jurisdiction. They laid out the principle that westward migrants could form "territories" and that territories could become states of the Union. Ohio would be the first state admitted under those terms, and the process would be continued until the admission of Alaska and Hawaii. Only Vermont, Kentucky, Tennessee, Maine, Texas, California, and West Virginia entered the Union directly rather than going through the territorial stage first. One major effect was to transform the significance of making state constitutions. At independence the states offered crucibles for vital debate about the most fundamental questions white Americans could imagine. That explains the enormous variety of constitutions that they produced. Now constitution making became a ritual, acted out on terms that for the most part were already laid down.[25]

The Ordinances of 1784 and 1787 provided for territories and states. The Ordinance of 1785 laid the basis for the interior's development. The boundaries of most colonial-era land grants had been haphazard, reflecting colonial America's uneasy combination of speculation and the need for lasting communities. Along the Atlantic coast there are still county and township lines as twisting as any that Europe has inherited from its medieval past. West of the Appalachian chain, however, the lines become straight, oriented directly toward the North Pole. Literally, they are imposed from above for the sake of quick sale, clarity of possession, and easy transfer. This grid pattern did not actually begin with the Ordinance of 1785; a map of New York that was drawn in 1774 shows straight lines and square townships already imposed upon the Adirondack Mountains. It was ironic that this was the part of New York least suitable for any such division.[26]

As of 1785, the national grid was a statement of intent rather than a description of reality. The defeat of the Six Nations was resounding; it reduced them from being proud possessors of land and reputation to beggars struggling for bare survival. Other nations, however, still possessed great holdings and the power to protect them. The Cherokees controlled much of western Georgia and the Great Smokies. South of them were Creeks and Seminoles; directly west were Chickasaws and Choctaws. To their northwest were Iroquoian- and Algonquian-speaking refugees in the village world that still defined the "middle ground."[27]

The plans of the United States for these people and their land were not necessarily malevolent. People as diverse as ordinary soldiers in Iroquoia in 1779 and George Washington thought that Indians could be made "civil," like whites, and that they would be the better for it. Most Indians had other ideas, and they still possessed the land. Many were giving serious thought to how they would remain upon what was theirs. When a combined Indian force defeated American troops at Fort Harmar, Ohio, in 1791, it seemed that the terms of their participation in the new order might remain the Indians' own.

The Republic's emissaries did come to realize that they could not act as conquerors of people who were not yet conquered. Even though the British were legally gone, they were not far away. Until 1795 they controlled forts within American territory along the boundary with Canada. They were happy to stir up troubles for the United States. Settlers, however, not soldiers or politicians, were the Indians' worst enemies, and they kept coming. The balance of power was tilting rapidly against the Indians, and it would not tilt back.

[V]

It was the case, proclaimed the constitution of Vermont in 1777, "that all men are born equally free and independent, and have certain natural, inherent and unalienable rights," and so certain conclusions had to be drawn. Hence, "no male person . . . ought to be holden by law, to serve . . . as a servant, slave or apprentice, after . . . the age of twenty-one years, nor female . . . after . . . the age of eighteen . . . unless they are bound by their own consent."[28] Massachusetts having become a republic with a constitution "favourable to the rights of mankind," said its chief justice in 1783, "slavery is . . . as effectively abolished as it can be."[29] "The unconstitutional bondage," wrote the Reverend Absalom Jones in 1797, "in which multitudes of our fellows in complexion are held, is to us a subject sorrowfully affecting [and] a direct violation of the declared fundamental principles of the Constitution." But "to encourage slaves to petition the House" of Representatives, said a congressman in reply, "would tend to spread an alarm throughout the Southern States; it would act as an 'entering wedge,' whose consequences could not be foreseen."[30] "Among the Romans," wrote Thomas Jefferson as early as 1782, "emancipation required but one effort. The slave, when made free, might mix with, without staining the blood of his master. But with us a second is necessary, unknown to history. When freed, he is to be removed beyond the reach of mixture."[31]

All these voices were addressing the now glaring contradiction between how the American Republic framed its claim to freedom and the continuing reality of racial slavery within it. They were the voices of people we can name and of people who remain anonymous, people who were black and people who were white, people who were prominent and people who were obscure. "How is it," asked Dr. Samuel Johnson of London in 1776, "that we hear the loudest *yelps* for liberty among the drivers of Negroes?"[32] The sarcasm was biting, but it was also a measure of the difference the Revolution had made. If the yelps had merely been for old-style British liberty there would have been no problem, no contradiction at all.

The numbers freed in Vermont in 1777 and in Massachusetts six years later were small. The closest we can get to a Vermont figure is the New York census of 1771. In that year the whole black population in New York was 19,883, 12 percent of the province's non-Indian population. But there were only nineteen black people in the two counties that declared their own independence and became Vermont six years later, out of a total population there that was nearing 5,000.[33] White Vermonters abolished the principle of slavery, but for practical purposes it had never existed among them. There were more African Yankees in Massachusetts, both numerically and in percentage; in 1764 they accounted for between 2 and 3 percent of the whole and for 5.2 percent of all Bostonians.[34] Nonetheless, they were not a large enough group for whites to perceive them as either a necessary economic prop while still enslaved or a threat to social order if freed.

Nonetheless, Vermont and Massachusetts became the first places in the American hemisphere to break the automatic assumption that a black person was a slave. Both states reversed the position entirely: anybody within them was free. The marriage that Americans had contracted between race and enslavement was at the beginning of its end, and both Vermonters and Massachusetts Yankees took the issue seriously. One Vermont "judge demanded a bill of sale from 'God Almighty' " before he would recognize a putative master's claim to have a slave returned. When a Connecticut minister came to a pulpit in Bennington and brought a slave with him, he violated "Vermont law and the policy of his church not to commune with anyone who owned a slave." Vermont's foremost figure, Ethan Allen, convinced the slave "to sue for her freedom."[35]

These people were pioneers. Black Americans who escaped with the British or who, like Absalom Jones, stretched the principles the whites proclaimed were pioneers as well. So was the white South Carolinian John Laurens when he proposed to "lead a corps of emancipated blacks in the defence of liberty."[36] They were defining the problem, however, not resolving it. They crossed the whole spectrum of opinion. Sir William Blackstone, Samuel Johnson, Lord Mansfield, Lord Dunmore, and Sir Henry Clinton were enemies of the American Revolution, but they all helped weaken slavery. Quakers stood neutral yet they became antislavery. The same Chief Justice William Cushing who decreed slavery's end in Massachusetts pronounced fiercely phrased death sentences upon leaders of Shays's Rebellion in 1787. The New York State legislature debated emancipation in 1785, its members lining up as proslavery or antislavery on vote after vote. Yet their votes had nothing to do with how they voted on any other issue of note. Slavery was a problem that people were coming to recognize, but it was also a political wild card. Its abolition remained a minority cause. In 1787, when the federal Constitution was written, only Pennsylvania had joined Massachusetts and Vermont in ending it, and abolition there would be gradual. The North Star shone only faintly. Slavery remained bound into the economy, society, and consciousness of all America, North as well as South.[37]

[VI]

The years 1787 and 1788, when the federal Constitution was written and ratified, were a time of definition. The Framers met in Philadelphia to solve problems of political representation and to create new public power. The foremost issue on their minds was the kind of people whom the Revolution had brought to power in the separate states and how they were using it. The clearest evidence that something was very wrong came from Massachusetts. On the surface it seemed that every problem of political society the Revolution raised was solved there. Massachusetts invented the device of a special convention to write a constitution and special gatherings of "the people" to ratify or reject what the convention produced. Its state constitution contained the original pregnant phrases "we the people" and "do ordain and establish." Massachusetts gave itself a strong governorship, state senate, and courts, and it separated them from one another. Annual elections would keep representatives from forgetting that the power they wielded belonged to their constituents, not them. Massachusetts abolished slavery immediately and directly, with no drawn-out "apprenticeships" and with no compensation for slave owners. It resisted paper money, so the 1780s inflation did not plague it. Even so, it experienced Shays's Rebellion. To the rebels it was a desperate and righteous defense of what their Revolution had gained. To the commonwealth's officials and others like them it was a fearful sign that republicanism was not going to work.[38]

The delegates who gathered in Philadelphia the following summer and wrote the United States Constitution thought that the states were the problem. The most powerful argument in the Constitution's support, James Madison's *Federalist*, no. 10, shows the diagnosis, by the remedy it prescribes. Madison asked how Americans could preserve their liberty against the corrosion of "faction" and self-interest. "Extend the sphere" of politics, he wrote, and interests would multiply until none could dominate the others. At the same time, "as each representative will be chosen by a greater number . . . it will be more difficult for unworthy candidates to practise with success the vicious arts by which elections are too often carried." Instead, the voters would pick "men who possess the most attractive merit and the most diffusive and established characters."[39] In a large republic the Americans would eliminate the effects of their selfishness and they would find rulers of genuine public spirit. They could not lose.

The Constitution of the United States is more than a political charter. It attempted much more than just solving problems that could not be worked out in the separate states. For two centuries it has provided a lens for viewing American society and a fulcrum for guiding society's development. It is American Scripture and the justices of the Supreme

Court are its high priests, possessed of the power to determine what it shall mean. In 1791, before the principle of judicial review was firmly established, President George Washington, who had chaired the convention, asked for his cabinet's opinions on how the Constitution should be read. Secretary of the Treasury Alexander Hamilton took on the problem of whether the future would have to be governed by what he and his fellow delegates at the convention had "intended" at the time. Hamilton maintained that

> intention is to be sought for in the instrument itself, according to the usual and established rules of construction. Nothing is more common than for laws to *express* and *effect*, more or less than was intended. If then a power . . . be deducible by fair inference from the whole or any part of the numerous provisions of the constitution of the United States, arguments . . . regarding the intention of the convention, must be rejected.[40]

What, then, does "the instrument itself" say about American society?

The Constitution declares itself "the supreme law of the land," which is much like Sir William Blackstone's assertion in 1765 that there "is and must be . . . a supreme, irresistible, uncontrolled authority, in which . . . the rights of sovereignty reside."[41] The difference was that sovereignty now belonged to a people that supposedly knew its own mind, rather than to a king who supposedly could do no wrong. During twenty years of revolution, however, Americans had demonstrated that they were of many minds, not one. They had wanted to protect their customs, not suppress them with a new supreme power, even one exercised in their name. Now this was changing. The United States would be "federal," not "composite" in the old sense. Its self-sovereign single people proclaiming one "supreme law of the land" would be much harder to resist than a distant monarch reigning over many distinct dominions.

The Constitution grants powers to Congress and denies others to the states, and taken together the grants and denials provide a vision of what that sovereign people would do. Article I, which lists the powers the central government was granted, has no precedent or model in any of the state constitutions written before 1787. Some of the powers were simple continuations of ones wielded before 1776 by the British Crown, such as making war and negotiating treaties.[42] But in a series of striking grants and denials, the Constitution establishes institutions and practices to surround, protect, and foster the national economy that had begun to take shape during the war. No state shall interfere with obligations of contract, which undid the clauses in state constitutions that had allowed, even mandated, embargoes to protect fragile local economies during a time of crisis. Nor shall any state make anything but gold or silver a legal tender for payment of debts, which undercut the paper money laws that most states had passed in order to cope with the severe depression that began in mid-1784 and lasted into 1787. Decisions of the courts of one state shall be accorded full "faith and credit" by the courts of the others, pointing toward rough uniformity in state-made commercial law. Congress, not the states, was to have the primary power to regulate interstate commerce. It could provide for a uniform bankruptcy law and it could protect the commercial rights of innovators with patents and copyrights. By controlling post offices and post roads it could enhance the flow of information, and perhaps promote the flow of goods. Here were the sinews of a common market, a large economic community oriented around trade and production, larger geographically than any other in the Western world, at that point or well into the future.

The Constitution had a vision of race as well as of economics. A few years after he made himself the foremost of the Constitution's Framers, James Madison of Virginia addressed the problem of political society posed by American people who were not white. Speaking in the House of Representatives on receiving a petition from North Carolina slaves against slavery, he was succinct. The black petitioners had simply "no claim" on Congress's "attention."[43] Federal judges would make that same point again and again in the future. Both Native Americans and African-Americans belonged in the United States or nowhere. But they did not participate in the "blessings of liberty" which the Constitution proposed to secure. They were not among the Republic's sovereign citizens. They were simply its subjects. So Madison and many others thought.

The Constitution does speak repeatedly to the condition of black people within the Republic at the time of its writing. It provided for federal aid to states against insurrections. It increased the political weight of slaveholding states by counting three-fifths of the slaves for representation, although the slaves could neither vote nor be elected to public office. The slave trade was a perceived abomination, but Congress could not cut it off for twenty years. Slaves escaping to the northern zone of freedom that was emerging would be returned to the South by the federal courts. A future government could not tax slavery out of existence by imposing export duties on what slaves produced, because no export duties would be allowed. These clauses were what the abolitionist William Lloyd Garrison had in mind half a century later when he called the

document a "covenant with death and an agreement with hell." The
Revolution had forced open a window on slavery. The national power
that the Constitution created would not be used to close that window,
but it would not be used to open it any wider.[44] So it was to be until
slavery itself finally was destroyed.

The word "slavery" is not used in the Constitution, but its presence
is clear. The word "Indian" is used only to exclude "Indians not taxed"
from any part in political representation and governance and to grant
Congress the power to regulate trade "with the Indian tribes." Nonetheless, the settlement affected Indians as fully as it did whites and slaves.
Congress would have "Power to dispose of and make all needful Rules
and Regulations respecting the Territory or other Property belonging to
the United States." This would be without "Prejudice" to the claims of
any particular state to federal land. There would not be protection, however, for the claims of Indian tribes. The Constitution's fourth article
provided that "new States may be admitted by the Congress into this
Union" but no "new State" was to "be formed or erected within the
Jurisdiction of any other State; nor . . . by the Junction of . . . Parts of
States, without the Consent . . . of the States concerned."

The Cherokee nation attempted to form its own jurisdiction within
the state of Georgia and to become an autonomous republic that was
associated with the United States but not subordinate to it or any state.
But in 1830 the Supreme Court held that the Constitution did not
support the Cherokees. Treaties with foreign countries would be "supreme law," paramount to the will of Congress or any state. Treaties
with Indian tribes would not be supreme even over state laws. They
would depend for their power on the goodwill of the more powerful
party. Some, particularly the beaten Catawbas and Iroquois, did attract
goodwill, at least to the extent that they were not stripped of the last
remnants of their land and forced to leave it. Most others did not.

[VII]

The federal Constitution was not the product of a malign conspiracy,
any more than the Revolution had been. It was a remarkably creative
response to the problems the independent states faced. The Constitution
presented a map of the future, a vision of what the new society should
be like. That vision was very different from the colonial society that had
been organized around the power of the British Crown. Unlike virtually

any previous republic and unlike many that followed it, what the Constitution created would last. The Framers and their supporters persuaded enough whites to accept their vision. They offered stability, after a long epoch of confusion and disruption. To the many people who came to its support, the Constitution seemed to complete the Revolution. Even whites who opposed it at first—probably a majority—came to accept its version of a "more perfect union."

The differences between the colonial order those people had destroyed and the republican order they were creating were profound. The former had been organized around the subjection of unequal subjects to a sovereign Crown. The latter was organized around the participation of equal citizens in a self-sovereignty they shared. By its nature and its rhetoric, the republican community of white Americans offered the possibility that its own limits and exclusions could be overcome, which perhaps is one reason for its enduring strength. Nonetheless, other people had produced other visions of the American future during the revolutionary epoch. They stated them clearly enough. They tried to realize those visions with moral argument, political organization, and military force. In 1787, however, those people were in no position to turn their visions into reality. Whatever possibilities the republican community might offer in principle, the reality of the new republican society was that its very real benefits would be purchased at a high very real price, which white Americans would not have to pay.

PART TWO

WHAT, THEN, WERE
THESE AMERICANS?

Why reclining, interrogating, why myself all drowsing?
What deepening twilight—scum floating atop of the waters,
Who are they as bats and night-dogs askant in the capitol?
What a filthy Presidentiad! (O South, your torrid sun! O
North, your arctic freezings!)
Are those really Congressmen? are those the great Judges? Is
that the President?
Then I will sleep awhile yet, for I see that these States sleep
for reasons;
(With gathering murk, with muttering thunder and lambent
shoots, we all duly awake,
South, North, East, West, inland and seaboard, we will surely
awake.)

—WALT WHITMAN

CHAPTER 5

MOUNTAINS, VALLEYS, AND PLAINS

TO most Americans the early nineteenth century seems a second Age of Discovery. The Lewis and Clark National Historic Trail has eighty markers and displays between its beginning at Wood River, Illinois, and its terminus at Ecola Creek, Oregon, marking major stops on the explorers' way. It is one of six such trails west of the Mississippi. The others celebrate traders who opened a route between Missouri and Santa Fe, Pony Express riders, forty-niners seeking California gold, Oregon settlers, and Mormons following the Lord to Utah. They recall the different ways western places turned into American states.

There is a historic place in Idaho called Lemhi Pass, where Meriwether Lewis and William Clark crossed the Continental Divide. Their expedition was exploring the newly purchased Louisiana Territory and what lay beyond. At the pass they entered country where Britain and Spain maintained legal claims, but where neither enjoyed control. As the party crossed, they were among Shoshoni Indians who thought all the land around was theirs. The Shoshonis' leader, Cameahwait, was the brother of the expedition's guide, Sacagawea.

It was all new to the travelers, but the Shoshonis were no strangers to Lewis and Clark's kind. Sacagawea's marriage to the French-Canadian Toussaint Charbonneau is evidence. So is the couple's first meeting with the expedition at Fort Mandan, more than seven hundred miles east of the divide, where the Missouri River bends south. Cameahwait gave the travelers horses to cross the Bitterroot Mountains. The Shoshonis had animals enough to lend. Perhaps they had obtained them at Santa Fe, founded by Spaniards in 1610, just as the French were building Quebec, the Dutch were possessing Albany, and the English were planting Jamestown. However the horses got to Idaho, they were descended from Spanish herds. The Shoshonis had probably known no Africans but the expedition included York, Clark's slave. Tradition holds that both York and the whites left offspring behind. If so, the Shoshonis would have accepted them as members of the community.[1]

The National Trails System does not specifically commemorate the tracks of black Americans into the Cotton Kingdom. The system does include the Natchez Trace, from central Tennessee to the Mississippi River at Natchez. Many slaves walked the Trace, but it is designated scenic, not historic. Where the Trace crosses northwestern Alabama, it intersects the Trail of Tears, the westward route of Cherokees when Georgia and President Andrew Jackson forced them out to go to what is now Oklahoma. Far to the west, the Juan Bautista de Anza Historic Trail honors the Spanish captain who found an inland route from Santa Fe to the mission communities along the California coast in 1774. His venture helped secure him the governorship of New Mexico, which he took up four years later. Traders going to Santa Fe from Missouri during the era of Lewis and Clark blazed the trail that still bears their destination's name.[2] That was long after Indians cut another westward track leading there, from the French settlement of Natchitoches, in Louisiana.[3] U.S. Route 82 roughly follows its course along the Red River, but it is not honored as a historic trail.

Like Columbus, Lewis and Clark discovered nothing. Their trek, those of other explorers like Zebulon Pike, and the Missourians' trading ventures to Santa Fe were signs that what already existed was about to be rearranged. President Thomas Jefferson had many reasons for dispatching Lewis and Clark on their epic journey. He took an active, impassioned part in transatlantic debate about America's merits and he wanted to reveal its spectacles to a gaping world. But President Jefferson also believed the United States ought to expand. The western Indians, mestizos, métis, Spaniards, French, and English who encountered Lewis and Clark understood that a new power was appearing in their world. The old American order had been defined by conflicting European interests, merchant capitalism, imported customs, frontier exchange, diplomacy, and independent-minded Indians. Increasingly, the new order would be defined by the United States.

As Lewis and Clark set forth, Americans east of the Mississippi were digging canals and building roads. They were patenting useful inventions and turning money into capital by pooling it in banks and insurance companies. The population of New York City in 1810 was three times its size in 1790. Power-driven machinery was turning in small factories. All the changes drew upon what the Republic was doing with its land, now that it was an independent nation, able to rule as it saw fit within its boundaries. The journeys of westering explorers and traders offered the clearest possible sign that those boundaries were not yet fixed.

[I]

When the Revolutionary War ended, land was the Republic's only material treasure. In 1779 New York seized loyalist holdings and declared its sovereignty "in respect of all property" inside its boundaries. That meant Iroquoia. Virginia, North Carolina, and Georgia made similar claims over Indians' land, all stretching to the Mississippi. West of the coastal states and north of the Ohio River, the whole self-defined American people made the same claim. Indians held possession, but what began to happen to the Iroquois at Fort Stanwix in 1784 proclaimed what awaited them all. Tribal titles would be "extinguished." In the most benevolent view of the future, Indian women would marry white men. The children would become American farmers, losing forever their color, languages, cultures, and gods. Indians would vanish, not by becoming extinct but by amalgamation.[4] But very few Indians wanted to lose their traditions and identities.

State and federal rulers alike made it their goal to use the new treasure to pay the Revolution's costs, while they also filled the land and encouraged sturdy personal independence. Land grants could meet the claims of soldiers and officers. Land sales would raise money to pay the public debt and keep taxes down. Either way, smallholders would come into possession of land and turn the wilderness into the world's garden. Nobody would lose, except the people whose land it had been. So the hope went.

People who won, won big. In Maine, which was part of Massachusetts until 1820, General Henry Knox used political connections and a good marriage to gain 576,000 acres. The commonwealth of Massachusetts claimed that it owned much of Iroquoia under its old royal charter. It and New York worked out an agreement that gave the land to Massachusetts, but as a property-holding corporation operating under New York law rather than under Massachusetts's own sovereignty. Two adventurers named Oliver Phelps and Nathaniel Gorham agreed to pay $1,000,000 for the whole of the Massachusetts claim. They failed to keep up payments, and much of the land passed to the Philadelphian Robert Morris, financial hero of the Revolution. He failed as well, and the tract fell into the hands of speculators in Holland. East of Seneca Lake, where New York claimed actual ownership of the land as well as legal sovereignty over it, the first thought was to use it to pay off revolutionary soldiers. In 1791, however, the state's commissioners began selling land "on such terms and in such manner as they shall judge." Farms for citizen soldiers and small tracts bought directly from the state disappeared as goals of state policy. The state possessed 7,000,000 acres when divestment began. It sold 5,500,000 acres within a year, to a mere thirty-five purchasers. More than 3,000,000 went to just one man.[5]

When Kentucky entered the Union in 1792, its land had already been granted by Virginia. Nonetheless, the Kentucky legislature granted the land again. Both states let grantees "locate" unclaimed land for themselves, wherever they could find it and put down markers. The result was chaos. Kentucky was "shingled" four times over with overlapping claims, and "one quarter of the entire state was claimed by twenty-one extensive speculators." The terms of Kentucky's separation from Virginia protected Virginia grants against interference. Nobody had any idea how to reconcile the overlaps.[6]

The most notorious speculation was in Georgia. In 1789 it tried to convey 25,400,000 acres to a land company "at less than a cent an acre." That failed, but in 1795 it sold 21,500,000 acres to another company at 1.25 cents per acre. Much of this land lay in Alabama and Mississippi and was held and used by Chickasaw and Choctaw Indians. In practice the Choctaws' land would belong to them until the treaties of Doak's Stand in 1820 and Dancing Rabbit Creek a decade later. The value of the Georgia grants lay in the right of first purchase, should Indians be cajoled, bribed, or simply forced to sell. The total land east of the Mississippi that came into public hands and was thus available for redistribution amounted to 237,000,000 acres. In all of human history no people had held such a treasure.[7]

In 1785 the Confederation Congress adopted the grid pattern for selling off federal lands. Land would be surveyed, not "located." Townships and sections would be clearly marked. One goal was order: the Kentucky disaster was no more than one instance of how old-order land grants worked. Another goal was revenue. Land that was clearly identified would be easy to sell, so cash would flow. A purchaser might contract for a six-mile-square "township" of 23,040 acres. whether the purchaser was an individual, a group of "proprietors," or the would-be founders of a town. Land could also be sold by individual "sections" of 640 acres, to become single-owner farms.[8]

The grid system ended the chaotic land policies of the colonial years, but it did not end vast acquisitions. By 1836 Solomon Sturges "had accumulated 173,000 acres" of Indiana land, including 32,000 in just one county. The Buckingham family had 103,000 acres in the state and the Ellsworths 110,000. On the banks of the Wabash River there were sixty-four owners with more than 2,000 acres each. Only twenty-one lived in Indiana.[9]

White Americans were heirs to the deep European tradition that large landholdings like these make a person "gentle." Legally and culturally, a colonial gentleman had been someone who did not have to support himself by direct manufacturing or commerce or tilling his own land. As late as 1769 Sir William Johnson sought the title of manor for his Mohawk Valley estate, so he could be its lord.[10] The dream of getting out of business and becoming a gentleman by acquiring land continued after the Revolution. Both Henry Knox and Robert Morris moved into landholding precisely so they could establish themselves at a new level of prestige.[11] But Morris ended in a debtors' prison and Knox nearly did.[12] The wreckage of their dreams also suggests the larger change underway.

We can see the change among New York's postrevolutionary great landlords. The "good patroon" Stephen van Rensselaer clung to the old ways and Rensselaerswyck turned into a morass of uncollected rents. But Philip Schuyler began writing leases for short terms, not the three lives or ninety-nine years of old. His leases reserved the right to build a dam and flood a tenant's land for the sake of "improvement." He would sell the land if the price became right. Schuyler sponsored early efforts to build a canal west from Albany along the course of the Mohawk River. Robert R. Livingston still played the seigneur at his Hudson River estate of Clermont, but he became the patron of Robert Fulton's efforts to build a steamboat.[13] Both men were stepping from the old ground of great estates and fawning tenants onto the treacherous but fertile soil of innovation and capitalist development.

Tenancy persisted. Touring western New York in 1802, the missionary John Taylor commented that

> the same evil operates here . . . as in many parts of this country—the lands are most of them leased. This must necessarily operate to debase the minds and destroy the enterprise of the settlers. . . . If men do not possess the . . . soil, they never will . . . feel independent. And . . . they will always be under the influence of their landlords.[14]

But the contrast between the admiring word "gentleman" and the disparaging phrase "idle rich" suggests the gulf between the old ethos of wealth and the new.[15] The mentality of Schuyler and Livingston reflected it. So did the visions of people who came to the landholders wanting to buy, not rent.

The great men were buying land to sell it again, not to build estates. We can call them speculators (the eighteenth century would have said "land jobbers") and condemn them for their greed. We also can call them developers and show how they encouraged settlers to move in. To Phelps and Gorham, western New York land was just a capital investment. Prospective purchasers were just as commercially minded as they, with no romantic desire to retreat into rustic self-sufficiency. In the Massachusetts and Connecticut towns that the purchasers were abandoning, the aftermath of the Revolution brought refinement and comfort, if a person could afford them.[16] Migrants wanted these. That meant selling what they produced for profit, in the open market.

But the markets of Albany and New York City were hundreds of miles to the east. So Phelps and Gorham created "city-towns" with all the amenities of New England. As in Worcester, Massachusetts, so in Canandaigua, New York, where settlement began in 1789. Within five years the town had a central square, a courthouse, a main street, and forty houses "attractively painted, and many surrounded by neat gardens and lawns." By 1800 there were seventy households, a steepled church, and more than forty businesses.[17] In northern New York the Beekman family could not rent their 30,000 acres on Lake Champlain, even on attractive terms. In 1785 they made the "reluctant decision . . . to prepare for the disposition of their property . . . to individual settlers." Nobody wanted to live with their requirements that tenants "build a frame house, clear a reasonable number of acres, plant an orchard, and cut no timber on land not leased." The time had come to sell.[18]

The South was not strikingly different. Great planters in the colonial era had been enmeshed in transatlantic capitalism. A person grew tobacco or indigo to sell it, not consume it. Nonetheless, they did fancy themselves as patriarchs and lords. The Virginia planter William Byrd II made the point in 1726, using prose that bordered on poetry:

I have a large Family of my own, and my Doors are open to Every Body, yet I have no Bills to pay, and half-a-Crown will rest undisturbed in my Pocket for many Moons together. Like one of the Patriarchs, I have my Flocks and my Herds, my Bond-men and Bond-women, and every Soart of trade amongst my own Servants, so that I live in a kind of Independence on every one but Providence.[19]

When a man like Byrd acquired land farther west it was at least partly to continue his patriarchy by guaranteeing prosperity to his offspring, and to offset how tobacco exhausted the soil by making sure that good land remained available. By the late eighteenth century, however, settlement had reached the Blue Ridge. The tobacco frontier was disappearing.[20]

White Southerners still wanted land and slaves. The Tayloes of Virginia solved the problem of running out of tobacco land by expanding into Alabama and switching to cotton.[21] They remained patriarchs, southern style. But nineteenth-century land sales suggest that simple market calculation, not long-term strategy, was more and more at work. The cotton market boomed three times between 1800 and 1860. With each boom, sales of public land surged. After the War of 1812 the place to be was Alabama. Settlers took up 209,000 acres in 1816 and more than 1,400,000 in 1818. Then panic set in and the boom collapsed. In 1832, 261,314 acres were sold in Mississippi and in 1835 more than 2,900,000. Then panic struck again and only 271,075 acres were sold in 1837.[22] Much the same pattern held during the final boom, just before the Civil War.

On the best soil many of these purchases were on a very large scale. A mere ten individuals took out "154,000 acres and 216 bought over a thousand acres each" in northern Alabama during the first boom. In 1850 the absentee planter Benjamin Roach had 488 slaves on properties scattered throughout Mississippi. Stephen Duncan had nearly 700 on five plantations in the delta county of Issaquena and on his home place near Natchez. But they also bought land to speculate in rising values, sometimes outside the South. The largest southern-owned landholding in Illinois in the mid-1850s was 20,661 acres, and there were twenty-nine southern holdings larger than 1,000 acres. Duncan, the greatest Mississippi planter of all, was accused (accurately) "of investing 'great amounts' in land and securities in the North or 'elsewhere out of the South.' "[23]

Northern or southern, eighteenth-century or nineteenth-, all these great landholders were mixtures, compounded in varying proportions out of the same elements. We can take William Byrd II as our benchmark. Though he was born in Virginia, Byrd spent the first part of his life trying desperately to find an upper-crust English bride and become an English gentleman. Finally he accepted that he was a Virginian. The commitment was complete. Westover, the home he built on the James River, is one of the earliest great Chesapeake dwellings. His history of Virginia's border with North Carolina ranks among the early South's most entertaining and original writings. His pen picture of himself, "my Flocks and my Herds, my Bond-men and Bond-women," is patriarchal imagery at its absolute purest. He had succeeded, he thought, at re-creating the English gentry ideal in the New World. At bottom the man was a colonial capitalist. He grew his tobacco for distant sales and invested the profits in more land and slaves. But he covered it well.

Henry Knox and Robert Morris got into land to make themselves gentlemen on the same model. But Knox put up a gimcrack mansion in Maine that proved as impermanent as Westover proved enduring. Philip Schuyler and Robert R. Livingston began as authentic Hudson Valley gentry. But they went on to promote canals and steamboats, the very symbols of modernity and commerce, as opposed to gentlemanly repose. The style of Nathaniel Phelps and Oliver Gorham was never patriarchal or gentlemanly. They were egalitarian Yankees. But for a time they became true princes, with their purchase of the whole Massachusetts claim in Iroquoia. Benjamin Roach made no personal commitment to the nineteenth-century Mississippi that gave him his wealth. It was just a place to do business, even if the business was growing cotton with slaves. Stephen Duncan made a large commitment there and became the essence of the Old South gentleman. But Duncan was Pennsylvania-born and he realized that the Old South might not last. For safety's sake he invested outside it as well. What binds all these men together is the part they took in turning the acres they acquired, which were not capital in any sense, into the landed capital that underpinned the American interior's rapid development.

[II]

Henry Knox's plans for Maine seemed beneficent, at least to him. He would provide what others needed: "barrel works, saw- and gristmills, wharves, coast[al] and West India vessels, stores, lime quarries and kilns, brickworks, fisheries, gardens, orchards, grain fields, canals, and breeding farms." These would employ "dozens of men." Knox was not prepared for the resentment and resistance that he provoked. Settlers insisted the land was theirs, because their labor was making it fruitful. They called themselves "Liberty Men," maintaining that they, not George Washington's former Secretary of War, were the true defenders of the Revolution. Then they became "white Indians." They donned Indian clothes, disrupted surveying, and terrorized the landlords' agents. There were 133 incidents between 1790 and 1809, when the uprising started to subside.[24]

Call them settlers, squatters, Liberty Men, or white Indians, almost all were from lower New England. At the same time, other Yankees were going to central and western New York, where they began to create "greater New England." These people built houses and barns, towns and churches, all in New England style. They turned the landscape of western New York and northern Ohio, Indiana, and Illinois into a cultural outpost of the Merrimack and Connecticut valleys.[25]

In 1784 one such man, named Hugh White, trekked from Middletown, Connecticut, to the upper Mohawk Valley, where he founded Whitestown, New York. The Iroquois had just abandoned the land, but he acquired it direct from New York State and they did not figure in the world he set out to create. His 1,500 acres was far more than he could have hoped for in Connecticut. Hugh White did not become either a would-be gentleman like Henry Knox or an insurgent. White did intend to become a patriarch, settling his sons on farms of their own within his tract. His ancestors included five successive men named Hugh White and the family had a long tradition of cohering around a father figure's control. Now, in a new place, it was his turn. This latest Hugh White made himself a businessman as well as a patriarch. He built sawmills. He fertilized his fields according to the best knowledge. His lumber and grain would be sold in distant markets. Hugh White's ancestors knew about commerce and took part in it. But his world was far more open than theirs. His grandson became an engineer, a man of innovation and change who acquired fame for his work on the Erie Canal and later on railroads. He became very much his own man, and the name he bore, Canvass White, was his own as well. In true Yankee style it honored a family with which the Whites had intermarried. But unlike the long succession of Whites named Hugh, this man felt no obligation to do with his life as his fathers had done before him. Nor would such a man pass that kind of burden on to sons of his own.[26]

[III]

In England and America the terms on which land could be owned presented a most serious issue in the eighteenth and early nineteenth centuries. In England the issue took the form of enclosures, as communal parish and manor rights gave way to absolute individual ownership. In America it meant replacing Indian terms of ownership, which allowed for many possible users at once, with white terms that in theory were exclusive. In both countries, land became a zero-sum commodity. What one person gained, another had to lose.

But Henry Knox's half million acres in Maine seemed empty to the Yankee settlers who became white Indians for a time. There was plenty for everybody, as long as one ignored the real Indians who already had lost it absolutely. The grants that shingled Kentucky seemed empty too. So did western New York and the Old Southwest. Henry Knox knew that his title was perfectly legal and that it could not be challenged in the courts. He eventually realized that he could make an accommodation with the Liberty Men and "white Indians." He could give them legal titles. They could give him peace, development, and rising prices. The squatters would buy the prospect of providing their own children with a material future on their own patriarchal terms. But like Knox's of himself as a beneficent gentleman, their vision of themselves as patriarchs providing for their families' futures was very close to its end.[27]

Accommodations like the one that settled matters between Knox and the settlers became the rule. Kentucky legislators understood that Virginia had saddled them with impossible contradictions. In 1797 they solved the problem by legalizing preemptions where "titles lay a long time dormant." Squatters could defeat unenforced landlord claims or win generous compensation if their own claims lost. The goal was the certainty and clarity that the federal grid system offered.[28]

Early in the nineteenth century the Holland Land Company gridded its holdings in western New York and appointed the highly able Joseph Ellicott as its chief agent. Ellicott took his role seriously. He understood that different kinds of land had different values and that this had to be recognized. In some places he agreed that the grid had to be tilted off true north, for the sake of equity. Nonetheless, the hope of the developers was that each successive tier of townships would fill before the next opened. In reality "decisions made by the settlers themselves" shaped "the spread of settlement." Settlers, not Ellicott or the Dutch owners he represented, "took possession of the land" and created "communities on the western New York wilderness."[29]

By the time of Joseph Ellicott's valiant stand for order among the invading Yankees, other whites were moving out of Kentucky onto the open prairie north of the Ohio River. These were not Yankees but rather southern plain folk, among them Tom and Nancy Lincoln, who settled in Indiana after the birth of their son Abraham. Like Ellicott acting for the Holland Land Company, the federal government intended to survey and open up the prairie states tier by tier, each tier following only when its predecessors had been filled. But one historian has called people like the Lincolns "American Tartars" who could not be stopped. Much like Liberty Men and white Indians farther east, they had their own ideas about how to distribute landed wealth. At Sugar Creek, Illinois, near Springfield, the first wave of settlers "deliberately set out to stake their claims in advance of the surveyors" and thus to subvert the whole project of "ordering the land in advance of settlement." By 1828 fully two-thirds of Illinois farmers were "squatters on the public domain."

These people developed strong "customs of association" which they intended to endow with the force of law. Again much like the squatters in Maine, they understood that statutory land titles could not be defeated. Nonetheless, "a kind of common-law was established . . . that the improvements on Congress land shall not be purchased by any person except he who made the improvement."[30] Even far to the west, the same rules applied. White Americans went to California in vast numbers after the discovery of gold in 1848. The territory was newly conquered by war with Mexico. According to the treaty that ended the war, Spanish- and Mexican-derived land titles were to be recognized. But the newcomers were little disposed to honor the treaty. Their mining communities worked out their own rules, and like customary titles on the Illinois prairie, these took on the effective force of law. After California became a state in 1850 its legislature recognized the miners' customs, and in 1865 Chief Justice Salmon P. Chase of the United States Supreme Court did the same, holding that "a . . . common law of miners . . . has sprung up on the Pacific coast." The following year Congress recognized "local mining customs and rules of miners when not in conflict with the laws of the United States and acknowledged and confirmed the miners' rights to their properties."[31]

The official goal of American land policy was to create a citizenry of individual freehold farmers. By and large, it succeeded. By 1860 there were 667,697 separate farms in the states and territories with public land. By 1880 that figure had multiplied more than threefold and three-quarters of those were farmed by the person who owned them. By this time, the goal of acquiring enough land to see to the next generation's needs had almost disappeared. When Congress amended federal land law in 1820 it reduced the minimum tract for purchase to only eighty acres, at $1.25 per acre, with full immediate payment. In 1862, after long pressure, it adopted the homestead policy, giving grants of 160 acres at no cost other than minimal fees. On land that was adequately watered, this would be enough for a family farm. It would not be enough for a patrimony.[32]

The net effect was to foster an understanding of the land in commercial terms. The goal of a property-holding citizenry, free of obligations and supporting themselves from their own efforts, was roughly what Thomas Jefferson had in mind when he wrote, in one of his most delicious phrases, that "those who labor in the earth are the chosen people of God, if ever he had a chosen people, whose breasts he has made his peculiar deposit for substantial and genuine virtue."[33] It is why the anonymous painter of an enchanting nineteenth-century farmscape called his work "He Who Tills His Land Shall Be Satisfied." The reality, however, was that the earth and what it could grow became subjects for sale in a world of entangling competition.

During the middle of the nineteenth century the government ratified this development by explicitly turning very large amounts of land into capital grants. These had two purposes. One was to foster a transport network in the West, based to some extent on publicly built canals but much more on privately built railroads. The other goal was to enrich the separate states by direct grants of public land to finance public higher education.

The original plan for the railroad lands was to take advantage of the grid system's checkerboard pattern. Along a right-of-way alternating sections would be deeded over. These sections would rise in value with the promise of easy railroad transportation. So could the sections still available from the government. Congress's intent was that these were to be sold for at least $2.50 per acre, double the normal minimum. What the railroads received was enormous, totaling 94,355,739 acres from the federal government, in addition to 51,133,620 from the states. Twenty percent of the whole acreage of Kansas fell into railroad hands and 15 percent of Nebraska. Almost a quarter of North Dakota belonged to railroad companies as well.

The total direct land grants south of Alaska dwarfed even these huge figures, amounting to 223,884,994 acres. The grants sponsored railroads, wagon roads, canals, and the draining of "seemingly unwanted" wetlands so that they could be made productive. Of sixty-four million acres given as swampland, Florida received 20,326,708 and Louisiana 9,504,412. Mississippi, Arkansas, Missouri, Illinois, Indiana, Iowa, Michigan, Wisconsin, and California all received swampland grants greater them a million acres. Another eleven million acres were handed out to establish universities. The vast bulk of this went to "the more populous and older states." New York used its university grant to finance not a public institution but rather Cornell, which became a unique public-private hybrid. Rhode Island's grant benefited Brown, which was and is entirely private.[34]

Public or private, the emergence of the land-grant universities demonstrated what the nineteenth-century Republic thought was good. Their purpose was not to pass on received culture to a narrow elite. Instead, in Ezra Cornell's phrase, it was to found institutions "where any person can find instruction in any study" and to encourage the innovations that the United States valued. They were of a piece with the Republic's massive investment in railroads, the most advanced technology of their day. Railroads and state universities alike were supposed to carry free individuals wherever they wanted to go, however far it might be from where they had begun. It was on this basis that the interior became "the West."

But "the rise of the West" was not simply the triumph of individualism that was proclaimed by Jefferson. The enormous size of the railroad land grants suggests not only the huge cost of the Republic's railroads, far beyond what any individual or small group could raise, but also the huge possibilities railroad construction presented for getting rich at the public trough. These fitted with the "incongruous land system" that the foremost historian of land distribution sees in the real West.[35] To appreciate what happened, however, we must understand that not everyone who went West went there free. We must understand as well that homesteaders, gold miners, planters, slaves, railroaders, and university builders alike were not conquering "virgin land," however empty it looked. All were imposing a new layer upon a landscape that already had its history.

[IV]

Reliable evidence about black people in the Old Southwest is hard to find. Not until 1850 did the United States census apply the same age categories to whites, free black people, and slaves. The censuses of 1830 and 1840 provide very precise breakdowns of young whites by five-year intervals, but they divide young black people only once, at the age of ten. The next cutting line was age twenty-four. The 1820 census put the cutting point at age fourteen. Censuses prior to that provide no age breakdown for black Americans at all.

The implication is clear. In the minds of the officials who designed the census, a white child passed through many stages along the route from birth to adulthood. These needed to be noted. Black children passed one threshold only, taking them from a world of play and light responsibilities to the unceasing demands of slave labor. The passage also marked where the prospect of being separated forever from parents, brothers, sisters, cousins, and friends grew considerably stronger. White Americans often migrated in their youth as well, but the comparison is irrelevant. For them it was a matter of families moving freely or individuals deciding equally freely to leave home. A slave who was sold from Virginia to Alabama had no more choice about it than that slave's ancestor had about leaving Africa.

Because the data are so weak, we can only guess how the slave population grew during the great surge westward and how black people took part in the surge. Nonetheless, we have some figures. Between 1790 and 1810, about 194,000 black people entered the United States, passed from one slave region to another, or both. More than 90,000 were newly transported Africans who came in through Charleston and Savannah. About 63,000 of these stayed near the port of entry, 15,000 in South Carolina and 48,000 in Georgia. About 18,000 were transported to Mississippi and Louisiana, where they joined some 3,000 who came from the West Indies, entering through Mobile and New Orleans. While the Africans and West Indians were being imported, another 98,000 African-Americans were transported from the Chesapeake Bay area. Seventy-nine thousand were taken to Tennessee and Kentucky and smaller numbers to the two Carolinas, Georgia, Alabama, Mississippi, and Louisiana.

Despite the legal closing of the slave trade in 1808, illegal slaving vessels brought perhaps 7,000 more Africans into the United States during the next decade. Finally satiated, South Carolina received none. Georgia took about 2,000 and Mississippi and Alabama 2,000 more. About

3,000 were taken to Louisiana, Arkansas, and Missouri. During those years 124,000 African-American slaves were sold or transported out of the Chesapeake states, 51,000 to Alabama and Mississippi, 26,000 to Louisiana, Arkansas, and Missouri, 24,000 to Kentucky, and smaller numbers to Georgia and Tennessee. The internal slave trade took about 13,000 straight west from North Carolina into Tennessee.[36] In total, then, about 338,000 slaves either entered the United States or were forcibly transported internally between 1790 and 1820. These represent 22 percent of the whole enslaved population in the year 1820. One enslaved person in every five, in other words, knew forced migration directly. Every single slave either experienced it or saw it happen to someone who was close.

After 1820 the African slave trade to North America was almost dead, but internal sales and transportation continued at an enormous rate. More than 100,000 slaves entered the booming cotton state of Mississippi during the 1830s. Nearly 97,000 entered Alabama during the same period, and 99,190 went to Texas between 1850 and 1859. In every census interval the greatest out-migrations were from Virginia: 22,767 between 1790 and 1799, 76,157 in the 1820s, 118,474 during the 1830s, 82,573 in the Old South's final decade.[37]

Without doubt, many slaves traveled because whole plantation communities were on the move. The tobacco land of Virginia and Maryland was worked out and masters were seeking rich soil in the Black Belt, the Mississippi/Yazoo Delta, northern Louisiana, or Texas, where cotton would grow. Yet even in these people's lives there may have been considerably more disruption than a first glance would suggest. A slave who belonged to the Tayloes of Virginia was not sold by being sent to the cotton lands that they began to open up in Alabama. But the sundering from that slave's Virginia home and from family who remained behind was probably permanent. Someone on a Yazoo County, Mississippi, plantation owned by Benjamin Roach was part of an empire that sprawled the whole width of the South. Any person within that empire could be shifted at Roach's whim and he was unlikely ever to shift that person back.[38]

Outright sale rather than forced migration with a planter or within a planter's holdings was what most slaves had to anticipate. Migration with a planter implied shifting a whole community, from the very young to the very old. Migration by sale implied selecting slaves for their youth and their strength. During the 1820s perhaps 70 percent of interregional slave migration was due to the domestic slave trade. During the 1850s the percentage was barely less. Thus about 115,000 persons were traded during the former decade and more than 200,000 during the latter. Land itself and the cotton it grew were fundamental commodities in the Old South's economy. So were slaves. Slave markets on the African coast were inseparable from how the institution began in America. Slave markets in Richmond, Charleston, Mobile, and New Orleans were vital to the spread of slavery. In Africa and America alike, the greatest burden was borne by the young.[39]

There were significant differences between the trade across the ocean and the trade across America. Domestic slaves were, of course, not piled into ships and were not subject to the frightful and dangerous middle passage across the Atlantic. Born in America, they knew English. They knew the rules of American slavery, including the oral traditions that their people had developed to help one another through the ordeal.[40] Their bodies were used to American diseases. During the main years of the African trade there was slavery everywhere in America that whites settled. When the domestic trade was in full swing, however, the North Star did point toward freedom. A slave had at least the possibility of permanent escape, a point that both the nineteenth-century white abolitionist Harriet Beecher Stowe and the twentieth-century African-American writer Toni Morrison made in their powerful and emotive fictional accounts of slavery.[41]

Not least in terms of difference from original African enslavement, the domestic trade transported the two sexes in roughly equal numbers. This meant that on the slave frontier in Mississippi or Texas it was much easier to found or refound families than it had been earlier in South Carolina or Virginia, when men greatly outnumbered women. In 1850, the numbers of slave men and women in Mississippi balanced almost perfectly, 154,674 men to 154,626 women. In the same year, white Mississippi men outnumbered white women 156,287 to 139,431.

Yet these figures may deceive. They show the possibility of finding new partners, but they also hint at the special stress of nineteenth-century slavery on black women. In the United States, white men outnumbered white women by about 500,000 in 1850 and in most states, North or South, East or West, the imbalance held. One of the very few exceptions was North Carolina, where white women outnumbered white men by 280,000 to 273,000; another was Massachusetts, where the figures were 501,000 women and 484,000 men. The obvious reason for these differences among whites is male migration, both from overseas to the seaboard states and from the seaboard to the West.[42] The whole slave population was balanced that year, standing at 1,602,000 men to 1,601,000 women. That balance was not reproduced evenly wherever slavery existed. Though the sex ratio in Mississippi was almost even in 1850, slave women in South Carolina outnumbered men by 197,000 to 187,000.

Slave women went West for the same reason as slave men: somebody else had decided that these people would expend their life's energy growing cotton. Compared with sugar, or perhaps rice, cotton imposed a relatively light burden, and masters knew it. Nonetheless, to go to the cotton frontier was to encounter roughly the same combination of low capital costs and high profits that had made the initial stages of tobacco and rice cultivation as difficult as they were for the servants and slaves who had grown those crops in the seventeenth and eighteenth centuries.

Forced migration to mid-nineteenth-century Mississippi meant entering the Mississippi/Yazoo Delta. This is the incredibly fertile, low, wet triangle of land defined by the two rivers whose name it bears. It was full of malaria-bearing mosquitoes, and whites entered it as little as they could, women far less than men. Slaves had no choice. Whichever their sex, they had to go.[43] These people were just as much makers of the moving American frontier as any New Englander who went to Maine or western New York, any Kentuckian who moved to Illinois, or any gold-hungry forty-niner bound for California.

As the frontier moved onto Indian and Spanish land, it carried both slavery and freedom. Between the Revolution and the Civil War, each was an essential element in the society of the United States, just as each had been essential to the colonial social order. That slavery was now identified with "the South" and free labor with "the North" foreshadowed the bloody, violent terms of slavery's destruction, as many a wise person both North and South was coming to understand. Nonetheless they were thoroughly intertwined. As the United States expanded, both its slavery and its freedom were imposing themselves upon ground that had not belonged to either of them when the free white men Meriwether Lewis and William Clark and Clark's slave whom we know as York stood with Sacagawea, Cameahwait, and Toussaint Charbonneau at Lemhi Pass.

[V]

To open the Maine frontier to the men who became white Indians required that real Abenaki Indians get out of the way. To open New York's frontier to Yankees meant destroying Iroquoia. The Illinois prairie was inhabited by Algonquian and Siouan speakers when Kentuckians started arriving. Less than the span of a normal life covered the whole period from 1820, when the Choctaws surrendered northern Mississippi, to 1862, when General Grant invaded it with his blue-uniformed Union army. Like many a Civil War general, including Robert E. Lee, Grant had first practiced his profession with the American army that invaded Mexico in 1846 and took one-third of that country as conqueror's booty. In every case except the last, the "frontier" meant transforming the conditions of people who already were subject to United States sovereignty and already part of its society and economy. In the last, it meant incorporating people who had no desire to become *Americanos del Norte* at all. These last were people to whom the world had extended recognition as part of another sovereign republic, with the protection of what Europeans and their offspring called international law.

During the first quarter of the nineteenth century the system of "frontier exchange" that had long set the terms of Indian/white relations in North America finally and irretrievably broke down. By this point Indians had little to offer that a white might want, beyond the knowledge possessed by a woman like Sacagawea or the horses that could be loaned by her brother. For a brief period, the fur trade ripped across the Rockies and the Cascades, controlled jointly from Canada by the Hudson's Bay Company and the Northwest Company and from New York City by John Jacob Astor's American Fur Company. The fur trade made Astor a rich man, as it had enriched many a chair-bound adventurer before him. The far-western Indians who now felt the trade's power became part of the world economy as surely as tribes who had harvested animals in the Maine forests, the Adirondacks, or the southern piney woods.

With the passing of the eastern and midwestern fur trade and the possibility of wartime alliance, there passed also the "middle ground." In 1790 the Lake Superior region was a "village world" of French-speaking métis, English-speaking whites, and Indian refugees from war, upheaval, and destruction to the east. It contained soldiers of both the American and British armies. In 1795 the British finally withdrew from the American forts that they had occupied since the Peace of 1783. Although the United States and Britain went to war again in 1812, and although most of that war was fought along the northern frontier, the time was past when Indians could use the wars of white Americans and Europeans in order to aid themselves. For half a dozen years before the War of 1812, Indian leaders tried to bring their people together and to keep links to the British open. The most successful were two brothers who belonged to the Kispoko Shawnees, the military leader Tecumseh and the religious prophet Tenskwatawa.

Tenskwatawa had a message that the Delaware prophet Neolin had preached before and that others would preach again: survival meant rejecting as much as possible of white America's ways. Christianity should be thrown off; cattle should be killed so that wild animals could flourish again. What Tenskwatawa preached led to blows with the Americans under his brother's leadership in 1811, at a place in Indiana called Tippecanoe. The battle was provoked by Indiana's governor, William Henry Harrison. The magic protection against white men's implements of war that Tenskwatawa had promised did not work, and he faded into obscurity, at least in white memory. It was otherwise for Harrison. Twenty-nine years later, in 1840, astute politicians dredged up the memory of Tippecanoe and used it to turn the aged Harrison into a national hero. Justified or not, the reputation he belatedly enjoyed as an Indian fighter helped make him President of the United States.

Tippecanoe was not the last armed struggle between Indians and whites in the Old Northwest. Tecumseh's defeat did signify, however, that whites could turn the land into farming country. The waves of grain that they intended to plant would be as foreign to the Indians as the Indians' world had been to most whites. Tippecanoe also signified that in the Old Northwest white frontierspeople who understood the Indians—even if they cheated them, hated them, and fought them— were giving way to people with no comprehension of Indians at all.[44] The Indians' marks were upon the land when squatters began settling down and federal surveyors arrived to run their long, straight lines. But neither squatters nor surveyors knew how to read the Indians' lines. These were inscribed in language other than the speech of private property, commercial agriculture, and speculation that squatters, surveyors, and dealers who grew rich from owning vast holdings of public property all understood.

The last war on the Illinois prairie was the futile attempt in 1832 of Sauk and Fox led by Black Hawk to cross the Mississippi from Iowa and retake the land. Only fourteen years separated that war from the American Republic's military conquest of New Mexico, Arizona, Utah, Nevada, and California. With its great seizure from Mexico and its simultaneous settlement of a boundary with British Columbia in the Far Northwest, the United States completed the reshaping of North American political and economic geography that began when the Lewis and

Clark expedition crossed Lemhi Pass into space that was not yet American.

In a very important way, conquering the northern third of Mexico was different from conquering Indian lands. To most whites, Indian treaties were just scraps of paper, regardless of their phrases of solemnity and permanence. American courts agreed. But the treaty that Joel Poinsett negotiated with Mexico at Guadalupe Hidalgo clearly qualified as international law. It became part of the "Supreme Law of the Land" that was defined by the federal Constitution. It protected the lands of missions and pueblos, which had been recognized under Spanish and Mexican law and which now became the responsibility of the United States. A Federal Land Commission was established in California in 1849 to work out the details.

The reality became clear, however, in 1851, when informal American policy toward Mexican landholdings became written American law. Despite the treaty, "which specifically promised full and complete protection of all property rights of Mexicans," the "burden of proof" was thrown upon claimants, who had to convince the new authorities that the land they occupied was really theirs. "Proof" was not easy, and it could mean employing American lawyers whose fees might amount to the value of the land. Despite the treaty and despite California's past as part of a recognized foreign country, much of its land became as available to migrants as that of any dispossessed Indian tribe.[45]

By 1850 the North American continent lay almost entirely open to the people of the east coast Republic. The legal bounds of the United States stretched from the Gulf coast and the Rio Grande to the forty-ninth parallel, and from Maine to the Pacific, defining the familiar outline of the modern lower forty-eight states. Citizens of the Republic called it their Manifest Destiny. Had some had their way, both Canada and Mexico would have been entirely conquered as well. The fact that expansion happened as fast as it did demonstrates the Republic's enormous energy. That same energy brought as much change within the expanding United States as upon its advancing edge.

CHAPTER 6

CAPITAL CITIES

A TRAVELER in the northeastern United States passes through many landscapes at once. Beneath all others lie the rocks, soil, and watercourses bequeathed by plate tectonics and glaciers. Indians carved the second landscape, almost invisible now except to an archeologist. A third landscape conjures up the English colonists and their revolutionary-era descendants. The fourth was the product of the Northeast's nineteenth-century industrial development. Finally comes the modern "built environment" of cities, highways, suburbs, tourist attractions, hiking trails, and ski areas. The nineteenth century's dams, canals, railways, and factory towns form the subject here. They are the historical signature of young American industrial capitalism.

Much of this landscape is abandoned now, or preserved in open-air museums. The mills of Lowell, Massachusetts, are a National Historic Park where rangers in Smokey Bear hats guide tourists and show how the machinery worked. Great buildings where yarn was spun and cloth woven stand empty or house successor businesses making consumer plastic ware. Only a few miles might separate gaunt factory shells and worker housing from the clapboard churches and dwellings of an earlier New England, as with the factory town of Naugatuck, Connecticut, and the postcard idyll of Litchfield. This time appearances deceive, for Litchfield only seems remote from the nineteenth century. It housed the young Republic's first law school and it produced the remarkable sisters Catharine Beecher and Harriet Beecher Stowe, who between them defined the terms of America's mid-century crisis. Yet the visual difference speaks to a larger truth. The Northeast underwent a profound disruption between 1790 and 1860. Towns like Naugatuck were the result.

[I]

The makers of the United States understood that their political decisions
would shape their whole society's future. The federal Constitution won
support in the port cities because it promised commercial prosperity.
Virtually nobody, rural or urban, North or South, on the coast or in the
interior, doubted that commerce would be central in the new Republic.
The issue was how. One possibility was slave-grown staples, continuing
what the colonial South had already become. Another was foodstuffs, on
Thomas Paine's premise in *Common Sense* that Americans would not suffer
while eating remained "the custom of Europe." Cities offered a third
possibility. Townsfolk celebrated the Constitution because it promised
to foster their manufactures and trade. There would be a common market
for what they could produce, and they would gain from trade within it.

Between then and the Civil War, the hope of manufactures turned
into the reality of industry. Each of the port cities stood alone in 1788,
surrounded by farming hinterland. By 1850 Boston's hinterland was defined by such industrial towns as Lynn, famous for its shoes, and Man-
chester, Lawrence, Lowell, Waltham, and Fall River, where factories
produced cloth. Boston was the port, the source of finance, and the headquarters for the companies that dominated these places. It became a
center of national finance as well, and it made goods itself. Some 3,000
Boston tailors cut ready-made clothing for just one firm. Boston refined
sugar. It smelted iron, brass, and copper. It fashioned musical instru-
ments, locomotives, steam shovels, and dredges.[1] Its population climbed
from 15,000 in 1770 to 177,000 by 1860. It filled in the wetlands
around its original peninsula, creating the city's present-day shape. Entrepreneurs poured much of their profit into the cultural monuments
that define Boston now as a great center of art and learning.[2]

By mid-century New York City's hinterland stretched to the Great
Lakes and included much of the cotton-growing South. With more than
800,000 people on Manhattan Island in 1860 and 266,000 more in
Brooklyn, New York City's own expensive real estate was part of the
reason for its wealth.[3] By this time Philadelphia had changed from a
farmland entrepôt to a big manufacturing city. It made goods as simple
as shoes and as complex as railway engines. Towns surrounding it spun
yarn, wove cloth, mined coal, and smelted iron. No longer the capital
of either Pennsylvania or the United States, it was nonetheless the Republic's second city, comparable to England's Birmingham in its size,
its complexity, and its subordinate relationship to somewhere else.[4]

Some people who engineered the great change are instantly recogniz-able, like Alexander Hamilton. Others linger at the edges of awareness: the factory builder Francis Cabot Lowell, the canal sponsor De Witt Clinton. Still others would remain obscure if historians had not recovered them: factory owner Daniel Lammot, furniture maker Duncan Phyfe. With a great deal of argument and dispute, people like these became a new social class, convinced they knew how to benefit both themselves and their society.

Alexander Hamilton often receives credit for envisioning American industrialization. In his eleventh *Federalist* paper he made his rapture plain:

> The world may politically, as well as geographically, be divided into four parts, each having a distinct set of interests. Unhappily . . . Africa, Asia, and America have successively felt [Europe's] domination. The superiority she has long maintained has tempted her to plume herself as the mistress of the world, and to consider the rest of mankind as created for her benefit. . . . Let Americans disdain to be the instruments of European greatness![5]

In the *Report on Manufactures* that he presented to Congress in December 1791, Hamilton turned from vision to practicality, showing the state of American manufacturing and arguing for federal sponsorship to foster its growth. But Congress rejected the *Report* and some of Hamilton's later actions point toward neocolonial subordination to Britain rather than toward American economic independence.[6] What Hamilton suggested, it took others to execute.

By Hamilton's time, the idea of using money as venture capital was gathering force. America had begun to develop banks, including two that Hamilton sponsored, the Bank of New York and the Bank of the United States. Early banking directed itself more toward short-term commercial needs than long-term investment. Nonetheless, it assumed there were better uses for a fortune than sinking it into land. The people who got involved in banking were the sort who already were investing in high-risk manufactures, like iron.[7] Englishmen who knew the secrets of water frames, spinning jennies, and spinning mules realized they could sell their knowledge in America, despite laws against exporting the machinery or the plans for it, and forbidding people who knew about it to leave Britain.

American capital, supplied by the Providence merchant Moses Brown, and English knowledge, brought by the Derbyshire migrant Samuel Slater, joined in a fertile union at Pawtucket, Rhode Island, in 1790. Their spinning factory was not much larger than a good-sized house and its workers were women and children, but, unlike previous false starts, it prospered. Slater eventually freed himself from the Browns. By his death in 1835 he was proprietor of fourteen textile mills, an iron foundry, and a machine shop.[8] His importance, however, is not his personal success. It is that his first venture survived where other attempts had failed, and that others followed.[9]

Had Rhode Island still been a British colony, the Brown-Slater partnership could not have happened. The British would have stopped it. Had there been no national common market, the factory probably could not have prospered. Moses Brown's conversion to the Quakers helped as well. Once upon a time the Browns had put their extra money into the slave trade, but as a Friend that option was closed and he sought a more moral use. Yet the long-staple cotton that the Pawtucket mill first spun came from the West Indies. The short-staple variety that replaced it came from Dixie. Northeastern industrialization only looks remote from what was happening in the South and the West. Every millworker handled cotton that slaves had also touched, grown on land that Native Americans had just lost.

For almost a quarter century following 1790 Britain and France were at war, which protected America's small, inefficient, crude factories against the vastly more efficient British industrial machine. At the war's end America still could not compete. Nonetheless, it had begun a self-sustaining process of both growth (greater size) and development (greater complexity). A new way of life was appearing.

In 1811, the Bostonian Francis Cabot Lowell toured the vastly more advanced factories of Britain. Deliberately playing the innocent American abroad, he persuaded his hosts to show him the secrets of power-loom weaving. The Briton Slater had been an industrial traitor. The American Lowell was a spy. He had a large fortune to invest, so he and like-minded men formed the Boston Associates to take industrialization into its next phase. They would build enormous factories to both spin and weave, employing the technology that Lowell had observed. They established their first at Waltham, just up the Charles River from Boston. Their greatest achievement was the city of Lowell, built from nothing at the falls of the Merrimack and named in the spy-tourist's honor. By 1840 Lowell had 20,000 people. Not many American cities were larger but it was just one of Boston's satellites.[10]

What the Boston Associates began foreshadowed American big business. In a gorge at Chester, Pennsylvania, where a creek descends a series of rapids to the Delaware River, another change was underway. There are watercourses like this from Delaware to Maine and much the same was happening in many of them. Ever since first colonization, people had been tapping Chester Creek's power and by the early nineteenth century the gorge held the ruins of gristmills and forges. Now cloth mills took their place. None became huge. Nor did their builders reach great prosperity as the nearby family of E. I. Du Pont de Nemours did. None of the mill communities of Rockdale, as the place became known, ever grew to more than a few hundred people. Nonetheless, what happened there and in places like it took American manufactures another step.

Pawtucket and Lowell began with pirated knowledge, but for manufactures to become genuinely self-driving, Americans had to become technological innovators. Mechanicians in mill towns like Rockdale began thinking very creatively about machinery. They learned to value their own innovations rather than what their elders had taught. None became an inventor-hero in the manner of Eli Whitney with his cotton gin, Robert Fulton with his steamboat, or Samuel F. B. Morse with his telegraph. But both they and the great figures of American invention show that creativity is not the work of lonely geniuses in their garrets. American innovations began to succeed because people with a common interest learned to share ideas and develop each other's insights.[11]

Some of the masters of the new emerging order were old-style gentry like Robert R. Livingston, who merely sponsored innovation. Some were merchants who bet their fortunes on it, like Brown, Lowell, or Rockdale's John S. Phillips. Still others were climbers. When Paul Revere rode to warn Concord, Massachusetts, in 1775 that "the Regulars are coming out," he was a working silversmith. By the end of his long life, his name was attached to a large metal business, which still exists. In 1808 the aged Revere personally developed a technique for rolling copper, and Robert Fulton used Revere's ideas to build boilers for steam engines. A man could rise by organizing others too. The New York City furniture maker Duncan Phyfe contributed nothing to his trade's techniques, but he did develop a high reputation for quality, to the point that other woodworkers joined him to share his good name. Neither Paul Revere nor Duncan Phyfe ever tried to become a "gentleman" in the old sense that drove Robert Morris. Both died rich men nonetheless.[12]

There was no single road to industrial society. Capital had to be amassed and invested. People had to get used to the idea that what was new was probably better. Old skills had to be used in new ways, under new conditions. For all the success of Revere or Phyfe, most people had little real prospect of improving their conditions or rising in the world. In some ways prospects narrowed. By the mid-nineteenth century a craftsman had little expectation that he would master his trade and preside over his own shop.[13] Whether we speak of capitalization, technology, or organization, the way that cities produced what people needed became fundamentally different from how they had made things "before." So did the ways that goods flowed from hand to hand, and information from mind to mind.

[II]

New York State's Erie Canal was one of the early nineteenth century's great public works. Building it meant generating public support and raising very large sums. It also meant solving difficult problems of engineering, with only amateur talent. There had been proposals to deepen the Mohawk River and build locks around its many rapids as early as 1724. In 1792 a Western Inland Lock and Navigation Company began carrying some of that work out. In 1807, Jesse Hawley, a flour dealer in western New York, raised a more ambitious idea: a canal from the Hudson to Lake Erie, with branches feeding it along the way. He thought it should be a federal project, but despite years of lobbying by New York officials in Washington, building the canal became New York's task alone. People called it Clinton's Ditch, from De Witt Clinton's hard work on its behalf as canal commissioner, mayor of New York City, and governor. But Clinton was no more the canal's sole creator than Samuel Slater was the creator of American industry.

Clinton's greatest achievement was financial. In 1817 he saw a bill through the legislature creating a public canal fund. The fund became a central element in how the state financed its entire development over the next quarter century. Canal surveyors estimated before construction began that the state needed to raise $7,000,000 to build it, which was one-third of New York's whole available capital in banking and insurance. Two London insurance companies invested in the first loan, but for the first three years most money came from New Yorkers. Of the sixty-nine subscribers to a loan in 1818 "fifty-one invested $2,000 or less, and . . . twenty-seven . . . less than $1,000."

Then the pattern changed. The state built the easiest sections first, across flat, rich land west of Utica. First water entered the canal by 1818 and when the middle section opened the next year revenue began to flow. Bigger American investors started buying state bonds and by 1824 New York canal certificates were trading in London. Investments came from as far away as China. But the early small investments by New Yorkers of middling means provided the seed money. When foreigners entered, it was to join in a going venture, not to establish one of their own. They paid for most of the difficult construction and the state assured scrupulously that they received their promised financial rewards, so they would invest again. But despite the overseas money that paid for most of its construction, the canal never fell under foreign control.[14]

Construction began on July 4, 1817, at the growing town of Rome, which had been Fort Stanwix in Indian country not long before. The junction with the Hudson was made by the end of 1823, and in 1825 the canal was open its whole length. Recognizing the canal's significance, Pennsylvania constructed a rival from the Delaware to the Ohio. Without the Erie's easy route along the Mohawk Valley and across the Lake Ontario plain, Pennsylvania had to build inclined planes across the Allegheny ridges. The "Main Line's" highest elevation was 2,200 feet, compared with the Erie's 650. It needed 174 locks, ninety more than its rival. There was no comparison between the routes and the whole northern interior now belonged to New York City. So heavy was the Erie's use that enlargement of it began as early as 1836.[15]

Small contractors organized the construction, except for one difficult rocky stretch. Canal engineers taught themselves and created the American civil engineering profession. One, John B. Jervis, "began as an axeman," and went on to work on the Delaware and Hudson Canal, the Croton Aqueduct, and New York's early railroads. Another, Canvass White, solved the problem of building through wetland by discovering a cement that grows harder under water. It took a 245-foot culvert to cross Irondequoit Creek, an aqueduct 802 feet long to span the Genesee River, and twenty-seven locks plus two long aqueducts to negotiate the final sharp drop from Schenectady to sea level at Albany.[16] Aztecs, Mayas, and Incas had built to this scale, but among white Americans there was no precedent. The longest previous American canal extended only twenty-seven miles.

Where the canal went, it brought change. By 1822 its Champlain branch had redirected the northern New York wood market from Mon-

treal to New York City and changed the nature of the wood trade. Wood
went to Canada as roughly squared timber, but New York City wanted
fully finished lumber, with a great deal more added value. In 1823, 1,329
canal boats arrived at Albany. In 1826, with the whole canal open, almost
7,000 did. The commissioners had projected eastbound traffic of 250,000
tons annually. The total in 1826 was 302,170. The canal created a wheat
belt 150 miles long and 40 miles wide across central New York. Population tripled along its route between 1810 and 1835.[17]

The Erie Canal was the product of a whole people's enterprise and
intelligence.[18] It was a material achievement and a cultural statement. It
was a stunning innovation and it was just part of something much larger.
By 1860 there were major canals in the Blackstone and Connecticut
valleys of New England, across central New Jersey, and from northeastern
Pennsylvania's anthracite coalfields to the Hudson. Canals reached up the
James, Potomac, and Susquehanna rivers from the Chesapeake. Both the
Erie Canal and the Pennsylvania Main Line had branches throughout
their states, and in 1858 the two systems were connected. The Illinois
and Michigan Canal linked the Great Lakes to the Mississippi.[19] The
total canal mileage leapt from 1,277 in 1830 to 3,698 twenty years later.
The Erie Canal created Schenectady, Utica, Rome, Syracuse, Rochester,
and Buffalo as cities of economic significance and considerable size. Erie,
Cleveland, Toledo, and Detroit became feeder ports sending grain to
Buffalo for shipment down the canal. The cost per ton-mile eastward
from Buffalo was 19.12 cents in 1817. It dropped to only .672 cents in
1859.

But the example proved deceptive. Even in New York, some branches
proved unprofitable. Whole state systems failed farther west and south.
As late as 1868, more tonnage was still moving over New York's canals
and rivers than over its railroads, but the great era of canal building was
over by 1840. In that year 3,326 miles of artificial waterway stood finished and there were 2,818 miles of completed track. By 1850 railway
mileage stood at 9,021 and in 1860 it was 30,626, representing a total
investment of $1,149,481,000. In that same year the nation had 88,296
miles of surfaced roads, 4,723,006 tons of oceangoing shipping, 462,123
tons of shipping on the northern lakes, and 167,739 tons on the western
rivers. Every one of those numbers conceals many human stories.[20]

The canal boom, then, was only the first phase in creating a national
transport network. Cotton manufacturers needed to receive raw cotton
and ship finished thread and cloth whatever the season. A canal was built

between Boston and Lowell, but it was never adequate. The Boston and Lowell Railroad replaced it as soon as engine and track technology allowed. Bostonians built a trunk line to Worcester and on to Albany in order to steal "a march on New York City in the great scramble for commercial advantage." Boston did become the western terminus for Britain's Cunard packets, the foremost transatlantic service.[21]

The Boston and Albany railroad led to trunk lines along the Erie Canal route and onward to Chicago. Rails ran across southern New York, from Philadelphia to Pittsburgh and Cincinnati, from Baltimore to St. Louis, from Norfolk to Memphis, from Charleston through Atlanta to Chattanooga, and from Chicago to New Orleans. Short connecting lines soon spanned the whole distance between Portland, Maine, and Wilmington, North Carolina.[22]

This enormous network transported an equally enormous national output. In 1820 the country produced 335,000 five-hundred-pound bales of cotton. In 1860 the figure was more than 5,300,000. In 1840 the United States mined 1,102,931 tons of soft coal and 967,108 of anthracite. It produced 321,331 tons of pig iron. The 2,284,631 spindles in its factories processed 236,525 bales out of a cotton crop that totaled 1,348,000 bales. In 1860 bituminous coal production was 6,494,280 tons, anthracite production was 8,115,842 tons, and 919,770 tons of pig iron emerged from American blast furnaces. Of that year's cotton crop, 845,410 bales went to American factories rather than their overseas competitors. American factories now held 7,235,727 spindles. In 1839 the corn crop was 377,532,000 bushels and the wheat crop was 84,823,000. In 1859 American farms produced 838,793,000 bushels of corn and 173,105,000 of wheat.[23]

There had not been a single power-driven spindle in the United States in 1790, nor a mile of railroad or hard-surfaced road or canal. Not a bale of short-staple cotton was available, and the main sources of nonhuman energy were wood, falling water, and the power of animals. A fast horse was the quickest way to carry a message. By 1860 raw materials, fossil fuel, and finished products sold in a national market, carried by a transport system as advanced as any of its day. The high-bulk products of farms, mines, and forests could be moved cheaply on canals, steamboats, and the merchant fleet. Passengers and expensive goods could travel at great speed on the railroads. Vital information could circulate at virtually the speed of light over American inventor Samuel F. B. Morse's telegraph. A uniquely American network of cities stretched from New York to San Francisco and from Chicago to New Orleans. Without all these changes in industry, marketing, transport, and communication, those cities and the unprecedented way of life they contained could not have come to be.

[III]

In 1790 President George Washington was among New York City's residents. Congress was meeting on Wall Street. Federal architecture was replacing the half-ruined cityscape left by war. The streets were full of people flaunting their New York style. Nonetheless, the city remained a second-level commercial center standing alone in farmland. A pedestrian could cross it in well under an hour's walk. Its 33,000 people filled in only Manhattan Island's lower tip. In the seventy years that followed, New York became a world city, with people piled so densely into its poorer parts that privacy did not exist. It directly dominated New York State, northern New Jersey, western New England, all the Great Lakes, the upper Mississippi Valley, and the Cotton Kingdom. Every other great city in the Republic became its tributary.

During its brief time as the nation's capital New York was only the nation's second city, with 11,000 fewer people than Philadelphia. In 1800 it had 60,000 people but Philadelphians still outnumbered New Yorkers by 9,000. In 1810, however, New York was first, with 96,000 to Philadelphia's 91,000. In 1820 New York had grown to 123,000 to Philadelphia's 112,000. A decade later its lead was 40,000 and in 1840 the gap rose to 92,000. New York's population in 1860 (including Brooklyn) was 1,080,330; Philadelphia's was 565,529.

Against all geographical logic, New York captured much of the commerce of the cotton South, including its transatlantic trade in both directions. But shipping could not have supported the city that New York was becoming. People with money to invest found that New York offered ever-widening possibilities. Banks, factories, mechanical inventions such as steamboats, canal bonds, land investment with an eye on speculative growth rather than safely retiring a fortune, urban real estate in a rising market, ironworks: all these and many more beckoned.[24] People migrated to New York from all over the United States. There were New England Yankees looking for opportunities other than farming in the expanding West or millwork in Lowell and Fall River. There were African-Americans making their way out of slavery as it collapsed in the North and began to rot along the South's upper edge. New York City's free black population rose from a scant 1,036 in 1790 to 7,470 in 1810. Philadelphia's was about 10,000 in 1810, 12,000 in 1820, and 14,600 in 1830.[25] Why they went to the larger cities is not hard to see. In 1826, one year before New York slavery finally ended, a writer in the Hudson River town of Kingston offered an opinion on the former slaves' future:

A few of this ill-fated race, more wise and faithful than the rest, still remain in their own chimney corners to spend their days in comfort; [while] the wicked ones, the thieves, the drunkards, and the bullies, are all gone to that paradise of negroes, *the City of New York*! There let them stay, a curse or blessing to those who made themselves so busy in their behalf.

But Kingston's black people had good reason to think that its chimney corners offered no refuge. In 1827 "a coloured boy" there got into trouble for burglary. The court sentenced him to life for his crime. About the same time, a white Kingston man was found guilty of "assault and battery with intent to kill." He got a prison term of just three years.[26]

In 1815 peace returned to Europe and the seas were finally safe for travelers. It still took time for migration to resume. In 1820 only 8,385 people made the journey to the United States. Eleven years later immigration stood at 22,633. Then it shot upward: 60,000 in 1832, 76,000 in 1836, 84,000 in 1840, 114,371 in 1845, 369,980 in 1850, and a pre-Civil War peak of 427,833 in 1854. That year's total would not be surpassed until 1880. Virtually all came from Britain, Germany, and Ireland. Britons were more than a quarter of the people who came in 1820. Their number reached its absolute prewar peak in 1854, at 58,749, but by then their proportion among immigrants was dwindling. Only 968 Germans came in 1820, but after 1836 their flow was never less than 10,000. Their peak, also in 1854, was 215,009.

The largest group came from Ireland. There were 3,614 Irish migrants in 1820. In 1828, 12,488 came, the first time that one group had more than 10,000 migrants in one year. Between 1834 and 1846 their numbers ranged from 12,645 to 51,752. English and Anglo-Irish landlords were driving these people out, much as had happened in the Scottish Highlands in the 1760s, or to Cherokees in the Appalachians, just before the great Irish migration began. There were 491,300 one-room dwellings in Ireland in 1841. Only 89,400 remained in 1871.[27]

At the end of the 1840s departure under pressure turned to flight in order to survive, when the Irish potato famine struck. Much like disease among Indians, the famine's effects were magnified by the weakness that long struggle against invaders had forced on Irish society. The potato blight could not have been avoided, but a society that was differently organized might have coped better. Instead, some 105,000 people fled to America in 1847, 113,000 in 1848, 159,000 in 1849, and 164,000 in 1850. The peak was 221,253 in 1851.[28] Almost all the Irish ended up in east coast cities, with absolutely no means to go farther and very little to offer beyond the power of muscles.

As New York City seized national predominance, other places passed the "urban threshold." The census listed 24 "urban" places (with more than 2,500 people) in 1790, 90 in 1830, 236 in 1850, and 392 in 1860. Only New York and Philadelphia had more than 25,000 people at the first census. In 1860 there were thirty-five places at least that size. Nine were greater than 100,000 and another seven had more than 50,000. The 201,655 townspeople of 1790 were only 5 percent of the recorded population. The 6,216,518 city folk of 1860 were almost a quarter of the whole American population.[29] The fifteen largest cities ranged from New York's million to the 50,666 people of Providence, Rhode Island.

But numbers alone do not make a city. The difference is the density and complexity that urban life makes possible and requires. What, then, was happening in these urban places that had only barely existed or not been there at all when the Republic first appeared?

In legal terms Albany, New York, had been a city ever since it received a colonial-era royal charter that gave it a mayor, a council, and the status of a corporation.[30] Until the Revolution it remained a self-enclosed, mostly Dutch community that served the British military in wartime and traded furs. It owed its postrevolutionary development to the West, and development began well before it became the eastern terminus of the Erie Canal, where goods were transferred from canal boats to river sloops and steamboats and oceangoing vessels.

Yankees crossing into New York after independence found Albany a good place to stay. Its 12,000 people in 1820 were nearly four times the number dwelling there in 1790. Dutch was still spoken in its streets, but New Englanders controlled its business life. It was handling as many as 200 river vessels at once. In 1817 it built a pier to accommodate 1,000 canal boats. By then it had fifty-eight manufacturing establishments, employing almost half its adult males. There were tanneries, breweries, distilleries, "air furnaces," a tobacco factory, hat shops, and brickyards. With the canal's completion came iron manufacturing, a wholesale lumber trade, and a large-scale printing business.[31]

In 1695 fortified colonial Albany filled only seventeen blocks. In 1770 it had grown to about forty. When it was mapped in 1794, the cartographer added out-of-town mansions and showed six separate churches and their burial grounds. The city had a market, courthouse, prison, and ferryhouse. But its fifty blocks displayed the same outline and occupied the same space as at the eve of independence. Colonial Albany had been a "city-state," ruled by its town fathers and by landlords like the Van Rensselaers. Now it had been through a revolution. For a time its most powerful man was Abraham Yates, self-taught lawyer, onetime cobbler of old shoes, and very much a man who had found his moment at independence. Practically alone among major towns, Albany was Antifederalist in 1788.

Five years after the Erie Canal was opened, another map revealed a wholly different Albany. The old city had become the core of a much larger place, with roughly one hundred new blocks. Function and class separated them. There was a downtown where people did business. Middle-class residences surrounded the business area. Beyond that was working-class housing, "a miserable collection of hovels" inhabited by "mostly mechanics," many of them young single males in boardinghouses. Like Boston or Philadelphia, Albany was in the grip of "metropolitan industrialization." Highly organized central shops and fully mechanized factories made its goods. If older-style artisan shops survived, their masters were probably working on contract for somebody else under the "putting-out" system. Master artisans' traditional autonomy was eroding so badly that one historian has called the situation "the bastard workshop."[32] Clothing, shoes, and furniture were becoming "sweated trades."

The nearby city of Troy displayed the new order even more strikingly. At the end of the eighteenth century Troy barely existed, but by 1860 it had 39,237 people. Only 611 were not white. More than thirteen thousand were foreign-born, primarily in Ireland although also in Germany and Britain. Twenty-three thousand more were of first-generation foreign descent. Troy had abundant free energy from falling water, and as early as 1807 a mill for rolling and slitting iron had opened below one of its cascades. By the eve of the Civil War, Troy was the foremost iron town in the Republic, created by the "gigantic Albany and Rensselaer Iron and Steel Company." Troy made the iron that clad the Union vessel *Monitor* when it dueled with the Confederate States ship *Merrimac* during the Civil War. In 1865 it opened the first Bessemer furnaces in the United States for making iron into steel. Later, as the American iron industry shifted its center to Pittsburgh, Troy's main industry became men's shirts, with women doing most of the work. Yet as late as the 1950s Troy still had steelworks and its air reeked with burning coke.[33]

When the Reverend John Taylor toured the Mohawk and Black River country in 1802, he drew maps of its major places. Little Falls had a few houses, a mill, and an octagonal church. There were forty-four houses and three churches in Whitestown, stretched out over "nearly one mile." Utica had eighty buildings and Rome fifty-five, still dominated by the looming bulk of Fort Stanwix. These were the only places that Taylor bothered to draw.

Someone making the same expedition a quarter century later would have filled page after page with sketches. In 1820 Syracuse had 1,814 people, Rochester 1,502, and Buffalo 2,095. In 1825 Lockport's people numbered 3,007. Rochester was moving toward the domination of flour milling it would enjoy for decades to come. Utica had become a commercial center of note. Its forward-looking "business leaders invited the local citizenry to purchase stock in a textile factory to be powered by steam." Three additional factories followed the initial Utica Cotton Works, with a total investment of $500,000. Together Utica's factories employed 1,200 people. Even as the frontier closed, western New York's "urban-industrial stage of local economic development" was underway and the main lines to the future were clear. In the old New York, city and countryside had been radically separated. Now New York State was a complex economic region, with a grand metropolis, second-level centers, a web of smaller places that were becoming cities rather than mere market towns, and a rich agricultural zone that was as commercial as New York City itself. All were linked by the best transport the age could offer. As with New York State, so with the nation itself.

[IV]

"The town is clean and pretty, and of course is 'going to be' much larger," wrote Charles Dickens of Columbus, Ohio, in 1842.[34] Dickens was nearing the end of a long journey and he was bored with American sameness. Beyond that phrase, the master of the nineteenth-century English novel offered no description of Ohio's capital. The town had been planned as early as 1817, laid out in straight lines and right angles around a single public square. With some variations that same theme would dominate the platting of towns and cities across the continent.

So much was that the case that model town plans appeared, to save developers the trouble of working out their own ideas. The Illinois Central Railroad generated a plan for towns along its right-of-way. Its tracks would cut each town in half, with Mulberry, Hickory, Walnut and Chestnut streets on one side and Oak, Locust, Poplar and Ash on the other. There would be an alley between each pair. Streets that crossed the track would be numbered each way from the depot: North First, South First, North Second, South Second. There was a space on the printed plat for the actual town name, as if it made any difference.

Not all model plans were so dreary. One drew inspiration from Pierre L'Enfant's Washington, D.C., with squares, circles, crosscutting boulevards, irregularly shaped blocks, and "scarcely a turn that will not surprise us with something unexpected." I. M. Papworth, who called himself "Architect to the King of Würtemburg" (presumably in Germany, though he seems as unlikely as Mark Twain's fictitious Duke of Bridgewater in *Huckleberry Finn*), proposed to build "a Rural Town, to be called Hygeia" on "The River Ohio." His plan had enormous squares, four of them contained within a huge circle. It had swirling lines and curving streets. Milan, Munich, London, and Paris all contain such patterns, but Hygeia was never built.[35] Inspired or depressed by what appeared instead, writers since Dickens have harped upon the theme of four-cornered tedium in midwestern urban America.

Had Dickens made his journey in 1860 he would have found six of the fifteen leading cities west of the Alleghenies. These were New Orleans, Cincinnati, St. Louis, Chicago, Louisville, and San Francisco, and not one was tedious. Only Cincinnati had a large proportion of its population in manufacturing, 18.3 percent of its 161,004 people. Only 3 percent of the 168,675 people of New Orleans were in manufacturing; fewer than 5 percent of Chicago's 109,260 people were, and only 2.6 percent of San Francisco's 56,802. All were places of note, but not for the same reasons as the port and industrial cities of the East. In their different ways, New Orleans, Chicago, and San Francisco show western urban variety and energy, with no four-cornered tedium at all.

New Orleans was a product of the slave system. Its earliest map dates from 1720, and a detailed map drawn in 1764 shows forty-four square blocks (the modern French Quarter) arranged around a central Place d'Armes (Jackson Square) dominated by the Église Paroissiale. According

to the map, eight platted blocks were wholly unoccupied. Partially surrounding the city was a canal, intended more for drainage into Lake
Pontchartrain than for protection. A map drawn "about 1770," shows
the city surrounded by a massive wall. When the city was mapped again
in 1815, eight of its buildings were monumental enough for individual
display. Now it had distinct zones, inhabited by different language and
ethnic groups, arranged along the Mississippi River's crescent curve. The
original French-speaking Catholic church was joined by two others, including one to serve the city's free *gens de couleur*. There was a school
where Ursuline nuns had a long tradition of educating the free black
community's daughters.[36]

The rights of these people had been guaranteed by treaty when the
United States took over Louisiana in 1803. There were 1,566 "free people
of color" in the city in 1805, 4,950 in 1810, 11,562 in 1830, and they
reached a peak of 15,072 in 1840. That was 3,000 fewer than the number
of slaves. In both New Orleans and Mobile, which also had Latin origins
and treaty protection, free black Creoles took care to distinguish themselves from slaves. It was a losing fight. The number in New Orleans
actually began to fall after 1840. Their proportion of the city's total
population dropped from 28.7 percent in 1810 to only 6.4 percent in
1860. That year New Orleans had 10,939 free blacks and 14,484 slaves,
matched against 144,601 whites.[37]

New Orleans needed only its location to grow. The city's site between
Lake Pontchartrain and the river was unpromising in some ways, rising
at its most elevated to only fifteen feet above sea level. Between the
natural levees that the Mississippi and Bayou Metarie raised on their
banks the land was below river level. But despite sandbars, swamps,
mosquitoes, snakes, alligators, and incessant waterlogging, despite competition from the Erie Canal and the railroads, the mouth of the great
river required a great port. New Orleans's nineteenth-century size and
prosperity sprang from the southern cotton and the northern grain that
the Mississippi system poured through it. Its colorful original architecture, its layout, and its legal system show its French origins. Its flora
bespeaks its tropical setting. Its language and cuisine show that this is
where Indians, French, Africans, Spaniards, English, and eventually white
Americans crossed paths.

The different fate of Charleston shows the advantage the Mississippi
provided. A mere fortification in 1704, Charleston was the fourth-largest
urban place in British America by the Revolution, and it contained the

greatest concentration of wealth. By the middle of the nineteenth century it was urbane, elegant, and well settled. Its population in 1861 was 48,409. Slightly more than half of these were white, 7.8 percent were free blacks, and 36.5 percent were slaves. Despite its elegance and wealth, however, Charleston was stagnant. Even earlier than Boston, it and the state of South Carolina set out to construct a long-distance railroad that would capture the trade of the interior. The line covered 136 miles to the interior town of Hamburg opposite Augusta, Georgia, on the Savannah River, and after its opening in 1833 it did bring a sizable proportion of the upland cotton crop to the port's wharves. By itself, however, upland cotton did not generate enough traffic to give the railroad a profit, not even combined with the flow of passengers and of westbound high-value, low-bulk manufactured goods. Nor, apparently, did the railroad stimulate a capitalist boom in property values, as the Erie Canal did in New York. Perhaps this was because of the sandy, pine-covered hills and swampland that lay along much of its course.

Despite the initiative that Charleston showed in building the railroad, it would not let the tracks enter its own bounds. Arriving cotton had to be hauled from the railhead to the docks by horse-drawn drays. The riverboats that served New Orleans were much more suited to that city's needs, and they contributed to its prosperity. Nonetheless, Charleston, New Orleans, Mobile, and their like showed the limits of the urban development within plantation society. During the 1830s, when the main northern cities were growing at breakneck pace and urban networks were springing up around them, Charleston increased its population only 2 percent.[38]

In 1830 a man named James Thompson drew the first plat of what became Chicago. "Section 9, Township 39, Range 14" was at the Lake Michigan end of a planned canal to the Mississippi. Kickapoo Indians were still contesting the ownership of land not far south. By 1836 the new city had 4,000 people. More important, as a sign of its future, it was already in its first great boom. A single well-placed plot rose from a selling price of $38,000 in 1833 to a valuation of $1,200,000 only three years later. The canal finally opened in 1848, the same year as the city's first railway. At that point Chicago's population was about 20,000. In 1860 the city had ten separate railway lines entering it, and a population of 100,000. No more than a swampy place when it was platted, it was already one of the Republic's great cities. After the Civil War it would defeat both Cincinnati and St. Louis for midwestern primacy, become the metropolis of the American interior, industrialize the handling of grain, pork, and timber, attract immigrants in great numbers, and become a major center of steelmaking and machine production.

Chicago's very first growth was akin to that of New Orleans, both in the importance of its placement in relation to the "Great West" and in what it did with the West's products. The difference was its ability to transcend itself, which New Orleans could not do. New Orleans needed only to be where it was in order to transfer cotton from steamboats to oceangoing ships and prosper. Given the extent of the Mississippi river system, the planters who grew the vast bulk of the South's great crop had no other choice and no other need. Aside from building artificial levees to provide wharf space and keep the river back, the capital cost of the cotton trade could be met by the individuals and partnerships that owned the steamboats and the oceangoing fleet. New Orleans was simply a place where bales were transferred, not one that would produce machines and finished goods or invest its capital in new and promising ways.

Chicago had to begin by promising a canal and attracting railroads. It had no capital. To finance canal and railways alike it had to persuade the federal government to give it land grants. The canal was a public venture and the railroads were private. But canal and railways alike required both capital and creative vitality. New Orleans was still ahead of Chicago in population in 1860, but during the preceding decade it had grown by only half Chicago's absolute number and at a much slower rate.

Even before the grain elevators, lumberyards, and slaughterhouses of the later nineteenth century, Chicago was hungry for steel. Among the products of the 5 percent of its people who were working in industry in 1860 were Cyrus McCormick's mechanical reapers. McCormick had moved from Virginia to Chicago in 1847. By 1850 his reapers were selling through much of northern Illinois, southern Wisconsin, and eastern Iowa and Missouri. In 1860 people were buying them all across the Midwest, most densely in a line of counties west of Chicago itself and fronting on the Mississippi north toward Minneapolis. Even if the grain that those machines cut was marketed via steamboats downstream through St. Louis and New Orleans, rather than on railroads to Chicago and eastward, the city that made the reapers would harvest the money that prosperous wheat farmers had to spend. Once Chicago invented grain elevators and the novel pattern of organizing the wheat market they represented, it would capture almost the whole grain market.[39]

San Francisco grew for a third reason, gold. Spaniards founded it for military reasons in 1776 as a *presidio*. The military camp soon gave rise to a separate *pueblo*, a farming and commercial settlement called Yerba Buena. The *pueblo* took the *presidio*'s name in 1847, after the United States seized California from Mexico. It had fewer than a thousand people, but because of the gold rush the population multiplied sixfold by the turn of the new decade. As heir to a legal Mexican entity, San Francisco was entitled by treaty to "four square leagues of land," which the United States government finally recognized as belonging to it in 1865. More important than the Spanish grant was rapid inflation of property values, on a par with Chicago's during the 1830s. San Francisco was entering a classic boom, where "even those who come in from the hills with a pocketful of gold generally give it up in a hurry—for drink, for women, even for goods and clothing at bonanza prices."[40]

Had the gold of the Sierra Nevada been the only source of west coast wealth, San Francisco would never have become much more than the little *pueblo* it was in 1847. The aged Luis Peralta, owner of the *rancho* land that is now the cities of Berkeley, Oakland, and Alameda, understood the point. When the gold miners came after 1848, Peralta advised his sons to "plant your fields, and reap; these be your best gold-fields, for all must eat while they live."[41] He was right. The thousands who poured into the state for gold left "the Mountains of the Mother Lode gashed and scarred like a deserted battlefield." They "continued to rifle California all through the nineteenth century." But even these "adventuring strangers . . . characterized by an essential selfishness and an underlying instability" needed food. If they could hold their land against squatters, the sons of Luis Peralta were in a position to provide it.

Migrants who failed in the search for gold, or who came with other ideas in mind, began to appreciate California's fertility. As public land started to become available, they began taking out entries in vast quantities. A total of 9,276,588 acres were taken up between 1866 and 1878.[42] In the long run, agriculture would contribute much more than mining to California wealth and to making San Francisco, Los Angeles, and its other cities what they became.[43]

Part of California's problem was to feed itself. Another part was to ship the food it could produce to the rest of the Republic. A third was for its burgeoning population to find ways to live with one another, both in their different groups and in the large entity that was their state. In this, if in nothing else, they faced a problem that they shared with every single person, of whatever race, class, condition, or sex, between the easternmost point in Maine and Big Sur, and between the Canadian border and the Florida Keys. Caught up in a society that could not stay still and separated from one another in almost every conceivable way, the people who lived within the Republic's bounds all tried to deal with the problem of establishing coherence in their lives. Whatever their differences, an astonishing number of them came up with very similar answers.

CHAPTER 7

"WITH IRON INTERLACED"

"THE Prairie States" is a very small piece of Walt Whitman's great celebration of his country and people, *Leaves of Grass*. In just six lines it hymns "a newer garden of creation . . . cities and farms, with iron interlaced, composite, tied, many in one . . . the crown and teeming paradise, so far, of time's accumulations, to justify the past."[1] Phrases like "a newer garden . . . to justify the past" were commonplace, almost clichéd, in poetry that celebrated eighteenth- and nineteenth-century America. Whitman sounded his own voice in his compelling image of "iron interlaced," strong in its delicacy, binding a teeming people. Immediately, he meant the national lattice of railways, but the image asked how his whole people held together. Whitman's great poetic project was to render his people as not-strangers to the entirety of themselves. Among his Americans there was no Other, no "them who do not belong: the ignoble, the nonkith, the nonkin, the people we do not marry, the alien within—the serf, the Jew, the Slav, the slave, the Negro, the people who cannot vote—who demarcate what we are."[2]

Reality was not so easy. The shared Americanness that Whitman rightly perceived offered ample possibilities for seeing somebody else as the Other that defined oneself. Tribal community, race, ethnicity, neighborhood, gender, and social class were among the answers people proposed to the problem of who they were and who was Other. But all their answers were provisional, both because their world would not hold still and because they could not help belonging among one another. Whitman's Americans were separate, but even in their separateness they were working out common answers to a problem they all faced.

Maturing capitalism was at the heart of their world, bursting with new opportunities and new problems. Capitalism is a complex mingling of social, political, and economic issues that people organize, and that organizes them. No society is entirely capitalist, because even now people need and find other ways besides the cash nexus to interact. The historical problem that capitalism presents is not easily resolved.[3] Nor are the civic issues it evokes. The right has its point to celebrate capitalism's strength and possibilities, including new possibilities for freedom. The left has its point to note its imbalances, its costs, and its shortfallings from what it promises. Capitalism drove the Republic to triumph. It also forced the Republic's people to consider the conditions of their own existence and, in the eighteenth century's apt phrase, to "govern themselves accordingly."[4]

[I]

Though the developing Republic was a disaster for almost all Indians, it did not render them impotent. Thomas Jefferson spoke for Presidents from Washington to John Quincy Adams when he told the Seneca Ganeodiyo (Handsome Lake), "We are always ready to buy lands but we will never ask but when you wish to sell." He offered a scenario: "Persuade our red brethren . . . to cultivate their lands, and their women to spin and weave. . . . You will soon see your women and children well fed and clothed, your men living happily in peace and plenty, and your numbers increasing from year to year." Then Indians would find it "advantageous . . . to sell a part, and lay the money in stocks and implements of agriculture."[5]

In the Revolution's aftermath Ganeodiyo's Senecas, once the proud "keepers" of Iroquoia's "western gate," became drink-ridden beggars in rural slums on land not valuable enough to justify evicting them. When their plight passed endurance Ganeodiyo sought and found an answer. Within the Iroquois tradition of prophetic dreams he discovered his *Gaiwiio* or Good Word and began to preach it. War was an impossibility. So was the old economy of men who hunted while women worked in the fields. The *Gaiwiio* borrowed from Christianity, including Catholic confession. It abandoned the Senecas' old morality, where marriages were easily broken but matrilineal families endured, and substituted the Christian morality of permanent sexual union. People who accepted the *Gaiwiio* gave up alcohol, which had been the symbol, the solace, and the reinforcement of their despair. The remedy worked. The reborn Senecas did not lose any more land or disintegrate or die out. They still survive.[6]

What worked for the Senecas did not necessarily work for anyone else.

Ganeodiyo did not preach the *Gaiwiio* to outsiders. Two other Indian prophetic movements whose founders had greater ambitions bracket the age of the Revolution. One was preached by the Delaware prophet Neolin in the early 1760s, and the other by the Shawnee prophet Tenskwatawa five decades later. Both movements failed. Neolin and Tenskwatawa wanted to stave off the whites, not just cope with what was going to be, as Ganeodiyo proposed. Neolin's people were exiles from the past, driven into the Ohio country by colonial conflicts. Neolin's call was "to live 'without any Trade or Connections to ye White people, Clothing & Supporting themselves as their forefathers did.' " Nonetheless, his followers would "pray to 'ye Son or Little God.' " His cosmos included the Christian ideas of heaven and hell. He could not escape the history that had made him.[7] Neither could Tenskwatawa. In his teaching Indian women married to whites should "be brought home . . . and their children . . . be left with their Fathers, so that nations might become genuine Indian." But "genuine Indian" was open to definition. Indians had honored age, but to Tenskwatawa "the old people no longer have anything to say. The young people now rule." Rejecting not only white men but the very beasts they had brought, his followers should slaughter their cattle. Tenskwatawa did not preach killing horses, however, though whites had supplied both species. He did call on his followers to kill their dogs, which were the only mammals that Indians had domesticated. Indian men should plant corn, despite its being women's traditional work.[8]

Both movements turned into attempts to wage concerted, intertribal war against whites, Neolin's as the "Conspiracy of Pontiac" of 1763 and Tenskwatawa's under his brother Tecumseh, who sought to organize all the tribes east of the Mississippi and who traveled as far as the Creek and Cherokee nations urging Indians to join him. The Indians lost both times, and Tecumseh's defeat marked the end of the "middle ground" that had set the terms of white-Indian relations in the western Great Lakes region since the middle of the seventeenth century. Unlike the *Gaiwiio*, the teachings of Neolin and Tenskwatawa disappeared, except from memory.

Cherokees, Creeks, Seminoles, Chickasaws, and Choctaws were given a longer time to work out their answers. By the 1820s Cherokees had changed from hunting to farming. They established a territorial republic within the state of Georgia, with its own constitution and terms of citizenship. Cherokees fended off repeated white efforts to expel them. They learned to write their own language without the Roman alphabet.

Some became Christians and these could read the Bible in Cherokee; others learned to use Christian missionaries and American laws for their own purposes. During the Revolution the Cherokees had sided for a time with the British, but they backed away from that and did not lose their land at the war's end. They refused Tecumseh's call to war against whites. They joined arms with the United States in 1812 against both British and Creeks. They understood the large course that history was taking. As they saw the matter, they did not have to figure among history's victims.

Cherokees did not face the whites absolutely united. Some sold tribal land for as little reward as a gun, a blanket, and some help moving West. Others sought the aid of the spirits in a futile Ghost Dance. Cherokees drank, quarreled, and murdered. As we have seen, in 1830 the state of Georgia and the federal government under President Andrew Jackson joined to drive them into Indian Territory, beyond the Mississippi, along the Trail of Tears. By 1840 most were gone from Georgia. But the Cherokee republic endured, even if it had to do so on new ground.[9] For Choctaws it was much the same. President Jackson made it plain that to remain a people they would have to follow their own trail of tears, without any regard to how they had fought with him against Creeks at Horseshoe Bend in 1814 and against the British at New Orleans the following year. The choice he presented was stark: depart together or remain individually as "citizens of color."[10] Most went. The Ouachita Mountains of Oklahoma are where the Choctaw Nation now lives.

After 1840 there were still Cherokees in the southern Appalachians and Choctaws in Mississippi. Some prospered, most notably the Choctaw Greenwood Leflore, who became master of a delta plantation. Both the city of Greenwood, Mississippi, "Cotton Capital of the World," and the county of Leflore honor his name. Leflore opposed secession and displayed the Stars and Stripes throughout the Civil War. But most Indians who stayed found that to a white Southerner a "citizen of color" was just a tolerated person, not a citizen at all.

[II]

To Easterners who imagined themselves sophisticated (northern and southern alike), the white people who dwelt nearest the Indians seemed much like Indians themselves. One group was "savage." The other approached savagery, as frontier life stripped their culture away.[11] Widely read captivity narratives made the point again and again that a white who fell into Indian hands could easily "go Indian." In his *Letters from an American Farmer* the French observer Hector St. John de Crèvecoeur argued that just living on the frontier was enough to make it happen. The world-famous legend of Daniel Boone made the same point.[12] Land rioters in early-nineteenth-century Maine and mid-nineteenth-century New York played on the imagery, becoming themselves "white Indians" with blankets, paint, and mock dialect.[13] The imagery had its basis in experience. Some pioneers (white and black alike) accepted Indian ways and took Indian identity.[14] Others hated Indians but still understood their world, creating the figure of the "Indian hater," one of the most enduring and compelling images in the whole mythology of the American West.[15] The notion that "the frontier" stripped away the veneer of civilization and left people free to start again was one of the most powerful elements in Frederick Jackson Turner's argument that the frontier was the key to understanding American history.[16]

Nonetheless, white men and women going West did not lose their culture and turn into frontier brutes, any more than Indians actually were forest or prairie brutes. Migrants wanted both self-advancement and community. Advancement would come as they farmed the rich soil beyond the Appalachians and began to sell their surplus. At first reaching the market meant no more than setting out occasionally with a herd of pigs, a few barrels of whiskey, or a flatboat loaded with grain to sell.[17] Later, with the triumph of technology, canals, steamboats, railroads, and telegraphs made taking part in commerce much easier. Until then, settlers dealt for the most part with one another.

"I had not been two years at the licks before a d—d Yankee came and settled *down within an hundred miles of me*," legend has the aged Daniel Boone saying as he retreated from overcrowded Kentucky into Missouri.[18] The West certainly attracted loners. But people sought sociability, including Boone. One powerful way was to reconstruct old customs. Newlyweds on the Illinois prairie might be treated to an unwelcome "shivaree" with "ole tin pans, kittles, whistles, cow-bells, horns en everything they could make a howlin' noise with." Shivaree was how prairie people pronounced "charivari," the French word for that kind of carrying-on. These people who were creating the American Great West would have learned the word from French Canadian survivors of the old middle ground. A shivaree might tease newlyweds, shame a wife beater or cuckold, or harass somebody who just was different. The word was

probably new to the pioneers; the custom was not new at all. In England
it was called "rough music." The American tradition of tarring and
feathering stemmed from it. By itself what happened to embarrassed
Illinois newlyweds might seem to mean little. In fact, it showed how
deeply these pioneers drew upon their own history in rituals of belonging. Today wedding parties sounding their car horns and guests show-
ering confetti upon the couple draw upon that history still. So, much
less happily, do people who drive someone who is "different"—a Jew, a
black person, a homosexual—from a community's midst.[19]

Pioneers could not be self-sufficient. They grew crops, made objects,
and rendered services in order to exchange them for what they could not
grow, make, or do for themselves. Sometimes they traded over great
distances under the rules of commerce, sometimes locally under the rules
of community. The more remote a community, the more likely that its
members would live by rules they worked out themselves. In that kind
of economy everyone usually was in debt to everyone else. Some people
kept careful accounts in a book; others just noted them on a painted
board. From kin and neighbors, a person might ask no interest. The
principal might not be paid for years, perhaps not before death forced a
reckoning of all the accounts a person ever accrued. A country store's
books might show long-distance exchanges of manufactured goods and
luxuries for cash or barter. They also might show local exchange in the
same language of mutuality that neighbors and kin employed. People
lived that way in western Massachusetts during the late eighteenth century, in the Hudson Valley during the early decades of the nineteenth,
on the Illinois prairies during the 1830s, and in Wisconsin two decades
later.[20] The difference was not an absolute contrast between community
among neighbors and contract among strangers. Nor, absolutely, was it
one between capitalism and some other way of organizing the world.
Neighbors and strangers, community and capitalism alike defined the
world, and the balance between them had to be struck again and again.[21]
It makes more sense to think of their America as a social formation that
contained contrasting possibilities than as a situation with only one set
of rules, despite there being a "supreme law of the land."

Every white and black community in America has begun with migration, free or forced. Virtually all Indian communities have known
migration too. People of all races crisscrossed the American landscape
during the nineteenth century. Otherwise, of course, the whole idea of
the moving frontier would have no basis. In Jacksonville, Illinois, "only
a minority . . . remained . . . for a decade" between 1850 and 1870.[22]

The image of nineteenth-century Americans as utterly restless people, constantly on the move, is very strong. Nonetheless, there still were people who found a place they wanted to be, formed binding ties, put down roots, and stayed.

In 1860 the white people of Trempealeau County, Wisconsin, included Canadian, English, Scottish, Irish, Norwegian, German, and American-born ethnic groups. They were young, and they were marrying. In Trempealeau that year, 296 American-born women married and so did 276 American-born men. Of these, 269 married somebody who was also American-born. For the English-born the numbers were twenty-seven women who married and thirty-four men, with twenty marriages in which both partners came from England. Thirty-three Irish-born women married, as did thirty-seven Irish-born men. In thirty-two of the couples both partners were Irish. Among the Germans thirty-five women married, thirty-five men did as well, and thirty-three marriages were of German to German. At this stage in Trempealeau's development neighbors could easily remain strangers. The small, immediate group was what equaled the community. Marriage meant confirmation that a man and a woman spoke the same language with the same accent, ate the same food, wore the group's clothes, and worshipped the group's God. Marriage was public acceptance of adulthood, with obligations that could not be shirked. A person who tried would face strong disapproval from people who counted.[23] Trempealeau was not unique. In 1850, 28 percent of the adult males in Jacksonville, Illinois, had adult male kin nearby; in 1860 the figure was 35 percent. Jacksonville's married men and women were likely to stay there and prosper; its single people moved on.[24] Even now there are farming families in Illinois who regard their land as sacred. Their great and first goal is to provide a future on that land for their children, not to get ahead themselves.[25]

White Southerners did the same. People in mid-nineteenth-century Orange County, North Carolina, built their lives around "family, kinship, and neighborhood." This was no frontier. Settlement had begun in 1752 and "forty-nine of the sixty most common surnames in 1850" had also been "recorded on the county's 1779 tax list." There was no need here for German to marry German or Irish to marry Irish. With little immigration there were not enough of any ethnic group to make ethnic matching possible. Instead, people married within their churches and among their immediate neighbors. Half the marrying couples grew up no more than "one to three miles" apart. Sixty percent of Orange's people who shared their name with seven or more male household heads in

1850 were still there in 1860. Only 46 percent of men who shared a name with fewer than four others remained.[26] Even migration did not break up communities. "Around 1853" a whole group moved from Edgefield County, South Carolina, to Bullock County, Alabama. Almost their first act when they arrived was to found a church. Massachusetts Puritans could not have shown better what they thought community was about.[27]

[III]

South of the Ohio River, pioneering meant that slavery grew. From Georgia to Texas, from the Ohio River to the Gulf of Mexico, the southern landscape was full of black people going West. For them, as it was for Indians and whites, the central issue was how to live with wrenching change. These people's roots ran deep. By the nineteenth century many had white and Indian ancestry as well as African.[28] Even the final victims of the African slave trade were in the United States before nineteenth-century European migration began. Their ancestors' arrivals predate those of almost all whites. Slaves had no property, except on white sufferance. But they did have traditions that had begun to develop almost as soon as their American captivity began.

Slave traditions could acquire great power, both among themselves and as a practical way to live with their captors. The most stable part of enslaved America was the South Carolina and Georgia lowlands and Sea Islands. These remained dangerous places, with alligators, poisonous snakes, and disease-bearing mosquitoes everywhere. The British actress Frances Kemble recorded a harrowing picture of how seacoast slaves lived during her sojourn on her husband's Georgia plantation in 1839. Modern scholars bear her out. On St. Helena Island, South Carolina, "sickness and death tormented all classes of people." The " 'great object' of health care . . . was 'to prolong the useful laboring period of a Negro's life.' "[29] Low-country slave communities survived despite the demanding conditions they faced.

But most lowland slaves did not face forced migration, since rice did not exhaust the land as tobacco did and constant flooding and draining replenished the soil. Unlike Virginians, rice planters had little reason to sell their slaves or move. In 1859 the mean size of a slave force along the Waccamaw River in South Carolina was 292 people, almost fifteen times the conventional number required for the master to have planter status.[30]

Waccamaw slaves formed not only a large community but a dense one, on terms that they, not whites, set when they could. Southern whites married neighbors and even cousins, but slaves married "out." They knew that even on a prosperous rice plantation the master's death could destroy a slave community, however secure it seemed. If bad times drove that master into bankruptcy the same would happen. Any slave could be sold anytime, merely at a whim. A master's generous wedding gift of slaves to a grown son or daughter could split slave families forever. When (not if) such things happened, there would be people to help the orphaned child and to support the adult whose spouse was gone.[31]

Rice planters used the task system of labor to make their slaves compete. When the day's task was done, the slave could quit or do more work for pay. Slaves realized that the goal was productivity, not slave welfare. Tasks done too quickly one year could be increased the next. Stronger workers had to go slow for the sake of weaker ones. So most refused a competition that none could really win and set their work pace together, often with music. Tasking did allow free time and rice slaves used it to generate their own economy. South Carolina law forbade slaves to hold property, but practice was another matter. South Carolina governor and Waccamaw planter Robert F. W. Allston swore solemnly to enforce the state's laws. Nonetheless, his slaves grew crops, caught fish, alligators, and birds, kept hens, and made goods. They traded it all, among themselves, in the market at nearby Georgetown, and even with Alston. The governor could not stop them, whatever the law required.[32]

There was no single way to be a slave, any more than to be an Indian or a white. Most nineteenth-century slaves produced not rice or tobacco but rather short-staple cotton in the vast territory between the Carolina and Georgia piedmont and East Texas. What actually happened to slaves as Cherokee, Creek, Choctaw, and Caddo country became the Cotton Kingdom remains almost unexplored.[33] Let us attempt a first answer by looking at the very heart of it, the state of Mississippi. The source will be the United States census for 1850. The bare statistics of Mississippi's white and black population that year open one window on what the slaves endured. Like other numbers from the time, they only seem daunting. Human life and death lie behind them.

Mississippi's nearly 48,000 square miles form a roughly shaped rectangle, stretching 332 miles from the Tennessee border to its southernmost point and 190 miles from east to west where it is widest. The state varied enormously in the middle of the nineteenth century. The Gulf coast meadows and nearby piney woods never became cotton country and never acquired large black populations. Plantation agriculture began near Natchez late in the eighteenth century. By 1850 the town had created its permanent image of wealth, elegance, and, at Natchez-under-the-Hill, decadence. Adams County, which surrounds the town, was dotted with places that were as much monuments to their owners' wealth as they were working plantations.[34]

Substantial numbers of white people lived in the Natchez district. Adams County had nearly 4,000. But it had 14,395 blacks at the same time. A spine of hills stretches up central Mississippi. Much of the soil is rich brown loam and loess, good for cotton as long as it does not erode. In mid-century the hill country contained only one substantial town, the state capital at Jackson. Racially, it was more balanced than the river counties, though whites remained the minority. In Carroll County there were 8,653 whites and 9,812 blacks. Farther north, plantations gave way to small farms and the racial balance shifted sharply in favor of whites. Lafayette County, which includes the university town of Oxford and would be the model for William Faulkner's fictional Yoknapatawpha, had 8,346 white people to only 5,719 black ones.

East of the hills, the Tombigbee River drains a rich cotton-growing lowland. Economically the Tombigbee basin belongs to Alabama and it exported its cotton through Mobile. Here the mid-century racial balance was like the counties around Natchez, with sizable white populations and much larger black ones. In Noxubee County there were 4,976 whites and 11,323 blacks. Finally, there is the Mississippi/Yazoo Delta, the enormous flat triangle bounded by the two rivers whose names it bears. The delta is reclaimed floodplain and before the Civil War much of it remained what whites called wilderness. Choctaw and Tunica Indians would have seen it differently.

In 1850 the delta was the cotton frontier, and the imbalance between the races there was staggering. Issaquena County had 369 whites and 4,105 blacks.[35] All Mississippi had only 930 free black people in 1850 out of a total black population greater than 309,000. Most dwelt in Natchez, Vicksburg, Jackson, and Columbus. In rural Mississippi counties as few as one or two African-Americans might be free. White Mississippians wanted no living examples to bear out what all slaves knew in their hearts anyway, that slavery and blackness did not have to go together.

Slavery was slavery and north of the piney woods all Mississippi grew cotton. But what it meant for the people involved varied enormously. The higher above sea level or the farther from river water where a steamboat could go, the more likely that a county would have sizable numbers of whites. In the North Central Hills the productivity rate might be less than two bales per worker, with foodstuffs accounting for the rest of the crop. In the Brown Loam and Loess Hills and around Natchez productivity was higher, varying between 2.65 and 4.56 bales. Every county in the Tombigbee basin produced more than four bales of cotton per slave. The highest rate of all belonged to Issaquena County, lying between the Yazoo and the Mississippi at the delta's southern tip, where almost nine bales were brought to market for every single slave of working age.

The delta still produces vast amounts of cotton, long after forests have begun reclaiming the worked-out, gullied soil of the hill counties. Production now is mechanized, but under slavery every step meant direct human labor. The delta has a well-justified reputation not just for the richness of its soil but also for its extreme unhealthfulness. Delta water does not run. It stands. Cholera, yellow fever, and malaria have been facts of delta life. Highly toxic pesticides are facts of life now. Antebellum whites avoided the delta if they could, however great its potential wealth. Black people went there because they had no choice. The full story of Mississippi slaves remains to be told. It is not accidental, however, that the delta is where the blues began.[36]

[IV]

Slaves could husk and polish Carolina rice after they picked it, perhaps using African techniques. They were using those techniques when rice culture was new, in the 1730s. They were still using them on the eve of slavery's destruction, in 1859. Once processed, the rice would be ready for somebody to cook, and it could be cooked just as readily in a slave's own pot as in the kitchen of a purchaser who lived an ocean away.[37] Slaves ginned and baled Mississippi cotton, just as they husked and polished Carolina rice. But for cotton that was only the start of a long, complex process of turning loose fibers into finished cloth.

Northern and English white people finished that process in highly mechanized factories. In England these people could properly be called a working class by the early nineteenth century. There, the innovations of the late eighteenth and early nineteenth centuries took place once and for all. English factory workers became a self-conscious group that would reproduce themselves and their distinctive culture for generation after generation, even to the present.[38] As with the English, the history of industrial working people in the United States began with cloth production. But its course has not been the same.

One reason is America's size. Wage-earning men and women in both Britain and America likened themselves to slaves, but it was not true in either place. They were not even under formal indentures and in both countries if they wanted to move they could. Moving in good times could be a way to negotiate for better pay and conditions. In bad times a person could go wherever there were rumors of jobs.[39] Moving could also be a way to leave the working class itself, by going where land could be had and a new start seemed possible. British workers who made that choice had to cease being British and instead become Australians, New Zealanders, Canadians, or Americans.

An American could leave the working class without departing the United States. A family that pooled what it earned and did not meet disaster might get its own land from the government or a speculator.[40] Many people held the hope. But the actual prospects for going West and succeeding were not high. Transportation, implements, fencing, breaking the soil, housing, seed, animals, and sheer survival for the first year or two all had to be paid for. Free workers were not bound to a place, which distinguished them from slaves. But most found that, like slaves, they had to "take root there" where they were, "or nowhere."[41]

That meant forming connections. "Class happens," the late English historian E. P. Thompson wrote, "when some people as a result of common experiences feel and articulate the identity of their interests as between themselves, and as against" others.[42] Class did "happen" that way in nineteenth-century America. So, however, did community, gender, and ethnicity. Rather than attempt a catalogue of places and situations, consider one thread that runs brightly through this whole skein, the experience of women within the new industrial economy.

That women worked in the market economy before it became industrial is no news. Artisan shops were likely to be family enterprises where husband, wife, daughters, sons, journeymen, and apprentices all took part. A widow who had mastered her late husband's trade might take over the business, as did Elizabeth Holt, who became New York State's official printer for several years just after independence. In smaller towns an artisan's family could run a farm as well as keep the shop going. By the late eighteenth century the north shore Massachusetts town of Lynn had become a cordwaining center. It shipped both well-made high-fashion shoes to Boston and crude slave footwear to South Carolina. Almost all its shoes were made in "ten-footers," small shops behind a family dwelling, with a barn nearby and fields to the rear. The master cordwainer could drop his shoemaking and attend to his cows or corn as need required. His wife was his partner. She was involved like him in making shoes, running the farm, and dealing with family demands.[43]

It sounds lovely, idyllic. From a shoemaking woman's point of view the idyll fades rapidly. Their primary task was to bind the shoes, not cut or last them, and

> binding shoes was not considered skilled work; shoebinders were not taught to make an entire shoe. Learning to bind shoes did not provide the shoemaker's daughter with a trade . . . The low wages paid to binders . . . reflected this lack of craft status. There was no reason for women to enter the ten footer . . . Neither did shoebinders share in the good times at the Nahant beaches, or in the gatherings of the militia and fire companies.[44]

Shoemaking wives and daughters lived in the same world and they worked in the same enterprises as their husbands, sons, and brothers. Very probably they did feel real solidarity with their male kin. Nonetheless, even within household production being a woman made a big difference to how a person experienced the economic world.

For many wage-earning women in the first half of the nineteenth century, work at home did not mean sharing work with male family members. By the middle of the nineteenth century New England merchants had organized large circles of "outworkers," almost all of them women on farms and in rural towns. No factory bells called these people to work; no power machinery set rhythms that their bodies had to follow. Yet the work could not stop, because if one consignment went uncompleted there might not be another and they needed the money. They bound shoes for some distant master cordwainer, not their farming husbands. They wove palm-leaf hats for the urban market. These women were working at home, but they were on their own. They were part of family enterprises only in the sense that they pooled what they earned for the whole family's sake.

Much the same was going on in New York City. By the 1830s tailoring, "artificial-flower making, fringe and tassel making, embroidery, mantua making, fancy bookbinding and parasol making . . . along with all manner of other fancy stitched, burnished and gilded manufactures," all got done in the same places people lived. This was "sweating," and in the city both sexes shared the work. Nonetheless, "men and women . . . occupied different positions within this cooperative group, much as they did in the family, with men at the top." Many New York women did outside work on their own, either because they did not live with families or because they went to work for "unmarried journeymen" who paid the women no more than "fixed wages."[45]

From Samuel Slater's first Pawtucket mill onward, "the sex" were among the makers of factory America. Almost from the start, Slater wanted to hire whole families rather than separate individuals. In fact, it worked out in a more complex way. By the 1820s male heads of families often refused to enter Slater's mills, although "all of the skilled and supervisory positions, such as mule spinner, dyer, dresser, machinist, and overseer . . . were filled by men." Married women tended to work "inside or around the home" rather than go into the factories as well, although they might do piecework. It was younger family members who normally went through the gates of a Slater mill. If whole families or a parent and child did work within the mill, they would be separated, so that the authority of parents and the authority of foremen did not clash.[46]

In the mills of Rockdale, Pennsylvania, a different pattern emerged. Here whole families would be hired; indeed, employment was hard to get for a man who was alone. Parents and children frequently worked in the same rooms. Families permeated the mills, and mill life permeated families. The companies supplied housing, in the form of whole houses, not "small apartments or dormitories" or boardinghouses. In Rockdale "the nuclear family was vitally necessary to . . . economic welfare" because workers could not live on their own, especially if they were women. In these mills "the mother and teen-age children evidently were almost as productive financially as the father" and "the patriarchal quality of family life" dwindled.[47]

The most famous instance of American female labor did not involve households, parents, wage pooling, or outside work. The "enterprising elite" who set out in 1821 to build a whole new town at the falls of the Merrimack River realized that the immediate area could not possibly supply them with a workforce. They knew that there were many young women in central and northern New England who might be brought into the factories, and they set out to recruit them. When Francis Cabot Lowell went on his spying mission in 1811 he found the machinery enchanting, but the condition of British working people revolted him. He genuinely wanted to do better. The Boston Associates also knew that they could not recruit New England women without real provision for their well-being. The result was the Lowell boardinghouses.

It would be easy to romanticize the boardinghouses where the first generation of Lowell mill women lived. Charles Dickens did so. The creator of the squalid fictional Coketown perceived no squalor when he visited Lowell. Instead its factory women were "all well dressed . . . healthy in appearance . . . and had the manners and deportment of young women, not of degraded brutes of burden." Their workrooms were airy and decorated with "green plants." Dickens solemnly declared that not "one young face . . . gave me a painful impression."[48]

Conditions in Lowell were far better than in Lancashire, but if Dickens had stayed longer or listened more he might have written otherwise. Almost a decade before his visit, the women had thought conditions bad enough to "turn out," or strike. When he passed through, a ferment was building among them for a ten-hour working day. He got no sense of it.

Nonetheless, working in the Lowell mills and living in the boarding-houses marked a major dividing line in these women's lives. They were subject to a strict regimen, both so that they would not be led into a city's temptations and to socialize them into meeting the company's demands. To a twentieth-century person the restrictive rules of the boardinghouses would chafe unbearably. Nonetheless, this was the first time in the whole history of white Protestants that large numbers of women assembled on their own as participants in the world. They were in Lowell as themselves, not as wives or daughters or sisters of somebody else. Like many other people in the expanding, transforming Republic, they found that their lives were changed and that they could not go home again. One who tried to do it summed up how she felt: "It is extremely dull here now, there is nothing at all interesting going on here, save the orthodox have a singing school, but *that*, *we* do not attend." Some Lowell women found that having their own liberty would always be better than being married. However, most did marry eventually. But the terms of their endearments could not be the same as those that worked for their mothers, or for their sisters who stayed at home.[49]

[V]

During the early nineteenth century factory workers were not the only women in Rockdale, Pennsylvania. Visually, each of its mill villages presented a perfect tableau of early industrial class relations. The mills sat at the bottom of the gorge. Just out of floodwater's way was worker housing. A larger house farther up the hill would be a foreman's residence. At the top of the gorge's bank stood the mansion of the owner, and near the house might stand a church. The churches of Rockdale were Protestant, perhaps Episcopalian, perhaps evangelical. They represented the deliberate effort of women of the factory-owning class to give moral cohesion to their communities in ways that transcended class lines. To a remarkable degree their effort succeeded. The "sisterhood" reached out to one another and formed a strong bond. They reached out to men of their own class, and an "infidel" male who did not think as they did stood no chance of acceptance in their society. They reached out to the women of the mill families, striving hard to bring them, their children, and their husbands into church fellowship. They did not succeed in every individual case. They did turn this small corner of industrializing America into a moral whole that found its terms of cohesion in "Christian Capitalism."[50]

What Rockdale women bearing such names as Anna Potts Lammot, Clementina Smith, and Sophie Du Pont set out to achieve served their needs. Except for one strike, Rockdale remained a peaceful place. But there is no need to accuse them of rank cynicism or manipulation. They were confronting a world that seemed to be running amok. It may well be that in a truly large entity common purpose will disappear and self-seeking will prevail. This has been the dilemma of republican thinking ever since the notion that people might govern themselves first began to emerge. The answer of people of all sorts in nineteenth-century America was to look for conditions that would generate solidarity among themselves, whatever the outright individualism and self-seeking they saw around them.[51]

In this curious way we can see why conditions among the urban poor, the squatters of the western frontier, and the most desperate of the people of the countryside, the slaves of the South, all led to roughly the same results. Individuals could not get by on their own, and the only way to survive was to cooperate with people who shared the same situation. The prairie frontier, a Mississippi plantation, a Lowell boardinghouse, and the streets of a burgeoning city all could be frightening places. Except for the boardinghouse, they could be tough, even violent places as well. In all of them people generated codes that gave them some control over their own lives.

The striking thing is how those codes keep appearing. In 1847 an

Irish mob in New York "gathered for a classic European charivari [against] a notorious minister, charged with . . . seduction and adultery." There were times when a person in trouble had to invoke that kind of intervention. A quarreling couple in working-class New York would be allowed by the neighborhood to go their own way, however loud or violent. But the ritual cry of "murder" was the signal for the community to step in and perhaps save a life.[52] Even in a big city the police and the fire department were rudimentary, and the kind of service they provided depended upon who and what one was. In smaller communities formal public services virtually did not exist and mutual self-help was the only way to accomplish what lay beyond an individual's or a family's own power.

In this sense almost all Americans, whatever their condition, faced the same problem. Their dominant culture and the laws that surrounded them rested firmly on private property and individualism. But men and women found that it was not good to try to live alone. Their personal lives and their relations were defined formally by a large-scale system of law. That law was proclaimed in statutes under the authority of the sovereign people. It was interpreted by professional jurists who formed a community of their own, bound together by published case reports and legal journals. Beyond the protection of life, the primary purpose of the law was to set the rules for property to be exchanged and developed. In theory those rules would operate uniformly, throughout the entire society.

But in practical terms the developing national capitalist structure intersected with individuals and groups in very complicated ways. Some people's response to their common human need for mutuality and sociability provided them with powerful means for controlling their whole world. Among the elite, like the Boston Associates or Rockdale's sisterhood and the men in their lives, a potent brew of power and influence appeared. Long-distance connections, a strong consciousness of family history, marriage for the sake of an alliance as much as for love, access to credit, participation in large institutions, the near-surety that a person who obeyed the conventions would not be allowed to sink, ready access to political office, gender relations that made women utterly dependent materially but immensely powerful as shapers of culture: these were its distinguishing marks. A person who possessed these marks and knew how to use them had reason to think the world was good.[53]

Most of these marks defined the southern planter class as well, and the two groups did intermingle. The Connecticut Yankee Eli Whitney invented the simple gin that made the Cotton Kingdom possible. The Georgia rice planter Pierce Butler spent most of his prosperous adulthood in Philadelphia, far from the human sources of his wealth.[54] The Mississippi cotton planter Stephen Duncan was northern-born, but when he heard in 1831 about Nat Turner's insurrection in Virginia, his response was realistic, hardheaded, and very southern: "We have here 5 blacks to one white; and within 4 hours march of Natchez there are 2200 able bodied male slaves. It behooves to be vigilant—but *silent*."[55]

That the owners of plantations and the owners of mills developed very similar ways is not surprising. In any society the elite can rule best and with least resistance if it is aware of its role and if it protects and extends its own interests. The two groups needed each other as well. The South Carolinian James Henry Hammond knew what he was saying when he proclaimed to Northerners that "you dare not make war upon cotton, cotton is king!"[56] But to rule by any means beyond sheer force, the elite must convince others that it does speak for all, as eighteenth-century Virginia planters succeeded in doing. By the mid-nineteenth century, many (not all) white Northerners were becoming convinced that the expansion of slavery threatened their futures. Many (not all) ordinary white Southerners believed just as firmly that they had a real stake in the slavery system. Here is one reason for Abraham Lincoln's dictum during his great debates with Stephen A. Douglas in 1858 that "a house divided against itself cannot stand." Douglas was convinced that the gaps of social class, regional interest, and gender awareness and the gulf between slavery and freedom could be bridged. Lincoln knew better.

How the women of the two ruling groups dealt with their respective worlds provides one key to how the American ruling elite came apart. Like their men, southern planter women and the women of the northern bourgeoisie had a great deal in common. Among both groups a woman was not expected to support herself. That would come from her husband's wealth. Women of the planter class and women of the bourgeoisie were equally influenced by the collection of ideas about sexuality that we now call Victorian.

But one major difference developed. Northern middle-class women organized to do things in the world. Southern planter women did not. In the North, women of the same class who set out to give cohesion to communities like Rockdale also set out to organize larger communities like New York City. They focused their campaigns at first on the issues of temperance, sexual purity, and prison reform; these causes led ultimately to campaigns for the abolition of slavery and for women's rights.

What the crusaders did worked better in a small town than in a big city, where it tended to degenerate into mere meddling.[57] Nineteenth-century northern middle-class women devoted enormous energy to social reform. Their efforts at betterment contributed mightily to the way that their own free-labor society justified itself.

Nonetheless, gender was central not only to well-meaning reform movements but to the whole pattern of northern class relations and to the process of sectional divergence and ultimate separation. Reform efforts in the North promised (in Northerners' eyes) to make a good society better. The great attack on slavery both transformed the South into an Other and held up a mirror in which the North could behold itself and admire what it saw.

Southern women of the planter class were just as important for their region's cohesion and self-definition as northern women of the bourgeoisie were to theirs. They too struggled to make the most of themselves and their talents and their energies. The cultural patterns that developed around them, however, were fundamentally different from what their northern counterparts generated around themselves. In imagery, at least, the Belle was the passive reason why her society existed, not an active participant in defining that society's goals.[58]

In one sense, then, the people of the young American Republic were as divided as any human group in history. The fundamental American division remained race. That issue had been present from the very beginning, although it did not become fully conceptualized until the late eighteenth century. In the mid-nineteenth century that division cut deep, whether the line was red and white, black and white, or red and black, but it was not the only line. The end of slavery in the postrevolutionary North created a line that was separating the sections, although it was hardly the case either that all white Southerners supported the plantation regime or that all white Northerners wanted to see black people free. The development of industrial society in the North was cutting yet another line, separating the social class that owned the new order from the social class that worked within it. Free or slave, North or South, owning class or working class, the world inhabited by women was not the same as the world inhabited by men. The line cut by gender zigged and zagged through all other social divisions.

Yet in the midst of all the confusion and tumult and small-scale efforts to organize a society that seemed to be verging on chaos, two themes did cut through. One was the need to form communities, if only on a small scale. This, however, is not peculiarly American. The other theme,

American indeed, was to endow both small communities and large ones with meaning in this world. From its very beginning, the United States had chosen to define itself in ideological terms. The issue of who actually did belong to "the people," who actually could lay claim to the Americans' "blessings of liberty," admitted of no easy answer. But the people who comprised the Republic found themselves unable to let the question go, no matter what kind of Americans they were.

CHAPTER 8

CITIZENS, SUBJECTS, AND SLAVES:
THE REPUBLICAN MOSAIC

"WE are now under the American flag, be it through our own choice or by force, and it is probable that we will remain thus always. We should then accept the events and vicissitudes of our age and familiarize ourselves with the new language, habits, and customs; thus we will not be dominated but equal in everything." So wrote the journalist Francisco Ramírez half a dozen years after his Mexican California became a state of the American Union. Ramírez was not usually so resigned. Perhaps, he speculated once, the solution was for Californios to emigrate below the new border to Sonora. Perhaps California could become "a protectorate of the European and Latin American nations whose citizens had settled" there.[1]

Californios, Nuevomejicanos, and Tejanos faced an extreme situation. A foreign army had conquered them and their own republic had given them away, although admittedly at gunpoint. Under the terms of the Treaty of Guadalupe Hidalgo of 1848 they retained genuine rights, including ownership of what Mexican law had recognized as theirs. They understood, however, that their lives had changed. Anglos were unlikely to give their laws, customs, and land titles the "full faith and credit" that the federal Constitution required among the states. English replaced Spanish, particularly in the courts where disputes would be resolved. When gold was discovered near Sacramento, the new authorities drove Hispanic people from the fields under a law "whose 'avowed purpose . . . was as far as possible to exclude foreigners from these mines, the God-given property of the American people.'" Some of the conquered still saw gain: "The liberty that we enjoy, the wealth and general prosperity, the moderation and fairness of our laws" stood in contrast to "the military despotism, the poverty, the edicts, the political convulsions that prevail in Mexico." Others saw none: "Despotism [and] crime have existed here since the day of the discovery of gold. . . . Brute force is the only law that is observed."[2]

These conquered Mexicans were facing the problem of belonging to a United States that wanted their land but not them. They shared the problem of belonging to America with many other people. The official language of American belonging has no qualifications at all. By the mid-nineteenth century reality was otherwise. It is a mere cliché to dismiss nineteenth-century American democracy as of no consequence, because it only included white males. On the contrary, as its great analyst Alexis de Tocqueville understood, democracy was more than voting. It was a social innovation of world interest and importance that touched everyone. Nonetheless, Hispanics, Native Americans, slaves, free black people, and women of every single group were excluded from one, another, most, or all of the blessings of American liberty. By the standards of the times these people may not have been "qualified" to take part in the Republic; it may be "anachronistic" to suggest that they should have been. By the Republic's own rhetoric, the exclusion rankled. American belonging, American exclusion: the tension of these polar opposites set the terms of civic culture between the Revolution and the Civil War. It was a tension that no person could avoid, whether that person was a citizen, a subject, or a slave.

The older colonial mosaic had been structured around an unashamed acceptance of inequality among different human conditions, whether the measure was property, gender, age, standing, class, or just membership in one community rather than another. The proclaimed equality and inclusiveness of the new order clashed starkly with how people actually experienced property, gender, age, standing, class, community, and, most especially now, race. Giving actual meaning to what the Republic proclaimed about itself and about the people within it required disputes about who "the people" were and about the terms on which they might act together. It required intellectual contortions in order to justify excluding people who were nothing if not American from some or all of the blessings of American liberty. It required coming to terms with new inequalities of possession, whether what was possessed was material objects or specialized knowledge.

Seeing how that happened is not easy. The new balance between equality and inequality worked itself out in fits and starts, not in a straight line. Nonetheless, by the middle of the nineteenth century certain points seemed clear. There was political equality among white men. There was a deep cleft between all who enjoyed full citizenship and people who "belonged" to American society as subjects and possessions, rather than as participants in its civic culture. Most subtly and least visibly, ways were being worked out of dealing with the undeniable inequalities of possession and power that persisted and grew among full citizens.

[I]

The United States Constitution uses the word "citizen" nine times, but in only three limited contexts. "No person except a natural born Citizen, or a Citizen . . . at the time of the Adoption of this Constitution, shall be eligible to the Office of President" (Article II). The federal courts can resolve "Controversies . . . between a State and Citizens of another State; —between Citizens of different States;—between Citizens of the same State claiming Lands under Grants of different States, and between a State, or the Citizens thereof, and foreign States, Citizens or Subjects" (Article III). Finally, "Citizens of each State shall be entitled to all Privileges and Immunities of Citizens in the several States" (Article IV). Not until the Fourteenth Amendment in 1868 would the supreme law actually define an American citizen as anyone "born or naturalized in the United States." The original federal Constitution provided no real definition of who actually belonged as the Republic took shape.

The original state constitutions do not help. Virginia's and New York's did not use the word "citizen" at all. Pennsylvania's employed it only to forbid that "any man, who acknowledges the being of a God, be . . . deprived or abridged of any civil right as a citizen, on account" of religious belief. Massachusetts used it only to protect "the right of every citizen to be tried by judges as free, impartial and independent as the lot of humanity will admit." Generally, these founding American documents employed other nouns: subjects, inhabitants, freemen, "Indians not taxed," "persons held to service," or "persons as any of the states now existing shall think proper to admit."[3] New York used the phrase "subjects of this state" in early proclamations, but that conjured up the old order's hodgepodge of inequalities. That may be all it did mean. As late as 1838 a North Carolina judge was holding that "the term 'citizen' as understood in our law, is precisely analogous to the term *subject* in common law."[4] The Revolution "invented the people," but it said very little about who "the people" were.[5] The closest we can get to an authoritative early statement is the naturalization act of 1790, which required that new citizens be white. But that said nothing about black or red people already in the country, and it was only a statute, not a constituting document.[6]

The French Revolution, not the American, provoked the issue of citizenship as a subject for discussion. When "Citizen" Edmond Genêt came to represent his government to the Washington administration he flaunted his egalitarian title to an age that still meant something by "Gent."[7] Imitating French practice, the Democratic-Republican Society of Pennsylvania decided in 1794 that "the appellation, 'Citizen,' shall, exclusively of all titles, be used in the correspondences of this Society." It was just a fashion, like wearing a *drapeau tricolore* or a Cap of Liberty. But fashion can have serious meaning, showing where a person stands on the largest issues of the time.[8]

President George Washington dismissed the Democratic-Republican Societies as "self-created," although the United States was self-created too. In the words of the Massachusetts constitution of 1780, "the body politic is formed by a voluntary association of individuals."[9] The Democratic-Republican Societies did not try to become formal bodies politic. They did insist that free individuals can associate themselves when and how they choose for any political purposes that may strike them.

During the 1790s the issue of what citizenship meant provoked two distinct positions. From one perspective "the people" ought to submit to the public authority they had made. Dissent was sedition. Any attempt at organization seemed like creating a selfish "faction." Opposition came close to treason. From the other perspective, republican rulers could reason badly. They could act out of mere self-interest. Political activity was always legitimate, not just at election time. Only active politics could turn the rhetoric of popular sovereignty into the reality of a genuinely self-sovereign people, free to criticize even themselves. Three issues were at stake: the extent of American public liberty, how and for what purposes people might organize, and the very nature of the body politic. In principle, the first two were worked out within the revolutionary generation's life span. The last was not.

Both civil liberties and people organizing themselves took sharper focus when Congress passed the Alien and Sedition Laws in 1798. The context was war, as relations with France deteriorated to the point of exchanging fire at sea. Men in power now saw dissent as outright disloyalty. Their "Alien Friends Act" excluded foreigners from American debate. Its intended targets included French exiles fleeing their own country's revolution, like the gunpowder maker E. I. Du Pont de

Nemours, and English people fleeing reaction, like the chemist and phi-losopher Joseph Priestley. The Sedition Act invoked the old English concept of "seditious libel" to criminalize any criticism of government. It did not protect Vice President Thomas Jefferson, who led the half-formed opposition. Its life ran only until the end of the administration of President John Adams. When Adams left office his successor, Jefferson, let the act die.[10]

"We are all Republicans, we are all Federalists," said Jefferson when he became President. It was a time to bind wounds, and Jefferson did not really mean what he said. Privately he thought his victory was a "revolution."[11] Adams agreed. Not able to bear defeat, he had departed quietly the day before his successor's inauguration. As Jefferson assumed power, he played the ordinary man. On inauguration day he breakfasted at the foot of his boardinghouse table, walked to the Capitol, and scorned the knee breeches and powdered hair that still marked a gentleman. But despite the pose, Thomas Jefferson was as much an eighteenth-century gentleman as either of the Presidents before him.[12]

Neither of Jefferson's points, fundamental consensus or revolutionary change, was correct. The election did not put a new kind of American in power or disrupt the Republic's institutions. One administration, "high" in tone, arrogant toward its opponents, closer to England than France, and centralist about the economy, was replaced by another op-posing it on all those points. The Republic had dealt with a problem nobody had foreseen: principled opposition and the transfer of authority without force. The 1800 election's great significance is that it both de-fined and broadened what American citizenship meant. Adams support-ers predicted terror and atheism if Jefferson won. Alexander Hamilton suggested that Governor John Jay manipulate New York's electoral vote to deny Jefferson victory, which Jay scornfully refused to do. The trauma faded and as old men Jefferson and Adams resumed their friendship, meditating about all they had accomplished and what had driven them apart. Not all American oppositions would end so well.

[II]

When farmers revolted in Massachusetts in 1786 and Pennsylvania in 1794, they had many precedents. Revolt had long been a way to make needs known and negotiate about what to do. Responding to revolt offered a way for rulers to both reward lesser people and discipline them.

That balance did not cease with the establishment of republicanism. Massachusetts sent militia to crush the Shaysites and the federal government dispatched troops against the Whiskey Rebels. Shaysite leaders walked to the gallows after hearing Chief Justice William Cushing pronounce ringing sentences of death, only to have the governor's carefully staged reprieve arrive at the very last moment. It was a piece of public theater that kings and their minions had been using for centuries. The strongest and most legitimate authority still had to show that it could accommodate. That tradition was already becoming outdated and within a generation the ideas of equal citizenship and organized political competition would replace it.

Even under the old order, however, the code phrase "rabble of sailors, negroes, and boys" had signified a crowd that would be firmly repressed. Mass executions of slave rebels in South Carolina in 1739 and in New York in 1712 and 1741 revealed a different sort of relationship between people who enjoyed power and people who were not supposed to have it than the one that lay behind the public theater of terror and mercy. In the new order as in the old, a rebellion that included the theme of race invited a response from authorities in which mercy would have no place.

In the year 1800 a Virginia slave named Gabriel hatched a plan for a rebellion. He was a literate blacksmith who understood his epoch. Perhaps he appreciated "the perishability of revolutionary time" and wanted to act against southern slavery before American conditions congealed. Apparently "about one thousand slaves, some mounted, armed with clubs, scythes, homemade bayonets, and a few with guns," did assemble. We do not know what they would have done, because bad weather foiled the plot and it was discovered.[13] In 1822 a free black Charleston sailor named Denmark Vesey hatched another plot. He was literate in several languages and had traveled widely. Like Gabriel, he knew that a black person did not have to be a slave. Again, as in the case of Gabriel, we do not know what he would have achieved, because a frightened slave betrayed him. His followers did collect or make hundreds of pike heads and daggers, and they made disguises. One report had it that they intended to kill anyone who opposed them. In 1832 Nathaniel Turner of Virginia planned rebellion again. Turner was a field worker, but he too could read and write. What drove him was neither awareness of the unfulfilled American Revolution nor knowledge of the outside world but rather his sense that slavery was an outrage to his living God. His plot was neither foiled nor betrayed. The slaves rose up and killed at least fifty-seven white people before militiamen captured them.[14]

All three leaders died on the gallows after public trials. So did fifteen of Gabriel's followers, thirty-seven of Vesey's, and nineteen of Turner's. Unable to contain himself, Judge Jeremiah Cobb went beyond the usual formula when he sentenced Turner: "The judgement of the Court, is that you . . . be hung by the neck until you are dead! dead! dead!"[15] It was public theater, like the near-executions of the Shaysites, but this play had no happy ending. No reprieve was expected; nor did one arrive. The slaves hanged. After the Turner rebellion there were no slave revolts of consequence until the Civil War raised the possibility that slavery itself might break up. Enslaved black Americans did not accept their situation. But active resistance had to take another form if it was to have an effect and not just be foolhardy vainglory. Much like Ganeodiyo's Seneca Indians, they faced a choice between sacrificing themselves in a grand conflagration or finding a way to cope with what they could not overthrow. Most coped with it, weakened it where they could, and waited until it became possible to do more.

Indians who turned to force against the United States had no communities behind them that needed to be terrorized into submission and then appeased with a dramatic gesture. Nor could anybody demand compensation for the loss of a Native's capacity to labor or reproduce, as a master could when the South's version of justice demanded that a slave should die. What Indians did have was land. An Indian "revolt" justified a war, and a justified war offered the very best means for taking what Indians had.

The Republic's first Indian war grew out of the Revolution's unfinished business. When British negotiators surrendered the whole area between the Appalachians and the Mississippi in 1783, western Indians called it betrayal. They had been allies of the British, they thought, and the British could not speak for them. They had not been defeated. Confident of their strength and aware of continuing British strength along the Canadian border, Indians in the country north of the Ohio River waited and considered, until the Republic moved prematurely against them. Then they went to war and in 1791 they inflicted humiliating defeats on Generals Josiah Harmar and Arthur St. Clair. Shock spread throughout the expanding settlements and back to the national government. Then, at Fallen Timbers in 1795, General Anthony Wayne avenged Harmar and St. Clair's defeat and finally "reduced Indians to subjects."

But to see "the confrontation . . . simply as a conflict between the new American state and Indian tribes misses the complexity of the relationships . . . involved." The war rearranged "organization and relationships" within the Old Northwest, but the Republic could not drive the Indians out, yet. The "middle ground" of conflicting strengths and necessary accommodation still endured.[16]

The battle of Tippecanoe in Indiana in the year 1811 was another matter. Tippecanoe grew from the prophet Tenskwatawa's attempt to redefine the terms of Indian-white engagement, and even of Indian existence. Indians lost at Tippecanoe, but their war merged into the larger dispute between Britain and the United States that became the War of 1812. In geopolitical terms, that war made little difference to anybody. The bombardment of Baltimore caused Francis Scott Key to write "The Star-Spangled Banner" while he watched from the deck of a British ship. The British captured Washington, D.C., and burned the Executive Mansion. When the Americans returned they painted the building to hide the damage, giving the White House its permanent name. There were victories and there were defeats. "We have met the enemy and they are ours"; "Don't give up the ship"; a victorious Andrew Jackson at New Orleans: these created powerful new American martial images. But they redrew no boundaries and toppled no governments. Inadvertently, perhaps, the great effect of the war was to guarantee that the United States would never take control of Canada. The Republic's Manifest Destiny would be to spread west, not north.

The war's end did mean, however, that "politically the consequence of Indians faded . . . and even their economic consequence declined with the fur trade." When the Kickapoo nation joined the British in 1812, the Republic's soldiers "destroyed" their "towns and stores" in Illinois. In 1813 American troops found "Kickapoo Town rebuilt and cornfields replanted," so "they burned summerhouses, huts, and maize." Meanwhile "the territorial legislature established a bounty of fifty dollars for the scalp of any Indian—man, woman, or child—who entered an American settlement with 'murderous intent.'" Kickapoos and white America came to blows for the last time in 1832, when the Indians crossed back from Iowa to retake their Illinois home. The result was "the slaughter and mutilation of Indian men, women, and children at Bad Axe River." This was not a conflict of position or politics or commerce or principle; it was "a war of extirpation."[17] Indian nations had a place on the "middle ground" but none in the "Great West."[18]

Indians in the South faced a different situation. West Florida had become a British possession in 1763, but the end of the Revolution returned it to Spain. The Louisiana Purchase meant that after 1803 New Orleans belonged to the United States. Creeks, Seminoles, Cherokees, Chickasaws, and Choctaws were under pressure not just from the east but from the north and west as well. Both Cherokees and Choctaws understood that war was a hopeless venture. Creeks thought otherwise, driven by their own discontent and tempted by Tecumseh to enter his northwestern confederacy. Cherokees who went to the Creek capital to hear Tecumseh speak were "dismayed to hear the message" he brought. They realized that dances, war clubs, and slaughtering cattle would not frighten whites off or deflect their bullets.[19]

But though the Creeks did accept Tecumseh's call to war, they were not naive. Other emissaries also visited them and they knew that the British wanted to recover Florida, which Spain still held. Though the main fighting of the War of 1812 took place along the Great Lakes, the British did establish a military presence all along the Gulf coast, near Creek country. The larger war proved too far away and too inconsequential to aid the Indians, however. The Creeks met massive defeat at Horseshoe Bend at the hands of Tennessee volunteers under Andrew Jackson, aided by both Cherokees and Choctaws. They accepted the end of their own war at the Treaty of Fort Jackson and "one of the greatest land rushes in the history of the American frontier" resulted. Alabama's white and black population shot from 9,000 in 1810 to 144,000 in 1820.[20] As in the Northwest, there was simply no compatibility between what white people wanted and the presence of Indians in numbers that counted, let alone the persistence of Indian ways.

Ironically, it was "acculturated" Creeks in western Georgia rather than traditional ones in more remote Alabama who faced the greatest immediate pressure. These "Lower Creeks" did not heed Tecumseh or fight on the British side. After the Revolution, the half-Creek, half-Scottish leader Alexander McGillivray had tried to lead them toward nationhood in the European sense by creating central authority over their village world. Nonetheless, "the trend toward Creek centralization was just that: a trend, more of a hope than a reality." As far as Georgia was concerned, all Indians had to depart, including these Creeks. The Georgia government warned them that "should a militia army be marched into the Indian territory, there is reason to apprehend that 'humanity' would not be inscribed on its banners."[21]

What Creeks attempted, Cherokees got close to achieving. They sought their own Cherokee Republic, perhaps to exist autonomously, perhaps to take full part in American life. Cherokees had no intention of gradually disappearing as their women married whites, their men died childless, and their children's skins grew pale. They wanted to remain a distinctive people. Like Creeks, they had to confront the determination of Georgia that there would be no Indian communities at all within the state's boundaries.

Cherokees were facing a change in the whole idea of American nationality. The Republic was abandoning its founding premise that "an American was a rational, civilized, more or less Christian citizen who was committed to republican ideology and to the rising greatness of the United States." Instead, it was adopting the view "that there was a hierarchy of races" and that "the new [white] race of Americans" was "superior to all others." Now "Americans discovered who they were by deciding who they were not, and those who were deciding were not black Africans or red Indians; this was a white man's country." The Cherokees had to go, just because of what they were.[22]

Pressure to expel Indians came from pioneers, states, and the central government. British negotiators tried to protect Indians who had been their allies as they ended the War of 1812. American diplomats would have none of it. Whites had "needed" Indian land before, to grow tobacco, rice, or wheat, or simply to live upon it their own way. Now Cherokee, Creek, Chickasaw, and Choctaw land was "needed" to appease the world's demand for cotton, which whites knew they could satisfy at great profit to themselves. Creeks, particularly, had already made a separate peace and become a wholly subject people. The long, long Indian strategy of using diplomacy to win what war could not achieve had reached its end.

After the war the administrations of James Monroe (1817–25) and John Quincy Adams (1825–29) kept pressing the southern tribes to withdraw. Whites would not mingle no matter what Indians did to adapt, even if they had sided with the Republic in war. Beyond the Mississippi lay "empty" wilderness that eastern Indians could make their own. By this time the assumption that the two races could not mingle was probably true, because whites intended to have it so. The assumption that the land beyond the Mississippi was empty was not true at all.

Nonetheless, the Monroe and Adams administrations still insisted that Indians had to consent to removal. Consent could be manufactured and there were many ways to do it, including splitting the leadership, taking advantage of Indian factionalism, and outright bribery. All these were done, and all had their effect. Andrew Jackson wanted to force "a cession of the whole area" of Cherokee land called the "Creek Path," without reference to the Cherokee National Council, which alone had constitutional power to negotiate. To him the Indians were "not aliens" but rather "the real subjects of the United States." It was an "absurdity" to negotiate with them by treaty as if they were French or English. The only task was to render them truly subject and force them out.[23]

Jackson would have become President in 1825 if the popular vote had created the electoral college majority it justified. With four candidates in the field, there was no electoral majority. After a long dispute in the House of Representatives, John Quincy Adams became President. Adams agreed with removing the Cherokees, and his chosen means was to make a treaty with other Cherokees who had already emigrated to Arkansas. Under Cherokee law the migrants had forfeited membership in the nation, but it did not matter to the white treaty makers. Arkansas was on the way to statehood and pressure was building there for the migrants to go still farther west. The western Cherokees exchanged their Arkansas land for 7,000,000 acres that were still more remote. Eastern Cherokees could join this new emigration, each receiving "a good Rifle, a Blanket, a Kettle, and five pounds of tobacco" as "just compensation" for the fertile soil, dense forests, and rich mineral deposits, including gold, that they would be giving up. Heads of families would receive $10 for each individual they took west as well. A campaign for enrollments met little success, partly because of Cherokee resistance, partly because the Adams administration was waning as the election of 1828 approached.[24]

Andrew Jackson finally became President in 1829 and he was more blunt. An act of Congress would send all Indians, North and South, beyond the Mississippi. Jackson was from Tennessee and was well acquainted with Alabama, Mississippi, and Louisiana; he had the South foremost in his mind. What he wanted became law in 1830.

In principle the Indian Removal Act continued the policies of the past. Tribes were recognized as legal entities; the President could "solemnly . . . assure . . . secure and guarantee" a "tribe or nation's" tenure upon its new western land. But the new grants would not give the absolute freehold that whites received when they bought public land. If "the Indians become extinct" a grant would "revert to the United-States."[25] Despite Jackson's own sense of the "absurdity" of Indian treaties, they would continue to be made for another four decades. But by the end of his presidency in 1837 the eastern Indians were virtually gone into what is now Oklahoma. Where they survived it was because they hid, as did some Cherokees in the depths of the Great Smoky Mountains in western North Carolina, or because they became complete dependents, like Catawbas in South Carolina, or because, like the New York Iroquois, they had reservation lands under state laws that they did not let go.

[III]

The achievement of Jackson's goal came not directly from him or from the Indian Removal Act but rather from confrontation between Georgia and the United States Supreme Court. Taking on the issue of sovereignty that the Cherokees posed, Georgia passed a law to extinguish tribal self-government and seize Indian lands beyond bare individual freeholds. Both Cherokee political authority and communal land were to be ended. Cherokees who remained would not be able to testify against a white, which meant they would have no legal redress against murder, assault, rape, or theft, unless a white saw the crime and would testify for them. Long before, toward the end of the seventeenth century, colonial Virginia had passed a similar law in regard to black people. It had been one of the major mileposts as Virginia changed from a society that had black servants within it to a society based fundamentally upon black enslavement.

The Cherokees responded in perfect American style. They brought a federal lawsuit, thus turning a political and social problem into a legal one. Their premise was that as an organized political society they enjoyed corporate standing under the Constitution, in the same manner as an American state or a foreign nation. They could sue Georgia on their own behalf. The case reached the Supreme Court, and in March 1831 Chief Justice John Marshall expressed great concern. Cherokee lands had been "assured . . . by the United States in solemn treaties repeatedly made and still in force. . . . A case better calculated [to win the Court's sympathy] can scarcely be imagined. A people once numerous, powerful, and truly independent . . . have yielded their lands . . . until they retain no more . . . than is deemed necessary to their comfortable subsistence. To preserve this remnant, the present application is made."

Marshall knew, however, that a decision for the Cherokees might be unenforceable—because of Georgia's own stance and President Jackson's hostility, because Georgia's neighbor South Carolina was in quasi-rebellion on a different issue, and because Marshall had campaigned against Jackson. The Chief Justice had spent three decades building up the Court's power. He had any politician's realistic sense that power deployed to no effect becomes power lost. He ended the dilemma by denying that Indian nations enjoyed standing under federal law. They were "domestic dependent nations," whose "relation to the United States resembles that of a ward to his guardian." "They look to our government for protection," Marshall wrote, and they "rely upon its kindness and its power; appeal to it for relief of their wants; and address the president as their great father." Nobody expected the "great father" to give the Cherokees aid; neither would they get it from the Court. The Cherokees were not citizens of anything that counted. It might be "true" that they had "rights," but the Supreme Court was "not the tribunal in which those rights are to be asserted." The injunction they sought was denied and the Cherokees were left to their fate.[26] Writing as the matter was unfolding, an outraged Alexis de Tocqueville summed up what many people thought that fate would be:

No doubt within a few years that same white population which is now pressing around them will again be on their tracks in the solitudes of Arkansas; they will suffer again from the same ills without the same remedies; and because sooner or later there will be no land left for them, their only refuge will be the grave.[27]

Cherokee Nation v. *State of Georgia* did not deny that Indians belonged to the United States. It simply stated that they belonged to it as subjects, not citizens. Twenty-six years later, in 1857, the Supreme Court again considered the problem of belonging in *Dred Scott* v. *Sandford*. Scott's master took him from Missouri into the free state of Illinois in 1834 and then into the free territory of Minnesota. It took twenty-three years for Scott's legal claim that his slavery was ended by his being taken to free territory with his master's consent to reach the Supreme Court. The master Scott sued was in fact a New Yorker, although he claimed ownership of Scott under Missouri law. Scott claimed federal standing to sue on the ground that he, a supposedly free Missourian, and the master were citizens of different states.

The goal was to resolve a large debate within northern antislavery. One group of abolitionists, centered on William Lloyd Garrison and Wendell Phillips, was convinced that American institutions were fundamentally tainted by slavery and that no political road could lead to slavery's end. The Constitution was "a covenant with death and an agreement with hell." The other group regarded American institutions as prejudiced toward freedom, not slavery. In the 1850s its greatest spokesman was the former slave Frederick Douglass. Despite asking the bitter question "What to the slave is your fourth of July?" in his greatest speech, Douglass wanted to believe that American institutions could work. A decision for Scott would establish the point.

When he finally decided the case, Chief Justice Roger B. Taney relied heavily on English precedent. He might have used it to avoid the case's implications altogether, noting that until West Indies slavery ended, a slave who won emancipation by entering England could be reenslaved where slavery did exist. Scott had returned to Missouri, and that might have closed the issue.

Taney, however, chose to address the whole problem posed by black people's presence within the Republic. He made a ritual bow to the plight of "that unfortunate race," but his fundamental position was that "neither the class of persons who had been imported as slaves, nor their descendants, whether they had become free or not, were acknowledged . . . as a part of the people" when the United States formed itself. Instead, they were "regarded as beings of an inferior order . . . and so far inferior, that they had no rights which the white man was bound to respect." This, Taney wrote, was a matter of "historical facts." Therefore no black person, free or slave, was part of the "posterity" for whom the Constitution was created. A white person might acquire "the personal rights and privileges guaranteed to citizens . . . by birthright or otherwise." People who stemmed from Africa, however, "were not intended to be embraced, in this new political family which the Constitution brought into existence, but were intended to be excluded from it." Scott was not a citizen of Missouri, the United States, or anywhere else. Like the Cherokees, he and his people had no claim to membership in the Republic or protection from its laws.[28]

One way to consider the Dred Scott case is to see it as a way point on the Republic's self-destructive journey to civil war. Another is to probe the history lesson that Taney tried to draw. As law and precedent stood, he had reason for his opinion. Since the naturalization act of 1790, public authorities had been tightening the legal criteria of American identity in one dimension while they loosened access to it in another. In practically any other society, public identity might not have proven a problem. Naturalization was a rare procedure that transferred allegiance to a new sovereign and claimed that sovereign's protection. The terms of American belonging were not the same. If the infant United States defined itself at all, it was not racially but rather in language that was ideological, and in practice that could be open-ended. Free black men and women were voting in New Jersey, and free black men were voting in New York, Pennsylvania, Delaware, Maryland, and North Carolina. A black Marylander ran for a seat in his state's house of delegates in 1792. He lost the election, but nobody denied him the right to try.[29]

Nor were Indians and blacks the only nineteenth-century Americans who were different from the Republic's white, overwhelmingly Protestant founders. The quarter century between *Cherokee Nation* and *Dred Scott* saw enormous Catholic immigration. Immediately after independence some states excluded any non-Protestant from voting and public office. If those laws showed the founders' intent, latter-day immigrants had no claim on political rights unless they were or became Protestant. Yet the Republic's doors remained wide open to newcomers and anti-Catholic legislation gradually died. White immigrants' naturalization as Americans became a right they could claim under law, not a rare favor granted by a sovereign to a would-be subject. American citizenship was open-ended and expandable, for European immigrants at least.

But for Californios excluded from the goldfields or for Indians and black people excluded from protection of the law, it was otherwise. They had been born under American jurisdiction or brought under it against their will and they violated the Republic's laws at their peril. They had no place else to go. By mid-century the clash between these subject people's situation and the freedom of its white citizens was glaring. Citizenship had replaced subjection as the dominant metaphor for American society. The attractiveness of the ideal was undeniable. That is why Californios, Nuevomejicanos, and Tejanos, British, Irish, and German immigrants, Dred Scott, and, in their special way, the organized, historical, self-constituted community of Cherokees laid claim to it. They all understood that citizenship could be a powerful tool as they tried to cope with their own plights. In the old order of formal and fundamental inequality, the status of subject had been such a tool as well. In Great Britain any subject, even the lowest, could claim the king's protection, exercised through his courts.

The old order was gone. With it was gone the age-old understanding that it was God's will for some to be "highe and eminent in power and dignitie; others meane and in subjeccion."[30] The condition of being an unwilling, unequal subject was not gone at all. White women understood that point; in both law and practice most remained subject to fathers and husbands. They were excluded from the polls and public office. Their rights to property remained limited. Their chances of losing child custody should there be a divorce were very high. Still, they at least had a

claim to standing under law, which meant they could claim both belonging and protection. For Indians, for black people both free and slave,
and for the people who had been taken from Mexico, the subjection was
far more complete. In the new order of equality among all citizens, to
be merely a subject of the sovereign American people was to be lower
and to have fewer rights than any Briton had in relation to the king.

[IV]

Six decades elapsed between the appointment of John Marshall as Chief
Justice and the end of his successor Taney's tenure. Their time in office
spanned the epoch from John Adams to Abraham Lincoln. Each Chief
Justice was a towering figure in American jurisprudence. *Cherokee Nation*
and *Dred Scott* were only two of the many important cases that the Supreme Court decided while they presided over it.

The power that Marshall and Taney gathered unto the Court realized
in practice what Thomas Paine had proposed as far back as *Common Sense*:
that the law itself be ceremoniously crowned. Law rather than any living
person should be treated with the public reverence due a king. During
the years of Marshall and Taney, law did flourish in the United States,
both as a political fact and as a social phenomenon. The handful of men
who served on the highest American bench were an enormous influence
on the development of American law. The law itself, meaning statutes,
received traditions, precedents, the decisions of judges, and the development of a self-conscious legal profession, influenced the pattern of
American society even more. We cannot understand the Republic's development without considering the law as a social entity in its own right.

The Revolution did not break the legal traditions that English colonists had brought with them. There would be no American *Code Napo-
léon*, completely redefining the terms of human relations. The first draft
of the Articles of Confederation proposed in 1776 that each "Colony
shall retain and enjoy as much of its present Laws, Rights and Customs,
as it may think fit."[31] Several of the original thirteen states specifically
continued English law. In the words of New York's constitution of 1777,
"such parts of the common law of England, and of the statute law of
England and Great-Britain, and of the acts of the legislature of the colony
of New-York" that were in effect on April 1, 1775, "shall be and continue the law of this state."[32] Anticipating the inadequacy of statutes
and the need to interpret traditional "Rights and Customs," New York

created a chancellorship as a separate judicial office that would deal with cases in equity, much as did the Lord Chancellor of England.

Nonetheless, American law was about to enter a period of astonishing creativity, building on what was happening in England but going in directions of its own. By the eve of independence English law was moving away from the notion that law should express what is absolutely right and toward the position that law just expresses what the government decides. Sir William Blackstone argued the point in his *Commentaries* on English law and American thinkers echoed it. To Justice James Wilson in 1790, "in every state, there must be somewhere a power supreme, arbitrary, absolute, and uncontrollable." Yet Wilson, perhaps the foremost legal thinker of the Revolutionary generation, drew back from Blackstone's full implications. Long experience, not mere will, was the ultimate test of what a government might enact or forbid. Carried to its logical conclusion, this meant that many specific customs, statutes, and practices, not a single constitution, comprised the land's supreme law. This was exactly how the ancient, unwritten British constitution might have been defined. Wilson had returned to the intellectual impasse of trying to impose limits on an absolutely sovereign authority that the British had forced upon the white colonists in 1765.

The state and federal constitutions represented massive acts of will by "one people" that had declared itself to be its own sovereign. In this sense, the documents were more in accord with Blackstone than with Wilson. They were also in accord with the development of a complex American society. In practical terms, local custom might be enough to govern a society that dealt only intermittently with the outside world, as many colonial-era communities had done. Custom could not cope with the needs of a society that was organized around relationships between strangers at long distance, as the United States was fast becoming. Hence the great importance of the Constitution's assertion of its own supremacy.

But the Constitution also harked back to another legal tradition. This held not that law was simply the will of the sovereign but rather that there is a higher law which is right because it is right and against which other laws can be measured. The time when higher law could be found in either divine revelation or long-standing custom clearly was over. But it could be found in this special, solemn expression of sovereign will that was a written American constitution. In effect, two separate traditions —of higher law that was right because it was right and of positive law that was right because the sovereign wished it to be so—proved able to merge in American practice. Adopting what pre-Blackstone English legal thinkers had regarded as the function of the High Court of Parliament, the Supreme Court would endeavor to "speak" the rightfulness of American law in terms of the Constitution (*jus dicere*), not to "make" law. Because all American law became subject in principle to the Court's review it could all be taken as "spoken" in the old sense of recognizable rightfulness, as well as "made" in the new sense of power doing what it chose. It would not be the case (as Blackstone thought was true of Parliament) that "if the parliament will positively enact a thing to be done which is unreasonable, I know of no power that can control it."[33]

In the same year that the federal Constitution was written New York State set out to codify its own statutes. Bill after bill in that year's legislative session was presented by the special committee that had been given the task. It was one of a number of projects to codify and clarify legislation at the state legislature. It satisfied a growing sense among American legislators that certainty and predictability were to be preferred to the semi-chaos that had characterized much colonial law and revolutionary practice.[34]

The abstract idea of constitutionalism and the project of codifying and rationalizing old laws provided the first two themes in the extended discussion of the relationship between law and society that began. Constitutional law as understood in the Supreme Court of Marshall and Taney provided the third theme in this legal canon. The fourth, perhaps the most immediately important for structuring development and guiding relationships, was shaped not so much in legislatures or before the Supreme Court as in ordinary, day-to-day courts of law as they dealt with one mundane case after another.

When Justice Wilson delivered his *Lectures on Law* in Philadelphia in 1791 he was imitating Blackstone and seeking to establish law as a subject for formal, academic debate. Chancellor James Kent of New York State did much the same when he set out to make his own *Commentaries* upon American law, first published in 1826. One consequence was to start transforming legal training from mere apprenticeship in a working practice into formal tuition in a law school, particularly the one that Tapping Reeve established in Litchfield, Connecticut. Another consequence was to change the makeup of American courtrooms. They ceased to be places where an honored layman presided while a lay jury determined both matters of law and matters of fact. Instead, courts became places where trained members of a professional elite decided the law on the basis of statute and precedent, while juries determined facts alone.

The professionalization of the bench and bar was of a piece with a larger professionalization that was underway in other fields. The founding of the Rensselaer Polytechnic Institute to train engineers in Troy, New York, in 1824 was as important a sign of the direction of American society as Justice Wilson's lectures, Chancellor Kent's commentaries, or the founding of the Litchfield Law School. Nonetheless, the legal profession placed itself right at the heart of defining the terms of American social and economic relations. This meant defining the necessarily uneven terms under which people who enjoyed formal legal equality would be members of American society.

The fundamental issue in most nineteenth-century courtrooms was property. How the United States acquired the vast landed property that its borders enclosed was a matter of diplomacy and war, decided for the most part within the presidency. How it divided that property among its citizens was a matter of civil policy, worked out in Congress and the state legislatures. How property holders were to relate to one another became a matter for the courts.

Throughout their history, white Americans have valued private property. What courts began deciding about the use of property marked a fundamental shift in what private property meant. The shift was by no means as great as the destruction of Indian notions of property in favor of white ones or, after the Civil War, abandoning the idea that some human beings could be the property of others. Nonetheless, the shift was essential to American society's enormous "release of energy" during the nineteenth century.

Legal historians have probed this problem deeply. Naturally, they have disagreed.[35] A few points do seem clear. One is that the law became a professional matter that required mastering a great deal of special knowledge, which amounted to property itself. A second is that both material and intellectual property shifted from being understood as the fundamental basis for membership in an ongoing community to being the basis for a process of ongoing change. A legal doctrine that gave primacy to the "quiet enjoyment" of property gave way to a doctrine holding that the demands of the future should take precedence over memories of the past or a desire to stay the same. If there had to be a choice between the developer and the owner, the developer would win. The third change was the "triumph of contract." By the middle of the nineteenth century the idea that contracts could be measured against general standards of rightness had given way to the idea that their validity depended on no more than the consent of the parties involved.

Finally, jurists changed the legal doctrine of tort in a way that significantly modified how property was understood. A tort is a noncriminal wrong that someone has suffered at another's hands. As the demands of technological change on material resources increased, the chances of committing a tort increased as well. Flooding the fields above a dam in order to power a mill; flooding fields and towns below should the dam break; diverting water that historically had been used by others; hot ashes from a passing train setting fire to a standing crop: all these are possible examples. Under the concept of law that was emerging, the injured party did not necessarily qualify for a legal remedy. If that party's "quiet enjoyment" of property was impaired, it might be the necessary price for the other party's creative use of what belonged to them. Only if there was demonstrable negligence did the injured party have grounds to claim compensation. There was no right, as custom once had allowed, to take direct action in order to end such "nuisances" altogether. In the political realm now there was no difference between the man who owned the dam and the man whose fields it flooded. In the economic realm each was equally free to do as he chose with what was his. But if the two came into conflict, the dam owner and what he stood for would win.[36]

Where the law is king, all citizens are equally subject to it, or so republican thinking runs. The contrast between British colonial belonging (in terms of ordered subjection) and American republican belonging (in terms of open citizenship) was very real. As much as any other element in the life of the young Republic, that contrast helps to explain both the extent and the tone of surging change that was American society's most visible characteristic. In particular, the contrast helps us to understand how the United States came to be marked not only by republican citizenship but also by its distinctive democratic capitalism, unique in the nineteenth-century world. The contrast is particularly strong in comparison to England, where class division proved permanently fixed. There the symbols of nationality are also the symbols of a social order that still expresses a fundamental belief in inequality. In the United States the equivalent symbols can express a mindless patriotism, but they can also express a genuine sense of possibility, openness, and legitimate outrage if these are thwarted.[37]

We should not be too smug, however, in our reading of the theme of American inclusion. The acquisitive and individualistic society that took shape in the early United States was genuinely popular, which is part of what made the Republic's exclusion of people who belonged to it as possessions rather than members seem so glaring, even then. Had American rhetoric not soared so high, perhaps, the failures would not seem so profound.

It is mere cliché to dismiss nineteenth-century America's claim that it was a democracy simply on the ground of what it did not do. It is a mere truism to suggest that in America the line of race cuts in the same way that the line of social class cuts elsewhere. What seems much more worthy of note is that in the young United States the category of race, defined by skin and culture, the category of class, defined by one's place in the order of production and exchange, the category of gender, springing from an accident of conception, and the category of citizenship that guaranteed political participation and access to the law all became hopelessly intertwined. By the century's second quarter race was deemed enough to justify absolute exclusion. Both gender and what Americans now call ethnicity—being a Californio in Los Angeles or Irish in Boston—seemed to justify partial exclusion in practical terms, if not in the absolute terms laid down in *Cherokee Nation* and *Dred Scott*.

In the year 1850, the American Republic was triumphant, but its triumph had a very real quality of being hollow. Public discussion in the decades before and after that date turned less and less on the triumph and more and more on the hollowness, on the yawning, widening gap between what the Republic proclaimed itself to be and what many different people were coming to feel that it actually was. It was a contradiction not to be endured.

PART THREE

A HOUSE BURST ASUNDER

Where another man, acting for the sake of so many "square feet of land" declaims about "the struggle for an idea," Lincoln, even when he is acting for the sake of an idea, speaks only in terms of "square feet of land." Indecisively, against his will, he reluctantly performs the bravura aria of his role as though asking pardon for the fact that circumstances are forcing him to "play the hero." The most formidable decrees which he hurls against the enemy . . . resemble—as the author intends them to—ordinary summonses sent by one lawyer to another on the opposing side. . . . And this is the character the recent Proclamation bears—the most important document of American history since the founding of the Union, a document that breaks away from the old American Constitution —Lincoln's manifesto on the abolition of slavery. . . . Truly in our day, when every little happening on this side of the Atlantic assumes an air of melodramatic portent, is there no meaning in the fact that everything of significance taking shape in the New World makes its appearence in such everyday form? . . . Never yet has the New World scored a greater victory than in this instance, through its demonstration that, thanks to its political and social organization, ordinary people of good will can carry out tasks which the Old World would have to have a hero to accomplish.

—KARL MARX

CHAPTER 9

THE CRISIS OF
TRIUMPHANT DEMOCRACY

D URING the quarter century after 1825 it seemed that the United States had developed a permanent way of life. The whole continent (south of Canada) lay open to Americans' Manifest Destiny of making it theirs. They would build both an "empire" of political liberty and a "fee-simple kingdom" of absolute private property.[1] The problem of class seemed solved. A free market for land necessarily meant that both vast holdings and small to middling ones would develop and that some people would have no property at all. But without feudal restrictions land could always be sold and holdings broken up, so there would be no European-style lordship and peasantry. In an earlier day the landless would have been disqualified from citizenship, because a man needed a stake in his community to participate in its affairs. Now the notions of citizenship and property holding were divorced. The lines that severed full participants from the rest were cut by gender and race. To most white men those divisions seemed no more than what nature intended.[2]

Strictly political problems seemed solved as well. The founding states and new ones would be equal partners, without the forced subordination that tore the old British Empire apart. When Tennessee's Andrew Jackson won the presidency in 1828 power seemed to shift peacefully from the east coast to the Mississippi Valley. During Jackson's epoch citizens took gleeful delight in the "public sphere" of parades, meetings, campaigns, elections, and officeholding. The sovereign "people" of the United States were not an abstraction. They were visible everywhere, exercising the "share in the government" that Alexander Hamilton called the essence of American liberty as early as 1784.[3] Here was the "democracy in America" that Alexis de Tocqueville observed with insight and foreboding. Here, we are told, was the Revolution's final, enduring consequence.[4]

But by 1850 the fabric that had seemed so strong was stretched and frayed. The decade that followed saw it shredded by pressures it could not contain. The crisis that tore American political democracy apart emerged from the very warp and weft of democratic American society.[5]

[I]

Andrew Jackson became President in 1829 not because he was the best man but thanks to open political partisanship. By the time of his election the raw material for political parties lay all about. Even before independence voters in Pennsylvania and New York were used to choosing among competitors and some politicians were saying that partisanship was positively good.[6] During the Revolution electors learned to intervene directly to get the government they wanted, and rulers learned to respond to pressure and to yield office when they lost.[7] Conflicting interests and clashing perceptions of what the Republic ought to be cried out for organization. People still hoped that partisanship would fade. Hence Washington's condemnation of the Democratic-Republican Societies of 1794 as "self-created"; hence Jefferson's inaugural address of 1801: "we are all Republicans; we are all Federalists." Hence the phrase "era of good feelings" that is still commonly applied to the presidency of James Monroe (1817–25), when organized dispute collapsed.[8]

Monroe won the presidency with only a single dissenting vote in the electoral college. When he left office it was clear that disorganization had brought chaos, not good feelings. In 1824 no candidate had an electoral majority and the House of Representatives chose the new President. Andrew Jackson had the greatest popular support, but John Quincy Adams won a majority in the House. When Adams made Henry Clay, another trailing candidate, his Secretary of State, people thought they saw why. Jefferson, Madison, and Adams himself all had preceded Clay in the State Department and the ambitious Clay seemed Adams's intended heir apparent. It looked like a corrupt bargain to thwart "the people's" choice of Jackson.

Three years later New York State's Martin Van Buren realized what had to be done and emerged as a first-order political innovator. "Draw anew the old party lines" and substitute *"party principle* for *personal preference* as one of the leading points" was his principle. "We must always have party distinctions," he wrote, and a political union "between the planters of the South and the plain Republicans of the North" would be

"natural and beneficial to the country," not least because it would suppress conflict "between free and slaveholding states." Van Buren understood that Jackson's

> election, as the result of his military services without reference to party &
> so far as he alone is concerned scarcely to principle would be one thing.
> His election as the result of a combined and concerted effort of a political
> party, holding in the main to certain tenets and opposed to certain pre-
> vailing principles, might be another and a far different thing.[9]

Jackson won. The people could speak, but they needed organization to
direct all their voices and discontents toward one single question: who
should be President? Republicanism presumed general virtue and goodwill, but democracy needed parties.

Jackson believed in weak government. But he strengthened the presidency enormously by making himself the chief shaper of public policy.
He expelled the eastern Indians beyond the Mississippi. He faced down
South Carolina over its claim that it could "nullify" a federal law. He
used the veto to intervene directly in economic and social development.
His argument on the economy was simple, and he put it with eloquence
in 1832: "There are no necessary evils in government. Its evils exist only
in its abuses. If it would confine itself to equal protection, and, as Heaven
does its rains, shower its favors alike on the high and the low, the rich
and the poor, it would be an unqualified blessing." It was not the central
government's business to build roads or canals or to operate a bank. It
was President Jackson's business, however, to run the government.

Van Buren succeeded Jackson and served one term. Late in life he
wrote an *Inquiry into the Origin and Course of Political Parties in the United
States*.[10] By then organized parties were the norm. Over the two decades
between the towering if deeply flawed Jackson and the undistinguished
President Franklin Pierce, the Van Buren-Jackson "Democracy" and their
"Whig" opponents contended on an even basis throughout the country.
In Congress "the shrine of party" determined where a senator or representative would stand on virtually any issue. Even local elections became
intensely partisan affairs.[11]

One reason was social class, in the new sense that industrial society
was giving to it. The Democrats absorbed the urban Workingmen's parties that flourished briefly at the end of the 1820s. Democrats also
wielded a class rhetoric of producers versus parasites with great effect.[12]
But Whigs learned to use the same rhetoric and they deployed it with

devastating effect against a supposedly "aristocratic" Van Buren during the presidential campaign of 1840. The two sides differed more deeply on whether the federal government should guide economic development. But neither of the elected Whig Presidents, William Henry Harrison and Zachary Taylor, served his full term. Each was succeeded by a feckless Vice President who carried very little through, least of all an economic program. Henry Clay was the only Whig politician with a real program, which he called "the American system." But Clay never won the presidency.

The two parties did differ in ethnic, cultural, and religious appeal. By the 1830s many German and Irish Catholics were entering the country and the Democrats reached out to them. Northern Whigs became the party of native-born Protestants and they played willingly if subtly on anti-immigrant feeling.[13] Yet on issues of race and slavery the party leaders were in complete harmony. Jackson was a major slaveholder. So was the Democratic President James K. Polk. So were the Whig Presidents John Tyler, who succeeded Harrison and eventually was elected to the Confederate Congress, and Taylor. So was the perennial Whig hopeful Clay. So were both of the era's Chief Justices, the old Federalist John Marshall, appointed by John Adams, and the Democrat Roger B. Taney, named by Jackson. Each party did have a northern former President who moved toward antislavery, the Whig John Quincy Adams and the Democrat Martin Van Buren, but only after each man had left office. Some of Adams's fellow New Englanders protested when Andrew Jackson sent the Cherokees down the Trail of Tears, but President John Quincy Adams had sought the same goal. For almost all politicians of all parties, the United States was white man's country.

Democracy's triumph in the age of Jackson was hollow, for reasons at the heart of American society. The crisis of the 1850s disrupted the two parties that had given form and discipline to white democracy, and with their disruption the road to civil war lay open. In that sense the great crisis between North and South was political. But the crisis drew its terrible swift energy from the most fundamental questions of social relations, social belief, and social development.

[II]

There was no single cause for the rending of the United States. The great contradiction was between free labor and slavery, as Harriet Beecher

Stowe understood in her powerful novel of 1852, *Uncle Tom's Cabin*. Abraham Lincoln expressed the same contradiction when he sought a seat in the Senate in 1858: "A house divided against itself cannot stand. I believe this government cannot endure permanently half slave and half free."[14] Lincoln lost that election, but two years later he won the presidency with only northern support. Within the South sectional feelings began hardening as early as 1820, when Missouri sought admission to the Union as a slave state. South Carolina tried to force the issue when it "nullified" the 1828 federal tariff. Yet the Tennessee slaveholder who was President confronted the Carolinians in the name of "our federal union" which "must be preserved."[15] The time was not ripe for white Southerners to stand together.

Southern cotton was northern industry's basic raw material, which provided ample reason to see the sections as not divided at all. Most politicians of both parties agreed, and while either Democrats or Whigs retained power the crisis could be put off. Slavery was a necessary cause of the Union's near-destruction. Destroying slavery instead of the Union was the Civil War era's great achievement. By itself, however, the slavery question could not disrupt the white democratic consensus. For that to happen a whole range of issues had to intersect.

Black Americans' opposition to slavery; a growing sense among northern whites, especially women, that moral people could make the world better; gender as a separate public issue; the tensions of class; white Southerners' increasing awareness of their difference from the North and Europe; the problems of conquering new territory; the large issue of what American liberty and equality meant: all these fed into the Republic's ordeal. More and more they intertwined until only one question remained to answer: could the Union survive?

[III]

African slaves showed their "fondness for freedom" throughout the history of enslavement, a point that whites appreciated from the beginning.[16] The original American Revolution pointed black Americans toward concerted attack upon what bound them. That did not have to mean armed insurrection. The bloody repression of the Gabriel and Denmark Vesey conspiracies and the Nat Turner insurrection showed that outright rebellion led to death. Whites had the weapons, the laws, the courts, the gallows, and the will to use them. For anybody who did not court martyrdom, another path would have to be followed. That path began in the communities that African-Americans built up, whether they were free or slave.

When the roughly 27,000 white people of Charleston, South Carolina, stood poised in 1861 to open war against the North, 21,400 black people dwelt among them. About 3,700 were free. Black Charlestonians had generated institutions of their own. They had African Methodist churches, a Brown Fellowship Society and a Friendly Moralist Society for people of light color, and a Humane Brotherhood for "dark" men. There were free black people who owned other blacks. Some of the people they held were spouses and children whom the "owners" were buying into freedom. Some were simply slaves.

Among the Charleston free black community's organizations was the Clionian Debating Society, which flourished between 1847 and 1851 to foster "learning and mental improvement." The Clionians were self-improving artisans, reminiscent of the Junto that Benjamin Franklin had organized in Philadelphia a century before. They argued about capital punishment, ancient Greek law, the future of the newborn French Republic of 1848, the relative merits of George Washington and Alexander the Great, and the principles of republicanism. Such people lived under immense pressure. White Charleston took every step to keep them and slaves apart and to isolate them from the North, but it was impossible. Free blacks mingled with slaves every day and "the flow of information" between them and northern black communities "never halted."

What they did against slavery had to be in secret. But we can get glimpses here and there of what linked African-Americans, whatever their condition and in defiance of the danger they faced. When black inmates of the Charleston city workhouse rebelled in 1849, one, who was a slave, chased the master from the building, calling him "Santa Anna." The reference was to the Mexican President who tried to prevent the secession of Texas from his own country and its annexation to the United States. Whether he deserved it or not, Santa Anna was a hated figure in the United States, especially in the South. That angry slave's invocation of his name offers a lightninglike flash on how people in his plight took information from the culture that surrounded them and used it for purposes of their own.[17]

The starting place for organized campaigning against slavery was among black people, in the South to the extent that it was possible and much more openly in the North.[18] The unbroken families, and the churches, fraternal societies, businesses, and neighborhoods that took

shape in northern cities, or even among free blacks in Charleston or
Mobile, were where dangerous words could be spoken, ideas developed,
and plans made. Race rioters drove black Philadelphians from the city's
celebration of independence on July 4, 1805. Obviously they could not
drive black Americans from their claim that what they endured was
wrong by America's best standards. The proof lies in how black communities made possible what had not been possible before: a militant,
determined drive to bring all slavery to an end.

Once, many people thought that freedom came to black Americans
only because white people finally brought it. Now the names of the major
black abolitionists are familiar: David Walker, Henry Highland Garnet,
Frederick Douglass, Sojourner Truth, Harriet Tubman.[19] Garnet's life
began in Maryland slavery. Subsequently it led through his family's self-
liberation and entry into the free community in New York City. The
young Garnet once watched while his father fled across rooftops to avoid
recapture. As an adult, Garnet became pastor of a black Presbyterian
church in Troy, New York, where he worked out his African-centered
ideas. He finally abandoned the United States and ended his days in
Africa.[20] Douglass's path likewise started in Maryland. While still a slave
he lost his most of his family to forced separation. With the aid of Anna
Murray, the free woman whom he married, he escaped to the North.
Like Garnet, he was a man of words, but he rejected the church and the
prospect of a pulpit, forging instead a speaking and writing career that
brought him world fame. Tubman neither sought nor won immediate
fame. Instead she quietly made journey after journey into the South and
helped slaves escape to the North. She, too, was a Marylander. The fact
that slavery was slowly disintegrating in their native state may have
helped Garnet, Douglass, and Tubman alike. So might the proximity of
the antislavery Quaker community in Philadelphia.[21]

These now-famous figures did not stand alone. Black communities
gave them shelter when they escaped, heard Garnet preach, and attended
Douglass's meetings and bought his newspaper. The great assault on
slavery started among the Americans who had the most to gain from
destroying it.[22]

For their goal to be won, however, there would have to be a revolution.
The revolution of 1776 had seen the collapse and replacement of the
institutions and principles of public authority among people who already
enjoyed personal freedom. It had opened the way for them to impose
their mark upon the continent. This new revolution would have to end
the entire southern social order. The destruction of the principle of mon-

archy within America had marked one social change. The destruction of slavery would mark another, but it would mean defeating forces far stronger and far more committed than any King George could ever have mustered.

Great revolutions do not happen because of just one group, whatever its grievances. In the words of one political scientist, "it takes more than one revolutionary group to make a revolution . . . one social group can be responsible for a coup, a riot, or a revolt, but only a combination of groups can produce a revolution."[23] Outnumbered, for the most part denied the vote, the legal system stacked against them, and certainly outgunned, African-Americans needed allies. In growing numbers they found them, until a coalition of militant abolitionists and more practical politicians took shape, able to force the issue onto the national agenda. Given slavery's social strength and economic and political power, given the prevailing racism, the change could not, perhaps, have happened any other way. What the antislavery coalition achieved was enormous. The coalition contained its own fault lines. They present one reason why the great coalition against slavery accomplished no more than it did, and why the end of slavery did not usher in the millennium of human perfection that slavery's more romantic opponents expected to see.

The starting place in the search for allies was in the revolutionary generation that was dying out during the years that spanned the Missouri Compromise, the Denmark Vesey conspiracy, the South Carolina nullification crisis, and the Nat Turner rebellion. The problem of slavery was perfectly apparent. On July 4, 1827, gradual emancipation finished its work in New York. The end of slavery was approaching in Connecticut as well, even though there would still be a few hundred slaves in New Jersey as late as 1850. But the manumission societies that had formed in the 1780s were moribund in the South and torpid in the North. Quakers had retreated into isolation from the world. The leading white antislavery element during the 1820s was a well-organized movement to colonize free black people in Africa. Prominent Southerners like Thomas Jefferson, James Madison, and Henry Clay supported colonization and Madison was the American Colonization Society's president. The idea of colonizing free black people was perfectly congruent with what Andrew Jackson imposed on the eastern Indians. Colonization and removal alike assumed that white Americans and people of color could not live together as equals.

Whether or not whites intended it, colonization addressed the fundamental problem of black American identity. Henry Highland Garnet saw that problem clearly from his Hudson Valley pulpit. Long after slavery, W. E. B. Du Bois pointed it out again with his notion that black Americans have a dual identity from which they cannot escape.[24] Where was home, in an Africa to which there might be a return or on the Atlantic's western shore? The contrasting choices of Garnet and Du Bois, who did return to Africa, and of Frederick Douglass, Booker T. Washington, Martin Luther King, Jr., and Malcolm X, who all came to identify themselves as American, show the possible answers.

A saying popular among slaves—"Take root there [wherever a person was] or nowhere"—may suggest how most saw the matter.[25] The American Colonization Society was an organization of whites who proposed to "aid" blacks, not black people doing things for themselves. Free black people proved very reluctant to migrate, unless it was to Canada to prevent recapture. We can get a sense of colonization's sheer impracticality simply from the numbers involved. The legal slave trade took about 110 years to bring approximately 360,000 Africans to North America. The first great wave of European immigration after independence, from 1820 to 1860, took four decades to bring 5,540,000 people. In 1830, when the colonization movement was at its most powerful and white immigration was about to accelerate rapidly, there were more than 2,300,000 black people in the United States, free and slave. Clearly, colonization was a hopeless venture either for the purpose of freeing the slaves or for freeing white Americans from the presence of black ones. Nor did anyone consider that whatever countries where former slaves might be sent might not be able—or willing—to deal with such a massive migration, any more than trans-Mississippi Indians wanted to give up their land in favor of the tribes Andrew Jackson expelled from the East.

The mass departure of black people did remain a live subject until slavery's end. Harriet Beecher Stowe considered it in *Uncle Tom's Cabin*. Abraham Lincoln considered it too as a rising politician and even as President. At the end of the 1820s another serious possibility emerged among white opponents of slavery: direct and immediate emancipation leading to full equality. This rested on two assumptions. One was that African-Americans belonged in the United States and nowhere else. The other was that there could be no compromise with slavery because it was essentially evil. There could be no delayed emancipation, no drawn-out "apprenticeship," no waiting for demography to do its slow work.[26]

This position became firmly associated with the white abolitionist William Lloyd Garrison. From the time he founded his newspaper *The*

Liberator in 1831 until slavery ended, Garrison poured his life into the cause. He became synonymous not only with "immediatism" but also with three other positions. He adopted a radical pacifism that would not crack until the stated northern purpose in the Civil War shifted from merely preserving the Union to destroying slavery. Believing that American public life was fundamentally tainted by slavery, he saw no point in political participation. He concluded that women had as good a right as men to take a full, public part in antislavery work and in the world.[27]

Garrison was one of a group of white men who made themselves highly visible in the antislavery crusade after 1830. Wendell Phillips, the brothers Lewis and Arthur Tappan, Gerrit Smith, Elisha P. Lovejoy, and Alton Parker are only a few of the others. Black abolitionists David Walker, Frederick Douglass, Henry Highland Garnet, and Harriet Tubman emerged from a larger community, and white crusaders also had a constituency. Garrison promised when he began *The Liberator* that he would "be heard." Both his printed voice within the paper's pages and his speeches at public meetings found their first audience among black people. When whites began to rally to abolitionism in numbers that counted, most were women.

Again, familiar names make the point. The roll call of antislavery leaders would be just as incomplete without Sarah and Angelina Grimké, Lucretia Coffin Mott, Lucy Stone, Abby Kelley, Susan B. Anthony, and Elizabeth Cady Stanton as it would without Douglass and Tubman, or Garrison and Phillips. Except for the Grimké sisters from South Carolina, these women were middle-class northern Protestants. Many pressures impelled them into the public sphere. One was a tradition of women's education and right to act publicly that reached to the revolutionary era. Elizabeth Cady of Johnstown, New York, was the granddaughter of a revolutionary leader. She got the best education an American girl of her time could have at Emma Hart Willard's Troy Female Seminary. She wanted desperately to follow her brother to Union College. She could not. He died young, and it was her name that became famous.

William Lloyd Garrison and Elizabeth Cady Stanton became strong critics of orthodox organized religion. Nonetheless, Evangelical Protestantism underpinned both abolitionism and the later women's movement. One reason was its profound sense that evil had to be confronted, not endured. Another was religion's "feminization," as women became the people most likely to do the church's work.[28] When the Grimké sisters emerged in 1836 as antislavery agitators in the North, a scandalized Congregational ministry of Massachusetts tried to stop them, but it failed. It was a sign of how power was shifting.[29] This change in the church emerged from a growing separation between a male middle-class world of work and a female middle-class world of domesticity. Middle-class women began to regard American cities as places that needed to be domesticated. When Utica, New York, was still called Whitestown, a Female Charitable Society took shape and other groups followed.[30] The New York City Tract Society and the Female Moral Reform Society there strove valiantly but with no great effect to bring the Bible into tenements and to root out prostitution.[31] In Rockdale, Pennsylvania, the "sisterhood" of factory owners' wives and daughters put themselves into so strong a cultural position that they masked the community's tensions in the name of "Christian capitalism."[32]

An army of women emerged from this matrix during the 1830s and set out to bring slavery to its end. At first they thought moral suasion would be enough, a point articulated most forcefully in Angelina Grimké's *Appeal to the Christian Women of the South*.[33] In 1835 and 1836 women sent so many antislavery petitions to Congress that it refused to heed them, commanding that they simply "lie upon the table" for members' perusal if they chose. But this "gag rule" only confirmed Garrison's indictment of the American political system as being fundamentally tainted by slavery. In 1839 the issue of women's active participation split the American Anti-Slavery Society into two groups. The next year a world antislavery congress in London not unexpectedly refused to seat American female delegates. Lucretia Coffin Mott was among the women it excluded, while Elizabeth Cady Stanton, wife of a delegate but just an observer herself, watched from the gallery.

[IV]

What began as the "woman question" within antislavery became the "woman movement" in 1848, when a convention gathered in Seneca Falls, New York. Mott, Stanton, and Susan B. Anthony organized it and among the delegates was Frederick Douglass. It published a "Declaration of Sentiments" modeled on the Declaration of Independence, with the deeds of men against women in place of those of George III against the colonists. The compliment to the American political tradition could not have been more clear.

The Seneca Falls women and the Africa-centered Henry Highland Garnet had to face the problem of American nationality. So too did Frederick Douglass. On July 5, 1852, Douglass addressed the subject, giving the most powerful speech of his life to a largely white audience in his adopted city of Rochester, New York. The Fourth of July, he told them, was *"yours*, not *mine. You* may rejoice, *I* must mourn. To drag a man in fetters into the grand illuminated temple of liberty, and call upon him to join you in joyous anthems, were inhuman mockery and sacrilegious irony." It seemed very much like Garrison's declaration seven years earlier that the Constitution was a "covenant with death and an agreement with hell." But Douglass had been controlled too long by white abolitionists and he needed to speak in his own voice. That was why he had moved from Boston, the white abolitionist headquarters, to Rochester and founded his own newspaper, *The North Star.* For all the Republic's flaws, he wanted it to be his: "Would you have me argue that man is entitled to his liberty? that he is the rightful owner of his own body? You have already declared it. Must I argue the wrongfulness of slavery? Is that a question for Republicans?" The speech was saturated with suppressed and angry patriotism. July 4 to white Americans was "what the Passover was to the emancipated people of God. . . . The Declaration of Independence is the RING-BOLT to the chain of your nation's destiny." But "what," Douglass asked,

> to the American Slave is your Fourth of July? I answer: a day that reveals to him . . . the gross injustice and constant cruelty to which he is the constant victim . . . your celebration is a sham; your boasted liberty, an unholy license; your national greatness, swelling vanity. . . . There is not a nation on the earth guilty of practices, more shocking and bloody, than are the people of these United States.

Yet it was clear what Douglass wanted. Closing the speech, he asserted that the federal "Constitution is a GLORIOUS LIBERTY DOCUMENT" (his emphasis) without "a single pro-slavery clause." It was a reading founded more on hope than close analysis and historical development. But Douglass thought that black America could make the Constitution the genuine instrument of freedom that it was supposed to be. Perhaps he was right at a level that went deeper than either exegesis or what the courts had held.[34]

In the same year Harriet Beecher Stowe published *Uncle Tom's Cabin.*

She and Douglass knew each other well; he even advised her about her descriptions of slave life. Frustrated sentimental domesticity stood for Stowe as frustrated patriotism did for Douglass. Her book became the single most powerful tract of the Civil War era. Southerners read it as avidly as Northerners and argued with what it said. *Uncle Tom* was not "great" writing like *Jane Eyre* or *Moby-Dick*. It was unconsciously but deeply patronizing toward "the lowly" for whose freedom Stowe wrote it. Her book touched very sensitive American nerves. Its significance is not that it describes the conditions of slavery; despite Douglass's advice and a great deal of library research it reveals how little Stowe knew about the South, white or black. Instead, *Uncle Tom* shows in bold outline the mentality of the largely female reform-minded readers Stowe wanted to reach. It reads much better as a novel about women's reforming energy than as a novel about black Americans' actual experience of slavery.[35]

Stowe constructed the novel around a fusion of morality and geography. She anchored the book in a Kentucky plantation and in a Quaker settlement across the Ohio River in Indiana. Both are places of domesticity. But in Kentucky slavery blights the prospect of family happiness. Separating Tom from his wife and children, the domestic slave trade sends him south to a terrible death. A second slave family escapes northward rather than see their child sold. Significantly for a book centered on gender, Stowe cross-dresses both the escaping woman, making her a temporary man, and the woman's young son. Slavery blights the white family too, coming between the Kentucky plantation's well-meaning but ineffectual master and his Christian wife. She cannot prevent what must happen to Tom but she aids the younger family on their way north.

As Tom descends into the heart of slavery, family life becomes ever more deformed. In New Orleans he finds himself in a poisoned paradise, where the serpent is a white woman who thinks only of herself. Finally, on the banks of the Red River, he enters a hellish world where all relationships are askew. This is the nightmare domain of the Man Alone who will kill him, Simon Legree, not a Southerner but a corrupted Yankee. But north of the Ohio, where slavery does not reach, women, men, and children can be together, and hardworking individuals can achieve what they will. Stowe's immediate injunction to the reader is to "feel right," which was appropriate for women readers barred from politics. Her larger theme was as patriotic as Douglass's frustrated love for the Republic. The free-labor, domesticated North represented what all the

Republic should be. Douglass had already said the same in his widely read autobiography.[36]

To Stowe and Douglass slavery was radically evil and the northern system was positively good.[37] That would be one of the strongest appeals of the Republican Party when it began to take shape after 1854.[38] The North was not the paradise of free labor, achievement, and sentiment that Stowe limned in her later chapters. It was riven with profound tensions, partly along the line of social class, and partly along the one that separated Stowe's kind of people from German Catholics and political refugees and the desperately poor Irish Catholics who were pouring into east coast ports. As early as the late 1830s Protestant crowds were storming Catholic churches and convents. By the time of Douglass's speech and Stowe's novel, the Irish were replacing the Yankee mill women of Lowell, Massachusetts. Even before that, conditions in the mills were deteriorating, with sporadic labor unrest in the 1830s and a powerful movement for a ten-hour working day the following decade.

Immigrant workers gravitated to the Democrats, who showed them sympathy, but who had none for slaves. The most powerful political leader that the new migrant workforce produced, New York City's Mike Walsh, was just as skilled at showing contempt for black people who worked as slaves as he was at expressing the anger of Irish people who worked under conditions of legal freedom and desperate poverty.[39] Abolitionists could be just as blind in the reverse direction. Frederick Douglass saw the conditions of the working class in England and of starving peasants in Ireland. But he missed his chance to bring the problem of slavery together with the problem of social class in a free-labor society.[40]

Douglass did foresee the war—as in his July 5, 1852, speech:

> From the round top of your ship of state, dark and threatening clouds may be seen. Heavy billows . . . disclose to the leeward huge forms of flinty rocks. . . . *Cling to this day—cling to it*, and to its principles, with the grasp of a storm-tossed mariner to a spar at midnight.[41]

Between them, Stowe and Douglass sketched out the issues along which the United States was coming apart: the great contradiction between slave and free; the militant Protestant belief, shared as much by the unbelieving Douglass as by the pious Stowe, that it was the Lord's work to make the world right; the insistence, which Douglass himself personified, that African-Americans must have a hand in making their freedom; the loving hatred, or hate-filled love, that they felt toward the Republic and its boasts; and the close interrelation of the cause of slaves and the cause of women. Reform was not a single movement. It was as much a coalition, as full of its own possibilities for coming apart, as any of the three great formations of the revolutionary period—the one that resisted British policy, the different one that actually broke the British Empire, and the third, different again, that created the United States.

In 1852, when Douglass spoke and Stowe wrote, most white Southerners still believed that they belonged in the United States. Most northern men thought that maintaining the Union was more important than any other issue. That is why both sections compromised one last time in 1850, when the question of admitting California as a free state without a slave state to balance it made the prospect of the Union failing seem very real.[42] Two elements were missing and had to be supplied before the fusion of white freedom everywhere and continuing black slavery in the South that the earlier revolution had brought about could be undone. One was the full conviction of white Southerners that the federal Republic had nothing left for them, that there was no way at all for them and northern whites to work together. The other was the translation of what Douglass and Stowe stood for into a political form that could win control of the United States government and take charge of American society.

[V]

The white South became a very separate section and an almost-nation slowly and with reluctance. The North became a section that identified itself with the united Republic's future and meaning just as slowly. Many people resisted the whole process. Throughout the Civil War era there were Northerners who favored the southern cause and Southerners who did the opposite. To speak, then, of "the South" and "the North" as the sectional conflict developed is to use a shorthand for parts of the nation that saw their values and interests in opposition to another part. To speak of the two sections coming apart is to describe the decay of what had seemed a solution to the problem of American political society. Half slave and half free the nation could not survive, as Lincoln saw. But as long as the two middle-period political parties, Democrats and Whigs alike, could treat the sectional issue as illegitimate and keep it out of electoral, congressional, and presidential politics, the reckoning could be postponed.

Only one southern white in four owned slaves. Fewer than half the slaveholders had a force greater than five. If the planter class is defined as the white families with more than twenty slaves, it comprised a bare quarter million whites, out of a total in 1860 of eight million. The vast bulk of these were "second planters," not "chivalry," as the greatest planters were known. Huge holdings did exist: every brick, every classical column, every terrace, and every garden that contributed to the elegance of Charleston or Natchez gives permanent testimony. But these were the exception. Most planters lived in comfort at best. The lives that small-holding second planters and nonslaveholding plain people lived had little to do with any plantation stereotype.

Nor had southern whites spoken with one political voice. Party competition was as real in Louisiana as in New York during the age of Jackson, Van Buren, Harrison, Tyler, Polk, Taylor, Fillmore, and Pierce. Nonetheless, differences were opening even while Whigs and Democrats continued to avoid the sectional issue. Whether southern whites owned slaves or not, they had a moral stake in the society that slaveholding produced. At bottom was the fear of insurrection. The entire structure of the South rested on the willingness of all whites to keep the slaves down by any means necessary. Planters understood that they could not rule fellow whites the same way. By 1850 the solution that Virginians had framed a hundred years before to the problem of white disorder had become general throughout the Cotton Kingdom. White Southerners formed a genuine community united around not only staple-crop production and slave labor but a genuine sense of self as against others.

Public rituals of power, subordination, inclusion, and sociability defined white southern public life. At the heart of it was the powerful belief in southern "honor."[43] Nobody denied that there was a difference between the planters and the rest, but a rich Southerner who put on airs became the butt of humor, not the object of respect. James Henry Hammond returned to South Carolina from Europe in 1837 laden with what a nouveau riche took to be treasures of art, but his neighbors "gazed at them with the apathy of Indians." Even in Adams County, Mississippi, with more millionaires than any other place in the country, a holding was a "place" and never an "estate."[44] The white South had immigrants. It had Jews and Catholics. It had industrialists and bankers.[45] It had growing towns which were starting to display the complexity of their northern counterparts.[46] It remained a largely native-born, Protestant society, cohering around the institution of slavery. More and more,

Southerners were defining slavery as a positive good for everyone, slaves included.

A brief look at three southern leaders will show how reluctant awareness of difference gave way to the belief that difference needed defending and how that yielded to militant pride. Thomas Jefferson finally realized how southern he was late in 1820, when the question of admitting Missouri as a slave state split the nation. Jefferson likened it to a "firebell in the night" and he feared for his country, Virginia, because "God is just." Nonetheless, this was when he "threw his weight behind slavery's expansion." He convinced himself that if the institution was "diluted" it might more easily be dissolved. It was a specious hope. The real effect was that Jefferson "bequeathed to the South the image of anti-slavery as a . . . mask for political and economic exploitation" by a rapacious, commercial North.[47]

John C. Calhoun of South Carolina began his public career just as Jefferson was finishing his. The young Calhoun was a nationalist. "War hawk" in 1812, Secretary of War and Secretary of State, senator, Vice President, ambitious for the White House, he became a sectionalist slowly. But when he did it was with his whole heart and the whole power of his considerable mind. The turning point was his state's attempt to nullify the "tariff of abominations" that a northern-controlled Congress imposed in 1828. Calhoun and many others were coming to understand that whatever the formal equality in Washington between southern and northern states, the South was becoming the North's economic colony. It had no particular reason to foster northern industrialization by paying higher prices for northern goods, particularly when England, its main trading partner, could provide what it needed better and cheaper. Though he was Jackson's Vice President, Calhoun challenged the President's intention that the law be enforced. He also embarked on abstract political thought, developing his idea of a "concurrent majority." This amounted to a restatement of the old theory of a "composite" polity that could bind many separate political entities together on terms that recognized and respected their differences, without any pretense at uniformity.[48] Yet Calhoun was reluctant to go further. In 1850, when his generation's public career was ending and he was on the edge of death, he helped patch together one last attempt at compromise.[49]

Where Calhoun hung back, James Henry Hammond pushed forward. He fancied himself Calhoun's successor as the spokesman for their state

and the whole South. As governor, congressman, and senator, he followed
Calhoun's political path, and he too wrote in defense of southern ways.
In 1852 he contributed to a major anthology defending the principle
and the practice of slavery. In 1857, during the furor over Dred Scott's
lawsuit for freedom, Hammond coined his most enduring phrase: "You
dare not make war upon Cotton. Cotton is King!" To some extent he
got the regional fame he craved; the Committee on Slaves and Slavery
of the legislature of distant Texas saw fit to reprint his writing.[50] Yet
even Hammond hung back in the final stages of the Union's breakup,
finding it difficult to accept completely the consequences of what he had
spent his public life seeking.[51]

As self-conscious sections, the white South and the free-labor North
made each other, each shaping perceptions of the other that made difference look like enmity. For Northerners the idea took shape of a "slave
power conspiracy" aimed at bending the United States government to
southern purposes. Southern control of the presidency and the Supreme
Court seemed to bear the point out. So did the foreign policy of President
James K. Polk of Tennessee, who made aggressive war on Mexico in
1846 and acquired land that seemed open to slavery, but who compromised with Britain over land in the Far Northwest, where only free labor
was likely to go. So did the whole direction of "normal" party politics.

The old system began to crack almost as soon as it took full shape.
In the elections of 1840 and 1844 outright opponents of slavery sought
the presidency as third-party candidates. They failed dismally at the
polls, attracting a bare 0.3 percent of the vote in their first campaign
and only 2.3 percent in their second. Still, they were raising the issue.
John Quincy Adams, now a representative from Massachusetts, launched
a campaign against the "gag rule" that required Congress to ignore
antislavery petitions. In 1844 he saw it repealed. In 1846 Congressman
David Wilmot, a Pennsylvania Democrat, proposed that slavery be barred
from any territory acquired from Mexico in President Polk's war. Whig
congressman Abraham Lincoln of Illinois agreed. In 1848 Martin Van
Buren, the very architect of the coalition between "planters" and
"plain republicans," sought the presidency on the basis of "Free Soil."
This meant opposition to slavery's expansion, not its existence, but it
was anathema to the South. Van Buren got nearly 11 percent of the
vote.[52]

During the next decade the old politics broke open. The well-known
story does not need a full retelling, but simply to look at the main areas

of disagreement will demonstrate that the issue was not just politics. In 1850 the white South traded acceptance of California as a free state, which meant conceding a free-state majority in both houses of Congress, for an act of Congress that put the central government firmly on the side of people trying to reclaim slaves from northern freedom. In 1854 the question of expanding the political union arose again, when Kansas sought admission. The rising Democratic star, Senator Stephen Douglas of Illinois, sought southern support for his presidential ambitions by proposing that the people of Kansas decide whether their new state would be free or slave. The result did not provide a democratic resolution of a difficult situation. Instead "squatter sovereignty" brought guerrilla warfare, the destruction of the Whigs, and defections from the Democrats. "Conscience" Whigs and some Democrats coalesced and became the Republican Party, which mounted its first presidential campaign in 1856 with support exclusively from the North.

In the same election a short-lived American Party roused hostility to immigration and ran former President Millard Fillmore, who had succeeded Zachary Taylor when Taylor died in office, for the White House. Much of its support came from Protestant artisans who saw in Catholic immigrants a reason why their own lives were deteriorating as the new industrial order advanced. In principle, these people were open to Republican blandishments, both because the Republicans inherited the northern Whigs' mantle as the party of native-born Protestants and because the new party promised prosperity. Republican politicians knew as well that they could attract support from traditionally Democratic midwestern farmers if they revived the idea that the central government should involve itself in economic development.

From all these sources—the belief even among Northerners who did not care about slavery that the South had seized the government and was subverting it, the complex tangle of nativism and social class that went into the American Party, and the prospect of an economically active state—emerged the Republican coalition that won the presidency for Abraham Lincoln in 1860. The party's slogan of "Free Soil, Free Labor, Free Men" was masterful. "Free Soil" harked back to Van Buren's 1848 campaign and promised opposition to the *Dred Scott* decision and slavery's expansion. "Free Labor" appealed to the pride and self-assertion that American workingmen had been manifesting since the Revolution. It also played on their fears. "Free Men" could be read as abolitionist, but it could also be read as promising to keep slaves away by confining them to the South, particularly after *Dred Scott* seemed to open the way for slaves to be taken wherever masters wanted to go. Whatever their ambiguities, the Republicans were intolerable to the South.[53]

Southerners developed a comparable image. In part they derived it from a thoroughly false sense of being descended from seventeenth-century English Cavaliers who had fled the Puritan Revolution. Sir Walter Scott's Waverley novels with their tales of castles and knighthood were immensely popular among Southerners who read for pleasure. Within this framework, Northerners became Roundhead descendants of the meddling Puritans who had overthrown Charles I and the gracious social order he represented.

Southerners rightly perceived the Yankee sense that the world could be made right, whatever the cost. The consequence, they thought, was the Yankee emigration to Kansas after 1854 and the emergence of the bloody-handed John Brown as a guerrilla fighter in Kansas two years later. Brown passed from notoriety into legend in 1859, when he embarked on an ill-conceived plan to raise a general slave insurrection. Militarily he got no further than an attempt to seize the federal arsenal at Harpers Ferry, Virginia. Federal troops under Robert E. Lee captured his tiny force and Virginia executed him for treason. To a growing number of Northerners Brown showed what a man of courage might attempt. To the vast majority of white Southerners he showed what the North intended.

Northerners' response to the Fugitive Slave Act of 1850 and the *Dred Scott* decision of 1857 also helped convince the South that the sections were enemies. Both the act and the decision attempted to resolve the sectional issue by showing where supreme authority stood; neither attempt succeeded. The Fugitive Slave Law led to United States marshals replacing private hunters as the men who would seek out former slaves and haul them off to their former owners. The *Dred Scott* decision denied even free black people the rights of citizenship, which meant that no African-American was safe. By the 1850s a far larger number of Northerners did see slavery as an abomination than two decades before, when the issue had begun to emerge. But they were still a minority. Other Northerners who did not like black people and did not care about slavery saw the Fugitive Slave Law and the *Dred Scott* decision as outrageous violations of the Constitution and simple justice. Many Northerners were simply racist and wanted no black people near them. For these last, *Dred Scott*'s protection of the right to take slave property anywhere seemed a genuine threat. To white Southerners it was all the same. By 1859 all Yankees might as well have been John Brown.

An organized black community that agreed with what Frederick Douglass said in his speeches; militant white women pushing into the public arena; the belief in perfection on earth; white antislavery that became progressively diluted but did not lose its soul; the immigration question; class antagonisms in a maturing industrial society; a white South that knew it was alone: all these came together between the Compromise of 1850 and Lincoln's election to the presidency. Lincoln took the position that legally the government could do nothing about slavery where it existed. But he was still antislavery.

Lincoln was surely no John Brown, but other Republicans found they admired that fierce old man. Lincoln believed in keeping the races apart, but other Republicans were not sure, and the party had the well-publicized support of Frederick Douglass. Most of all, the Republicans posed the possibility of the South losing the grip on the center of national politics that it had held since national politics began.

Lincoln himself contributed mightily to the demise of the old politics and the social order it had expressed and protected. Debating Stephen A. Douglas in 1858, he made his opponent concede that the people of a territory could keep slavery out if they wanted to. That was all that Douglass had said four years earlier when he proposed that the people of Kansas themselves settle the slave/free issue as their territory was becoming a state. It had been enough then to mark Douglas as a "dough-face," a "northern man with southern principles," like President Franklin Pierce or his successor, James Buchanan. By 1858 that was not enough for the South. Lincoln had trapped Douglas into rejecting *Dred Scott*. When the Democratic Party gathered in Charleston (of all places) to nominate a presidential candidate in 1860, Douglas was the northern delegates' favorite, but Southerners could not stomach him. The party split. Four candidates ran, including the southern Democrat John Breckinridge, the would-be compromiser John Bell, the northern Democrat Douglas, and the Republican nominee, Lincoln. With a minority vote at the polls Lincoln won in the electoral college.

Lincoln did not become President to abolish slavery. Nonetheless, his election had as much significance for American society as the election of Andrew Jackson thirty-two years before. Jackson's victory of party had resolved, at least seemingly, what remained of the American Revolution's leftover business. This victory of a different kind of party, and the breaking of the Union that resulted, came about because the greatest issue of all had not been resolved. It also came about because during the middle decades of its first century the complex, tangled United States raised problems its founders could only have dimly foreseen. The decade and a half after Lincoln's accession to the White House saw the United States confront not just civil war, which was grim enough, but every social problem that had been raised since Europeans and Africans first arrived.

CHAPTER 10

"ENGAGED IN A GREAT
CIVIL WAR"

"AS I would not be a *slave*, so I would not be a *master*," mused Abraham Lincoln sometime in 1858. This conveyed Lincoln's "idea of democracy. Whatever differs from this, to the extent of the difference, is no democracy."[1] Two years later, when Lincoln won the presidency with a minority popular vote in a four-way race, South Carolina "seceded" rather than submit. Ten states followed it. The seceding South formed the Confederate States of America. President Lincoln adroitly maneuvered the Confederacy into firing on the Union's Fort Sumter, in Charleston Harbor. "And," as he said, "the war came."[2]

Thinking both of northern Democrats and of the nonseceding slave states of Delaware, Maryland, Kentucky, and Missouri, Lincoln defined the war in terms of the nation, not in terms of antislavery. That remained his stated policy until late in 1862. But even in 1858 Lincoln had been sure that "this government cannot endure, permanently half *slave* and half *free*."[3] The slave owners seceded both because a man who opposed them had become President and because his election showed their political irrelevance. Southern slavery—the primitive springboard of American modernity, the only special interest that the federal Constitution explicitly protected, the last legally recognized "privilege held by grant of prescription, whereby men enjoy some benefit beyond the ordinary subject"—was reaching its moment of crisis. The South knew it, whatever candidate Lincoln said.[4]

"As I would not be a *slave*, so I would not be a *master*." Lincoln made the point to himself as he thought his way through the sectional crisis and prepared to debate Stephen A. Douglas in their 1858 campaign for the U.S. Senate. He was addressing more issues, perhaps, than he consciously realized. Decades before, in his earliest major address, Lincoln faced the difficulty that went with belonging (as he thought) to a lesser, younger generation that could not attain the mastery its forebears had known.[5] His parents and grandparents had waged the Revolution, establishing mastery over themselves and their world. To them, only a master of land, or skills, or a family, or slaves could stand truly free. Such freedom virtually required that somebody else not be free, either partly or wholly: wives, sons and daughters who had not left home, apprentices, or "persons held to service" as the Constitution delicately put it.

"We the People" of 1787 had been an assemblage of independent masters. For a person of the right color and sex, the way to mastery and thus to full membership among "the people" lay open, particularly once the seizing of Indian land began in earnest. Sons would not have to wait for their fathers' deaths to stand on their own, as their colonial and European ancestors had done. A nation that controlled its house would be built of men who controlled their productive lives and their personal households. In 1790 full citizenship and mastery went together, North as much as South.

By Lincoln's time, those two ideas had come apart. Lincoln's immediate reference was to mastery over slaves. The annexation of Texas, the conquest of the Southwest from Mexico, whether settlers could take slavery into new territories, the *Dred Scott* rulings that slaves taken to free states still remained slaves and that neither free nor enslaved black Americans had legal rights: these had made the issue increasingly salient for many people and Lincoln became their voice. In a good society neither slavery nor mastery of slaves had a place.

Slaves had no trouble agreeing. People who did not really care about slavery were having their own problems with the notion that full humanity meant mastery in one or another old-fashioned sense. "Free Soil, Free Labor, Free Men" was the Republicans' winning slogan.[6] Among their natural constituents were midwestern farmers who wanted public aid to build roads, canals, and railroads that would get their crops to market. They wanted a federal homestead law and public sponsorship of higher education as well. For these the time was almost over when the head of a farming family could use his mastery over property to dominate adult sons. The Republicans understood the point. In office they delivered "internal improvements," a Homestead Act that promised to set the younger generation entirely free of its parents, and land grants for state universities "where any person can find instruction in any study."[7]

The Republicans won both capitalists and workers in the industrial Northeast. Much more than the Democrats, the new party addressed American industry's need for fostering and protection. Within the industrializing sector many people still worked in small shops, but now that meant outwork and piecework, not complete control by master artisans. In wholly mechanized factories, apprenticeship leading to mastery of a craft and a shop had no place. The new division was not between masters and aspirants to mastery. It was between owners or bosses and workers.[8]

Many industrial workers were women, whose rewards (if not skills) were usually lower than men's. Old-style mastery had been possible for women only in widowhood, and generally not even then. In 1860 shoemaking women in Lynn, Massachusetts, went on strike under the slogan "American Ladies Will Not Be Slaves." Yet Lynn elected Republican factory owner John B. Alley to Congress that year. Although no woman could vote, the Republicans had a particular attractiveness for northern women of the antislavery sort. An increasing number of such women were deciding that the mastery of husbands and fathers was of a piece with the mastery of southern men over slaves. They found it equally malign. They had been saying so in public since the Seneca Falls convention of 1848.

Lincoln's "idea" of democracy survives only as a scrap in his papers. But what he meant resonated with his whole society. The Civil War, over which Lincoln presided, touched every group and person in that society: black, red, or white; female or male; southern or northern; farming, industrial, or commercial; capitalist or worker; slave, subject, or citizen. Beginning over the political question of winning the presidency, it escalated into the constitutional question of secession and then became a general social crisis. The revolution of 1776 had become a general crisis too, but in a much simpler society with a different agenda. Both American revolutions forced changes in the most profound social sense, even though each promised much that remained unfinished when the revolution was over.[9] This chapter and the one to follow will not attempt a narrative account of the Civil War and Reconstruction. There are many such already.[10] Instead, they will explore the epoch's meaning for the hugely complex society of mid-nineteenth-century United States.

[I]

The Civil War's bare statistics of mobilization, destruction, and death are overwhelming by any standard short of our own bloody century's. This was the first great war in which mechanized industry allowed the rapid, large-scale production and even more rapid transport of whatever an army required. Perhaps 6,000,000 of the roughly 7,000,000 white Southerners had no direct interest in slavery. Yet 900,000 white males served in the Confederates' army, without counting old men and boys in the state militias. By one estimate, "nearly four-fifths of all white southern men of military age" saw active service. More than 250,000 died. All the American fatalities in the Revolution, the War of 1812, the wars against Mexico and Spain, World War I, Korea, and Vietnam total 279,721. The Confederacy lost almost as many in just four years.

The Union lost far more. About 2,000,000 men wore its uniform, including nearly 190,000 who were black. Some of those black soldiers were free Northerners who volunteered, were drafted, or became a rich man's paid substitute. Others were Southerners who rejected their own slavery and set out to end that way of life. Men who served in the Union forces account for only about 40 percent of northern whites of military age, which measures both the difference that black soldiers made and the far greater population of the northern and border states. About 360,000 died in service. The official total of all Civil War military deaths, South and North, white, black, and Indian, was 618,222.[11] Roughly one soldier died for every six slaves the war freed. Taking North and South together, the casualty rate per 10,000 people was 181.7. This was half again as much as in the Revolution, more than six times the rate in World War II, and 64.9 times the rate in Vietnam. What happened to the Indians after the invasion of the hemisphere and to Africans during the slave trade dwarfs that total. No other American disaster comes close to the Civil War.[12]

Statistics of other sorts lie beneath this ocean of patriotic gore. In 1861 the South had 9,000 miles of trunk-line railroads and the North had 22,000. The South had 18,000 factories, employing about 100,000 people, both free and slave. The North had 110,000 industrial establishments and their workforce was thirteen times the South's. Both sections had advanced metallurgy. But the famous Tredegar Iron Works of Virginia did not compare with the northern iron centers of Troy, New York, and, increasingly, Pittsburgh, Pennsylvania.[13] What would become the great southern steel center, Birmingham, Alabama, had not even begun to be developed, although its coal and ore were known.[14] Both sections could raise large amounts of finance. But northern banks, investment firms, insurance companies, and chartered corporations vastly outstripped the South's in size, complexity, flexibility, and access to foreign capital.

The symbolic key, perhaps, is Jay Cooke, railroad man, banker, speculator, and financier. He emerged from Philadelphia to organize northern finance much as Robert Morris had emerged from the same city to organize the finance of the Revolution. Both ended their lives bankrupt and in disgrace, but that is not the point. However much wealth its great planters enjoyed, southern society could not produce anybody like these men. Morris's career shows how the vitality of eighteenth-century merchant capitalism underpinned American independence. Cooke's demonstrates the far greater vitality of its nineteenth-century industrial descendant.[15]

A tenth of Southerners dwelt in towns, as opposed to a quarter of Northerners. Of the twenty largest cities in 1860 the seceding states could claim only New Orleans. The Crescent City was an overgrown port for outbound cotton and inbound finished goods, not a center of capital or industry. Its 168,675 people formed the sixth-largest urban center in the country, but they were barely a sixth of the combined population of New York City and Brooklyn. Only three other slaveholding cities, Baltimore, Louisville, and St. Louis, ranked among the twenty largest, and these were in states that did not leave the Union.[16]

On the face of it, the historical problem of the Civil War would seem uncomplicated. Outnumbered, outgunned, outproduced, and fighting for a cause that the civilized world was coming to abhor (whatever anybody said otherwise), the South had to lose.[17] But material and numerical superiority do not guarantee victory, as the war in Vietnam shows. At times northern will seemed about to break, even among people who believed that slavery deserved to be destroyed and that a war against it was holy. Defeating the South meant destroying its whole civilization. Both the Union army and slaves who finally found their moment to seize freedom had a hand in that destruction. So, in a sense, did white Southerners, by embarking on a war that they could not ultimately win but in which all the destructive force their enemy could muster was required for their defeat.

[II]

Initially the North's position was that the South was rebelling against legitimate authority, not waging war against another power. Both sides did agree to be bound by the laws of war, so that the wounded, the captured, bearers of flags of truce, and holders of neutral citizenship could claim protection. But where the issue could be defined in terms of race rather than military practice, law did not count, North or South. Mass hangings in Mississippi in 1861 and in Texas and Minnesota in 1862 and a great riot in New York City in 1863 show how.

The Mississippi hangings were at Second Creek in rural Adams County, near Natchez. This was well-settled land. Its white people came as close as anyone to living out the romantic plantation myth and its black people had dwelt and labored for decades beneath a "mountain of pain." By 1861 the Natchez district's great cotton era was over. Its rich loess hills were gullied and eroding. Scrub forests were already starting to reclaim the land. Its premier resident, Stephen Duncan, drew most of his income from plantations well upriver in the delta county of Issaquena, where "more than 700 of his 1,036 slaves" had lived as early as 1850.[18] Pennsylvania-born and no fool about southern prospects, Duncan also put sizable funds into northern railroads and steamship lines and United States bonds. He continued to invest in the North throughout the war.[19]

Stephen Duncan could invest his way out of danger, whether it was the decay of Adams County cotton culture or the threat that had been growing for decades against the way of life he had chosen. Mississippi slaves had little option, not even to flee. Both Tennessee and Kentucky lay between their state and freedom. When war broke out Adams County slaves decided that the time was coming to strike, right where they were. The slaves knew about Fort Sumter. They knew when Union troops began advancing up the Mississippi. "Freedom was at our door," said one, as their "plan" was taking shape. Their discovery, their informal "examination" by "gentlemen of the neighborhood," and the hangings of at least ten men that followed have left only the barest record.

The slaves borrowed from white culture. One proposed to assume the name and rank of Winfield Scott, the Virginian who was Yankee general-in-chief. Others would be "president," "governor," "lieutenant," and "printer." But they had their own ideas about freedom. One, called Orange, told his interrogators that "whipping colored people would stop." Another said that "he would blow down a white man who called him a damn rascal." Reversing the terrible sexual logic that had left all black women vulnerable to any white man, some expected to make the white women of the district their own: *"Which one of the ladies was you going to take, boy?"* None of it came to fruition. Instead, the ones whom "the committee" interrogated died suspended from trees in September 1861. A little less than two years later the white people of Natchez surrendered to Union forces without a fight in order to save their lovely town, and slavery in Adams County ended.[20]

The forty-two men who were hanged for being Unionists in October 1862 at Gainesville, Texas, were white. They represented about a fifth of the suspected dissidents swooped up between Dallas and the Red River by the secessionist state government's militia. Cotton growing would spread into that part of Texas after the war, but in 1862 these counties lay at the very edge of the South. Just north of them, beyond the Red River, was Indian Territory, inhabited by the Chickasaws and Choctaws who had owned all of Mississippi not long before.

We can see these people more clearly than the victims at Second Creek, because they left tax, census, and militia records. A historian's careful research has resurrected both them and the fifteen jurymen of the "Citizens Court" who ordered that they be executed. The hanged men were not Yankees who had strayed unluckily into the wrong place. Of the thirty who were not Texas-born, twenty-six had moved from other southern states. Like most westering whites, they had stayed in latitudes and climates they knew. They had had the option to go north, as young Abraham Lincoln's family had done when they left Kentucky. They had not taken it. Although only one of the victims is listed as owning a slave, there seems little reason to think they had any real quarrel with slavery, whatever their reasons for the "Unionism" that cost them their lives.

Four of the fifteen jurymen who ordered the hangings were northern-born, and two of these had risen to some prominence. One was a lieutenant colonel of secessionist volunteers and the other a legislator, militia officer, and large landholder. The Texas county of Montague still honors the latter's name. Six jurymen held slaves, but none was a "planter" by the conventional twenty-slave rule. The jurors were men of standing. The most prosperous was a rancher who had eight slaves tending his 5,700 cattle and a total worth of $64,150. Other jurymen had holdings of between $10,000 and $20,000, including thousands of acres of grazing land. The victims were of a different order. The highest known property holding among them was $10,400. Other holdings ranged between $5,775 and a mere $12. That there was a difference in class, or at least condition, between the jurors and the men they hanged is clear. What is more important is how the hangings expressed the absolute certainty of people committed to secession that any challenge would be crushed, whatever the challengers' color.[21]

On December 26, 1862, thirty-eight Sioux Indians were hanged by the Union army at Mankato, Minnesota. It could have been far more. In the words of missionary Stephen Riggs, who "helped write up the results" of the trials that had condemned the Indians, "it almost made me sick to . . . attach to three hundred and three" names "the penalty *'to be hung.'*" The reduction in the others' sentences had come after a review in Washington ordered by President Lincoln himself.

The Sioux were hanged on gallows, not trees. Their formal, court-mandated, presidentially approved executions came about because the Sioux rebelled in 1862 against conditions they regarded as intolerable. Their greatest grievance was the government's delays in paying the annuities on which they had become dependent. Their rebellion was serious and it led to attacks on whites living along the Minnesota River. Some of the people the Sioux attacked died. In the national press the raids turned into a "most terrible and exciting Indian war" involving not just Sioux but also Chippewas, Winnebagos, Snake Indians, Blackfeet, and even Utes as far away as Denver. A "few thousand people" would be "at the mercy of 50,000 Indians"; the whole Dakota Territory "will be depopulated"; only "prompt action can stop the terrible massacre." Lincoln's personal secretary construed the rebellion as a general Indian war, called for a thousand cavalry to be deployed away from the conflict in the South, and advised that "as against the Sioux it must be a war of extermination." Between Blue and Gray the rule was that a person who surrendered or was taken prisoner became a noncombatant. The great Confederate prison camp at Andersonville saw terrible suffering, but it was not a death camp. When the Confederacy tried to treat captured black soldiers as merely rebellious slaves, which would have rendered them liable to death, the Lincoln administration moved to protect them. But on the Sioux front in Minnesota the laws of war did not apply and outright "extermination" of a vanquished foe was not beyond contemplation.[22]

The great New York City riot of 1863 involved not tens or hundreds of people but tens of thousands. One hundred and nineteen people died in the street violence, and reportedly more than three hundred sustained serious wounds. Five Union regiments put the violence down, after being rushed to the city direct from the war-turning battle of Gettysburg. The riot ranks among the most serious urban uprisings in American history, comparable to the Detroit and Newark uprisings of 1967 and the Los Angeles rebellion of 1992. It might have changed the course of history. Its most sophisticated student thinks it "fair to speculate . . . that if

Confederate General Robert E. Lee had pushed north from Gettysburg at the moment rioting erupted . . . European intervention would have stalemated the war." Instead, the defeated Lee "escaped south across the Potomac" from Gettysburg on July 13, the very day the riot began.[23]

The largest number of deaths took place among the working-class Irish immigrants who formed the great bulk of the rioters. But the real victim was the city's black community. The Irish were desperately poor immigrants and the blacks, just as poor, were slavery's survivors. The riot should not be construed, however, as simply a clash between two ethnic groups scrambling for the limited space at the bottom of the social ladder. New York's German, Jewish, and Chinese communities also became involved. Echoing a tradition that reached back to colonial times, houses of prostitution were attacked, although the women themselves were not injured. Rioters broke machines, in emulation of the well-known Luddite machine smashing of early-nineteenth-century England. Employers and prominent Republicans had their dwellings sacked. Only the intervention of a Catholic priest prevented the destruction of Columbia College. Columbia students were the sons of the city's largely Protestant, largely Republican well-to-do. Many such youths did go to the war, but any of them who wanted to escape the draft could afford to hire a substitute, as the law permitted. A working-class Irish immigrant, who might not even have citizenship, could not.

The rioting began when the federal government began drafting men into a Union army that no longer could attract volunteers. The Irishmen who formed the core of the rioters had come to America without the tradition that military service was a patriotic duty. The British military that they knew in Ireland was not their army. It was an occupying force imposed upon their land by an alien people and government that they hated.

Running through the riot was the fundamental dispute between Republicans and Democrats that had made Lincoln's election intolerable to the South. Almost all the Irish who had come to New York since 1830 had gravitated to the Democratic Party for reasons that had nothing to do with the slavery dispute, but that put them in the party of the slaveholders. Part of the reason for the Republicans' rise was the hostility of native-born Protestants to people like the Irish. Now a Republican administration that drew its support from people who did not like the Irish sought to draft them for a cause in which many simply did not believe. By the time the North began drafting men there was no question that going to the front meant running a very high risk of dying or being maimed. The winning strategy that General Ulysses S. Grant was shaping required little more than that the North keep sending more men against a South whose own supply was starting to run out. It had already worked for Grant at Shiloh and Vicksburg, in Mississippi, and he would shortly bring it to bear in Virginia against Robert E. Lee. The rioters knew what they faced.

At the bottom of the riot lay the problem of race, however refracted it was through lenses of class, politics, and culture. The draft riot did not create hostility against New York City's black community; it intensified it. The two themes, hostility to conscription and hostility to blacks, began to merge when a crowd set fire to the Colored Orphan Asylum, expressing its "desire not merely to destroy but to wipe clean the tangible evidence of a black presence." Other rioters attacked "black men and boys in the tenement district along the downtown waterfront." Rioters drove black longshoremen from the docks, hostlers from livery stables, and cartmen from the streets. They charged into tenements where black people dwelled and destroyed businesses that served them. A black man trying to escape disguised in his wife's clothes was beaten "senseless" before the crowd dumped him in the East River. A sailor who was merely looking for directions as he debarked from his vessel was caught by a gang, each of whose members "came up . . . to perform an atrocity—to jump on him, smash his body with a cobblestone, plant a knife in his chest—while the white audience . . . watched with . . . shock, fascination, and . . . a measure of approval."[24]

Whether the killing happened at Second Creek, Mississippi, Gainesville, Texas, Mankato, Minnesota, or in the "bloody 6th" ward of working-class New York, it shows the intensity of racial tensions in Civil War America. By 1863, immigration, white ethnicity, party politics, urbanization, and social class had all been added to the underlying problem that had begun to be posed when the first Europeans and Africans arrived. Reflecting on the problem of race and slavery, Thomas Jefferson once said that he "trembled" for his country when he remembered that "God is just." Delivering his gemlike second inaugural address on March 4, 1865, Abraham Lincoln commented that even in 1861 everyone had known that slavery "was, somehow, the cause of the war." With the South's defeat nearly accomplished and with slavery almost destroyed, Lincoln expanded Jefferson's meditation on divine vengeance:

> If we suppose that American Slavery is one of those offences which, in the providence of God, must needs come, but which, having continued

through His appointed time, He now wills to remove, and that He gives to both North and South, this terrible war, as the woe due to those by whom the offence came . . . until all the wealth piled up by the bond-man's two hundred and fifty years of unrequited toil shall be sunk, and until every drop of blood drawn with the lash, shall be paid by another drawn with the sword . . . so still it must be said "the judgments of the Lord, are true and righteous altogether."[25]

Yet to see the war simply as a conflagration, and to cast people of color as just that conflagration's victims, is to miss its significance for the shape and development of American society. Let us turn to another theme: how people who lived through so major an event influenced its course and changed its direction, and how they became different because of it. Most of all, that means how, and at whose hand, American slavery finally ended. But emancipation was not the only change that the Civil War wrought, and African-Americans were not the only people whom the war changed.

[III]

Perhaps because freedom proved so limited and bitter, the excitement, magnitude, and historical importance of slavery's destruction is not easily grasped. As Lincoln admitted, everyone understood when the war began that slavery, not the Union, was the underlying issue. Yet he had good reasons to define the war at first in terms of the Union. Maryland and Kentucky posed the two central problems. If Maryland followed Virginia out of the Union, Washington, D.C., would be lost. The danger was real. On his way to assume the presidency, Lincoln passed through Baltimore incognito in the small hours of the morning. When war began, Baltimore people rioted against Union troops passing through. Had Kentucky followed Tennessee, antiwar and prosouthern sentiment in Ohio, Indiana, and Illinois might have pushed those states into neutrality. With either Washington lost or the Midwest neutral, the powers of Europe might have intervened. The administration certainly feared they would. But despite having his reasons to construe the war in nationalistic terms, Lincoln was never a friend to slavery or an enemy of the slaves.[26]

What is most striking about Lincoln's original terms of engagement is that they failed. On January 1, 1863, he used his power as commander in chief to achieve what a civilian President could never do: proclaim the emancipation of every slave in all the areas that were under arms against the Republic. The actual, immediate effect was extremely limited. Where the Confederacy endured, slavery endured as well. Nor did Lincoln proclaim freedom for slaves in the border states or where secession already was subdued. It was on slavery's farthest northern extreme, in Kentucky, that it died hardest, persisting even when the war was over and Lincoln himself was dead.

Nonetheless, the moment of emancipation was exhilarating. Knowing what Lincoln intended to do—he had announced his intention months before—longtime campaigners against slavery gathered in Boston on New Year's Eve 1862. The majority were black, including Frederick Douglass. But whites were there too, including the poet John Greenleaf Whittier, the novelist Harriet Beecher Stowe, and the essayist Ralph Waldo Emerson. An orchestra played the final movement of Beethoven's Ninth Symphony, the Ode to Joy, which had first been written by the German poet Johann Schiller as an ode *"an die Freiheit,"* to freedom. Six thousand people waited in two locations for the news. Some were in the Tremont Street Church, where antiabolitionist rioters had broken up a meeting against slavery only three years before.

When the news of Lincoln's formal proclamation finally arrived from Washington, the celebrants knew that unless Union arms failed, slavery would die. They rejoiced without restraint. To Frederick Douglass, faith finally had been kept with "jubilee." After the whites went home, black celebrants moved to the Twelfth Baptist Church, "shouting and singing" as Beethoven yielded to " 'Glory Hallelujah,' 'Old John Brown,' 'Marching On,' and 'Blow Ye, the Trumpet Blow!'—till we got up such a state of enthusiasm that almost anything seemed witty—and entire appropriate to the occasion."[27]

American slavery's victims did not emancipate themselves, but they had not waited passively. Without them, Lincoln might not either have needed to proclaim emancipation or been able to do it. His proclamation brought only the possibility of freedom, not its reality. Realizing freedom required more than Beethoven or "Old John Brown." African-Americans did not receive their long-denied freedom and membership in the only nation they knew as a gift. They claimed it on the same terms that the nation had claimed its own freedom in 1776, as a matter "of right."[28]

[IV]

However important the rise of the Republicans had been for the anti-slavery movement, "black abolitionists viewed politics through issues, not political parties." They understood what Lincoln's party offered, and they also understood its limits. Men like Frederick Douglass had a tortured relationship of hope and frustration with both the Republicans and the Lincoln administration.[29] Writing in the New York *Weekly Anglo-African* in 1859, the black abolitionist William James Watkins said that "there are but two parties in this Republic. . . . composed . . . of all those at the North or at the South, at the East or at the West, who are *opposed* to slavery; and . . . of all those who are *in favor* of this accursed evil." In published opinions, private correspondence, and meetings in tiny churches, black people applauded John Brown's failed war against slavery in 1859. When real war came, they insisted that "the only salvation of this nation is *Immediate Emancipation*."[30] But free people were only a tiny minority of African-Americans. The real question is how the people whom slavery held responded once slavery's end became a thinkable, realistic possibility.

The slaves were no fools. They understood who had the weapons and numbers. They knew that even a black majority could easily be surrounded. John Brown assumed correctly in 1859 that to end slavery in the United States would require force. Brown also assumed that slaves would rally to him once he established an Appalachian base, despite having no preparation, arms, or organization. The honor that accrued to this angry white man among blacks is a tribute to his bravery and determination. That they did not do what he expected them to do is both the mark of his plan's fatal weakness and a tribute to the slaves' common sense.

When the war came, slaves were ready to act. The Union navy quickly won control of the Confederate coast and began pushing into rivers, bays, and estuaries. In 1860 a South Carolina slave called Scipio told "a northern visitor . . . that nearly all the blacks would fight for their freedom if they had the opportunity." "Suppose," he said, "dat one quarter of dese niggas rise—de rest keep still—whar den would de white folks be?"[31] Opportunity arrived in the very first weeks of war at Fortress Monroe, Virginia, on the point between the James and York rivers. Union troops held it throughout the war, and slaves "fleeing Confederate service and offering their labor to the Union cause" confronted Union commander Benjamin Butler when he arrived in May 1861. Butler was a Democrat who had actually wanted Jefferson Davis for President of the United States in 1860. How slaves forced this unlikely man to accept them, employ them, and guarantee their freedom is a measure of the difference they made to the whole war.

Butler knew that slaves crossing his lines had been commandeered by the Confederacy to build fortifications. The slaves knew that the Confederates' intent was to ship "women and children South," which was every slave's nightmare. So men, women, and children alike found their way across the pickets. Butler had already made up his mind to use "the services of able bodied men and women who might come within my lines." Now he had to face the "question . . . can I receive the services of a Father and a Mother and not take the children?" To pose the question was to answer it, both militarily, because receiving the slaves would weaken the Confederacy, and in its "humanitarian aspect." Butler knew that a major "political question" was involved. But the law of war regarded an enemy's militarily usable property as "contraband," and he applied the term to these black Virginians. It became the standard term for people who crossed the lines to be shed of slavery.[32]

These Contrabands were not American citizens: the Supreme Court's ruling in Dred Scott still stood. Butler thought to send receipts to masters, "presumably so that masters could later reclaim their slaves and perhaps compensation." But they were slaves no longer. By the end of July, Butler realized that they had "become . . . men, women, and children[,] no longer under ownership of any kind . . . free, manumitted, sent forth from the hand that held them, never to be reclaimed." Butler had become a liberator, in almost the same place where the British governor Lord Dunmore had proclaimed freedom eighty-four years earlier for rebels' slaves who took up arms on behalf of King George.

Now, however, there were two differences. One was the enormous pressure in the North and the outside world toward abolition. The other was that Butler was not on a ship in Chesapeake Bay. He, his troops, and the Contrabands had a permanent hold on Virginia soil. Fortress Monroe became what John Brown tried to create, a place where slaves could rally. The slaveholder James Cook wrote to his representative in the Confederate Congress that the losses were "heavy" and that

> several of the fugitives were very intelligent negros—familiar with the country occupied by our forces & with the navigation of the River—such will give valuable information to the Enemy. The labour of all of them is much in demand by the Abolition Army.

"Intelligent negros" who knew the land and whose knowledge would be of military use; an "Abolition Army" at a point (1861) when Lincoln's policy was simply to preserve the Union: Cook's terms show that, like the slaves, he was no fool about the people involved or the issues at stake.[33]

Tidewater slaves who crossed Confederate pickets to Fortress Monroe and ventured onto the bay to reach Union vessels; the fortress and vessels that offered safety; Butler and other officers who received and "rationed" the refugees: these marked only a beginning. Preoccupied in 1861 and early 1862 with the problem of keeping the border states of Maryland, Kentucky, and Missouri from joining the Confederacy, the administration was determined not to let antislavery become the war's stated rationale and purpose. Lincoln did accept Butler's definition of slaves who rallied to the Union as "contrabands." The First Confiscation Act, which he signed in August 1861, made both what Butler had done and its rationalization under the strict laws of war the basis of federal policy toward such people. But the administration would not go further. It repudiated General John C. Frémont when he tried to use martial law to free the slaves of all Missouri rebels. Secretary of War Simon Cameron, who backed Butler and who proposed arming black men, was "banished to an ambassadorship in Russia." Generals Henry Halleck, Don Carlos Buell, and John A. Dix simply turned away slaves who came seeking freedom.

The Contrabands, Butler, and the slaveholder James Cook, not the likes of Halleck, understood where events were pointing. Union troops who "stormed ashore at Port Royal" in the South Carolina Sea Islands in November 1861 bore "assurances that slave property would be respected." But their commanders could "employ captured or fugitive slaves . . . much as Butler had done." The troops found "few slaveholders to assure." They had fled, but slaves had "thwarted their owners' frantic attempt to evacuate them." These were Gullah speakers whose families had been growing long-staple cotton and rice in the coastal islands since colonial times. Now their slavery was over and Port Royal became the site of a remarkable experiment in which free black people showed how well they could do on their own small farms.[34]

The Lincoln administration took some time to work out its winning policy of tightening a ring of blockading naval vessels, river gunboats, and advancing armies around the Confederacy whatever the cost. One effect was to make what lay west of the Mississippi River irrelevant. Texas more or less escaped the war, and slavery did not end there until

"Juneteenth," black Texans' name for June 19, 1865, when the proclamation of freedom finally came. Masters east of the Mississippi tried to "refugee" slaves farther south, farther inland, farther from wherever the "Abolition Army" advanced. Because the Confederate troops fought with enormous determination under very talented officers, many masters retained control for a long time. "A considerable portion of the South's antebellum slave population" were still slaves at the war's end. Yet from the moment that black Virginians began "refugeeing" themselves as hostilities broke out, ending slavery was their war aim. By the time Lincoln made it an official goal, it was clear that slavery was already breaking up, under enormous pressure from within.

By late 1864 even Confederate President Jefferson Davis was beginning to refer to slaves as "persons." In March 1865, near the very end of the war, the Confederate Congress accepted the idea of enlisting and freeing black soldiers, as opposed to the forced black labor that it had been exacting since the war's beginning.[35] At first, black labor had been all that the Union army, the federal government, and the northern electorate would accept. By 1863, however, black men on the northern side were becoming soldiers, doing under military discipline what the 1861 Mississippi plotters had set out to do under their own "General Scott," now that it seemed (in the words of one of the Mississippians) that "freedom was at our door."[36]

[V]

Nearly 190,000 black men served in the Union army. Their record shows what slavery's destruction meant. The census of 1860 recorded 4,441,830 black people of both sexes and all ages in the United States, 488,070 of them free, the rest enslaved. If every free black male in the North donned a blue uniform, regardless of age or health, they would not quite account for the number of black men who actually fought for the Union. Since age and health disqualified many black Northerners from service, the importance of former slaves to the Union's military effort becomes clear. Black men wanted an active part in the struggle, with rifles rather than shovels in their hands. Their difficulty was to convince the North's leaders and white citizens to let them do it.[37]

Ironically, black military units first appeared in the deepest South and under the Confederate flag in 1861. These sprang from the communities of free people of color who had long dwelled in Mobile and New Orleans.

Dating back to each city's pre-American days, these communities had rights that were protected by the treaties with Spain and France that ceded West Florida and Louisiana to the United States. In 1861 they organized Native Guards, under their own officers. The same Benjamin Butler who had commanded at Fortress Monroe led the Union's capture of New Orleans in 1862. While white Louisiana troops fled, the Native Guards offered him their services. After some hesitation, he accepted them into Union ranks, under their own officers. They fought with courage in May 1863 at Port Hudson, Louisiana, the first battle that pitted black Unionists against white Confederates.[38]

The *gens de couleur* of New Orleans were an "elite—light-skinned, educated, propertied, and cosmopolitan." Many owned slaves; some sent their children to France for schooling. That these most privileged of all southern people of color did not flee Butler with the rest of the Confederate garrison is another indication of the southern system's weakness. Less privileged, poorer, often illiterate African-American men found that both Northerners and Southerners erected high obstacles to keep them out of the military struggle.

But the barriers could not stand. In an "unofficial letter" of "friendly advice," the northern general-in-chief told his friend commanding the Department of the Tennessee in March 1863 how matters stood. The writer was Henry Halleck, who had turned would-be Contrabands away two years before. The recipient was U. S. Grant, whose own spouse owned slaves. It was "good policy" to use the former slaves "to the very best advantage we can," Halleck wrote, and he expected Grant to "use your official and personal influence to remove prejudices on this subject." The "character of the war had changed" and the North "must either destroy the slave-oligarchy, or become slaves themselves." The government had "adopted a policy, and we must cheerfully and faithfully carry out that policy." An anonymous "Colored Man" in New Orleans offered more advice, in words that he wrote out with difficulty: "Declare freedom at onc and give us Somting to fight for Black Soldiers Black officers and all white rebles will Soon run them in or out of the union." About the same time Mary Duncan, Unionist daughter of the great Mississippi cotton family, protested her outrage that "all the male negroes" had been removed from her family's estates by army "pressgangs." These were people who were "freed and working for us on wages," but it was still, she thought, a "violation of our rights." It also meant the Duncan family's losing its cotton crop on their "*nine* estates on the river."[39]

In 1864 the adjutant general, Lorenzo Thomas, reported to the Sec-

retary of War on raising "Colored Troops." Iowa had provided one regiment, Arkansas six, Tennessee five, and Mississippi eight. There were
ten regiments from Louisiana, three from Alabama, one from Florida.
Fifteen regiments had enlisted in Kentucky. The 56,310 black soldiers
on whom he reported were infantrymen, light and heavy artillerymen,
and cavalry. Even "more troops" could have been raised "but for the
pressing demands" for laborers. Where troops of both races came together, blacks did whatever shovel work was needed and General Thomas
had tried "in vain" to "correct" this. The regiments had no black officers.
They suffered from inadequate medical care, until abolitionist physicians
were recruited from New England. Nonetheless, black men were becoming corporals and sergeants and "the prejudice in the Army against their
employment as troops . . . since their fighting qualities and manliness
have been fully shown . . . has greatly changed."[40]

As Thomas understood, what the black soldiers actually did is what
changed the "prejudice." They did not remedy it all. The adjutant general saw one central issue, the insistence of white commanders that black
troops would be used for labor, as if they were mere auxiliaries, while
white soldiers fought, much as the British had used white New England
militiamen more than a century before. In some theaters of the war this
was never remedied. West of the Mississippi River there was never much
serious fighting. On the river's eastern shore the worst of it—Shiloh and
Vicksburg—was over before the black units really began to form. Nor
did black soldiers fight at Antietam, Maryland, in 1862, the most bloody
single day of the whole war. The most successful northern commander,
U. S. Grant, never really believed that black troops could be worthy
fighters. Neither did William Tecumseh Sherman, who simply refused
to have black troops with him on his march from Atlanta to the sea.[41]

In terms of visibility, 1863 was the most important year for black
combatants. At Port Hudson and Milliken's Bend, Louisiana, and at Fort
Wagner, South Carolina, they showed that they would not quit under
severe fire and cut through white stereotypes maintaining that blacks
were naturally cowardly. The list of places where they fought during the
last, grinding phase of the war includes Fort Pillow, where victorious
Confederates massacred them, Nashville, which ended southern hopes in
Tennessee, Saltville, Virginia, where former slaves won "respectful silence" at the battle's end from white troops who had jeered them at its
start, lesser engagements in both Carolinas and Florida, and the trench
warfare at Petersburg and Richmond that finally brought the war to an
end.[42]

[VI]

Black troops who faced Confederates were casting off the psychological burden that two hundred and fifty years of forced submission had piled upon them. They took even greater risks than their white comrades. The massacre of black troops who surrendered at Fort Pillow took place under the command of Confederate general Nathan Bedford Forrest, a slave trader before the war and the founder of the Ku Klux Klan after it. For a time it was Confederate policy to treat black prisoners as rebellious slaves and whites with them as fomenters of insurrection, rendering both subject to the penalty of death. The Lincoln administration threatened retaliation, and it did end "prisoner exchanges . . . when the south excluded black soldiers from the exchange." In practice, capture by the Confederacy came to mean not execution but rather a return to slavery or, if the soldier had been free before enlistment, enslavement.[43]

The different treatment accorded black and white prisoners of war in the South had its northern counterpart in soldiers' pay. Despite promises of equal treatment, it became War Department policy to treat black soldiers as militiamen, rather than regular troops, paying them $10 per month, with a $3 deduction for the costs of their uniforms, rather than at the regular soldiers' rates of between $13 for a new private and $21 for a top sergeant. A black noncommissioned officer got the same pay as a private, which meant that whatever his rank he earned less than the newest white recruit. The issue became a major black grievance. In part the matter was practical. Whether they had been born free or in slavery, black soldiers were not likely to be men of any significant property and many had families to support. The principle, however, was what stung. The famous 54th Massachusetts Regiment, which had been recruited among free Northerners and which was decimated when it led the action at Fort Wagner, refused to accept any pay as long as the differential held. The regiment's white abolitionist officers supported their men. Not all the protests against inequality had officers' support. When a company of the black 3rd South Carolina Volunteers refused duty, the sergeant who led the protest, William Walker, was tried for mutiny and " 'shot to death with musketry' . . . in the presence of the Brigade."[44]

The murder and reenslavement of black prisoners of war by the South prefigured the reestablishment of white supremacy when the war and Reconstruction were finally over. Unequal pay, menial duties, and the North's virtual refusal to give officer rank to black soldiers were signs that the end of slavery was not going end black inequality. The struggle continued; it merely took a new phase. The fact that black people forced their way into the merely constitutional struggle between North and South helped transform it into open conflict over what everyone knew to be the real issue, freedom and slavery. The entry of black men made the northern army the genuinely "abolition" force that Southerners saw it as being as early as 1861. Southern men who escaped as runaway slaves returned to the ground of their degradation as victorious uniformed conquerors, showing themselves, people they had left behind, and their former masters that the old ways were gone. Nonetheless, the wartime reluctance of the North first to accept them into the struggle or then to treat them as equal participants bespoke a truth about race relations above the Chesapeake and the Ohio that white Southerners did understand, however self-serving were the ways in which they had used it before slavery ended. Slavery was gone. But along both the ancient lines of race and gender and the new lines of class and section in what was becoming a fully capitalist society, inequality endured.

CHAPTER 11

IN ONE, MANY

FORT Sumter in 1861, like Lexington Green in 1775, reduced all questions to just one: which side to choose. From the simplicity of that stark question new complexity emerged. Twice in their history Americans have disputed with arms whether to be a people at all. Both times, that issue has yielded to the problem of what kind of people to be. Both wars set agendas not of peace but rather for postwar strife. Each agenda included old questions that remained unresolved and new ones that had lain beyond the edge of imagination. In characteristically American style, the framing of the questions became political and constitutional, but they probed the very heart of society.

The stillness that fell at Appomattox on April 9, 1865, signaled that great issues finally had been resolved. The Republic would not be dismembered, whatever the pretensions of the separate states to sovereignty. The Old South was dead and its two defining social classes, the masters and the slaves, were ceasing to exist, at least in terms of one's claim to actually own the other. What Abraham Lincoln passed to his hapless successor, Andrew Johnson, came much closer to how Lincoln had defined democracy in 1858—a society with neither slaves nor masters— than what the equally hapless James Buchanan had passed to Lincoln four years, one month, and eleven days before.

Under the needs of a great war and the rule of an activist party, a powerful central state was emerging. Before the war the federal government's role in American society had been largely negative. The Republic had provided shared citizenship, military and civil protection, coherent law, the outlines of a common market, and international respectability, but little more. Virtually the only people who directly felt its power had been those Indians it succeeded in driving beyond the Mississippi, the Mexicans it conquered, and the escaped slaves its federal marshals recaptured after the passage of the Fugitive Slave Law of 1850. Jefferson and Jackson, the two most significant Presidents between Washington and Lincoln, agreed that government should do the least it could. The only President with an active national program, John Quincy Adams, failed. Henry Clay shared Adams's vision, but he never entered the White House other than as another man's cabinet officer or invited guest.

By 1865 the federal government had power to influence every American life and not just in matters of war. The Morrill Land Grant Act of 1862 put it in the business of higher education. The first railroad to the Pacific was underway and would be finished in 1869. All the transcontinental lines except the Great Northern were built with federal sponsorship through land grants. The railroads crossed lands where men and women could acquire federal land free at 160 acres per applicant, under the Homestead Law that the Republicans passed in 1862. The lines also crossed vast acreages that were not free for the taking at all. These could only be bought at greatly enhanced prices, whether direct from the government, from private speculators, or from the railroads.

President James Buchanan's Washington, D.C., had been a large village with a few public buildings, where Congress assembled for short terms and where a handful of clerks served government departments. President Andrew Johnson's Washington was a city of officials. In March 1865, the Bureau of Refugees, Freedmen, and Abandoned Lands, better known as the Freedmen's Bureau, became the first federal venture into welfare. Under it nearly half a million "former slaves and free blacks" participated "in some form of federally sponsored free labor in the Union-occupied South."[1] A veterans' service followed. The Department of Agriculture began defining a new governmental role in the economy. There was an enormous national debt that bore equally enormous implications for forming and using capital. Northerners had paid income taxes, though only as a wartime measure. The wartime government crushed dissent, by defeating the South, suppressing the New York draft riots, and imprisoning or exiling some 13,000 antiwar Copperheads.[2]

The issue now was not whether there would be a strong, active national power. It was who would benefit from the power the government had gained, even if peace meant that some power would ebb away. There were many claimants. Nothing was resolved about former slaves, beyond ending slavery. Nor was there certainty about the former masters. The future of the Indian nations was just as much in doubt. Wartime experience had presaged two different possibilities for them. Indian regiments fought under Indian officers on both sides. These were "soldiers," not "warriors," and the honor they earned pointed toward one future. The hangings on the Minnesota frontier in 1862 and the destruction by Colorado militia of a defenseless Cheyenne camp at Sand Creek two years later pointed toward another.[3]

For the war's duration, patriotism dampened tensions of region, interest, gender, and class within the coalition the Republicans had assembled. When war ended and patriotic fervor passed, the time for self-sacrifice seemed over.[4] If what followed became known as the "Great Barbecue," it was because there was a great deal of pork for the roasting. War was over, but struggle did not stop in any sense, economic, political, cultural, or even military.

[I]

Not all the problems of the Reconstruction era focused on the South, but it presented the most complex and pressing issues. White Southerners had failed in their bid for separate nationhood. The wealth they had poured into the war was dissipated, gone indeed with the wind. Southern factories, railroads, and cities were wrecked. But the South had two strengths: its rich land and a great body of potential labor power, including both former slaves and white "plain folk." Before the war, slaves and land had formed most of the South's capital. Now black Southerners were free persons, and they had a sharp sense of what freedom should mean. No longer bound to a place, freed people began to journey. Perhaps it was just for the joy of being on the road without a pass. Perhaps it was for the far more serious reason of finding parents, children, and spouses whom slavery had torn away.[5] They solemnized their marriages before ministers or Yankee magistrates. Like Jane Barnwell, they picked their way through the moral rubble that slavery had made of their personal lives. When Barnwell lost her husband, Martin, to the slave traders she had married Ferguson, who knew that Martin remained Jane's great love. Now came their moment of truth, for Martin who "is my husband . . . an' the father of my child" returned to her. Ferguson would accept it, she knew. He understood the issues and he was *"a man."* The extent to which that problem troubled former slaves shows how seriously they had taken the difficulties of being married "till death or Buckra do you part."[6]

Men and women who had been slaves found themselves becoming free workers. The earliest communities that emerged from Deep South slavery, the Gullahs of the Georgia and South Carolina coast and islands, became the subjects of intense interest on the part of Yankees who wanted to solve their problems for them and make money from them. One possibility was becoming laborers on reorganized plantations, under northern investors. Well-meaning, self-seeking, or both, Northerners began casting themselves for that role as early as 1861.[7] But the former slaves knew whose labor and blood were mixed with the southern soil, in the classic Lockean formulation that gave good title to land. They had built the South. Their vision of a good world was not one of growing cash crops. Their absolutely free choice would probably have been an African-American variation on how white plain folk already lived: free-hold mixed-cropping that grew most of what a family needed and something to sell or trade as well, without becoming trapped by a single staple crop.[8]

The possibility seemed open. The government never actually used the words "forty acres and a mule" that have come to symbolize it, but in practice that was how coastal and Sea Island land was parceled out as the Yankees advanced. Everybody assumed that secessionists who abandoned their land forfeited it, as loyalists had forfeited their land during America's earlier revolution, or as Indians were deemed to forfeit the land anytime the United States waged a "just" war upon them. By early 1864 islanders were seeking to preempt the soil. In January 1865 General William Tecumseh Sherman issued "Special Field Order Number 15," which "reserved and set apart" all the "islands from Charleston, south, the abandoned rice fields along the rivers for thirty miles back from the sea, and the country bordering the St. Johns river, Florida . . . for the settlement of the negroes now made free." Sherman had refused black troops, but now he offered black autonomy, in the precise sense that American ideology had long enshrined. The islands and lowlands of South Carolina and Georgia could become a perfect realization both of Thomas Jefferson's idyllic vision of a yeoman republic where "the small landholders are the most precious part" and of what the Homestead Act intended for the West.[9]

It did not happen. Part of the reason may be the sheer tragedy of Lincoln's assassination on Good Friday 1865, because it made Andrew Johnson President. A poor white Southerner, Johnson based his policy on little more than to make the secessionist planter "Chivalry" grovel and then to extend complete forgiveness. Lincoln had also pointed that way, however, when he proposed to reestablish civil government and property rights once 10 percent of white men renewed allegiance. More-over, many powerful Republicans balked on principle at seizing Confed-erates' land. Property in human beings was illegitimate, they thought, but property in land or goods was sacred.

The complex political maneuvering that followed among former Con-federates, the Johnson administration, and the Republicans' radical wing has been well described elsewhere.[10] The story leads through Kentucky's last-ditch attempt in 1865 to hold on to slavery, attempted reenslave-ment in all but name by briefly restored white governments, the Thir-teenth Amendment to the Constitution that ended slavery for good, antiblack riots in Memphis and especially New Orleans, the emergence of the Ku Klux Klan, Congress's strong civil rights bill and Johnson's veto of it, Congress's response with its own program of Reconstruction under military control, and its further response with the impeachment of Johnson in 1868 for "high crimes and misdemeanors."

The Senate failed to convict Johnson by just one vote. The disgraced President served out his term and was succeeded by Ulysses S. Grant, the victorious Union general. Grant enjoyed overwhelming black support and during his eight-year presidency military Reconstruction remained federal policy. Actual support for either Reconstruction's agents or their constituents weakened steadily. When final "Redemption" came at the accession of Grant's successor, Rutherford B. Hayes, in 1877, it did not lead to instant white supremacy and racial segregation. These came later. It did, however, restore the entire South to white control, except in scattered localities.[11]

The enduring monuments of the political struggle were the three Reconstruction amendments to the Constitution. The Thirteenth ratified the abolition of slavery that black energy, the Emancipation Proclama-tion, and northern military victory had achieved. The Fourteenth over-turned the *Dred Scott* decision's exclusion of black people from the American polity and from legal rights under the Constitution. It made "all persons born or naturalized in the United States . . . citizens of the United States and of the State wherein they reside." It seemed, at least, to protect the "privileges and immunities" of citizenship, for under its terms no "person" could be deprived of "life, liberty, or property" with-out "due process of law." For the purpose of apportioning representation in Congress, black Americans would be counted as whole human beings, rather than three-fifths of what whites were. The amendment also re-pudiated the Confederate debt and denied any possibility of compensation for the loss of slave property. The Fifteenth Amendment forbade the states to infringe male citizens' right to vote on the ground of their "race, color, or previous condition of servitude."

On paper, the achievement was striking. In practice, only the Thirteenth Amendment had a lasting effect. By the 1880s the Supreme Court was construing both the Fourteenth and the Fifteenth Amendment in the most narrow possible ways, culminating in the 1896 *Plessy* v. *Ferguson* decision, which held that states could impose "separate but equal" facilities upon the two races. Not until the National Association for the Advancement of Colored People, a Supreme Court of very different composition, and the Southern Christian Leadership Conference forced the "Second Reconstruction" of the 1950s and 1960s would those decisions be overturned and the first Reconstruction's promise of legal and political equality begin to approach reality.[12]

[II]

Nonetheless, a "New South" began to emerge. One possible change was that the defeated states be remade in the image of the middle-class capitalist North. What had been bare tendencies during the time of slavery would become the main lines of development. In the long run, this happened, but not very fast. Edgefield County, South Carolina, the home of John C. Calhoun, James Henry Hammond, and several successive planter-politicians named Wade Hampton, had over half the investment capital that South Carolinians put into cotton manufacturing in 1860. But after the war there was no surge of development there. Mill building in the southern piedmont did not begin until the 1870s and did not really flourish until decades later. There were 10,000 textile workers in the whole South in 1870, "the same number as in 1850 and 1860," and only 17,000 in 1880. By 1900, however, there were 98,000, roughly a third of the national workforce in the industry.[13]

The immense deposits of coal and iron ore in northern Alabama that became the basis of Birmingham's steel industry were well known, and debate about what to do with them was underway as soon as the war ended. Not until 1879, however, did Birmingham begin to be more than "a real estate boomtown at a railroad crossing." Even as Birmingham's full "industrial development was getting underway," Mobile's principal newspaper was reminding "its readers that agriculture was the true basis of Alabama's economy." By the 1880s the incredibly rich lands of the Mississippi/Yazoo Delta were crisscrossed with railroads, but the tracks had no other purpose than to get cotton to market.[14] "Southern manufacturing did not fit . . . the general pattern" of nineteenth-century industrial development. Despite "impressive strides" in a few industries, notably cigarettes, furniture, and textiles, "most southern industrial workers labored in forests and mines," extracting raw materials rather than transforming them. Cotton would remain king.[15] The possibilities existed; the tendencies were real. But for the most part the destruction of slavery did not lead to remaking the region in the northern conqueror's image.

What it brought instead was "one kind of freedom" that worked itself out with local variations all the way from the Virginia southside to the Texas plains. At its heart was cotton, touching more people and more places than it ever had before.[16]

Broadly, the outlines of the New South are simple to describe. Cotton production increased. Black people grew much of it, with almost no chance of escaping from it. Former masters wanted to retain the old plantation style, but gang labor was no longer possible. There were two reasons for this. Blatant use of "vagrancy" laws, year-long forced contracts, and involuntary apprenticeship of young blacks marked the first stage in the defeated planters' campaign to regain control in 1865. It proved too blatant both for the former slaves and for white Northerners. It was one reason why a Radical Congress intervened in 1866 and 1867 to protect the former slaves' civil rights and put the areas of worst abuse under military control. Had there been a massive redistribution of plantation ownership at that point, or had there been a serious attempt to resettle the former slaves on public land, the subsequent course of southern development might have been very different.

The social compromise that was worked out instead had three ingredients. The first was continued white control of the land. The second was effective black control of the details of cotton production, by substituting family-based sharecropping and tenant labor for old-style gangs. This ended "the plantation" as a coherent social unit, marked by planter control and immediate racially defined authority over black life. It also ended the picture that plantations presented of gentry elegance and patriarchal authority from one perspective and neo-African communities under alien domination from the other.[17] The great houses would remain, but the black workers would live either in their own settlements or on scattered farms.

The third element was a new kind of discipline, to replace the departed power of overseers and drivers. This took two forms. One was outright terror, enforced both by local officials who had the power to arrest and imprison and by groups like the Ku Klux Klan and the Knights of the White Camellia. Continuing the traditions of the slavery-era "patrollers," these night riders used costumes and pageantry to frighten supposedly superstitious blacks. If those failed, burning houses or barns, destroying crops and killing livestock, and murder would follow. The other form was using economic power to lock the former slaves into growing cotton. The means for this was country stores, which acquired monopolies on credit, on the supply of necessary goods, and on the purchase of what small farmers had to sell, backed by state crop lien laws that let creditors take out mortgages on growing crops. In that situation, the creditors acquired enormous power over what crops would be grown. It amounted to peonage, and it was a major element in defining the conditions of southern black rural life until cotton became a mechanized crop in the mid-twentieth century. What the former slaves gained from sharecropping had one merit: now a black family could control its internal life. It was a poor imitation of "forty acres and a mule," however, and it offered virtually no prospects for a family that wanted to improve its situation.

All this happened where there already had been cotton, plantations, and slaves. Cotton culture also spread into places it had only begun to touch before the war. It engulfed white plain folk who had previously stood apart from it. In economic and material terms, many of these found themselves facing material conditions not much different from those of the former slaves, including effective debt peonage. They had the immense advantage of being white. They gave rise to a tradition of white populism that produced such redoubtable political figures as Tom Watson of Georgia, "Pitchfork Ben" Tillman of South Carolina, James K. Vardaman and Theodore Bilbo of Mississippi, Huey Long of Louisiana, and ultimately George Wallace of Alabama and Lyndon Johnson of Texas. Nonetheless, their conditions could approach those of their black fellows. The haunting photographs of white southern poverty during the 1930s that Walker Percy took for *Let Us Now Praise Famous Men* and the pen picture that John Steinbeck limned in *The Grapes of Wrath* make the point as well as a stack of statistics.[18]

On this basis, the distinctive region that was "the South" reestablished its participation in the national and world commercial economy. How did it work in practice? Let us look at some variations on the main theme, working from Virginia to Mississippi.

Southampton County, Virginia, was the site of Nat Turner's attempted slave insurrection in 1832. It lies south of Chesapeake Bay, bounded by two rivers that flow into North Carolina's Albemarle Sound. During the last years of slavery it had both an overall black majority and a substantial free black population. It lay far enough south for cotton and it began growing the crop around 1830. It also produced pork commercially. Orchard and garden crops, grains, and potatoes figured in its mid-nineteenth-century output. Tobacco did not.

After the war, diarist Daniel W. Cobb recorded the changes he saw there. Cotton prices soared briefly and farmers rushed to plant the crop. Many were former slaves, whose insistence on controlling their time and families bothered the traditionalist Cobb. On his own place, black tenants abandoned "the old slave quarters in the yard." They built "new homes in the woods" for themselves, that "followed a pattern observed widely across the south at this time." They also plunged into debt, and that brought disaster when "cotton prices tumbled just as the 1870 crop reached market."

The price collapse did not kill black independence. Shocked when a coalition of "the Nigars in Town" and "radacal whites" elected a Vermont carpetbagger to Congress, boycotted in 1871 by blacks who preferred to settle "with those where stors are located," Cobb tried running his place with white wage labor. It was not a success, and neither was his return to "negrow hands" the following year. Although he felt warm enough toward his tenants to visit a "negrow school exhibition," Cobb died that autumn, a bitter and unreconstructed man.[19] There had been "real changes" in Southampton, but it remained a divided world, locked more than ever into producing its cash crop.

Two regions in Georgia present contrasting but complementary pictures. In the central part of the state lie the counties of Houston, Twiggs, Bibb, Crawford, Monroe, and Jones. Some of their land is on the "flat coastal plain," some on "the gently rolling hills of the lower Piedmont." The soil is rich. The region began with yeoman settlement but it was plantation country by slavery's end, centered on the market town of Macon, where three railroads met. Macon lay on the route of Sherman's March to the Sea, but freedom there did not come with that cataclysm. Instead, "it developed slowly over the course of the war . . . with countless small struggles that in the end decisively shaped the outcome of events." By war's end the former slaves "understood that freedom was not an absolute state so much as a contest that might sway backward as well as forward."

During the postwar years central Georgia moved into what its historian calls "agrarian capitalism." In this new scenario the freed people would be a "rural proletariat," wholly dependent upon the owners of the land. Whatever social unevenness the slavery-era order had provided would be ironed out. Central Georgia slavery had not been airtight. Instead, much of the labor that produced its cotton had been done on a tasking basis, emulating practice in the rice-growing lowlands and coastal islands of Georgia and South Carolina. This left considerable room for the slaves to develop customs that had no basis in law but that had a firm basis in their lives. Of these, free open-range herding on unused land and harvested fields and free hunting were central. These customs, like the informal right to cultivate their own small plots, permitted slaves to develop quasi-independent family economies and gave them the means for local exchange. These same herding and hunting customs were also central to how nonplantation white people supported themselves. In the antebellum era such customs had been protected by a fencing law that obliged "planters to enclose their crops" rather than "stock owners to pen their animals," a practice that reached back to 1759.

When Democrats regained control of Georgia in 1872 they commenced an assault on such traditions. The state legislature adopted a local-option law on fencing that permitted a reversal of open-range herding. Instead of agriculturalists having the obligation to fence animals out if they wanted to protect their crop, stock owners would be required to fence their animals in. The era when it was a customary right to graze animals on unused land, whoever owned it, was over. In forty-two Georgia counties a ban was imposed on nighttime trading. Night had been when slaves did their informal trading before the war and it was the only time most farmers could set fieldwork aside. Banning trade at night concentrated all commerce in the hands of planters and store owners. Sharecropping was defined in law as "merely another mode of wage labor, rather than a form of tenure," so that "croppers got their share only after landlords and furnishing merchants had taken theirs." Free access to land "for the purposes of gathering wood, hunting, and fishing" came to an end. Henceforth the landowner's permission would be required.[20]

Before the war Georgia's "up-country," centered on Atlanta, had been a different sort of place. Its black population was smaller, and "plantation-size units were few and far between." Among its yeomen, even more than in central Georgia, local custom had established the terms and rhythms of most people's lives. Up-country crops were mixed. Small farmers there did grow cotton, but in small amounts, not enormous quantities as staple-crop specialists. In 1860 the two counties of Jackson and Carroll produced 1,594 bales and 3,982 bales, respectively. Their major crop was corn, with 290,684 bushels and 331,692 bushels, respectively.

Reconstruction brought a striking transformation. In absolute terms, corn production stayed much the same, with Jackson County growing 295,641 bushels in 1880 and Carroll County producing 370,892. In per capita terms, however, these crop figures marked a sharp drop, from 27.4 bushels to only 19.6 in Jackson and from 27.6 to 21.9 in Carroll. Cotton production shot up, to 9,482 bales in Jackson County and 9,300 in Carroll, tripling the former county's per capita production and doubling the latter's. In Jackson County a farm of fewer than twenty-four acres was producing only half a bale on average in 1860 and producing two bales in 1880. Production on farms of between one hundred and two hundred acres was 3.8 bales in 1860 and 13.4 in 1880. Up-country farmers were continuing to raise grain and livestock, but a dramatic shift was happening in their lives.

The shift began because high postwar prices offered good reason to move into cotton. But the up-country's poorer soils and shorter growing season required fertilizer, particularly guano. This could readily be had on credit through country stores, and by 1873 up-country farmers were buying large quantities of it. Georgia's fertilizer consumption tripled between 1874 and 1881, bringing both increased productivity to old plantation regions and the up-country's leap into the crop. In the up-country as in central Georgia there resulted a sharp assault on traditional customs like hunting and herding on the open range. Commercial debt climbed just as sharply, provided and administered through the same country stores that brought the guano in and shipped the cotton out. Many of the people affected were white plain folk, members of what had been a freestanding yeomanry. Access to larger markets brought benefits, but it also enmeshed these people in a situation from which they could not extricate themselves.

They too became bound by crop lien laws that effectively denied them either ownership of what they grew or choice about what to grow. A creditor would offer to finance cotton and fertilizer, but not food crops. Corn and bacon became commercial commodities that had to be bought out of the surplus that remained after the cotton was sold, not items that a farming family produced to consume itself and exchange with its neighbors. Within "fifteen years the Upcountry moved from the periphery into the vortex of the market economy." Here lay the "roots of southern populism," and that late-nineteenth century political movement proved attractive to black people and whites alike. It was neither the first time nor the last when the shared experience of class overbalanced for a time the separating experience of race in southern life.[21]

Virginia, the Carolinas, and Georgia were old societies that had time to develop thick webs of local custom. Away from the coastal states, what Reconstruction proposed to change had much more shallow roots. In the Alabama Black Belt, plantation society dated not from the seventeenth or eighteenth century but only from the land sales of the late 1810s. In much of Mississippi, it dated from the 1830s. In Arkansas, northern Louisiana, and East Texas, slavery's time was shorter still. Much of the Mississippi/Yazoo Delta remained wild forest and wetland during the war. The novelist William Faulkner gave one picture of what capitalist transformation meant in these places after Reconstruction. In his fictional Yoknapatawpha County, Mississippi, the aristocratic Sartoris family gives way to the Snopeses, poor whites who climb the ladder of wealth and power with neither grace nor conscience. Reality was more complex.

In central Alabama planters never lost control. Subverting the Freedmen's Bureau, they organized the Ku Klux Klan as their instrument to control the former slaves. They wanted labor, and the Klan told former slaves that "they would be killed on their way" if they tried to leave. Here the replacement of gang labor by sharecropping meant "a substantial defeat" for the planters, but it also brought "a repressive system of labor allocation and control, based . . . on informal agreements . . . to limit competition for labor, on state laws which established legal obstacles to the free market in labor, and on the intermittent use of terror." These planters faced a substantial challenge from merchants who proposed to replace them as the middlemen between the black cotton growers and the market. When they resumed full control of the state at Reconstruction's end, they passed a crop lien law that gave primacy to landlords rather than merchants over tenant and sharecropper production. In 1883 Alabama established the "Anaconda" mortgage, which "gave the landlord the right to take not only his tenant's crop . . . but also his furniture, household goods, and personal effects," again with primacy over merchant claims. The following year merchants' liens became illegal "in all but one of the twelve counties where the population was more than 75 percent black, and in all but four of the twenty counties that were more than 50 percent black." As early as 1866 an Alabama planter had predicted that "the nigger is going to be made a serf, sure as you live. It won't need any law for that. Planters will have an understanding among themselves . . . then what's left for them? They're attached to the soil, and we're as much their masters as ever."[22] His fellows did their best to see the prediction come true.

The Natchez district of Mississippi had been the early heartland of Mississippi Valley cotton production. Such towns as Natchez and Port Gibson provide, in brick, stone, and intricately worked wood, elegant monuments to the district's vitality. The district became the home of Mississippi's "cotton nabobs," including both the Unionist Stephen Duncan and Confederate President Jefferson Davis. But "enterprising Yankees [who] flocked to the district" after the war "found the former slaveowners more than willing 'to let others try the experiment,' " and "by 1866 most of the great cotton estates bordering the Mississippi . . . were in the hands of lessees."

Much of the old elite did survive, however, and former slaves had virtually no chance of acquiring land. Their only choices were to work for wages or on shares. The largest difference between the Black Belt and the Natchez area was the emergence in the latter of a significant merchant group, trading directly with former slaves, not with the whites who owned or leased plantations. Mississippi's crop lien law did not give legal priority to landlords over merchants. In practice, however, the result was much the same as it was in Alabama, when small traders and planters who remained worked out an accommodation among themselves. From the black point of view it made little difference. Mississippi store records show markups on consumer goods sold to tenants and sharecroppers of between 22 and 100 percent, except for the absolutely basic foodstuffs of flour and sugar. This is completely in line with the "dual price" system that a general economic history of the post-Civil War South finds at the "roots of southern poverty."[23]

Finally, let us look at the delta, "the most southern place on earth." Before the war it was already distinct from the rest of Mississippi. Its black population enormously outnumbered its whites in 1860. Of the towns that now mark its map, Clarksdale, "the home of the blues," and Greenwood, "the cotton capital of the world," did not even exist. Cotton production reached as much as eight bales per slave.[24] The problem facing postwar delta landowners was not to control the existing black population; it was to attract new people who would build levees against flooding, drain swamps, cut forests, and open even more of the enormously fertile land to cotton. The task was not completed until well into the twentieth century. The need for labor put delta landowners into

competition with their own sort farther east in Mississippi and in Alabama. In the Mississippi hill country, whites turned to terror to prevent
"their" blacks from responding to the delta's temptations. The delta was
no paradise. It had always been an unhealthy place, and it still is. The
delta is the homeland of the blues, the great musical outpouring of black
American pain and endurance. Nonetheless, immediately after the war
it offered former slaves real possibilities that other southern places could
not match.

The lasting monument to those possibilities is the all-black town of
Mound Bayou founded on 1,500 acres of rich Bolivar County land in
1887 by the black entrepreneurs Isaiah Montgomery and Benjamin
Green and the Louisiana, New Orleans, and Texas Railroad. Mound
Bayou grew from Montgomery's earlier efforts to build a self-governing
and profitable black community at Davis Bend, the estate south of Vicksburg that had belonged to the family of the Confederate President.
Mound Bayou was one of a series of such towns west of the Appalachians,
and its founding was of a piece with the movement of hopeful "Exodusters" from the South to the open lands of Kansas. These towns and
the Exoduster movement are likewise monuments to postwar hope.[25]

Reconstruction in the delta, like slavery there, awaits a fully detailed
modern account.[26] It does seem that "even in the wake of Redemption,
the Delta's future by no means lay wholly in the hands of its white
landlords." Sharecropping was the main means of production even at the
end of the 1870s. People could bargain, not just accept what a planter
or merchant determined. During Reconstruction "tenants who could fur-
nish themselves" might keep up to three-quarters of the crop. In the
words of a Department of Agriculture report of 1870, a former slave's
great "desire" was "to become a proprietor." For a time "labor-hungry
Delta planters . . . urged their friends and neighbors to refrain from the
wholesale repression and violence against blacks that was so common in
other parts of the state." They risked violence themselves when they tried
to lure black people from the hill country. But the difference was only
one of time. By the end of the century, black delta people who ventured
near a train station with the idea of departing risked violence as much
as any black Alabamian had risked when he headed for the delta at the
end of the war. Black disenfranchisement was nearly total, and solid
control by white planter-businessmen was established.[27]

The South is not just one of many American regions. It is where the
European and African presence began. Its existence after the Revolution
as one of the dwindling number of slave areas in the world presented

the largest social problem the young Republic had to face. Its cotton drove the early northern industrial transformation. By its productive capacity, the South affected the whole nation. Nearly until the war, Southerners gave the nation its political leadership as well.

In the South, far more than the Northeast or the Midwest, the uniquely American drama of red, white, and black continued to have three sides, even after Andrew Jackson's supposed expulsion of the tribes beyond the Mississippi. Creeks, Cherokees, Chickasaws, and Choctaws all did remain. Both the full reality of Cotton Kingdom slavery and the continuing impact of Indian ways east of the Mississippi after 1830 still await their historian. Within the overall pattern of the South's "unfinished revolution" after the Civil War there was a great deal of variation. We can no longer to speak of a single "Reconstruction" South, any more than of a single "slave" South. But from Maryland to Texas these ten densely packed years worked out the final resolution of what began as Virginians started edging toward enslaving the Africans among them more than two centuries before. Enslavement then had been unproblematic, just part of the world's uneven way. The end of slavery proved extremely problematic. What remained unfinished as American society abolished the slave system haunts it to the present day.[28]

[III]

The decade after Appomattox was a time of general crisis. As the Republic reached its first century the totally "modern" issues posed by the problems of class, community, formal legal equality, and great economic disparity in any industrial society became more apparent. So did the issue of gender inequality, raised in the first American Revolution and left totally unresolved by the second. So, in a final violent burst of what had begun when the earliest Europeans and Africans arrived, did the problem of what the Indian nations were to do if they did not propose to simply die.

The Republican Party did not begin as the political instrument of an emerging industrial ruling class. Its appeal to northern workers was genuine. The leading Republican in the shoe town of Lynn, Massachusetts, was the wealthy manufacturer John B. Alley, yet Republicans "made headway among workingmen by appealing to their antislavery sentiments and flattering them as the bone and sinew of society, as its producing classes." In the iron city of Troy, New York, Republicans ran the former president of the molders' union for the State Assembly in 1860. In the campaign of 1872 posters showed President Grant under "the workingman's banner" and called him "the Galena [Illinois] Tanner." In Worcester, Massachusetts, the "City of Diversified Industries," neither of the two "mainstream political parties consistently championed working-class candidates or causes."[29]

The Republicans were in search of an enduring perspective and identity and they became the political home of many sorts of people. Let the remarkable Benjamin F. Butler of Massachusetts, who became a key figure among Reconstruction-era "radicals," show what was possible. Before the war Butler had been a "Negro-baiting Buchanan Democrat." He owed his generalship in the Union army to the Lincoln administration's need for the support of his sort. This was the very Butler who found himself in command of the Union toehold at Fortress Monroe, Virginia, in 1861, who faced the question of slaves crossing his lines, and whose decision to keep them and call them Contrabands marked a point of some note as slavery began to die.

As Union commander in New Orleans, Butler "courted the sympathies of the workers, most of whom he knew had been antisecession Douglas Democrats." After the war, Butler replaced John B. Alley as Lynn's congressman. He identified himself with both maximum federal support for the former slaves and labor reform. He addressed a massive trade union rally in Boston late in 1865. Massachusetts "labor reformers" found it "heartening" when Radicals assumed "full control" of the Republican state convention and "Butler himself presided." At the same time "regular Republicans and workingmen's caucuses shared offices and libraries and divided . . . the seats on the . . . city committees."

Congressman Butler resisted the Johnson administration's attempt to reduce the supply of paper currency that wartime needs had required. Keeping money "easy" was popular with his worker constituency, but Butler found himself allied as well with both financier "Jay Cooke . . . and numerous Democrats." More orthodox Republicans came to regard him as "the most complete representative" of their party's "corruption and degeneration." In 1868 they tried to replace him with the Harvard-educated Boston aristocrat Richard Henry Dana, Jr. Dana won enormous support from bankers and manufacturers but only 9 percent of the vote. Butler returned to Congress with the support of two-thirds of the electorate. Nonetheless, Dana's challenge was a sign of the direction that the Republicans were beginning to take.[30]

A tangled party politics of class generated itself in the war's after-math all over the nearly mature industrial North and the commercial-agricultural West. Butler's own community of Lynn became a chartered city and built an imposing city hall. Critics noted that the new building had offices for officials, a meeting room for the city council, courtrooms, and jail cells, but no place now where "the public" could gather. When a business-oriented mayor took office in 1862, one result was to create a police force and a fire service that served the business community. When shoe workers struck in 1878, another business mayor saw that the police escorted strikebreakers to factories. A Workingman's Party mayor followed exactly the reverse policy during another strike in 1885. In Troy, New York, two separate police forces, one responsive to employers and one to workers, literally faced each other across barricades in 1882.[31]

Class was not the only issue, because ethnicity and religion have been central elements throughout the history of American society. In England the lessons about identity, discipline, time, and belonging that went with becoming working class were learned at the beginning of industrializa-tion and passed on in a tradition that still endures. America has seen group after group learn those lessons, each virtually unable to commu-nicate with its predecessor. Almost the same problems of control and resistance in New England textile factories in the 1830s emerged again in their southern counterparts half a century later. They emerged yet again in the developing automobile industry in the early twentieth cen-tury.[32] In the 1950s the "worker city" of Troy, New York, had separate Catholic churches for its Irish, German, French-Canadian, Lebanese, and Italian communities, all within little more than a mile. Worship, leisure and social space, free time and enjoyment, as much as outright class conflict were present in the industrial cities of the postwar era, working themselves out in churches, at ballparks, and in taverns as well as on picket lines.[33] Likewise present is what one historian has called "civic capitalism," which has led in its time not only to urban monuments like the Victorian city hall that Lynn built but also to capitalists' genuine commitment to a community's well-being.[34]

Nonetheless, if there was ever an era when social class became a na-tional issue and when class consciousness spanned both miles and culture, it was the decades that began with the Civil War's end. The clearest evidence is the great and enormously violent railroad strike of 1877, the very year that Redemption signaled the end of southern Reconstruction. Both late-nineteenth-century labor strife and racial segregation lie outside this book's framework. But the same people were involved as the era of class and ethnicity in the North and segregation in the South displaced the era of civil war and slavery's destruction.

[IV]

At the end of Reconstruction the issue of women's rights seemed to be both established and lost. The gains that American women had made since Elizabeth Cady Stanton and Lucretia Coffin Mott called their convention at Seneca Falls in 1848 were striking. Middle-class women were earning college degrees. They had so strong a presence in medicine that Henry James assumed that a woman doctor would be freely accepted in his novel of feminism, *The Bostonians*. Nursing and schoolteaching became largely female professions. Women forced their way into caring for sick and wounded soldiers during the Civil War. Teachers owed a great deal to the campaigning of Catharine Beecher, sister of Harriet Beecher Stowe. But they also owed to her a general perception that a profession dominated by women deserved lower rewards than one dominated by men.[35]

For a middle-class white woman, there were possibilities that simply had not existed before. In the South as well as the North, women had emerged as a force "in public." The totality of the war that the North waged upon their world had a huge impact upon southern white women. They became nurses and "government girls" in the Confederacy's Richmond bureaucracy of 70,000. They took charge of farms and plantations. When the war's demands brought shortages, southern white women turned to traditional notions about the economics of the good small community. Rioting, seizing necessary supplies, and setting "just" prices, they acted almost exactly as Northerners had done during the Revolution. White women in conquered New Orleans showed their contempt for northern troops so strongly that the Yankee commander ordered that "when any female shall by word, gesture, or movement, insult or show contempt for any OFFICER or PRIVATE of the UNITED STATES she shall be regarded and held as liable to be TREATED as A WOMAN OF THE TOWN PLYING HER VOCATION." The commander was Benjamin Butler.[36]

What happened in New Orleans demonstrates the complex relationship between gender and other issues during the Civil War and Reconstruction eras. Women forced an enlargement of "the public sphere" in places as different and remote from one another as New York, New Orleans, and San Francisco. Before the war, public gender politics was necessarily intertwined with the problem of race and slavery.[37] After the war the two issues separated. The white New Orleans women who jeered Butler's troops had no intention of challenging the racial status quo, but they were opening up new social space in which they could act themselves.[38]

The link between gender and race was broken in the North as well. Confronted in 1865 by the resurgent white South's attempt to reestablish slavery in all but name, Radical Republicans responded by forbidding any state to deny the vote to male citizens because of race or previous slavery. This was the first mention of gender in the United States Constitution; previous denials of voting to women had been by state laws. Republicans insisted it was "the Negro's hour" and women could wait their turn. Women's movement leaders like Elizabeth Cady Stanton and Susan B. Anthony saw it differently. Their roots and the Republicans' were in the same soil; they had buried their own issue for the war's duration. They also understood that they were living through a revolutionary time, when long-established practices might be open to fundamental change. They realized also that if they did not seize it such a time would "perish."[39] So in 1867 they broke with the Republicans and moved toward a different feminist politics, with increasing room for southern white women and decreasing room for any women of color. The close friendship between Stanton and Frederick Douglass was ruptured, although Stanton found when Douglass died in 1895 that her grief was intense.[40]

Women who were not middle class experienced the Civil War's aftermath in different ways. For former slave women it meant not only the very real danger of rape but also trying to withdraw from field labor. This was not a matter of emulating the ways of whites; instead, it was part of the "process by which black people ceased to labor for their masters and sought instead to provide directly for one another." Poverty-stricken former slaves were under no illusions that women's productive labor would not be necessary for survival. They did quarrel with the assumption, shared by Yankees and former Confederates alike, that "black wives and mothers should continue to engage in productive labor outside their homes." From a black woman's point of view, one of the advantages of sharecropping was that "economic matters and family affairs overlapped to a considerable degree." In the context of emancipation, survival within families counted for more than personal autonomy that individualism offered.[41] In the context of the developing national economy that solution to an earlier problem posed new problems of its own.

Still another picture was emerging among women of the white working class, complicated always by ethnicity and religion. Even before the war, the original gains in terms of personal autonomy that some members of the first generation of factory women had made were being dissipated. By mid-century, Irish and German migrants were entering the mills, the women among them doing so as family members who contributed to collective household economies, rather than as free individuals on the model of the Lowell mill girls. As Quebecois, Slavs, Eastern European Jews, and Italians followed the original migrant groups, that continued to be the case. Working-class women began to appear in the series of movements that pointed after the war toward union formation on a national scale, beginning with the shoe industry's Knights of St. Crispin. As with the issue of race, the problem of gender presented a distinctively American complication for class politics, raising issues that remain unresolved to the present day. The Republic's first hundred years had seen gender emerge as a visible issue, not to be ignored. But the question of where gender stood alone and where it intertwined with the other categories that also shaped different kinds of American women's lives was only beginning to unfold.[42]

[V]

The decade after Appomattox saw changes of staggering magnitude in American society. The nation recovered from self-immolation. A race that had been entirely subject to another found itself in possession of "nothing but freedom." An industrial working class gave rise to a continent-spanning labor movement. Farmers in both the West and the South began to find their own political voice. Women who claimed to speak for their sex came to the conclusion that their own interests had to stand separate. Other women rejected that conclusion in the name of loyalties that went beyond gender. All of these issues drew their power from the collision between the Republic's unequal social realities and the premises of its rhetoric, a rhetoric strong enough to underpin its people's claim to be a distinct nation.

As these questions fermented, the oldest American issue of all, the place of Indians in a world that had been entirely theirs, was reaching its resolution. White Americans ever since that time have liked to dwell upon the image of a fort, a cavalry regiment, a wagon train, or a cabin surrounded by savage hordes bent on destroying all that was holy and civilized. But it takes no imagination at all to realize that the western Indians—the Sioux, Cheyennes, Arapahos, Comanches, Apaches, Navajos, Zunis, Nez Percé, and the rest—were utterly and finally surrounded, and that they knew it. Their way of life truly had reached the end of possibility.[43]

CODA

THE VEXED, UNANSWERED
QUESTION

A T the end of Reconstruction, one R. M. Devens published a huge
volume that he called *Our First Century*.[1] Its 1,004 pages offered "a
Popular Descriptive Portraiture of the . . . Great and Memorable Events
of Perpetual Interest in the History of our Country . . . Splendidly
Illustrated with . . . Plates, Portraits, and other Embellishments." Among
the "embellishments" was a figure of Time, with his fatal scythe lowered
while he traced the outline of the United States upon the globe. It was
a sign, perhaps, that what Time was drawing would endure.

The familiar topics, from George Washington to the southern surrender at Appomattox, were all there in Devens's book. So too were subjects
like "The Wonderful Dark Day—1780," a "Sublime Meteoric Shower"
of 1833, and "unrivaled Performances by Paul Morphy, the American
Chess champion" in 1858. Each seemed important enough to Devens for
a chapter of its own. *Our First Century* was pure nineteenth-century Amer-
icana. It evoked naive patriotism. It was saturated with humbug. It also
hinted at the proud complexity that Walt Whitman wrote into his great
poem of the same epoch, *Song of Myself*: "Do I contradict myself? Very
well, then, I contradict myself. (I am large. I contain multitudes.)"[2]

Devens celebrated American ingenuity: "Whitney's Extraordinary
Cotton-Gin . . . Fulton's Triumphant Application of Steam to Navigation
. . . Morse's Invention of the Electric Telegraph." He had no sense,
however, that American inventiveness had happened because of people
thinking together about problems they shared. Instead, echoing the dominant belief of the time, one of his steel engravings portrayed a solitary
"inventor toiling in his garret." Devens also reported American disasters.
The image of fire, in particular, kept recurring. Experimental guns exploded; steamships caught fire at sea; whole cities burned; schoolchildren
died in the crush as they fled a blaze they only imagined had broken

out. Perhaps it was Devens's way of dealing with the emotions left over from the great, genuine conflagration that had nearly destroyed the whole Republic only a decade before.

Whatever its hidden burden, the dominant mood of *Our First Century* was triumph. The United States had survived. Never had there been a military coup, or suspension of the Constitution, or armed eviction from the White House, or forced dissolution of Congress. Nor has there been yet. At its founding, the American Republic had stood alone in a monarchical world. All experience predicted that, like every previous republic, it would fail. By its first centennial, the Republic enjoyed imitators through much of its own hemisphere. Kings, queens, and emperors still reigned over most of Europe, but the vision of republicanism was thriving even there. France was on the point of overthrowing its last monarch, the emperor Napoleon III. Within another half century, Ireland, Germany, Austria, Russia, Estonia, Latvia, Lithuania, Poland, and Czechoslovakia would follow, as would China. By the second centennial of the United States, republics would be the normal political form around the globe. What Devens celebrated had inaugurated a worldwide change. If that change was for humanity's good, Americans were not the only people with reason to celebrate.

Devens's Americans were almost entirely white and male. Although one chapter told of the "Greatest Defeat and Victory of American Arms in the Indian Wars" in 1791, the book said nothing about the expulsion of the eastern tribes beyond the Mississippi or how some tribes managed to remain. It had a chapter on how an American army conquered Mexico, but nothing on the history and culture of the people whom that conquest brought into the United States. There was nothing about slavery's nineteenth-century expansion, or about how some black Americans set out to build their own version of American freedom at the same time. The book showed Abraham Lincoln proclaiming slavery's end and freed people rejoicing. But it gave no hint that African-Americans had a hand in destroying slavery, or about the role that white women took in the long campaign to abolish it, or about how those women began considering their own situation as well as the slaves'. All these might as well not have happened. If Devens's book represented American historical consciousness, these memories had been firmly repressed.

What is actually destroyed may be gone. But what is repressed has a way of coming back, in history as much as in psychology. July 4, 1876, was marred by a past that refused to disappear. Women suffragists disrupted the ceremonies in Philadelphia, at which the guest of honor (oddly enough) was the emperor of Brazil. Black America was represented there by not much more than a bust of Frederick Douglass, which amounted only to "an ironic memorial to a job not done" as white America gave up on Reconstruction's ten-year effort "to rebuild the nation along a fundamentally more egalitarian line."[3] In Hamburg, South Carolina, a July 4 celebration by black militiamen led to the militiamen being besieged in their armory, where five of them "were murdered in cold blood." Democratic governor Daniel H. Chamberlain called it "atrocity and barbarism."[4]

Only a few days before the centennial July 4, a combined force of Sioux, Cheyennes, and Arapahos defeated the 7th Regiment of the United States Cavalry at Little Big Horn, which the victors knew as Greasy Grass. When George Armstrong Custer and his troops perished there, all white America was shocked. The shock was understandable, but there was virtually no prospect that such a thing would happen again. The few thousand Indians who united against Custer did not compare with the more than 100,000 who had already accepted reservation status, and even these could not have defeated a white America that was forty times as populous. The victory that Tashunca-uitco (Crazy Horse) and Ta tan'ka I-yo-ta'-ke (Sitting Bull) led was tactically brilliant. Historically, however, it was futile. Exile or surrender remained the Indians' only real possibilities.

Even surrender did not offer permanent protection, as Sitting Bull and his fellow Hunkpapa Sioux learned fourteen years later. When fellow Sioux acting under white control killed the fifty-nine-year-old chief during an attempt to arrest him, it precipitated the final "battle" of the Plains Wars, at Wounded Knee, South Dakota. It was no battle at all, just indiscriminate killing. Both white soldiers assigned to the reconstituted 7th Cavalry and black soldiers who belonged to the all-African-American 9th Cavalry took part. The white soldiers, at least, reckoned afterward that Little Big Horn was avenged.

About the same time that R. M. Devens was writing his enormous celebratory book, a Texas woman named Ann Bell Shelton was also considering how American history added up. She paid no attention to Reconstruction's historic failure, and it does not seem that woman suffrage interested her. She was part Cherokee Indian and she identified with the Cherokee nation. Even that identity posed problems. The Cherokees had split during the Civil War, and she sprang from the group that had chosen the southern side. Stand Watie, who had led the pro-South wing and held a Confederate generalship, was her uncle. Very probably, her own family had owned black slaves. At least possibly, she had African ancestry as well as Indian and European. Even if she did not, she certainly knew Indians who did.[5]

Despite thinking of herself as Cherokee, Shelton had not stayed among her people. A widow, she was living in 1876 in the Texas town of Roxton, where she had "moved . . . in order to find work as a schoolteacher among whites" so that she could support her four children. The notion of a nineteenth-century Texas town hiring a self-identified Indian woman to teach its children may seem surprising. But southern history has its surprises. Colonel Richard Johnson, Vice President of the United States under Martin Van Buren, had lived in an interracial common-law marriage on his Kentucky plantation and he tried to introduce his part-black daughters into Washington, D.C., society.[6] The Choctaw Greenwood Leflore remained in Mississippi after most of his people followed the Trail of Tears. He served in both the Mississippi House of Representatives and State Senate before the Civil War. Once, when a white colleague provoked him with a pretentious speech in Latin, he responded with a whole hour of oratory in Choctaw.[7]

The Civil War split that aligned some Cherokees with the Confederacy and others with the Union is a measure of how closely the Cherokees themselves had aligned with the dominant culture's ways and contradictions, despite the Trail of Tears. Equally revealing is the fact that when slavery ended some southern Indians had considerable trouble with the idea that freed men and women might want citizenship in the Indian nations that had held them as slaves. Choctaws finally came to terms with the idea; Chickasaws proved "uncompromising" in their refusal.[8]

Ann Bell Shelton herself was thoroughly attuned to the whites' ways. She wrote excellent English. She was a convinced Christian. In 1880, when defeated Sioux refugees seemed about to enter Indian Territory, she distanced herself carefully from "that wild, savage element." Nonetheless, she knew that she remained an Indian. In 1876 she found herself wishing that "the whole of us, from the pure Indians to the last one with the millionth part of a drop of blood, could be cut off in a moment and the vexed question stopped forever."[9] Even her choice of how to measure "race" bespoke what history had done. The notions that "blood" conveyed identity and that a "millionth part of a drop" was enough to make a person not-white were not absolute standards. They were simply how white America had come to understand the idea of mixing ancestries and cultures.[10]

The "vexed question" would not disappear, not for Indians like Ann

Bell Shelton who more or less adopted white ways and perspectives, not for others who kept the richness of their ancestral culture alive.[11] Nor would the parallel question of black and white disappear, however far the Republic retreated from what the end of the Civil War had seemed to promise to former slaves. Officially, the "closing" of the western "frontier" was still a decade and a half away in 1876, when Shelton was giving her muted cheer for the Sioux and R. M. Devens was working on his book. Not until 1890 would the "Indian" question be completely resolved on the principle that, save for reservations, America belonged to whites. Full racial segregation in the South was about a decade and a half away as well. Even after the "frontier" was gone and Jim Crow was fully established, the Republic could not turn its attention wholly away from its red and black people, if only because of the almost pornographic quality that racially focused violence has possessed within American culture.[12]

The late nineteenth century's resolution of the issues of red-white, white-black, and red-black on the premise that America is indeed a white person's country did prove strong. It lasted for the best part of a century, while white Americans turned almost all their creative attention elsewhere. They were building a fully developed industrial society. They were struggling to resolve that society's problems and contradictions. They were securing its place in a complex, often hostile world.

But what seemed resolved about American society at the nineteenth century's end came unstuck again in the twentieth. Perhaps that is because from the beginning of what we call America all its people have been shaping the country while they also shaped themselves and one another. Perhaps it is for reasons of American belief, given the Republic's founding premise that human beings are equal, whatever their differences may be. Perhaps it is because red and black Americans proved not only too strong to disappear but also strong enough to recover from degradation and historic defeat. Whatever the reasons, the questions of identity and distinctiveness that were first raised when black and white people from the Old World and red people from the New World met remain open, even now.

NOTES

PREFACE

1. Sir Denis Brogan, *The American Character* (New York: Alfred A. Knopf, 1944); Richard Hofstadter, *The American Political Tradition and the Men Who Made It* (New York: Alfred A. Knopf, 1948); Ralph Barton Perry, *Characteristically American: Five Lectures Delivered at the University of Michigan* (New York: Alfred A. Knopf, 1948); David Potter, *People of Plenty: Economic Abundance and the American Character* (Chicago: University of Chicago Press, 1954); Clinton Rossiter, *The American Quest, 1790–1860: An Emerging Nation in Search of Identity, Unity, and Modernity* (New York: Harcourt Brace Jovanovich, 1971); Michael Kammen, *People of Paradox: An Inquiry Concerning the Origins of American Civilization* (New York: Alfred A. Knopf, 1972).

2. For an overview of development of thinking about the Revolution, compare Edmund S. Morgan, *The Birth of the Republic* (Chicago: University of Chicago Press, 1961); Bernard Bailyn, *The Ideological Origins of the American Revolution* (Cambridge, MA: Harvard University Press, 1967); Alfred F. Young, ed., *The American Revolution: Explorations in the History of American Radicalism* (De Kalb: Northern Illinois University Press, 1976); and Edward Countryman, *The American Revolution* (New York: Hill and Wang, 1985).

3. Countryman, *The American Revolution*.

4. Edward Countryman, "The Uses of Capital in Revolutionary America: The Case of the New York Loyalist Merchants," *William and Mary Quarterly*, 3rd ser., XLIX (1992), 3–28.

5. Pauline Maier, "The Revolutionary Origins of the American Corporation," *William and Mary Quarterly*, 3rd ser., L (1993), 51–84.

6. Young, *The American Revolution*.

7. Alfred F. Young, ed., *Beyond the American Revolution: Further Explorations in the History of American Radicalism* (De Kalb: Northern Illinois University Press, 1993).

8. Gordon S. Wood, *The Radicalism of the American Revolution* (New York: Alfred A. Knopf, 1992).

9. This is not to deny my enormous respect for a long series of sophisticated

studies in the Marxian tradition. See, as instances, William Appleman Williams, *The Contours of American History* (Chicago: Quadrangle Books, 1966); Herbert G. Gutman, *Work, Culture and Society in Industrializing America* (New York: Alfred A. Knopf, 1976); and Sean Wilentz, *Chants Democratic: New York City and the Rise of the American Working Class, 1788–1850* (New York: Oxford University Press, 1984).

10. James Fenimore Cooper, *The American Democrat; or, Hints on the Social and Civic Relations of the United States of America* (Cooperstown, NY: H. & E. Phinney, 1838).

11. Ms. Linda Williams Tomlinson, now a doctoral student at Clark Atlanta University.

12. Christopher Morris, *Becoming Southern: Vicksburg and Warren County, Mississippi, 1790–1860* (New York: Oxford University Press, 1995).

13. See Wood, *Radicalism of the American Revolution.*

14. Bank Veto Message, July 19, 1832, in Richard Hofstadter, ed., *Great Issues in American History* (2 vols.; New York: Vintage Books, 1958), I, 291–95.

15. It is more than appropriate here to acknowledge the pioneering work of Gary B. Nash in approaching American history this way. See his classic volume *Red, White, and Black: The Peoples of Early America* (Englewood Cliffs, N.J., Prentice-Hall, 1974) and his 1995 presidential address to the Organization of American Historians, "The Hidden History of Mestizo America."

1. A COLLISION OF HISTORIES

1. Barbara Jeanne Fields, "Slavery, Race, and Ideology in the United States of America," *New Left Review*, 181 (May–June 1990), 95–108, and Evelyn Brooks Higginbotham, "African-American Women's History and the Metalanguage of Race," *Signs: Journal of Women in Culture and Society*, XVII (1992), 251–74. My thanks to Neil Evans and Carroll Smith-Rosenberg, respectively, for pointing these articles out to me.

2. Edmund S. Morgan, *American Slavery, American Freedom: The Ordeal of Colonial Virginia* (New York: W. W. Norton, 1975), Chapter 8.

3. Ibid., p. 101.

4. Francis Jennings, *The Invasion of America: Indians, Colonialism and the Cant of Conquest* (New York: W. W. Norton, 1976), p. 28.

5. Quoted in Alfred W. Crowby, "Virgin Soil Epidemics as a Factor in the Aboriginal Depopulation in America," *William and Mary Quarterly*, 3rd ser., XXXIII (1976), 289–99.

6. Thomas Best (1623), quoted in Morgan, *American Slavery, American Freedom*, p. 128.

7. T. H. Breen and Stephen Innes, *"Myne Owne Ground": Race & Freedom on Virginia's Eastern Shore, 1640–1676* (New York: Oxford University Press, 1980), pp. 7–18.

8. Morgan, *American Slavery, American Freedom*, p. 298; Philip D. Curtin, *The*

Atlantic Slave Trade: A Census (Madison: University of Wisconsin Press, 1969), p. 119.

9. James H. Merrell, *The Indians' New World: Catawbas and Their Neighbors from European Contact Through the Era of Removal* (Chapel Hill: University of North Carolina Press, 1989), passim, esp. pp. 144, 207, 216, 244–45.

10. Allan Kulikoff, *Tobacco and Slaves: The Development of Southern Cultures in the Chesapeake, 1680–1800* (Chapel Hill: University of North Carolina Press, 1986), pp. 40–42, 319–34.

11. Curtin, *Atlantic Slave Trade*, pp. 53, 59.

12. Orlando Patterson, *The Sociology of Slavery: An Analysis of the Origins, Development, and Structure of Negro Slave Society in Jamaica* (Rutherford, NJ: Fairleigh Dickinson University Press, 1969).

13. Daniel H. Usner, Jr., *Indians, Settlers, and Slaves in a Frontier Exchange Economy: The Lower Mississippi Valley Before 1783* (Chapel Hill: University of North Carolina Press, 1992).

14. Curtin, *Atlantic Slave Trade*, pp. 156–58. See also Daniel C. Littlefield, *Rice and Slaves: Ethnicity and the Slave Trade in Colonial South Carolina* (Urbana: University of Illinois Press, 1991 [orig. pub. 1981]); Margaret Washington Creel, *"A Peculiar People": Slave Religion and Community-Culture Among the Gullahs* (New York: New York University Press, 1988).

15. Joyce E. Chaplin, "Tidal Rice Cultivation and the Problem of Slavery in South Carolina and Georgia, 1760–1815," *William and Mary Quarterly*, 3rd ser., XLIX (1992), 29–61.

16. Peter H. Wood, *Black Majority: Negroes in Colonial South Carolina from 1670 Through the Stono Rebellion* (New York: Alfred A. Knopf, 1974).

17. Alice Hanson Jones, *Wealth of a Nation to Be: The American Colonies on the Eve of the Revolution* (New York: Columbia University Press, 1980), and *American Colonial Wealth: Documents and Methods* (3 vols.; New York: Arno Press, 1977).

18. Winthrop D. Jordan, *White Over Black: American Attitudes Toward the Negro, 1550–1812* (Chapel Hill: University of North Carolina Press, 1968), p. 116.

19. Philip J. Greven, Jr., *Four Generations: Population, Land and Family in Colonial Andover, Massachusetts* (Ithaca: Cornell University Press, 1970, pp. 23–28.

20. John Winthrop, "Christian Charities, A Modell Thereof" (1630) in Edmund S. Morgan, ed., *The Founding of Massachusetts: Historians and the Sources* (Indianapolis: Bobbs-Merrill, 1964), pp. 190–204.

21. Ibid.

22. David Grayson Allen, *In English Ways: The Movement of Societies and the Transferal of English Local Law and Custom to Massachusetts Bay in the Seventeenth Century* (Chapel Hill: University of North Carolina Press, 1981).

23. R. H. Hilton, *Bond Men Made Free: Medieval Peasant Movements and the English Rising of 1381* (New York: Viking Press, 1973).

24. Jan Lewis, *The Pursuit of Happiness: Family and Values in Jefferson's Virginia* (New York: Cambridge University Press, 1983), p. 3.

25. Robert G. Pope, *The Half-Way Covenant: Church Membership in Puritan New England* (Princeton: Princeton University Press, 1969).

26. Darrett B. Rutman and Anita Rutman, *A Place in Time: Middlesex County, Virginia, 1650–1750* (2 vols.; New York: W. W. Norton, 1984).

27. Creel, *"A Peculiar People,"* Chapters 8–10; Patterson, *Sociology of Slavery*; Gwendolyn Midlo Hall, *Africans in Colonial Louisiana: The Development of an Afro-Creole Culture in the Eighteenth Century* (Baton Rouge: Louisiana State University Press, 1992), esp. Chapters 4–8.

28. Philip D. Morgan, "Work and Culture: The Task system and the World of Lowcountry Blacks, 1700 to 1880," *William and Mary Quarterly*, XXXIX (1982): 563–99.

29. Merrell, *The Indians' New World*.

30. Edward Countryman, *A People in Revolution: The American Revolution and Political Society in New York, 1760–1790* (Baltimore: Johns Hopkins University Press, 1981), Chapters 1 and 4.

31. Francis Jennings, *Empire of Fortune: Crowns, Colonies & Tribes in the Seven Years War in America* (New York: W. W. Norton, 1988), p. 81.

32. In addition to Jennings, *Empire of Fortune*, and the preceding volumes by the same author (*The Invasion of America* [1975] and *The Ambiguous Iroquois Empire* [1984]), see Daniel K. Richter, *The Ordeal of the Longhouse: The Peoples of the Iroquois League in the Era of European Colonization* (Chapel Hill: University of North Carolina Press, 1992).

33. Richard White, *The Middle Ground: Indians, Empires and Republics in the Great Lakes Region, 1650–1815* (Cambridge: Cambridge University Press, 1991).

34. In addition to Usner, *Indians, Settlers, and Slaves*, see Richard White, *The Roots of Dependency: Subsistence, Environment and Social Change Among the Choctaws, Pawnees, and Navajos* (Lincoln: University of Nebraska Press, 1983), Chapters 1–5.

35. Peter H. Wood, "The Changing Population of the Colonial South: An Overview by Race and Region, 1685–1790," in Wood, ed., *Powhatan's Mantle: Indians in the Colonial Southeast* (Lincoln: University of Nebraska Press, 1989), 35–103, esp. Table 1, pp. 38–39; White, *The Middle Ground*, 14, 43.

36. J. Leitch Wright, Jr., *Creeks and Seminoles: Destruction and Regeneration of the Muscogulge People* (Lincoln: University of Nebraska Press, 1986); White, *The Middle Ground*, pp. 145, 226.

2. BRAUDEL'S AMERICAN MOSAIC

1. Fernand Braudel, *The Perspective of the World {Capitalism and Civilization, 15th–18th Centuries*, Vol. III], trans. Siân Reynolds (London: Fontana, 1985), p. 426.

2. Frederick Jackson Turner, "The Significance of the Frontier in American History," in his *Frontier and Section: Selected Essays*, ed. Ray Allen Billington (Englewood Cliffs, NJ: Prentice-Hall, 1961), p. 44.

3. See Jay Gitlin, "On the Boundaries of Empire: Connecting the West to Its Imperial Past," in William Cronon, George Miles, and Jay Gitlin, eds., *Under an Open Sky: Rethinking America's Western Past* (New York: W. W. Norton, 1992), pp. 71–89.

4. Ramón A. Gutiérrez, *When Jesus Came, the Corn Mothers Went Away: Marriage,*

Sexuality, and Power in New Mexico, 1500–1846 (Stanford: Stanford University Press, 1991).

5. See Gwendolyn Midlo Hall, *Africans in Colonial Louisiana: The Development of an Afro-Creole Culture in the Eighteenth Century* (Baton Rouge: Louisiana State University Press, 1992), and Daniel H. Usner, Jr., *Indians, Settlers, and Slaves in a Frontier Exchange Economy: The Lower Mississippi Valley Before 1783* (Chapel Hill: University of North Carolina Press, 1992).

6. Richard White, *The Middle Ground: Indians, Empires and Republics in the Great Lakes Region, 1650–1815* (Cambridge: Cambridge University Press, 1991), Chapter 8, pp. 315–66.

7. Philip D. Curtin, *The Atlantic Slave Trade: A Census* (Madison: University of Wisconsin Press, 1969), Table 39, p. 137.

8. Margaret Washington Creel, *"A Peculiar People": Slave Religion and Community-Culture Among the Gullahs* (New York: New York University Press, 1988), pp. 43 (quoting Walter Rodney), 39–40.

9. Bernard Bailyn, *The Peopling of British North America: An Introduction* (New York: Alfred A. Knopf, 1986), Chapter 1; Bernard Bailyn, *Voyagers to the West: A Passage in the Peopling of America on the Eve of the Revolution* (New York: Alfred A. Knopf, 1986), Figure 4.1, p. 99, Table 4.3, p. 100.

10. Sharon V. Salinger, *"To Serve Well and Faithfully": Labor and Indentured Servants in Pennsylvania, 1782–1800* (Cambridge: Cambridge University Press, 1987), Table A.1, pp. 172–73, Table A.2, pp. 175–76.

11. Bailyn, *Voyagers to the West*, Part III, pp. 241–352, Part V, pp. 495–637; David Hackett Fischer, *Albion's Seed: Four British Folkways in America* (New York: Oxford University Press, 1989), pp. 605–782.

12. For the front view and Mulberry's architecture, see Richard McLanathan, *Art in America: A Brief History* (London: Thames & Hudson, 1973), p. 52; I have taken the view from the rear from a reproduction in John Mack Faragher et al., *Out of Many: A History of the American People* (Englewood Cliffs, NJ: Prentice-Hall, 1994), p. 94. The original is at the Gibbes Museum of Art.

13. Jacob M. Price, "Economic Function and the Growth of American Port Towns," *Perspectives in American History*, VIII (1974), pp. 123–63.

14. Marcus Rediker, *Between the Devil and the Deep Blue Sea: Merchant Seamen, Pirates, and the Anglo-American Maritime World, 1700–1750* (New York: Cambridge University Press, 1987).

15. Compare E. P. Thompson, *Whigs and Hunters: The Origin of the Black Act* (London: Penguin Books, 1977 [orig. pub. 1975]), with Stuart A. Marks, *Southern Hunting in Black and White: Nature, History and Ritual in a Carolina Community* (Princeton: Princeton University Press, 1991).

16. Anthony F. C. Wallace, *The Death and Rebirth of the Seneca* (New York: Vintage Books, 1972 [orig. pub. 1969]), p. 34; Patricia Galloway, " 'The Chief Who Is Your Father': Choctaw and French Views of the Diplomatic Relation," in Peter H. Wood, ed., *Powhatan's Mantle: Indians in the Colonial Southeast* (Lincoln: University of Nebraska Press, 1989), pp. 254–78; White, *The Middle Ground*, pp. 50–52.

17. Charles W. Akers, *Called unto Liberty: A Life of John Mayhew, 1720–1766* (Cambridge: Harvard University Press, 1964).

18. Ephesians 6:5; Matthew 22:21; Romans 13:1–2.

19. See David Brion Davis, *The Problem of Slavery in Western Culture* (Ithaca: Cornell University Press, 1966), esp. Chapter 10 and Epilogue, "John Woolman's Prophecy."

20. Jennifer Tolbert Roberts, *Athens on Trial: The Antidemocratic Tradition in Western Thought* (Princeton: Princeton University Press, 1994).

21. See Bernard Bailyn, *The Ideological Origins of the American Revolution* (Cambridge, MA: Harvard University Press, 1967), and J. G. A. Pocock, *The Machiavellian Moment: Florentine Political Thought and the Atlantic Republican Tradition* (Princeton: Princeton University Press, 1975).

22. Richard S. Dunn, "Black Society in the Chesapeake, 1776–1810," in Ira Berlin and Ronald Hoffman, eds., *Slavery and Freedom in the Age of the American Revolution* (Charlottesville: University Press of Virginia, 1983), p. 50.

23. This is not intended to contradict the important argument of Peter H. Wood, " 'Liberty Is Sweet': African-American Freedom Struggles in the Years Before White Independence," in Alfred F. Young, ed., *Beyond the American Revolution: Further Explorations in the History of American Radicalism* (De Kalb: Northern Illinois University Press, 1993), pp. 149–84.

24. Robert V. Wells, *The Population of the British Colonies in America Before 1776: A Survey of Census Data* (Princeton: Princeton University Press, 1975), pp. 277–79.

25. Marylynn Salmon, *Women and the Law of Property in Early America* (Chapel Hill: University of North Carolina Press, 1986).

26. Gordon S. Wood, *The Radicalism of the American Revolution* (New York: Alfred A. Knopf, 1992), Part I.

27. See Francis Jennings, *The Ambiguous Iroquois Empire: The Covenant Chain Confederation of Indian Tribes with English Colonies from Its Beginnings to the Lancaster Treaty of 1744* (New York: W. W. Norton, 1984).

28. Fragment, conjecturally dated August 1, 1858, in *The Collected Works of Abraham Lincoln*, ed. Roy P. Basler et al. (9 vols.; New Brunswick, NJ: Rutgers University Press, 1953), II, p. 532.

29. Mary Rowlandson, *The soveraignty & goodness of God . . . being a narrative of the captivity and restauration of Mrs. Mary Rowlandson* (Cambridge, MA: Samuel Green, 1682); see also June Namias, *White Captives: Gender and Ethnicity on the American Frontier* (Chapel Hill: University of North Carolina Press, 1993), and John Demos, *The Unredeemed Captive: A Family Story from Early America* (New York: Alfred A. Knopf, 1994).

30. See Sung Bok Kim, *Landlord and Tenant in Colonial New York: Manorial Society, 1664–1775* (Chapel Hill: University of North Carolina Press, 1978), and Gregory A. Stiverson, *Poverty in a Land of Plenty: Tenancy in Eighteenth-Century Maryland* (Baltimore: Johns Hopkins University Press, 1977).

31. Micah 4:4.

32. See James T. Lemon, *The Best Poor Man's Country: A Geographical Study of Early*

Southeastern Pennsylvania (Baltimore: Johns Hopkins University Press, 1972), and Richard L. Bushman, "Massachusetts Farmers and the Revolution," in Richard M. Jellison, ed., *Society, Freedom, and Conscience: The American Revolution in Virginia, Massachusetts, and New York* (New York: W. W. Norton, 1976).

33. Allan Kulikoff, *Tobacco and Slaves: The Development of Southern Cultures in the Chesapeake, 1680–1800* (Chapel Hill: University of North Carolina Press, 1986).

34. Thomas M. Doerflinger, *A Vigorous Spirit of Enterprise: Merchants and Economic Development in Revolutionary Philadelphia* (Chapel Hill: University of North Carolina Press), p. 17.

35. See W. J. Rorabaugh, *The Craft Apprentice: From Franklin to the Machine Age in America* (New York: Oxford University Press, 1986).

36. Gary B. Nash, *The Urban Crucible: Social Change, Political Consciousness, and the Origins of the American Revolution* (Cambridge, MA: Harvard University Press, 1979), Table 3, p. 395.

37. Rediker, *Between the Devil and the Deep Blue Sea.*

38. See Edward Countryman, "The Uses of Capital in Revolutionary America: The Case of the New York Loyalist Merchants," *William and Mary Quarterly*, 3rd ser., XLIX (1992), 3–28.

39. Max Weber, *The Protestant Ethic and the Spirit of Capitalism*, trans. Talcott Parsons (London: G. Allen & Unwin, 1930), p. 20.

40. Custom: David Grayson Allen, *In English Ways: The Movement of Societies and the Transferal of English Local Law and Custom to Massachusetts Bay in the Seventeenth Century* (Chapel Hill: University of North Carolina Press, 1981). Compare E. P. Thompson, "Custom, Law, and Common Right," in his *Customs in Common: Studies in Traditional Popular Culture* (New York: New Press, 1991), pp. 97–184. See also Jeanette Neeson, *Commoners: Common Right, Enclosure, and Social Change in England, 1700–1820* (Cambridge: Cambridge University Press, 1993). Political practice: Jack P. Greene, *The Quest for Power: The Lower Houses of Assembly in the Southern Royal Colonies, 1689–1776* (Chapel Hill: University of North Carolina Press, 1963). Witchcraft: John Putnam Demos, *Entertaining Satan: Witchcraft in the Culture of Early New England* (New York: Oxford University Press, 1982). Neo-feudalism: Rowland Berthoff and John M. Murrin, "Feudalism, Communalism, and the Yeoman Freeholder: The American Revolution Considered as a Social Accident," in Stephen G. Kurtz and James H. Hutson, eds., *Essays on the American Revolution* (Chapel Hill: University of North Carolina Press, 1973), pp. 256–88. Crowds: Dirk Hoerder, *Crowd Action in Revolutionary Massachusetts, 1765–1780* (New York: Academic Press, 1977).

41. See Kim, *Landlord and Tenant*; Patricia U. Bonomi, *A Factious People: Politics and Society in Colonial New York* (New York: Columbia University Press, 1971); Edward Countryman, *A People in Revolution: The American Revolution and Political Society in New York, 1760–1790* (Baltimore: Johns Hopkins University Press, 1981).

42. Countryman, *A People in Revolution*, Chapter 1.

43. Quoted in Pauline Maier, *From Resistance to Revolution: Colonial Radicals and the*

Development of American Opposition to Britain, 1765–1776 (New York: Alfred A. Knopf, 1972), p. 24.

44. "A Citizen," *Albany Gazette*, December 14, 1786; see also Gary Kulik, "Dams, Fish and Farmers: Defence of Public Rights in Eighteenth-Century Rhode Island," in Steven Hahn and Jonathan Prude, eds., *The Countryside in the Age of Capitalist Transformation* (Chapel Hill: University of North Carolina Press, 1985), pp. 25–50.

45. Morton J. Horwitz, *The Transformation of American Law, 1790–1860* (Cambridge, MA: Harvard University Press, 1977); William E. Nelson, *Americanization of the Common Law: The Impact of Legal Change on Massachusetts Society, 1760–1870* (Cambridge, MA: Harvard University Press, 1975).

3. COLONIAL REVOLTS, AMERICAN REVOLUTION

1. For a narrative account of the Revolution based on recent scholarship, see Edward Countryman, *The American Revolution* (New York: Hill and Wang, 1985).

2. Sir William Blackstone, *Commentaries on the Laws of England*, quoted in Bernard Bailyn, *The Ideological Origins of the American Revolution* (Cambridge, MA: Harvard University Press, 1967), p. 202.

3. Quoted in John Brooke, *King George III* (London: Panther, 1974 [orig. pub. 1972]), p. 108.

4. *Proceedings of the Congress at New York*, in Edmund S. Morgan, ed., *Prologue to Revolution: Sources and Documents on the Stamp Act Crisis, 1764–1766* (Chapel Hill: University of North Carolina Press, 1959), pp. 66–69.

5. H. G. Koenigsberger, "Composite States, Representative Institutions and the American Revolution," *Historical Research* LXII (1989), 135–53. My thanks to Neil Evans for pointing this article out to me.

6. Maryland Resolves, September 28, 1765, and *Proceedings of the Congress at New York*, in Morgan, *Prologue to Revolution*, pp. 52–53, 66–69.

7. See Marc Egnal, *A Mighty Empire: The Origins of the American Revolution* (Ithaca: Cornell University Press, 1988).

8. David Brion Davis, *The Problem of Slavery in the Age of Revolution, 1770–1823* (Ithaca: Cornell University Press, 1975), pp. 485–98.

9. Sylvia Frey, *Water from the Rock: Black Resistance in a Revolutionary Age* (Princeton: Princeton University Press, 1991), p. 194.

10. Morris to Mr. Penn, May 20, 1774, in Peter Force, comp., *American Archives* (9 vols.; Washington, DC: M. St. Clair Clarke and Peter Force, 1837–53), 4th ser., I, p. 343.

11. Alfred F. Young, *The Democratic Republicans of New York: The Origins, 1763–1797* (Chapel Hill: University of North Carolina Press, 1966), p. 15.

12. Gary J. Kornblith and John M. Murrin, "The Making and Unmaking of an American Ruling Class," in Alfred F. Young, ed., *Beyond the American Revolution: Further Explorations in the History of American Radicalism* (De Kalb: Northern Illinois University Press, 1993), pp. 27–79.

13. See Pauline Maier, *From Resistance to Revolution: Colonial Radicals and the Devel-*

opment of American Opposition to Britain, 1765–1776 (New York: Alfred A. Knopf, 1972).

14. Ibid., pp. 128–29.

15. Dirk Hoerder, *Crowd Action in Revolutionary Massachusetts, 1765–1780* (New York: Academic Press, 1977); Gary B. Nash, *The Urban Crucible: Social Change, Political Consciousness, and the Origins of the American Revolution* (Cambridge, MA: Harvard University Press, 1979). My thanks to Alfred F. Young for verifying that the victim John Gray was a rope worker who had been at the fight on March 2.

16. Robert A. Gross, *The Minutemen and Their World* (New York: Hill and Wang, 1976); Richard L. Bushman, *King and People in Provincial Massachusetts* (Chapel Hill: University of North Carolina Press, 1985); Alfred F. Young, "English Plebeian Culture and Eighteenth-Century American Radicalism," in Margaret Jacob and James Jacob, eds., *The Origins of Anglo-American Radicalism* (London: George Allen & Unwin, 1984), pp. 185–212.

17. Rhys Isaac, *The Transformation of Virginia, 1740–1790* (Chapel Hill: University of North Carolina Press, 1982); Edward Countryman, *A People in Revolution: The American Revolution and Political Society in New York, 1760–1790* (Baltimore: Johns Hopkins University Press, 1981); Richard Alan Ryerson, *The Revolution Is Now Begun: The Radical Committees of Philadelphia, 1765–1776* (Philadelphia: University of Pennsylvania Press, 1978); Steven Rosswurm, *Arms, Country, and Class: The Philadelphia Militia and the "Lower Sort" During the American Revolution* (New Brunswick, NJ: Rutgers University Press, 1987).

18. Eric Foner, *Tom Paine and Revolutionary America* (New York: Oxford University Press, 1976).

19. Geo. Turnbull to General Thomas Gage, September 30, 1769, in Gage Papers, Clements Library, University of Michigan. My thanks to Woody Holton for calling this document to my attention. See Holton, "The Ohio Indians and the Coming of the American Revolution in Virginia," *Journal of Southern History*, LX (1994), 453–78.

20. Anthony F. C. Wallace, *The Death and Rebirth of the Seneca* (New York: Vintage Books, 1972 [orig. pub. 1969]); Barbara Graymont, *The Iroquois in the American Revolution* (Syracuse: Syracuse University Press, 1972); Isabel Thompson Kelsay, *Joseph Brant, 1743–1807: Man of Two Worlds* (Syracuse: Syracuse University Press, 1984).

21. William G. McLoughlin, *Cherokee Renascence in the New Republic* (Princeton: Princeton University Press, 1986); J. Leitch Wright, Jr., *Creeks and Seminoles: Destruction and Regeneration of the Muscogulge People* (Lincoln: University of Nebraska Press, 1986); Richard White, *The Roots of Dependency: Subsistence, Environment, and Social Change Among the Choctaws, Pawnees, and Navajos* (Lincoln: University of Nebraska Press, 1983); Richard White, *The Middle Ground: Indians, Empires, and Republics in the Great Lakes Region, 1650–1815* (Cambridge: Cambridge University Press, 1991); Edward J. Cashin, "But Brothers, It Is Our Land We Are Talking About": Winners and Losers in the Georgia Backcountry," in Ronald Hoffman et al., eds., *An Uncivil War: The Southern Country*

During the American Revolution (Charlottesville: University Press of Virginia, 1985), pp. 240–75.

22. James H. Merrell, *The Indians' New World: Catawbas and Their Neighbors from European Contact Through the Era of Removal* (Chapel Hill: University of North Carolina Press, 1989).

23. See Winthrop D. Jordan, *White Over Black: American Attitudes Toward the Negro, 1550–1812* (Chapel Hill: University of North Carolina Press, 1968; Edmund S. Morgan, *American Slavery, American Freedom: The Ordeal of Colonial Virginia* (New York: W. W. Norton, 1975); Peter H. Wood, *Black Majority: Negroes in Colonial South Carolina from 1660 Through the Stono Rebellion* (New York: Alfred A. Knopf, 1974); Peter H. Wood: " 'Liberty Is Sweet': African-American Freedom Struggles in the Years Before White Independence," in Alfred F. Young, ed., *Beyond the American Revolution: Further Explorations in the History of American Radicalism* (De Kalb: Northern Illinois University Press, 1973), pp. 149–84.

24. Frey, *Water from the Rock*, p. 47.

25. Adams quoted in Sidney Kaplan and Emma Nogrady Kaplan, *The Black Presence in the Era of the American Revolution* (Amherst: University of Massachusetts Press, 1989), p. 25.

26. Clinton's Proclamation, June 30, 1779, in Ibid., p. 78.

27. Nash, *Urban Crucible*, p. 59; Christine Leigh Heyrman, *Commerce and Culture: The Maritime Communities of Colonial Massachusetts, 1690–1750* (New York: W. W. Norton, 1984), pp. 225–26.

28. *New-York Gazetteer*, December 3, 1783.

29. Barbara Clark Smith, "Food Rioters and the American Revolution," *William and Mary Quarterly*, 3rd ser., LI (1994), 3–38.

30. Mary Beth Norton, *Liberty's Daughters: The Revolutionary Experience of American Women, 1750–1800* (Boston: Little, Brown, 1980).

31. Robert R. Palmer, *The Age of the Democratic Revolution: A Political History of Europe and America, 1760–1800*, Vol. I: *The Challenge* (Princeton: Princeton University Press, 1959), p. 188.

32. James Kirby Martin, *Men in Rebellion: Higher Government Leaders and the Coming of the American Revolution* (New Brunswick, NJ: Rutgers University Press, 1973).

33. Wallace Brown, *The King's Friends: The Composition and Motives of the American Loyalist Claimants* (Providence: Brown University Press, 1965).

34. Mary Beth Norton, *The British Americans: The Loyalist Exiles in England, 1774–1789* (Boston: Little, Brown, 1972).

35. Janice Potter, *The Liberty We Seek: Loyalist Ideology in Colonial New York and Massachusetts* (Cambridge, MA: Harvard University Press, 1983), p. ix.

36. Esmond Wright, "The New York Loyalists: A Cross-Section of Colonial Society," in Robert A. East and Jacob Judd, eds., *The Loyalist Americans: A Focus on Greater New York* (Tarrytown, NY: Sleepy Hollow Press, 1975), p. 89.

37. Quoted in Countryman, *A People in Revolution*, p. 285.

4. THE REVOLUTION AND THE REPUBLIC

1. Mary Beth Norton, *The British Americans: The Loyalist Exiles in England, 1774–1789* (Boston: Little, Brown, 1972).

2. James St. G. Walker, *The Black Loyalists: The Search for a Promised Land in Nova Scotia and Sierra Leone, 1783–1870* (New York: Dalhousie University Press/ Holmes & Meier, 1976).

3. "An Account of . . . the County of Ontario," in Edmund Bailey O'Callaghan, ed., *Documentary History of the State of New York* (4 vols.; Albany: Weed, Parsons, 1850), II, 1113.

4. This argument is derived and toned down from Marc Egnal, *A Mighty Empire: The Origins of the American Revolution* (Ithaca: Cornell University Press, 1988).

5. Old Tassel and Drayton quoted in Edward J. Cashin, " 'But Brothers, It Is Our Land We Are Talking About,': Winners and Losers in the Georgia Backcountry," in Ronald Hoffman et al., eds., *An Uncivil War: The Southern Backcountry During the American Revolution* (Charlottesville: University Press of Virginia, 1985), pp. 240–75, quotes at pp. 240, 251–52.

6. Philip D. Curtin, *The Atlantic Slave Trade: A Census* (Madison: University of Wisconsin Press, 1969), Table 65, p. 218; Robert William Fogel and Stanley L. Engerman, *Time on the Cross: The Economics of American Negro Slavery* (2 vols.; Boston: Little, Brown, 1974), I, 24. Curtin's estimate is conservative. See also Paul E. Lovejoy, "The Volume of the Atlantic Slave Trade: A Synthesis," *Journal of African History*, XXIII (1982), 473–502. My thanks to Dennis D. Cordell for this reference.

7. Quoted in Carl L. Becker, *The Declaration of Independence: A Study in the History of Political Ideas* (New York: Vintage Books, n.d. [orig. pub. 1922]), p. 135.

8. Charles Royster, *A Revolutionary People at War: The Continental Army and American Character, 1775–1783* (Chapel Hill: University of North Carolina Press, 1979); James Kirby Martin and Mark Edward Lender, *A Respectable Army: The Military Origins of the Republic, 1763–1789* (Arlington Heights, IL: Harlan-Davidson, 1982).

9. Barbara Clark Smith, "Food Rioters and the American Revolution," *William and Mary Quarterly*, 3rd ser., LI (1994), 3–38; E. P. Thompson, "The Moral Economy of the English Crowd in the Eighteenth Century" and "The Moral Economy Reviewed," in his *Customs in Common: Studies in Traditional Popular Culture* (New York: New Press, 1991), pp. 185–351; Edward Countryman, *A People in Revolution: The American Revolution and Political Society in New York, 1760–1790* (Baltimore: Johns Hopkins University Press, 1981), Chapter 6.

10. Robert F. Jones, "William Duer and the Business of Government in the Era of the American Revolution," *William and Mary Quarterly*, 3rd ser., XXXII (1975), pp. 393–416.

11. Gary J. Kornblith and John M. Murrin, "The Making and Unmaking of an American Ruling Class," in Alfred F. Young, ed., *Beyond the American Revolution:*

Explorations in the History of American Radicalism (De Kalb: Northern Illinois University Press, 1993), pp. 27–79.

12. Quoted in Countryman, *A People in Revolution*, p. 123.

13. J. G. A. Pocock, ed., *Three British Revolutions: 1641, 1688, 1776* (Princeton: Princeton University Press, 1980).

14. Douglass to Washington (June 1776), in Peter Force, comp., *American Archives* (9 vols.; Washington, DC: M. St. Clair Clarke and Peter Force, 1837–53), 4th ser., VI, pp. 745–46.

15. See Edmund S. Morgan, *Inventing the People: The Rise of Popular Sovereignty in England and America* (New York: W. W. Norton, 1988); Winthrop D. Jordan, "Familial Politics: Thomas Paine and the Killing of the King, 1776," *Journal of American History*, LX (1973–74), 254–308; Gordon S. Wood, *The Radicalism of the American Revolution* (New York: Alfred A. Knopf, 1992).

16. Constitution of New Jersey (Burlington, NJ: Isaac Collins, 1776, Evans no. 14912), Article 13.

17. [Alexander Hamilton], "A Second Letter from Phocion to the Considerate Citizens of New-York, Containing Remarks on Mentor's Reply," in Harold S. Syrett et al., eds., *The Papers of Alexander Hamilton* (27 vols.; New York: Columbia University Press, 1961–87), III, p. 545.

18. Orlando Patterson, *Freedom*, Vol. I: *Freedom in the Making of Western Culture* (New York: Basic Books, 1991), p. 405.

19. Thomas Jefferson, "Notes on the State of Virginia," in Merrill D. Peterson, ed., *The Portable Thomas Jefferson* (Harmondsworth, Middlesex: Penguin Books, 1977 [orig. pub. 1975]), p. 164.

20. Richard Alan Ryerson, "Republican Theory and Partisan Reality in Revolutionary Pennsylvania: Toward a New View of the Constitutionalist Party," in Ronald Hoffman and Peter J. Albert, eds., *Sovereign States in an Age of Uncertainty* (Charlottesville: University Press of Virginia, 1981), pp. 95–133, quotes at pp. 130, 133.

21. For Pennsylvania, see Ryerson, "Republican Theory"; for New York, see Countryman, *A People in Revolution*, Chapters 7–9.

22. The most recent studies of Shays's Rebellion are contained in Robert A. Gross, *In Debt to Shays: The Bicentennial of an Agrarian Rebellion* (Charlottesville: University Press of Virginia, 1993); for the "perishability of revolutionary time," see David Brion Davis, *The Problem of Slavery in the Age of Revolution, 1770–1823* (Ithaca: Cornell University Press, 1975), pp. 306–26.

23. Alfred F. Young, "The Framers and the 'Genius' of the People," *Radical History Review*, XLII (1988), pp. 8–23.

24. Francis Jennings et al., eds., *The History and Culture of Iroquois Diplomacy: An Interdisciplinary Guide to the Treaties of the Six Nations and Their League* (Syracuse: Syracuse University Press, 1985), pp. 200–3.

25. Compare Gordon S. Wood, *The Creation of the American Republic, 1776–1787* (Chapel Hill: University of North Carolina Press, 1969); J. R. Pole, *Political Representation in England and the Origins of the American Republic* (New York: St.

Martin's Press, 1966); and Peter S. Onuf, *Statehood and Union: A History of the Northwest Ordinance* (Bloomington: Indiana University Press, 1987).

26. This is the map drawn by Claude Joseph Sauthier and contained in O'Callaghan, ed., *Documentary History*, Vol. I.

27. Richard White, *The Middle Ground: Indians, Empires, and Republics in the Great Lakes Region, 1650–1815* (Cambridge: Cambridge University Press, 1991).

28. Constitution of Vermont (1777), Article I.

29. Chief Justice William Cushing, quoted in Arthur Zilversmit, *The First Emancipation: The Abolition of Slavery in the North* (Chicago: University of Chicago Press, 1967), p. 114.

30. Quoted in Sidney Kaplan and Emma Nogrady Kaplan, *The Black Presence in the Era of the American Revolution* (Amherst: University of Massachusetts Press, 1989), pp. 270, 272.

31. Jefferson, "Notes on Virginia," p. 193.

32. Quoted in Davis, *Problem of Slavery in the Age of Revolution*, p. 275.

33. O'Callaghan, ed., *Documentary History*, I, 697.

34. Robert V. Wells, *The Population of the British Colonies in America Before 1776: A Survey of Census Data* (Princeton: Princeton University Press, 1975), Table III-4, p. 81.

35. Michael A. Bellesiles, *Revolutionary Outlaws: Ethan Allen and the Struggle for Independence in the Early American Frontier* (Charlottesville: University Press of Virginia, 1993), pp. 172, 235.

36. For Laurens, see Davis, *Problem of Slavery in the Age of Revolution*, p. 79.

37. This argument is derived primarily from Davis, *Problem of Slavery in the Age of Revolution*.

38. See Wood, *Creation of the American Republic*, and "Interests and Disinterestedness in the Making of the Constitution," in Richard Beeman et al., eds., *Beyond Confederation: Origins of the Constitution and American National Identity* (Chapel Hill: University of North Carolina Press, 1987), pp. 69–109; Pole, *Political Representation*, Chapters 13–15; Countryman, *A People in Revolution*, Chapters 9–10.

39. [James Madison, Alexander Hamilton, and John Jay], *The Federalist*, ed. Clinton Rossiter (New York: New American Library, 1961), no. 10, pp. 77–84, quotes at pp. 82–83; Adam Smith, *An Inquiry into the Nature and Causes of the Wealth of Nations* (London: Penguin Books, 1982 [orig. pub. 1776]). For the best modern discussion of the liberalism/republicanism problem, see Joyce Appleby, *Liberalism and Republicanism in the Historical Imagination* (Cambridge, MA: Harvard University Press, 1992).

40. Alexander Hamilton, "Final Version of an Opinion on the Constitutionality of an Act to Establish a Bank," *Papers of Hamilton*, VIII, p. 111.

41. Sir William Blackstone, *Commentaries on the Laws of England*, quoted in Bernard Bailyn, *The Ideological Origins of the American Revolution* (Cambridge, MA: Harvard University Press, 1967), p. 202.

42. This argument is influenced by Jerrilyn Greene Marston, *King and Congress: The*

Transfer of Political Legitimacy, 1774–1776 (Princeton: Princeton University Press, 1987).

43. Madison quoted in Kaplan and Kaplan, *Black Presence*, p. 272.

44. See Paul Finkleman, "Slavery and the Constitutional Convention: Making a Covenant with Death," in Beeman, ed., *Beyond Confederation*, pp. 188–225.

5. MOUNTAINS, VALLEYS, AND PLAINS

1. For the trails, see Lewis and Clark Trail Center, Nebraska, *Concept Plan: Environmental Assessment* (U.S. Department of the Interior, National Park Service, May 1991), p. 11; for overviews of the Lewis and Clark expeditions, see David Lavender, *The Way to the Western Sea: Lewis and Clark Across the Continent* (New York: Harper & Row, 1988), and James P. Ronda, *Lewis and Clark Among the Indians* (Lincoln: University of Nebraska Press, 1984); for the region's history before Lewis and Clark, see A. P. Nasitir, ed., *Before Lewis and Clark: Documents Illustrating the History of the Missouri, 1785–1804* (Lincoln: University of Nebraska Press, 1990 [orig. pub. 1952]); for York, see Robert B. Betts, *In Search of York: The Slave Who Went to the Pacific with Lewis and Clark* (Boulder: Colorado Associated University Press, 1985).

2. David J. Weber, *The Spanish Frontier in North America* (New Haven: Yale University Press, 1992), pp. 230–31, 251–53.

3. See Helen Hornbeck Tanner, "The Land and Water Communication Systems of the Southeastern Indians," in Peter H. Wood et al., eds., *Powhatan's Mantle: Indians in the Colonial Southeast* (Lincoln: University of Nebraska Press, 1989), pp. 6–20, and endpaper map.

4. See Bernard Sheehan, *Seeds of Extinction: Jeffersonian Philanthropy and the American Indian* (Chapel Hill: University of North Carolina Press, 1975).

5. Alan Taylor, *Liberty Men and Great Proprietors: The Revolutionary Settlement on the Maine Frontier, 1760–1820* (Chapel Hill: University of North Carolina Press, 1990), Chapter 2; Alfred F. Young, *The Democratic Republicans of New York: The Origins, 1763–1797* (Chapel Hill: University of North Carolina Press, 1967), Chapter 11.

6. Paul W. Gates, "Tenants of the Log Cabin," in his *Landlords and Tenants on the Prairie Frontier: Studies in American Land Policy* (Ithaca: Cornell University Press, 1973), pp. 13–47, quote at p. 17.

7. Paul W. Gates, *History of Public Land Law Development* (Washington, DC: Government Printing Office, 1968), pp. 54–55; Richard White, *The Roots of Dependency: Subsistence, Environment, and Social Change Among the Choctaws, Pawnees, and Navajos* (Lincoln: University of Nebraska Press, 1983), pp. 113–15.

8. William Wyckoff, *The Developer's Frontier: The Making of the Western New York Landscape* (New Haven: Yale University Press, 1988), Chapter 2.

9. Paul W. Gates, "Land Policy and Tenancy in the Prairie Counties of Indiana" and "Land Policy and Tenancy in the Prairie States," in *Landlords and Tenants*, pp. 108–39, 140–69; Gates, *Fifty Million Acres: Conflicts over Kansas Land Policy, 1854–1890* (Ithaca: Cornell University Press, 1954); Gates, "California

Land Policy and Its Historical Context: The Henry George Era," in *Four Persistent Issues: California's Land Ownership Concentration, Water Deficits, Sub-State Regionalism, Congressional Leadership* (Berkeley: University of California Institute of Governmental Studies, 1978), pp. 1–30; Malcolm J. Rohrbaugh, *The Land Office Business: The Settlement and Administration of American Public Lands, 1789–1937* (New York: Oxford University Press, 1968); W. W. Robinson, *Land in California: The Story of Mission Lands, Ranchos, Squatters, Mining Claims, Railroad Grants, Land Scrip, Homesteads* (Berkeley: University of California Press, 1948).

10. See Gordon S. Wood, *The Radicalism of the American Revolution* (New York: Alfred A. Knopf, 1992), pp. 24–43; Edward Countryman, "The Uses of Capital in Revolutionary America: The Case of the New York Loyalist Merchants," *William and Mary Quarterly*, 3rd ser., XLIX (1992), 3–28; Thomas M. Doerflinger, *A Vigorous Spirit of Enterprise: Merchants and Economic Development in Revolutionary Philadelphia* (Chapel Hill: University of North Carolina Press), Chapter 1.

11. Tamara Plakins Thornton, *Cultivating Gentlemen: The Meaning of Country Life Among the Boston Elite, 1785–1860* (New Haven: Yale University Press, 1989); Philip L. White, *The Beekmans of New York in Politics and Commerce, 1746–1877* (New York: New-York Historical Society, 1956).

12. Wood, *Radicalism of the Revolution*, pp. 211–12; Taylor, *Liberty Men*, p. 41.

13. Edward Countryman, *A People in Revolution: The American Revolution and Political Society in New York, 1760–1790* (Baltimore: Johns Hopkins University Press, 1981), pp. 264–65; George Dangerfield, *Chancellor Robert R. Livingston of New York, 1746–1813* (New York: Harcourt, Brace & World, 1960), pp. 403–22 and passim.

14. "Journal of the Rev. John Taylor, on a Mission Through the Mohawk and Black River Country, in the Year 1802," Edmund B. O'Callaghan, ed., *Documentary History of the State of New York* (4 vols.; Albany: Weed, Parsons, 1850), III, p. 1136.

15. Paul W. Gates, "Frontier Landlords and Pioneer Tenants," in his *Landlords and Tenants*, pp. 238–302.

16. Robert A. Gross, *The Minutemen and Their World* (New York: Hill and Wang, 1976), Chapter 7. See also Richard L. Bushman, *The Refinement of America: Persons, Houses, Cities* (New York: Alfred A. Knopf, 1992).

17. William H. Siles, "Pioneering in the Genesee Country: Entrepreneurial Strategy and the Concept of a Central Place," in Manfred Jonas and Robert V. Wells, eds., *New Opportunities in a New Nation: The Development of New York After the Revolution* (Schenectady: Union College Press, 1982), pp. 33–68.

18. Philip L. White, *Beekmantown, New York: Forest Frontier to Farm Community* (Austin: University of Texas Press, 1979), pp. 16–18.

19. Quoted in Rhys Isaac, *The Transformation of Virginia, 1740–1790* (Chapel Hill: University of North Carolina Press, 1982), pp. 39–40.

20. Allan Kulikoff, *Tobacco and Slaves: The Development of Southern Cultures in the Chesapeake, 1680–1800* (Chapel Hill: University of North Carolina Press, 1986), Chapter 4.

21. Richard S. Dunn, "Black Society in the Chesapeake, 1776–1810," in Ira Berlin and Ronald Hoffman, eds., *Slavery and Freedom in the Age of the American Revolution* (Charlottesville: University Press of Virginia, 1983), pp. 73–74.
22. Gates, *Public Land Law Development*, pp. 138, 166.
23. Edward Countryman, "The Price of Cotton: The Human Cost of Slavery in Mid-Nineteenth Century Mississippi" (paper presented at the symposium of the Milan, Italy, Group in Early United States History, June 19–23, 1992), pp. 12–13; William K. Scarborough, "Heartland of the Cotton Kingdom," in Richard Aubrey McLemore, ed., *A History of Mississippi*, Vol. I (Hattiesburg: University and College Press of Mississippi, 1973), pp. 310–51; Gates, *Public Law Land Development*, p. 39; Gates, "Southern Investments in Northern Lands Before the Civil War," in *Landlords and Tenants*, pp. 72–107, quote at p. 99.
24. Taylor, *Liberty Men*, pp. 61–101, 181–207, 227–28.
25. Wyckoff, *Developer's Frontier*; Michael Kammen, " 'The Promised Sunshine of the Future': Reflections on Economic Growth and Social Change in Post-Revolutionary New York," in Jonas and Wells, eds., *New Opportunities in a New Nation*, pp. 109–43; Paul E. Johnson, *A Shopkeeper's Millennium: Society and Revivals in Rochester, New York, 1815–1837* (New York: Hill and Wang, 1978), Chapter 1.
26. Mary P. Ryan, *Cradle of the Middle Class: The Family in Oneida County, New York, 1790–1865* (Cambridge: Cambridge University Press, 1981), Chapter 1.
27. Taylor, *Liberty Men*, Chapter 9.
28. Gates, "Tenants of the Log Cabin," pp. 21–26.
29. Wyckoff, *Developer's Frontier*, pp. 43–52, 125.
30. John Mack Faragher, *Sugar Creek: Life on the Illinois Prairie* (New Haven: Yale University Press, 1986), pp. 43, 53–55.
31. Robinson, *Land in California*, Chapter 10, quotes at pp. 140–41.
32. Gates, *Landlords and Tenants*, p. 12; Gates, *Public Land Law Development*, pp. 140–41 and Chapter 15.
33. Thomas Jefferson, "Notes on the State of Virginia," in Merrill D. Peterson, ed., *The Portable Thomas Jefferson* (Harmondsworth, Middlesex: Penguin Books, 1977 [orig. pub. 1975]), p. 217.
34. Gates, *Public Law Land Development*, Chapters 13–14.
35. Ibid., Chapter 16.
36. These figures are drawn from Allan Kulikoff, "Uprooted Peoples: Black Migrants in the Age of the American Revolution, 1790–1820," in Berlin and Hoffman, eds., *Slavery and Freedom*, Table 1, p. 149, Table 2, p. 152.
37. Michael Tadman, *Speculators and Slaves: Masters, Traders, and Slaves in the Old South* (Madison: University of Wisconsin Press, 1989), Table 2.1, p. 12.
38. See Dunn, "Black Society in the Chesapeake," and Countryman, "The Price of Cotton."
39. These figures are drawn from Tadman, *Speculators and Slaves*, pp. 29–31 and Appendix 3, pp. 237–47.
40. See particularly Herbert G. Gutman, *The Black Family in Slavery and Freedom, 1750–1925* (Oxford: Basil Blackwell, 1976), esp. Chapter 5.

41. Stowe, *Uncle Tom's Cabin* (New York: New American Library [orig. pub. 1852]); Toni Morrison, *Beloved* (New York: Signet Books, 1991 [orig. pub. 1987]).

42. These figures are drawn from the U.S. census for 1850. My thanks to James McMillan for pointing out the obvious explanation in terms of immigration.

43. These points are drawn from Christopher Morris, *Becoming Southern: Vicksburg and Warren County, Mississippi, 1790–1860* (New York: Oxford University Press, 1995); James C. Cobb, *The Most Southern Place on Earth: The Mississippi Delta and the Roots of Regional Identity* (New York: Oxford University Press, 1992); David Lewis Cohn, *Where I Was Born and Raised* (Boston: Houghton Mifflin, 1948); and Countryman, "The Price of Cotton." My thanks to Christopher Morris for allowing me to see *Becoming Southern* in manuscript.

44. Richard White, *The Middle Ground: Indians, Empires and Republics in the Great Lakes Region, 1650–1815* (Cambridge: Cambridge University Press, 1991), Chapters 10–11; Faragher, *Sugar Creek*, Chapter 4. See also James H. Merrell, *The Indians' New World: Catawbas and Their Neighbors from European Contact Through the Era of Removal* (Chapel Hill: University of North Carolina Press, 1989), Chapter 5.

45. Robinson, *Land in California*, Chapter 8.

6. CAPITAL CITIES

1. Oscar Handlin, *Boston's Immigrants, 1790–1880* (Cambridge, MA: Harvard University Press, 1991 [orig. pub. 1941]), pp. 77–80.

2. See Arthur M. Johnson and Barry E. Supple, *Boston Capitalists and Western Railroads: A Study in the Nineteenth-Century Railroad Investment Process* (Cambridge, MA: Harvard University Press, 1967), and Ronald Story, *Harvard & the Boston Upper Class: The Forging of an Aristocracy, 1800–1870* (Middletown, CT: Wesleyan University Press, 1980).

3. Robert Greenhalgh Albion, *The Rise of New York Port (1815–1860)* (New York: Columbia University Press, 1939), and Elizabeth Blackmar, *Manhattan for Rent, 1785–1850* (Ithaca: Cornell University Press, 1989).

4. Diane Lindstrom, *Economic Development in the Philadelphia Region, 1810–1850* (New York: Columbia University Press, 1978); Cynthia J. Shelton, *The Mills of Manayunk: Industrialization and Social Conflict in the Philadelphia Region, 1787–1837* (Baltimore: Johns Hopkins University Press, 1986); Anthony F. C. Wallace, *Rockdale: The Growth of an American Village in the Early Industrial Revolution* (New York: W. W. Norton, 1978); Anthony F. C. Wallace, *St. Clair: A Nineteenth-Century Coal Town's Experience with a Disaster-Prone Industry* (New York: Alfred A. Knopf, 1987).

5. [Alexander Hamilton, James Madison, and John Jay], *The Federalist*, ed. Clinton Rossiter (New York: New American Library, 1961), no. 11, pp. 84–91, quotes at pp. 85, 91.

6. This is the argument of John R. Nelson, *Liberty and Property: Political Economy*

and Policymaking in the New Nation, 1789–1812 (Baltimore: Johns Hopkins University Press, 1987).

7. Edward Countryman, "The Uses of Capital in Revolutionary America: The Case of the New York Loyalist Merchants," *William and Mary Quarterly*, 3rd ser., XLIX (1992), pp. 3–28.

8. Barbara J. Tucker, *Samuel Slater and the Origins of the American Textile Industry, 1790–1860* (Ithaca: Cornell University Press, 1984), p. 93.

9. Jonathan Prude, *The Coming of Industrial Order: Town and Factory Life in Rural Massachusetts, 1810–1860* (Cambridge: Cambridge University Press, 1983).

10. Robert F. Dalzell, Jr., *Enterprising Elite: The Boston Associates and the World They Made* (Cambridge, MA: Harvard University Press, 1987).

11. Wallace, *Rockdale*, Chapter 5.

12. *Dictionary of American Biography*, s.v. Revere, Paul; Sean Wilentz, *Chants Democratic: New York City and the Rise of the American Working Class, 1788–1850* (New York: Oxford University Press, 1984), pp. 36–37.

13. Alan Dawley, *Class and Community: The Industrial Revolution in Lynn* (Cambridge, MA: Harvard University Press, 1976); Wilentz, *Chants Democratic*; Bruce Laurie, *Artisans into Workers: Labor in Nineteenth-Century America* (New York: Hill and Wang, 1989).

14. Nathan Miller, *The Enterprise of a Free People: Aspects of Economic Development in New York State During the Canal Period, 1792–1838* (Ithaca: Cornell University Press, 1962), Chapters 5–6, quote at p. 88.

15. Ronald E. Shaw, *Erie Water West: A History of the Erie Canal, 1792–1854* (Lexington: University Press of Kentucky, 1966); George Rogers Taylor, *The Transportation Revolution, 1815–1860* (New York: Rinehart, 1951).

16. Shaw, *Erie Water West*, pp. 89, 95, 123–39.

17. Philip L. White, *Beekmantown, New York: Forest Frontier to Farm Community* (Austin: University of Texas Press, 1979), pp. 45–46; Shaw, *Erie Water West*, p. 239. As I was in the very last stages of this manuscript, plans were announced for a "major restoration" of the canal as a recreation area, to replace commercial traffic that has almost totally ended. Ironically, the sponsor is the New York State Thruway Authority. Joseph Berger, "New York Planning Major Restoration for the Erie Canal," *New York Times*, June 30, 1995, p. 1.

18. In addition to Miller, *Enterprise of a Free People*, see Daniel Calhoun, *The Intelligence of a People* (Princeton: Princeton University Press, 1973), which investigates modes of thinking in early industrial New York.

19. Taylor, *Transportation Revolution*, p. 60.

20. U.S. Bureau of the Census, *Historical Statistics of the United States, 1789–1945* (Washington, DC: Government Printing Office, 1949), Series K, 168–69, 1–17, 18–27, 174–75, 124–26, pp. 200–20.

21. Taylor, *Transportation Revolution*, pp. 35, 87; Dalzell, *Enterprising Elite*, p. 87; Johnson and Supple, *Boston Capitalists and Western Railroads*; Handlin, *Boston's Immigrants*, p. 100.

22. Taylor, *Transportation Revolution*, pp. 79, 87.

23. Bureau of the Census, *Historical Statistics*, Series E, 218, pp. 108–9; Series G, 13, 16, p. 142; Series J, 179, p. 187; Series E, 182, 187, p. 106.

24. See Albion, *New York Port*; Taylor, *Transportation Revolution*, pp. 388–92; and Countryman, "Uses of Capital."

25. Shane White, *Somewhat More Independent: The End of Slavery in New York City, 1770–1810* (Athens: University of Georgia Press, 1991), p. 156; Gary B. Nash, *Forging Freedom: The Formation of Philadelphia's Black Community, 1720–1840* (Cambridge, MA: Harvard University Press, 1988), p. 213.

26. Stuart Blumin, *The Urban Threshold: Growth and Change in a Nineteenth-Century American Community* (Chicago: University of Chicago Press, 1976), pp. 35–36.

27. Handlin, *Boston's Immigrants*, pp. 31, 46.

28. Bureau of the Census, *Historical Statistics*, Series B, 304–10, p. 34.

29. Ibid., Series B, 145–59, p. 29.

30. For "public" corporations in colonial British America, see Pauline Maier, "The Revolutionary Origins of American Corporations," *William and Mary Quarterly*, 3rd ser., L (1993), pp. 51–84.

31. David G. Hackett, *The Rude Hand of Innovation: Religion and Social Order in Albany, New York, 1652–1836* (New York: Oxford University Press, 1991), pp. 78–82.

32. Wilentz, *Chants Democratic*, pp. 107–42.

33. Daniel J. Walkowitz, *Worker City, Company Town: Iron- and Cotton-Worker Protest in Troy and Cohoes, New York, 1855–84* (Urbana: University of Illinois Press, 1978), pp. 23–24.

34. Charles Dickens, *American Notes, for General Circulation*, ed. John S. Whitley and Arnold Goldman (Harmondsworth, Middlesex: Penguin Books, 1972 [orig. pub. 1842]), p. 236.

35. John W. Reps, *The Making of Urban America: A History of City Planning in the United States* (Princeton: Princeton University Press, 1965), pp. 290–91, 392–93, 359.

36. Ibid., pp. 81–87; Peirce F. Lewis, *New Orleans: The Making of an Urban Landscape* (Cambridge, MA: Ballinger Publishing, 1976); John Preston Moore, *Revolt in Louisiana: The Spanish Occupation, 1766–1770* (Baton Rouge: Louisiana State University Press, 1976), p. 162.

37. Joseph Logsdon and Caryn Cossé Bell, "The Americanization of Black New Orleans, 1850–1900," in Arnold R. Hirsch and Joseph Logsdon, eds., *Creole New Orleans: Race and Americanization* (Baton Rouge: Louisiana State University Press, 1992), pp. 201–61, figures from Table 1, p. 206. My thanks to New Orleans native Jeremy du Quesnay Adams for a very informative conversation about New Orleans history and to James McMillan for a term paper he wrote on the Mobile Creole community.

38. Reps, *Making of Urban America*, pp. 175–80; Edmund L. Drago, *Initiative, Paternalism, and Race Relations: Charleston's Avery Normal Institute* (Athens: University of Georgia Press, 1990), pp. 9 ff.; William H. Pease and Jane H. Pease, *The Web of Progress: Private Values and Public Styles in Boston and Charleston, 1828–1843* (Athens: University of Georgia Press, 1991 [orig. pub. 1985]), pp.

56–62, 217; Orville Vernon Burton, *In My Father's House There Are Many Mansions: Family and Community in Edgefield, South Carolina* (Chapel Hill: University of North Carolina Press, 1985), pp. 15–18, 30–33.

39. Reps, *Making of Urban America*, pp. 300–2; William Cronon, *Nature's Metropolis: Chicago and the Great West* (New York: W. W. Norton, 1989), pp. 310–18.

40. Edmund S. Morgan, *American Slavery, American Freedom: The Ordeal of Colonial Virginia* (New York: W. W. Norton, 1975), p. 110.

41. Quoted in W. W. Robinson, *Land in California: The Story of Mission Lands, Ranchos, Squatters, Mining Claims, Railroad Grants, Land Scrip, Homesteads* (Berkeley: University of California Press, 1979 [1948]), p. 133.

42. Paul W. Gates, *History of Public Land Law Development* (Washington, DC: Government Printing Office, 1968), p. 441.

43. Kevin Starr, *Americans and the California Dream, 1850–1915* (New York: Oxford University Press, 1973), p. 65.

7. "WITH IRON INTERLACED"

1. Walt Whitman, "The Prairie States," in *Leaves of Grass* (New York: New American Library, 1955), p. 316.

2. Orlando Patterson, *Freedom*, Vol. I: *Freedom in the Making of Western Culture* (New York: Basic Books, 1991), p. 405; see also three splendid articles in the *William and Mary Quarterly*, 3rd ser., LII, no. 2 (April 1995), that all bear on this theme: Martin H. Quitt, "Trade and Acculturation at Jamestown, 1607–1609: The Limits of Understanding" (pp. 227–56); Richard Godbeer, " 'The Cry of Sodom': Discourse, Intercourse, and Desire in Colonial New England" (pp. 259–86); and Eve Kornfeld, "Encountering the 'Other': American Intellectuals and Indians in the 1790s" (pp. 287–314).

3. See Michael Merrill, "Putting 'Capitalism' in Its Place: A Review of Recent Literature," *William and Mary Quarterly*, 3rd ser., LII (1995), 315–26.

4. The phrase, with all its double entendre, was frequently used in election proclamations.

5. Thomas Jefferson to Handsome Lake, November 3, 1802, in Merrill D. Peterson, ed., *The Portable Thomas Jefferson* (Harmondsworth, Middlesex: Penguin Books, 1977 [orig. pub. 1975]), pp. 305–7.

6. Anthony F. C. Wallace, *The Death and Rebirth of the Seneca* (New York: Vintage Books, 1972 [orig. pub. 1969]).

7. Richard White, *The Middle Ground: Indians, Empires and Republics in the Great Lakes Region, 1650–1815* (Cambridge: Cambridge University Press, 1991), p. 279.

8. Ibid., pp. 508–9.

9. William G. McLoughlin, *Cherokee Renascence in the New Republic* (Princeton: Princeton University Press, 1986).

10. Richard White, *The Roots of Dependency: Subsistence, Environment, and Social Change*

Among the Choctaws, Pawnees, and Navajos (Lincoln: University of Nebraska Press, 1983).

11. Kornfeld, "Encountering the 'Other.' "

12. June Namias, *White Captives: Gender and Ethnicity on the American Frontier* (Chapel Hill: University of North Carolina Press, 1993), and John Demos, *The Unredeemed Captive: A Family Story from Early America* (New York: Alfred A. Knopf, 1994); J. Hector St. John de Crèvecoeur, *Letters from an American Farmer* (New York: Signet, 1973 [orig. pub. 1782]), pp. 194–222; John Mack Faragher, *Daniel Boone: The Life and Legend of an American Pioneer* (New York: Henry Holt, 1992).

13. Alan Taylor, *Liberty Men and Great Proprietors: The Revolutionary Settlement on the Maine Frontier, 1760–1820* (Chapel Hill: University of North Carolina Press, 1990). Henry Christman, *Tin Horns and Calico: A Decisive Episode in the Emergence of Democracy* (New York: Henry Holt, 1945); the most recent account is John Reeve Huston, "Land and Freedom: The Anti-Rent Wars, Jacksonian Politics, and the Contest over Free Labor in New York, 1785–1865" (Ph.D. diss., Yale University, 1994).

14. See James Axtell, "The White Indians of North America," in his *The European and the Indian: Essays in the Ethnohistory of Colonial North America* (New York: Oxford University Press, 1981), pp. 168–206; Jack D. Forbes, *Africans and Native Americans: The Language of Race and the Evolution of Red-Black Peoples* (Urbana: University of Illinois Press, 1993); Namias, *White Captives*; J. Leitch Wright, Jr., *Creeks and Seminoles: Destruction and Regeneration of the Muscogulge People* (Lincoln: University of Nebraska Press, 1986); Philip Joseph Deloria, "Playing Indian: Otherness and Authenticity in the Assumption of American Indian Identity" (Ph.D. diss., Yale University, 1994).

15. White, *The Middle Ground*, Chapters 1 and 9; Herman Melville, *The Confidence Man: His Masquerade* (Evanston: Northwestern University Press, 1984 [orig. pub. 1857]), Chapter 26, pp. 144–45; Richard Slotkin, *The Fatal Environment: The Myth of the Frontier in the Age of Industrialization, 1800–1890* (New York: Atheneum, 1985). Compare how two of the greatest mid-century Westerns handle this theme: John Ford's *The Searchers* (1956) and (in ironic reversal), Clint Eastwood's *The Outlaw Josey Wales* (1976).

16. Frederick Jackson Turner, "The Significance of the Frontier in American History," in his *Frontier and Section: Selected Essays*, ed. Ray Allen Billington (Englewood Cliffs, NJ: Prentice-Hall, 1961 [orig. pub. 1893]), pp. 37–62.

17. John Mack Faragher, *Sugar Creek: Life on the Illinois Prairie* (New Haven: Yale University Press, 1986), Chapters 8 and 11.

18. Quoted in Henry Nash Smith, *Virgin Land: The American West as Symbol and Myth* (New York: Vintage Books, n.d. [orig. pub. 1950]), p. 58; emphasis in the original.

19. Faragher, *Sugar Creek*, p. 82 and Chapter 6; see also E. P. Thompson, "Rough Music," in his *Customs in Common: Studies in Traditional Popular Culture* (New York: New Press, 1991), pp. 467–538; Natalie Zemon Davis, "The Reasons of Misrule" and "The Rites of Violence," in her *Society and Culture in Early*

Modern France: Eight Essays (Stanford: Stanford University Press, 1975), pp. 97–123, 152–87.

20. Christopher Clark, *The Roots of Rural Capitalism: Western Massachusetts, 1780–1860* (Ithaca: Cornell University Press, 1990), Chapters 1–2; Thomas S. Wermuth, " 'To Market, to Market': Yeoman Farmers, Merchant Capitalists and the Transition to Capitalism in the Hudson River Valley, Ulster County, 1760–1840" (Ph.D. diss., State University of New York, Binghamton, 1991); Faragher, *Sugar Creek*, Chapter 14; Michael Merrill, "Cash Is Good to Eat: Self-Sufficiency and Exchange in the Rural Economy of the United States," *Radical History Review*, III (1977), pp. 42–71; James A. Henretta, "Families and Farms: Mentalité in Pre-Industrial America," *William and Mary Quarterly*, 3rd ser., XXXV (1978), pp. 3–32; Merle Curti, *The Making of an American Community: A Case Study of Democracy in a Frontier County* (Stanford: Stanford University Press, 1959), pp. 115–16.

21. For a particularly astute discussion of the theme of balance, see Bruce H. Mann, *Neighbors and Strangers: Law and Community in Early Connecticut* (Chapel Hill: University of North Carolina Press, 1987). See also James A. Henretta, *The Origins of American Capitalism: Collected Essays* (Boston: Northeastern University Press, 1992), and Allan Kulikoff, *The Agrarian Origins of American Capitalism* (Charlottesville: University Press of Virginia, 1992).

22. Don Harrison Doyle, *The Social Order of a Frontier Community: Jacksonville, Illinois, 1825–70* (Urbana: University of Illinois Press, 1983), p. 95.

23. Curti, *Making of an American Community*, Table 11, p. 105.

24. Doyle, *Social Order of a Frontier Community*, pp. 108–18 and Table 12, p. 267.

25. See Sonya Salamon, *Prairie Patrimony: Family, Farming, and Community in the Midwest* (Chapel Hill: University of North Carolina Press, 1992).

26. Robert C. Kenzer, *Kinship and Neighborhood in a Southern Community: Orange County, North Carolina, 1849–1881* (Knoxville: University of Tennessee Press, 1987), pp. 9–14, and Tables 1–3, pp. 163–65.

27. Orville Vernon Burton, *In My Father's House Are Many Mansions: Family and Community in Edgefield, South Carolina* (Chapel Hill: University of North Carolina Press, 1985), p. 117.

28. See Forbes, *Africans and Native Americans*, esp. Chapter 10.

29. Frances Anne Kemble, *Journal of a Residence on a Georgian Plantation in 1838–1839*, ed. John A. Scott (Athens: University of Georgia Press, 1984 [orig. pub. 1852]); Theodore Rosengarten, *Tombee: Portrait of a Cotton Planter* (New York: William Morrow, 1986), Chapter 9, quotes at pp. 180–81; I am drawing here as well on work in progress by Larry H. Hudson, Jr., of the University of Rochester and William Dusinberre of the University of Warwick.

30. Charles Joyner, *Down by the Riverside: A South Carolina Slave Community* (Urbana: University of Illinois Press, 1984), Table 1, p. 19.

31. Herbert G. Gutman, *The Black Family in Slavery and Freedom, 1750–1925* (Oxford: Basil Blackwell, 1978), Chapters 2 and 5.

32. Philip D. Morgan, "Work and Culture: The Task System and the World of

Lowcountry Blacks, 1700 to 1880," *William and Mary Quarterly* XXXIX (1982), pp. 563–99; Joyner, *Down by the Riverside*, Chapter 4.

33. For a fine beginning, see Christopher Morris, *Becoming Southern: Vicksburg and Warren County, Mississippi, 1790–1860* (New York: Oxford University Press, 1995).

34. Winthrop D. Jordan, *Tumult and Silence at Second Creek: An Inquiry into a Civil War Slave Conspiracy* (Baton Rouge: Louisiana State University Press, 1993).

35. All of these figures are drawn from the U.S. census for 1850 and 1860.

36. This account is drawn from U.S. census for 1850 and 1860; John Hebron Moore, *The Emergence of the Cotton Kingdom in the Old South: Mississippi, 1770–1860* (Baton Rouge: Louisiana State University Press, 1988, particularly Chapter 5 and Chapter 6); David L. Cohn, *Where I Was Born and Raised* (Boston: Houghton Mifflin, 1948); James C. Cobb, *The Most Southern Place on Earth: The Mississippi Delta and the Roots of Regional Identity* (New York: Oxford University Press, 1992); and Countryman, "The Price of Cotton" (see above, note 23 in Chapter 5). My own intention of exploring Mississippi slavery at length should be clear.

37. See Joyner, *Down by the Riverside*, Chapter 2.

38. See E. P. Thompson, *The Making of the English Working Class* (New York: Vintage Books, 1966 [orig. pub. 1963]).

39. See particularly Jonathan Prude, *The Coming of Industrial Order: Town and Factory Life in Rural Massachusetts, 1810–1860* (Cambridge: Cambridge University Press, 1983), Chapter 5.

40. Anthony F. C. Wallace, *Rockdale: The Growth of an American Village in the Early Industrial Revolution* (New York: W. W. Norton, 1978), pp. 65, 423.

41. Gutman, *Black Family in Slavery and Freedom*, Chapters 3 and 4.

42. Thompson, *English Working Class*, p. 9.

43. Alan Dawley, *Class and Community: The Industrial Revolution in Lynn* (Cambridge, MA: Harvard University Press, 1977).

44. Mary H. Blewett, *Men, Women, and Work: Class, Gender, and Protest in the New England Shoe Industry, 1780–1910* (Urbana: University of Illinois Press, 1988), p. 18.

45. Ibid., Chapter 3; Clark, *Roots of Rural Capitalism*, pp. 184–89; Christine Stansell, *City of Women: Sex and Class in New York, 1789–1860* (Urbana: University of Illinois Press, 1987 [orig. pub. 1986]).

46. Barbara J. Tucker, *Samuel Slater and the Origins of the American Textile Industry, 1790–1860* (Ithaca: Cornell University Press, 1984), pp. 141–43; Prude, *Coming of Industrial Order*, pp. 117–18.

47. Wallace, pp. 66–67. See also Thomas Dublin, *Transforming Women's Work: New England Lives in the Industrial Revolution* (Ithaca: Cornell University Press, 1994).

48. Charles Dickens, *American Notes, for General Circulation*, ed. John S. Whitley and Arnold Goldman (Harmondsworth, Middlesex: Penguin Books, 1972 [orig. pub. 1842]), pp. 115–16.

49. Thomas Dublin, *Women at Work: The Transformation of Work and Community in*

Lowell, Massachusetts, 1826–1860 (New York: Columbia University Press, 1979), Chapters 3 and 5, quote at p. 56.

50. Wallace, *Rockdale*, Chapters 7 and 8.

51. The argument here is drawn in part from Natalie S. Glance and Bernardo A. Huberman, "The Dynamics of Social Dilemmas," *Scientific American*, March 1994, pp. 76–81.

52. Ibid., pp. 80–83; Arthur K. Moore, *The Frontier Mind* (Lexington: University Press of Kentucky, 1957), p. 112; Rhys Isaac, *The Transformation of Virginia, 1740–1790* (Chapel Hill: University of North Carolina Press, 1982), p. 98.

53. In addition to Wallace, *Rockdale*, see Mary P. Ryan, *Cradle of the Middle Class: The Family in Oneida County, New York, 1790–1865* (Cambridge: Cambridge University Press, 1981), and Stuart M. Blumin, *The Emergence of the Middle Class: Social Experience in the American City, 1760–1900* (Cambridge: Cambridge University Press, 1989).

54. Malcolm Bell, Jr., *Major Butler's Legacy: Five Generations of a Slaveholding Family* (Athens: University of Georgia Press, 1987).

55. Duncan quoted in Jordan, *Tumult and Silence*, p. 1.

56. E. N. Elliott, *Cotton is king, and pro-slavery arguments: comprising the writings of Hammond, Harper, Christy, Stringfellow, Hodge, Bledsoe, and Cartwright, on this important subject* (Augusta, GA: Pritchard, Abbott & Loomis, 1860); Drew Gilpin Faust, *James Henry Hammond and the Old South: A Design for Mastery* (Baton Rouge: Louisiana State University Press, 1982).

57. Stansell, *City of Women*, Chapter 4.

58. See Kathryn Kish Sklar, *Catharine Beecher: A Study in American Domesticity* (New Haven: Yale University Press, 1973).

8. Citizens, Subjects, and Slaves: The Republican Mosaic

1. Quoted in John Chavez, *The Lost Land: The Chicano Image of the Southwest* (Albuquerque: University of New Mexico Press, 1984), pp. 49–50.

2. Ibid., quoting Josiah Royce (p. 47), *El bejareño* (p. 51), and Francisco Ramírez (p. 47).

3. Constitutions of Virginia, Pennsylvania, and Massachusetts, in J. R. Pole, ed., *The Revolution in America, 1754–1788* (London: Macmillan, 1970); constitution of New York in William A. Polf, *1777: The Political Revolution and New York's First Constitution* (Albany: New York State Bicentennial Commission, 1977).

4. Judge William Gaston, *State* v. *Manuel* (1838), quoted in James H. Kettner, *The Development of American Citizenship, 1608–1870* (Chapel Hill: University of North Carolina Press, 1978), p. 317; emphasis in the original.

5. Edmund S. Morgan, *Inventing the People: The Rise of Popular Sovereignty in England and America* (New York: W. W. Norton, 1988).

6. Kettner, *American Citizenship*, p. 236; see also Judith Shklar, *American Citizenship: The Quest for Inclusion* (Cambridge, MA: Harvard University Press, 1991).

7. See Stanley Elkins and Eric McKitrick, *The Age of Federalism* (New York: Oxford University Press, 1993), pp. 330–36.

8. Philip S. Foner, ed., *The Democratic-Republican Societies, 1790–1800* (Westport, CT: Greenwood Press, 1976), passim, quote at p. 74.

9. Constitution of Massachusetts, preamble, in Pole, *The Revolution in America*, p. 479.

10. The standard account is James Morton Smith, *Freedom's Fetters: The Alien and Sedition Laws and American Civil Liberties* (Ithaca: Cornell University Press, 1966).

11. "All Republicans:" First Inaugural Address (March 4, 1901), *Jefferson Writings*, ed. Merrill D. Peterson (New York: Viking Press, 1984), pp. 492–96, quote at p. 493; "revolution": Jefferson to John Dickinson, March 6, 1801, and Jefferson to Joseph Priestley, March 23, 1801, in ibid., pp. 1084–86.

12. For the best argument to this effect, see Kenneth A. Lockridge, *On the Sources of Patriarchal Rage: The Commonplace Books of William Byrd and Thomas Jefferson and the Gendering of Power in the Eighteenth Century* (New York: New York University Press, 1992).

13. David Brion Davis, *The Problem of Slavery in the Age of Revolution: 1770–1823* (Ithaca: Cornell University Press: 1975), pp. 306–26; Douglas R. Egerton, *Gabriel's Rebellion: The Virginia Slave Conspiracies of 1800 and 1802* (Chapel Hill: University of North Carolina Press, 1993); Herbert Aptheker, *American Negro Slave Revolts* (New York: International Publishers, 1952 [orig. pub. 1943]), p. 221. See also Eugene D. Genovese, *From Rebellion to Revolution: Afro-American Slave Revolts in the Making of the New World* (New York: Vintage Books, 1981 [orig. pub. 1979]).

14. Aptheker, *Slave Revolts*, pp. 267–76, 293–324.

15. Quoted in ibid., p. 302.

16. Richard White, *The Middle Ground: Indians, Empires and Republics in the Great Lakes Region, 1650–1815* (Cambridge: Cambridge University Press, 1991), p. 420 and Chapter 11.

17. Ibid., pp. 516–17; John Mack Faragher, *Sugar Creek: Life on the Illinois Prairie* (New Haven: Yale University Press, 1986), Chapter 4, quotes at pp. 32, 35.

18. William Cronon, *Nature's Metropolis: Chicago and the Great West* (New York: W. W. Norton, 1991).

19. William G. McLoughlin, *Cherokee Renascence in the New Republic* (Princeton: Princeton University Press, 1986), p. 187.

20. J. Leitch Wright, Jr., *Creeks and Seminoles: Destruction and Regeneration of the Muscogulge People* (Lincoln: University of Nebraska Press, 1986), Chapters 6 and 7, quote at p. 185.

21. Ibid., pp. 115–17, 241–42.

22. McLoughlin, *Cherokee Renascence*, pp. xv–xvii.

23. Jackson quoted in ibid., p. 260.

24. Ibid., Chapters 13 and 20.

25. The full text of the law is reprinted in Vine Deloria, Jr., ed., *Of Utmost Good Faith* (New York: Bantam Books, 1972 [orig. pub. 1971]), pp. 62–63.

26. *Cherokee Nation v. State of Georgia*, 5 Peters Reports 1 (1831) 75; see also Kettner, *American Citizenship*, pp. 287–300.

27. Alexis de Tocqueville, *Democracy in America*, ed. J. P. Mayer and Max Lerner, trans. George Lawrence (2 vols.; London: Collins, 1968), p. 417.

28. *Dred Scott* v. *Sandford*, 19 *Howard Reports* 393 (1857); for a full discussion, see Don E. Fehrenbacher, *The Dred Scott Case: Its Significance in American Law and Politics* (New York: Oxford University Press, 1978). Taney's opinion did not stand alone, of course. As early as 1838 the chief justice of Mississippi flatly rejected the comity ("full faith and credit") clause of the federal Constitution when he refused an Ohio court decision that "would have freed the black mistress and mulatto son of one of the state's white citizens." Kettner, *American Citizenship*, p. 307.

29. Benjamin Quarles, "The Revolutionary War as a Black Declaration of Independence," in Ira Berlin and Ronald Hoffman, eds., *Slavery and Freedom in the Age of the American Revolution* (Charlottesville: University Press of Virginia, 1983), pp. 283–301.

30. John Winthrop, "Christian Charitie, A Moddel Hereof," in Edmund S. Morgan, ed., *The Founding of Massachusetts: Historians and the Sources* (Indianapolis: Bobbs-Merrill, 1964 [1630]), pp. 190–204, quote at p. 190.

31. Reprinted in Pole, *Revolution in America*, p. 41.

32. New York State constitution of 1777, Article 35, reprinted in William A. Polf, ed., *1777: The Political Revolution and New York's First Constitution* (Albany: New York State Bicentennial Commission, 1977), p. 58.

33. Blackstone, *Commentaries on the Laws of England*, quoted in Gordon S. Wood, *The Creation of the American Republic, 1776–1787* (Chapel Hill: University of North Carolina Press, 1969), p. 264.

34. For this theme, see Wood, *Creation of the American Republic*, Chapter 10; for one instance, see Edward Countryman, *A People in Revolution: The American Revolution and Political Society in New York, 1760–1790* (Baltimore: Johns Hopkins University Press, 1981), Chapter 9. A full discussion of the codification project would be a major contribution to American legal history.

35. This argument is drawn from James Willard Hurst, *Law and the Conditions of Freedom in the Nineteenth-Century United States* (Madison: University of Wisconsin Press, 1964 [orig. pub. 1956]); Morton J. Horwitz, *The Transformation of American Law, 1790–1860* (Cambridge, MA: Harvard University Press, 1977); and J. R. Pole, "Property and Law in the American Republic," in his *Paths to the American Past* (New York: Oxford University Press, 1979), pp. 75–108. I am aware of the differences among their interpretations, but the net effect of their discussions is to invite a focus upon changes in the practice and function of nineteenth-century American law and changes in the large pattern of society and development. See also Stanley N. Katz, "The Problem of a Colonial Legal History," in Jack P. Greene and J. R. Pole, eds., *Colonial British America: Essays in the New History of the Early Modern Era* (Baltimore: Johns Hopkins University Press, 1984), pp. 457–89, and Gary Kulik, "Dams, Fish, and Farmers: Defense of Public Rights in Eighteenth-Century Rhode Island," in Steven Hahn and Jonathan Prude, eds., *The Countryside in the Age of Capitalist Transformation* (Chapel Hill: University of North Carolina Press, 1985), pp. 25–50.

36. See Kulik, "Dams, Fish, and Farmers," and Horwitz, *Transformation of American Law*, 74–78. My use of "his" is deliberate here, to reflect the unequal access to property between women and men.

37. See Gordon S. Wood, *The Radicalism of the American Revolution* (New York: Alfred A. Knopf, 1992), Part III.

9. THE CRISIS OF TRIUMPHANT DEMOCRACY

1. See Ernest Lee Tuveson, *Redeemer Nation: The Idea of America's Millennial Role* (Chicago: University of Chicago Press, 1968); Frederick Merk, *Manifest Destiny and Mission in American History: A Reinterpretation* (New York: Alfred A. Knopf, 1963); and Henry Nash Smith, *Virgin Land: The American West as Symbol and Myth* (New York: Vintage Books, n.d. [orig. pub. 1950]).

2. This point has a genuine basis in American social fact. The absence of any principle of entail in American landholding since the Revolution has left even the largest tracts at permanent risk of division by inheritance or sale. Although the principle of incorporation offers an immortality to property which entail can no longer provide, a survey of the largest corporations over fifty-year intervals turns up surprisingly little continuity. Any criticism of the American social order must take account of these points, not simply slide over them. My thanks to Anne-Elizabeth Wynn for pressing this issue forcefully when my graduate reading group discussed a draft of this book and for pointing out the special 75th anniversary issue of *Forbes* magazine (September 14, 1992), which addresses many of these issues. For the contrary argument, see Richard Sennett, *The Hidden Injuries of Class* (New York: Vintage Books, 1973 [orig. pub. 1972]).

3. "A Second Letter from Phocion to the Considerate Citizens of New-York, Containing Remarks on Mentor's Reply" (April 1784), *The Papers of Alexander Hamilton*, ed. Harold C. Syrett et al., (27 vols.; New York: Columbia University Press, 1961–87), III, 545. On American applications of Jürgen Habermas's notion of the public sphere, see Mary P. Ryan, *Women in Public: Between Banners and Ballots, 1825–1880* (Baltimore: Johns Hopkins University Press, 1990), and David L. Waldstreicher, "The Making of American Nationalism: Celebrations and Political Culture, 1776–1820" (Ph.D. diss., Yale University, 1994).

4. Alexis de Tocqueville, *Democracy in America*, ed. J. P. Mayer and Max Lerner, trans. George Lawrence (2 vols.; London: Collins, 1968); Gordon S. Wood, *The Radicalism of the American Revolution* (New York: Alfred A. Knopf, 1992).

5. For political disruption, see Roy Franklin Nichols, *The Disruption of American Democracy* (New York: Macmillan, 1948).

6. Alan Tully, *Forming American Politics: Ideals, Interests, and Institutions in Colonial New York and Pennsylvania* (Baltimore: Johns Hopkins University Press, 1994).

7. See Edward Countryman, *A People in Revolution: The American Revolution and Political Society in New York, 1769–1790* (Baltimore: Johns Hopkins University Press, 1981), Chapters 7–9; J. R. Pole, *Political Representation in England and the Origins of the American Republic* (New York: St. Martin's Press, 1966), Part

III, pp. 169–384; and Richard Alan Ryerson, "Republican Theory and Partisan Reality in Revolutionary Pennsylvania: Toward a New View of the Constitutionalist Party," in Ronald Hoffman and Peter J. Albert, eds., *Sovereign States in an Age of Uncertainty* (Charlottesville: University Press of Virginia, 1981), pp. 95–133.

8. George Dangerfield, *The Era of Good Feelings* (New York: Harcourt, Brace, 1952); Robert V. Remini, *The Era of Good Feelings and the Age of Jackson: 1816–1841* (Arlington Heights, IL: AHM Publishing, 1979).

9. Van Buren to unidentified recipient, January 13, 1827, *Papers of Martin Van Buren*, microfilm edition (Washington, DC: Library of Congress, 1960), ser. 2, reel 7. Much of the argument that follows draws on Joel H. Silbey, *The American Political Nation, 1838–1893* (Stanford: Stanford University Press, 1991).

10. New York: Augustus M. Kelley Publishers, 1967 (orig. pub. 1867).

11. Joel H. Silbey, *The Shrine of Party: Congressional Voting Behavior, 1841–1852* (Pittsburgh: University of Pittsburgh Press, 1967) and *Ideology and Voting Behavior in the Age of Jackson* (Englewood Cliffs, NJ: Prentice-Hall, 1973).

12. For the best account, see Sean Wilentz, *Chants Democratic: New York City and the Rise of the American Working Class, 1788–1850* (New York: Oxford University Press, 1984), Chapter 5.

13. See Lee Benson, *The Concept of Jacksonian Democracy: New York as a Test Case* (Princeton: Princeton University Press, 1961).

14. Lincoln, Speech at Springfield, Illinois, June 16, 1838, in *The Collected Works of Abraham Lincoln*, ed. Roy P. Basler et al. (9 vols.; New Brunswick, NJ: Rutgers University Press, 1953), II, 461.

15. See William W. Freehling, *Prelude to Civil War: The Nullification Controversy in South Carolina, 1816–1836* (New York: Harper & Row, 1968 [orig. pub. 1965]).

16. See Peter H. Wood, *Black Majority: Negroes in Colonial South Carolina from 1670 Through the Stono Rebellion* (New York: W. W. Norton, 1975 [orig. pub. 1974) and "'Liberty Is Sweet': African-American Freedom Struggles in the Years Before White Independence," in Alfred F. Young, ed., *Beyond the American Revolution: Explorations in the History of American Radicalism* (De Kalb: Northern Illinois University Press, 1993), pp. 149–84.

17. Edmund L. Drago, *Initiative, Paternalism, and Race Relations: Charleston's Avery Normal Institute* (Athens: University of Georgia Press, 1990), Chapter 1.

18. For the conditions that bound free black Southerners, see Ira Berlin, *Slaves Without Masters: The Free Negro in the Antebellum South* (New York: Pantheon, 1974).

19. See Benjamin Quarles, *Black Abolitionists* (New York: Oxford University Press, 1969).

20. Sterling Stuckey, *Slave Culture: Nationalist Theory and the Foundations of Black America* (New York: Oxford University Press, 1987), Chapter 3.

21. See William S. McFeely, *Frederick Douglass* (New York: W. W. Norton, 1991), Chapters 6–9.

22. See Benjamin Quarles, *Black Abolitionists* (New York: Oxford University Press, 1969), and C. Peter Ripley et al., eds., *The Black Abolitionist Papers* (5 vols.; Chapel Hill: University of North Carolina Press, 1991).

23. Samuel P. Huntington, *Political Order in Changing Societies* (New Haven: Yale University Press, 1977), p. 277.

24. W. E. B. Du Bois, *The Souls of Black Folk* (New York: Alfred A. Knopf, 1993 [orig. pub. 1903]).

25. Herbert G. Gutman, *The Black Family in Slavery and Freedom, 1750–1925* (Oxford: Basil Blackwell, 1976), Chapters 3–4.

26. For three decades it has seemed to historians that colonization died as a serious proposal when Garrisonian abolitionism emerged, thanks to the early scholarship on antislavery of David Brion Davis. See his "The Emergence of Immediatism in British and American Antislavery Thought," *Mississippi Valley Historical Review* XLIX (1962), 209–30.

27. For the best short discussion in a vast literature on abolitionism, see James Brewer Stewart, *Holy Warriors: The Abolitionists and American Slavery* (New York: Hill and Wang, 1976).

28. See Ann Douglas, *The Feminization of American Culture* (New York: Alfred A. Knopf, 1977).

29. Gerda S. Lerner, *The Grimké Sisters from South Carolina: Rebels Against Slavery* (Boston: Houghton Mifflin, 1967).

30. Mary P. Ryan, *Cradle of the Middle Class: The Family in Oneida County, New York, 1790–1850* (New York: Cambridge University Press, 1981); Nancy A. Hewitt, *Women's Activism and Social Change: Rochester, New York, 1822–1872* (Ithaca: Cornell University Press, 1984).

31. Christine Stansell, *City of Women: Sex and Class in New York, 1789–1860* (Urbana: University of Illinois Press, 1987 [orig. pub. 1986]), Chapter 4.

32. See above, Chapter 7, and Anthony F. C. Wallace, *Rockdale: The Growth of an American Village in the Early Industrial Revolution* (New York: W. W. Norton, 1978).

33. Angelina Grimké, *Appeal to the Christian Women of the South* (New York: American Anti-Slavery Society, 1836).

34. Frederick Douglass, "What to the Slave Is the Fourth of July?: An Address Delivered in Rochester, New York, on 5 July, 1852," in John Blassingame, ed., *The Frederick Douglass Papers* (5 vols.; New Haven: Yale University Press, 1979–92), V, 359–88. For the issue of the continuing expansion of the idea of American freedom under pressure, see David Brion Davis, *Revolutions: Reflections on American Equality and Foreign Liberations* (Cambridge, MA: Harvard University Press, 1990). For court decisions before the *Dred Scott* case, see James H. Kettner, *The Development of American Citizenship, 1608–1870* (Chapel Hill: University of North Carolina Press, 1978), pp. 300–25.

35. I developed this reading independently, but modern scholarship supports it. See Jane P. Tompkins, *Sensational Designs: The Cultural Work of American Fiction,*

1790–1860 (New York: Oxford University Press, 1985), and Joan D. Hedrick, *Harriet Beecher Stowe: A Life* (New York: Oxford University Press, 1994).

36. Harriet Beecher Stowe, *Uncle Tom's Cabin, or, Life Among the Lowly*, ed. John William Ward (New York: New American Library, 1966 [orig. pub. 1852]); Frederick Douglass, *Narrative of the Life of Frederick Douglass, an American Slave*, ed. David W. Blight (New York: St. Martin's Press, 1993 [orig. pub. 1845]).

37. See Eric Foner, *Free Soil, Free Labor, Free Men: The Ideology of the Republican Party Before the Civil War* (New York: Oxford University Press, 1968).

38. Ibid.

39. See Wilentz, *Chants Democratic*, Chapter 9.

40. McFeely, *Frederick Douglass*, Chapters 11–12.

41. Douglass, Fifth of July Speech, *Douglass Papers*, V, p. 364; emphasis Douglass's.

42. See Holman Hamilton, *Prologue to Conflict: The Crisis and Compromise of 1850* (New York: W. W. Norton, 1966 [orig. pub. 1964]).

43. Bertram Wyatt-Brown, *Southern Honor: Ethics and Behavior in the Old South* (New York: Oxford University Press, 1982).

44. Drew Gilpin Faust, *James Henry Hammond and the Old South: A Design for Mastery* (Baton Rouge: Louisiana State University Press, 1982), pp. 228–29; Winthrop D. Jordan, *Tumult and Silence at Second Creek: An Inquiry into a Civil War Slave Conspiracy* (Baton Rouge: Louisiana State University Press, 1993), Chapter 1.

45. Larry Schweikart, *Banking in the American South from the Age of Jackson to Reconstruction* (Baton Rouge: Louisiana State University Press, 1987).

46. See Christopher Morris, *Becoming Southern: Vicksburg and Warren County, Mississippi, 1790–1860* (New York: Oxford University Press, 1995).

47. See John C. Miller, *The Wolf by the Ears: Thomas Jefferson and Slavery* (New York: Free Press, 1977); David Brion Davis, *The Problem of Slavery in the Age of Revolution, 1770–1823* (Ithaca: Cornell University Press, 1975), p. 184.

48. See H. G. Koenigsberger, "Composite States, Representative Institutions and the American Revolution," *Historical Research*, LXII (1989), pp. 135–53, and above, Chapter 2.

49. For the most recent study, see John Niven, *John C. Calhoun and the Price of Union: A Biography* (Baton Rouge: Louisiana State University Press, 1993).

50. *The Pro-Slavery Argument; as Maintained by the Most Distinguished Writers of the Southern States* (Charleston: Walker, Richards & Co., 1852); E. N. Elliott, *Cotton is king; and pro-slavery arguments: comprising the writings of Hammond, Harper, Christy, Stringfellow, Hodge, Bledsoe, and Cartwright on this important subject* (Augusta, GA: Pritchard, Abbott & Loomis, 1860); Texas State Legislature, House of Representatives, Committee on Slaves and Slavery, *A Report and Treatise on Slavery and the Slavery Agitation* (Austin: J. Marshall, 1857).

51. See Faust, *James Henry Hammond*, Chapter 16.

52. For third-party voting, see Silbey, *The American Political Nation*, Table 11.1, p. 210.

53. This argument is drawn from Joel H. Silbey, *The Transformation of American Politics, 1840–1860* (Englewood Cliffs, NJ: Prentice-Hall, 1967); David Brion Davis, *The Slave Power Conspiracy and the Paranoid Style* (Baton Rouge: Louisiana

State University Press, 1970); Robert William Fogel, *Without Consent or Contract: The Rise and Fall of American Slavery* (New York: W. W. Norton, 1989), Chapters 9–10; and Foner, *Free Soil, Free Labor, Free Men*.

10. "ENGAGED IN A GREAT CIVIL WAR"

1. Fragment, conjecturally dated August 1, 1858, in *The Collected Works of Abraham Lincoln*, ed. Roy P. Basler et al. (9 vols.; New Brunswick, NJ: Rutgers University Press, 1953), II, 532; emphasis Lincoln's.
2. See Kenneth M. Stampp, *And the War Came: The North and the Secession Crisis, 1860–1861* (Baton Rouge: Louisiana State University Press, 1950).
3. Speech at the Republican state convention, Springfield, Illinois, June 16, 1858, in *Works of Lincoln*, ed. Basler et al., II, 461; emphasis Lincoln's.
4. Quote from James Cowell and Thomas Manly, *The Interpreter* (2nd ed.; London, 1684, unpaginated; microfilm ed., Ann Arbor, MI: University Microfilms International, 1961).
5. "Address Before the Young Men's Lyceum of Springfield, Illinois," January 27, 1838, *Works of Lincoln*, ed. Basler et al, I, 108–15.
6. Eric Foner, *Free Soil, Free Labor, Free Men: The Ideology of the Republican Party Before the Civil War* (New York: Oxford University Press, 1968).
7. This phrase, of course, is drawn from the motto of Cornell University, New York State's land-grant institution. Ezra Cornell's full statement, which the university adopted, is "I would found an institution where any person can find instruction in any study." There is a saying among Cornellians that when asked whether the institution would not be flooded with students, he responded, "Not where I'm going to found it."
8. See Bruce Laurie, *Artisans into Workers: Labor in Nineteenth Century America* (New York: Hill and Wang, 1989). For working-class Republicanism (in the sense of the political party, not the revolutionary era belief) I am drawing on unpublished work by John Cumbler of the University of Louisville.
9. See Eric Foner, *Reconstruction: America's Unfinished Revolution, 1863–1877* (New York: Harper & Row, 1988).
10. For the Civil War the best is James M. McPherson, *Battle Cry of Freedom: The Civil War Era* (New York: Oxford University Press, 1988). Its counterpart for what followed is Foner, *Reconstruction*.
11. On Indians as soldiers, fighting for both sides, see W. Craig Gaines, *The Confederate Cherokees: John Drew's Regiment of Mounted Rifles* (Baton Rouge: Louisiana State University Press, 1989); William G. McLoughlin, *After the Trail of Tears: The Cherokees' Struggle for Sovereignty, 1839–1880* (Chapel Hill: University of North Carolina Press, 1993), Chapters 7–8; Lawrence M. Hauptman, *The Iroquois in the Civil War: From Battlefield to Reservation* (Syracuse: Syracuse University Press, 1993).
12. These figures are drawn from Maris A. Vinovskis, "Have Social Historians Lost the Civil War? Some Preliminary Demographic Speculations," in Vinovskis, ed., *Toward a Social History of the American Civil War: Exploratory Essays* (Cam-

bridge: Cambridge University Press, 1990), pp. 1–30, esp. pp. 3–7; Orville Vernon Burton, "Sectional Conflict, Civil War, and Reconstruction," in Mary Kupiec Cayton et al., eds., *Encyclopedia of American Social History* (3 vols.; New York: Charles Scribner's Sons, 1993), I, 131–55; and Ira Berlin et al., eds., *Freedom: A Documentary History of Emancipation, 1861–1867*, Series II: *The Black Military Experience* (Cambridge: Cambridge University Press, 1982). See also Ira Berlin et al., *Slaves No More: Three Essays on Emancipation and the Civil War* (Cambridge: Cambridge University Press, 1992).

13. Compare Robert S. Starobin, *Industrial Slavery in the Old South* (New York: Oxford University Press, 1970), and Daniel J. Walkowitz, *Worker City, Company Town: Iron- and Cotton-Worker Protest in Troy and Cohoes, New York, 1855–84* (Urbana: University of Illinois Press, 1978).

14. Jonathan M. Wiener, *The Origins of the New South: Alabama, 1860–1885* (Baton Rouge: Louisiana State University Press, 1978), Chapters 5–6, esp. pp. 162–63.

15. On the limits of southern banking, see Larry Schweikart, *Banking in the American South from the Age of Jackson to Reconstruction* (Baton Rouge: Louisiana State University Press, 1987).

16. Burton, "Sectional Conflict, Civil War, and Reconstruction," p. 133; Howard P. Chudacoff, *The Evolution of American Urban Society* (Englewood Cliffs, NJ: Prentice-Hall, 1975), Table 2, p. 56.

17. For essays on the problem of southern defeat, see Gabor S. Boritt, ed., *Why the Confederacy Lost* (New York: Oxford University Press, 1992).

18. James C. Cobb, *The Most Southern Place on Earth: The Mississippi Delta and the Roots of Regional Identity* (New York: Oxford University Press, 1992), p. 10.

19. Michael Wayne, *The Reshaping of Plantation Society: The Natchez District, 1860–1880* (Baton Rouge: Louisiana State University Press, 1983), pp. 37–38.

20. Winthrop D. Jordan, *Tumult and Silence at Second Creek: An Inquiry into a Civil War Slave Conspiracy* (Baton Rouge: Louisiana State University Press, 1993), pp. 179–80, 231, 284–302, quote at p. 162. The emphasis is Jordan's, in his reconstruction of the questions that are implied in the recorded statements of the Second Creek slaves to their interrogators.

21. See Richard B. McCaslin, *Tainted Breeze: The Great Hanging at Gainesville, Texas, 1862* (Baton Rouge: Louisiana State University Press, 1994), Appendices A and B, pp. 195–210.

22. This discussion is drawn from June Namias, *White Captives: Gender and Ethnicity on the American Frontier* (Chapel Hill: University of North Carolina Press, 1993), Chapter 6, quotes at pp. 228–29, 217.

23. For casualties, see Ernest A. McKay, *The Civil War and New York City* (Syracuse: Syracuse University Press, 1990), pp. 208–9; quotation from Ivor Bernstein, *The New York City Draft Riots: Their Significance for American Society and Politics in the Age of the Civil War* (New York: Oxford University Press, 1990), p. 3.

24. Bernstein, *New York Draft Riots*, pp. 26–36.

25. *Works of Lincoln*, ed. Basler et al., VIII, 332–33.

26. For the fullest defense of Lincoln in these terms, see James M. McPherson,

Abraham Lincoln and the Second American Revolution (New York: Oxford University Press, 1990), esp. Chapters 1–3.

27. See William S. McFeely, *Frederick Douglass* (New York: W. W. Norton, 1991), pp. 215–16; David W. Blight, *Frederick Douglass' Civil War: Keeping Faith in Jubilee* (Baton Rouge: Louisiana State University Press, 1989), Chapter 5.

28. The phrasing "of right" comes at the end of the Declaration of Independence, "that these United Colonies are and of right ought to be free and independent states." The usage seems antiquated, but it implies a stronger case, measured against a standard of absolute correctness, than the phrase "a right" can convey.

29. Blight, *Douglass' Civil War*, pp. 50–58; McFeeley, *Douglass*, pp. 208–14.

30. "The Issue Plainly Stated" (September 5, 1859); Thomas Hamilton, "Breaking into a State" (November 19, 1859); John A. Copeland, Jr., to John A. Copeland, Sr., and Delilah Copeland, November 26, 1859; Resolutions of the Second Baptist Church, Detroit, Michigan, December 2, 1859; James McCune Smith to Gerrit Smith, August 22, 1861 (emphasis in the original): *The Black Abolitionist Papers*, ed. C. Peter Ripley et al. (5 vols.; Chapel Hill: University of North Carolina Press, 1985–92), V, pp. 30–33, 14–42, 43–45, 51–53, 113–16. (Emphasis in the original)

31. Quoted in Charles Joyner, *Down by the Riverside: A South Carolina Slave Community* (Urbana: University of Illinois Press, 1984), p. 230.

32. Butler to Lieutenant General Scott, May 27, 1861, *Freedom: A Documentary History of Emancipation, 1861–1876*, Series I, Vol. I: *The Destruction of Slavery*, ed. Ira Berlin et al. (Cambridge: Cambridge University Press, 1985), pp. 71–72, 77. Butler first used the term "contraband of war" in July 1861. Editorial note 5, ibid., p. 61.

33. Editorial Comment, ibid., p. 61; Butler to Secretary of War Simon Cameron, July 30, 1861, quoted in ibid., pp. 74–75; Jas. W. Cook to Hon. J. M. Mason, August 27, 1861, ibid., p. 77.

34. Berlin et al., *Slaves No More*, pp. 22–28, quotes from p. 25; Willie Lee Rose, *Rehearsal for Reconstruction: The Port Royal Experiment* (New York: Random House, 1964).

35. Berlin et al., *The Destruction of Slavery*, pp. 680–82.

36. Jordan, *Tumult and Silence*, p. 162.

37. Figures drawn from U.S. Department of Commerce, *Historical Statistics of the United States, 1789–1945* (Washington, DC: Government Printing Office, 1949), Series B, 40–47, 48–71, p. 27.

38. Berlin et al., *The Black Military Experience*, pp. 279, 305–7, 518.

39. H. W. Halleck to Major General U.S. Grant, March 31, 1863, in Berlin et al., *The Black Military Experience*, pp. 143–44; "Statements of an Anonymous New Orleans Black," September (?) 1863, ibid., pp. 153–57; Mary Duncan to General Thomas, June 2, 1863, ibid., pp. 146–48.

40. Lorenzo Thomas to Hon. Edwin M. Stanton, November 7, 1864, ibid., pp. 168–72.

41. William S. McFeely, *Grant: A Biography* (New York: W. W. Norton, 1981), pp. 178, 179, 238–40, 356–59.

42. A narrative history of what black troops did remains to be written. The present fullest account is Berlin et al., *The Black Military Experience*, Chapter 11.

43. See ibid., Chapter 12.

44. The equal-pay issue is the subject of ibid., Chapter 7. See particularly the records of Walker's trial and execution, pp. 391–94; Corporal James Henry Gooding to Abraham Lincoln, September 28, 1863, pp. 385–86; and Col. E. N. Hallowell to Governor John A. Andrew of Massachusetts, November 23, 1863, p. 387.

11. IN ONE, MANY

1. Ira Berlin et al., eds., *Freedom: A Documentary History of Emancipation, 1861–1867*, Series I, Vol. III: *The Wartime Genesis of Free Labor: The Lower South* (Cambridge: Cambridge University Press, 1990), p. 77.

2. My argument about the emergence of a modern, active, powerful state is derived from David Montgomery, *Beyond Equality: Labor and the Radical Republicans, 1862–1872* (New York: Vintage Books, 1972 [orig. pub. 1968]).

3. June Namias, *White Captives: Gender and Ethnicity on the American Frontier* (Chapel Hill: University of North Carolina Press, 1993), Chapter 6; W. Craig Gaines, *The Confederate Cherokees: John Drew's Regiment of Mounted Rifles* (Baton Rouge: Louisiana State University Press, 1989); William G. McLoughlin, *After the Trail of Tears: The Cherokees' Struggle for Sovereignty, 1839–1880* (Chapel Hill: University of North Carolina Press, 1993), Chapters 7–8; Lawrence M. Hauptman, *The Iroquois in the Civil War: From Battlefield to Reservation* (Syracuse: Syracuse University Press, 1993).

4. See Montgomery, *Beyond Equality*; Alan Dawley, *Class and Community: The Industrial Revolution in Lynn* (Cambridge, MA: Harvard University Press, 1976); Anthony F. C. Wallace, *Rockdale: The Growth of an American Village During the Early Industrial Revolution* (New York: W. W. Norton, 1978), Chapter 9.

5. See Leon F. Litwack, *Been in the Storm So Long: The Aftermath of Slavery* (New York: Alfred A. Knopf, 1969), Chapter 6.

6. The fullest discussion is Herbert G. Gutman, *The Black Family in Slavery and Freedom, 1750–1925* (Oxford: Basil Blackwell, 1976), Chapter 9; Jane Barnwell quoted in ibid., p. 422; emphasis in the original.

7. For one instance, see Samuel H. Terry to Salmon P. Chase, December 18, 1861, in Berlin et al., *The Wartime Genesis of Free Labor: The Lower South*, pp. 119–21.

8. See particularly Charles Joyner, *Down by the Riverside: A South Carolina Slave Community* (Urbana: University of Illinois Press, 1984), Chapter 8; compare also John Scott Strickland, "Traditional Culture and Moral Economy: Social and Economic Change in the South Carolina Low Country, 1865–1910," and Steven Hahn, "The 'Unmaking' of the Southern Yeomanry: The Transformation of the Georgia Upcountry, 1860–1890," in Steven Hahn and Jonathan Prude, eds., *The Countryside in the Age of Capitalist Transformation: Essays in the Social History*

of Rural America (Chapel Hill: University of North Carolina Press, 1985), pp. 141–78, 179–204.

9. "Preempted Land on the J. F. Chaplain Place" (diagram, January 25, 1864); J. M. Fairfield to Dr. Wm. H. Brisbane, February 15, 1864; Special Field Orders No. 15, January 15, 1865, Berlin et al., *Wartime Genesis of Free Labor: The Lower South*, pp. 289–91, 338–40; for developments in the Sea Islands, see Willie Lee Rose, *Rehearsal for Reconstruction: The Port Royal Experiment* (New York: Random House, 1964); Jefferson to James Madison, October 28, 1785, in Jefferson, *Writings*, ed. Merrill D. Peterson (New York: Viking Press, 1984), quote at p. 842.

10. See particularly Eric Foner, *Reconstruction: America's Unfinished Revolution, 1863–1877* (New York: Harper & Row, 1988).

11. Edward L. Ayers, *The Promise of the New South: Life After Reconstruction* (New York: Oxford University Press, 1992); C. Vann Woodward, *Origins of the New South, 1877–1913* (Baton Rouge: Louisiana State University Press, 1951).

12. On the Supreme Court's role in undercutting the Reconstruction amendments, see Foner, *Reconstruction*, Chapter 11. For the eventual reversal of what the Court did, see Richard Kluger, *Simple Justice: The History of Brown v. Board of Education and Black America's Struggle for Equality* (New York: Alfred A. Knopf, 1976), and Taylor Branch, *Parting the Waters: America in the King Years, 1954–63* (New York: Simon and Schuster, 1988).

13. Orville Vernon Burton, *In My Father's House There Are Many Mansions: Family and Community in Edgefield, South Carolina* (Chapel Hill: University of North Carolina Press, 1985), pp. 33–34; Jacquelyn Dowd Hall et al., *Like a Family: The Making of a Southern Cotton Mill World* (Chapel Hill: University of North Carolina Press, 1987), p. 3; Ayers, *Promise of the New South*, p. 111.

14. Robert L. Brandfon, *Cotton Kingdom of the New South* (Cambridge, MA.: Harvard University Press, 1967); James C. Cobb, *The Most Southern Place on Earth: The Mississippi Delta and the Roots of Regional Identity* (New York: Oxford University Press, 1992), Chapter 4.

15. Jonathan M. Wiener, *Social Origins of the New South, 1860–1885* (Baton Rouge: Louisiana State University Press, 1978), Chapter 6, quotes at pp. 168, 182; Ayers, *Promise of the New South*, p. 105.

16. What follows will draw its interpretive structure from Roger L. Ransom and Richard Sutch, *One Kind of Freedom: The Economic Consequences of Emancipation* (Cambridge: Cambridge University Press, 1977). See also Maris Vinovskis, ed., *Toward a Social History of the American Civil War: Exploratory Essays* (Cambridge: Cambridge University Press, 1990).

17. The absence of an emphasis upon the African imprint on eighteenth-century Virginia's land mars Rhys Isaac's otherwise splendid interpretation of the patterns Virginians made. See Isaac, *The Transformation of Virginia, 1740–1790* (Chapel Hill: University of North Carolina Press, 1982), pp. 18–42. My emphasis on the African impact is drawn from several sources, including John W. Blassingame, *The Slave Community: Plantation Life in the Antebellum South* (New York: Oxford University Press, 1979); Charles Joyner, *Down by the Riverside: A*

South Carolina Slave Community (Urbana: University of Illinois Press, 1984); and conversations with Patricia Galloway of the Mississippi Department of Archives and History, Jackson.

18. James Agee and Walker Evans, *Let Us Now Praise Famous Men: Three Tenant Families* (Boston: Houghton Mifflin, 1969 [orig. pub. 1941]); John Steinbeck, *The Grapes of Wrath* (New York: Viking Press, 1939).

19. See Daniel W. Crofts, *Old Southampton: Politics and Society in a Virginia County, 1834–1869* (Charlottesville: University Press of Virginia, 1992), pp. 48–49, 279–82.

20. Joseph P. Reidy, *From Slavery to Agrarian Capitalism in the Cotton Plantation South* (Chapel Hill: University of North Carolina Press, 1992), Chapters 1–3 and 9, quotes at pp. 223, 225, 226; for the 1759 law, see Steven Hahn, *The Roots of Southern Populism: Yeoman Farmers and the Transformation of the Georgia Upcountry, 1850–1890* (New York: Oxford University Press, 1983), p. 60.

21. See Hahn, *Roots of Southern Populism*, Chapters 2 and 4. Crop data drawn from Tables 4.2, p. 147, and 4.3, p. 150. Compare Hahn's conclusions regarding up-country transformation with Reidy, *From Slavery to Agrarian Capitalism*, p. 9.

22. Wiener, *Social Origins of the New South*, Chapters 2–4, quotes at pp. 63, 69, 102, 103, 41.

23. Michael Wayne, *The Reshaping of Plantation Society: The Natchez District, 1860–1880* (Baton Rouge: Louisiana State University Press, 1983), Chapters 3–6, quote at p. 61. On price markups, compare ibid., Table 23, p. 189, with Ransom and Sutch, *One Kind of Freedom*, Appendix D, pp. 237–43. For tenant turnover, see Wayne, *Reshaping of Plantation Society*, Appendix II, pp. 208–9.

24. See Edward Countryman, "The Price of Cotton: The Human Cost of Slavery in Mid-Nineteenth Century Mississippi" (paper presented at the 1992 symposium of the Milan, Italy, Group on Early United States History).

25. See Kenneth Marvin Hamilton, *Black Towns and Profit: Promotion and Development in the Trans-Appalachian West, 1877–1915* (Urbana: University of Illinois Press, 1991), and Nell Irvin Painter, *Exodusters: Black Migration to Kansas After Reconstruction* (Lawrence: University Press of Kansas, 1986 [orig. pub. 1976]).

26. The two best modern accounts of the postbellum delta are Brandfon, *Cotton Kingdom of the New South*, which is primarily concerned with economic transformation and pays little attention to either former slaves or new black migrants, and Cobb, *Most Southern Place on Earth*, which deals with Reconstruction in some detail but only as part of a synoptic account of the development of regional identity.

27. Cobb, *Most Southern Place on Earth*, Chapter 4, quotes at pp. 68, 71.

28. This point was made to me by a major student of the Choctaws, Patricia Galloway, during conversations in Jackson, Mississippi, in November 1992. Faulkner hints at the issue by the importance he gives to Indian figures in his accounts of delta hunting, most notably his classic novella "The Bear."

29. Dawley, *Class and Community*, pp. 100–2; Daniel J. Walkowitz, *Worker City, Company Town: Iron- and Cotton-Worker Protest in Troy and Cohoes, New York,*

1855–84 (Urbana: University of Illinois Press, 1981 [orig. pub. 1978]), p. 94; William S. McFeely, *Grant: A Biography* (New York: W. W. Norton, 1981), p. 382; Roy Rosenzweig, *Eight Hours for What We Will: Workers & Leisure in an Industrial City, 1870–1920* (Cambridge: Cambridge University Press, 1983).

30. Montgomery, *Beyond Equality*, pp. 75–76, 90, 114, 265, 360–66; on the Boston elite, see the excellent study by Ronald Story, *Harvard and the Boston Upper Class: The Forging of an Aristocracy, 1800–1870* (Middletown, CT: Wesleyan University Press, 1980).

31. Dawley, *Class and Community*, pp. 124–27, 188, 206; Walkowitz, *Worker City, Company Town*, pp. 233–37.

32. Compare the title essay in Herbert G. Gutman, *Work, Culture, and Society in Industrializing America* (Oxford: Basil Blackwell, 1978), pp. 3–78, with E. P. Thompson, *The Making of the English Working Class* (New York: Vintage Books, 1966 [orig. pub. 1963]).

33. Rosenzweig, *Eight Hours for What We Will*. See also Sam Bass Warner, *The Private City: Philadelphia in Three Periods of Its Growth* (Philadelphia: University of Pennsylvania Press, 1968), Part II, and Elizabeth Blackmar and Roy Rosenzweig, *The Park and the People: A History of Central Park* (Ithaca: Cornell University Press, 1992).

34. See John T. Cumbler, *A Social History of Economic Decline: Business, Politics, and Work in Trenton* (New Brunswick, NJ: Rutgers University Press, 1989).

35. Kathryn Kish Sklar, *Catharine Beecher: A Study in American Domesticity* (New York: W. W. Norton, 1976 [orig. pub. 1973]).

36. Mary P. Ryan, *Women in Public: Between Banners and Ballots, 1825–1880* (Baltimore: Johns Hopkins University Press, 1990), pp. 3–4, 141–52; Catherine Clinton, *The Other Civil War: American Women in the Nineteenth Century* (New York: Hill and Wang, 1984), pp. 81–89.

37. See particularly Suzanne Lebsock, *The Free Women of Petersburg: Status and Culture in a Southern Town, 1784–1860* (New York: W. W. Norton, 1985 [orig. pub. 1984]). Christopher Morris, *Becoming Southern: Vicksburg and Warren County, Mississippi 1790–1860* (New York: Oxford University Press, 1995) addresses the same theme.

38. This is one of the major arguments of Ryan, *Women in Public*.

39. My reference is to David Brion Davis, *The Problem of Slavery in the Age of Revolution, 1770–1823* (Ithaca: Cornell University Press, 1975), Chapter 30, "The Perishability of Revolutionary Time," pp. 306–26.

40. Ellen Carol DuBois, *Feminism and Suffrage: The Emergence of an Independent Women's Movement in America, 1848–1869* (Ithaca: Cornell University Press, 1978); for Stanton and Douglass, see William S. McFeely, *Frederick Douglass* (New York: W. W. Norton, 1991), pp. 382–83.

41. Gutman, *Black Family in Slavery and Freedom*, pp. 386–87; Jacqueline Jones, *Labor of Love, Labor of Sorrow: Black Women, Work, and the Family from Slavery to the Present* (New York: Basic Books, 1985), pp. 45–46, 82, and passim.

42. This argument is derived in good part from Mary H. Blewett, *Men, Women, and Work: Class, Gender, and Protest in the New England Shoe Industry, 1780–*

1910 (Urbana: University of Illinois Press, 1988). See also Susan Porter Benson, *Counter Cultures: Saleswomen, Managers, and Customers in American Department Stores, 1890–1940* (Urbana: University of Illinois Press, 1986.

43. Compare (for the record of white cultural remembering) Richard Slotkin, *The Fatal Environment: The Myth of the Frontier in the Age of Industrialization, 1800–1890* (New York: Atheneum, 1985) and *Gunfighter Nation: The Myth of the Frontier in Twentieth-Century America* (New York: Atheneum, 1992) with (for the Indian memories) Roxanne Dunbar Ortiz, *The Great Sioux Nation: Sitting in Judgment on America* (New York: American Treaty Council Information Center, 1977), and Peter John Powell, *People of the Sacred Mountain: A History of the Northern Cheyenne Chiefs and Warrior Societies, 1830–1879* (2 vols.; New York: Harper & Row, 1981).

CODA: THE VEXED, UNANSWERED QUESTION

1. R. M. Devens, *Our First Century: Being a Popular Descriptive Portraiture of the One Hundred Great and Memorable Events in the History of Our Country, Political, Military, Mechanical, Social, Scientific and Commercial: Embracing also Delineations of all the Great Historic Characters Celebrated in the Annals of the Republic; Men of Heroism, Statesmanship, Genius, Oratory, Adventure and Philanthropy* (Springfield, MA: C. A. Nichols, 1878). My thanks to Evonne von Heussen-Countryman for finding this in an English antique store and surprising me with it.

2. Walt Whitman, *Leaves of Grass,* ed. Gay Wilson Allen (New York: Signet, 1955 [orig. pub. 1881]), p. 96.

3. William McFeely, *Frederick Douglass* (New York: W. W. Norton, 1991), pp. 288–89.

4. Eric Foner, *Reconstruction: America's Unfinished Revolution* (New York: Harper & Row, 1988), p. 571.

5. For Shelton, see William G. McLoughlin, *After the Trail of Tears: The Cherokees' Struggle for Sovereignty, 1839–1880* (Chapel Hill: University of North Carolina Press, 1993), pp. 378–80. For Stand Watie, see ibid., passim, esp. pp. 181–82, 210–16. For Indians and Africans, see Jack D. Forbes, *Africans and Native Americans: The Language of Race and the Evolution of Red-Black Peoples* (Urbana: University of Illinois Press, 1993); and three volumes by Daniel D. Littlefield: *Africans and Creeks: From the Colonial Period to the Civil War* (Westport, CT: Greenwood Press, 1979); *Africans and Seminoles: From Removal to Emancipation* (Westport, CT: Greenwood Press, 1977); and *The Cherokee Freedmen: From Emancipation to American Citizenship* (Westport, CT: Greenwood Press, 1978).

6. Bertram Wyatt-Brown, *Southern Honor: Ethics and Behavior in the Old South* (New York: Oxford University Press, 1982), pp. 311–12.

7. R. Halliburton, Jr., "Chief Greenwood Leflore and His Malmaison Plantation," in Samuel J. Wells and Roseanna Tubby, eds., *After Removal: the Choctaw in Mississippi* (Jackson: University Press of Mississippi, 1986), pp. 56–63.

8. See the three volumes by Littlefield, above, in note 5, and Angie Debo, *The*

Rise and Fall of the Choctaw Republic (Norman: University of Oklahoma Press, 1961 [orig. pub. 1934]), pp. 101–9.

9. Quoted in McLoughlin, *After the Trail of Tears*, p. 379.

10. Compare the arguments in Forbes, *Africans and Native Americans*, and Winthrop D. Jordan, *White Over Black: American Attitudes Toward the Negro, 1550–1812* (Chapel Hill: University of North Carolina Press, 1968).

11. See David W. Penney, *Art of the American Indian Frontier: The Chandler-Pohrt Collection* (Seattle: University of Washington Press, 1992).

12. See the trilogy by Richard Slotkin: *Regeneration Through Violence: The Mythology of the American Frontier, 1600–1860* (Middletown, CT: Wesleyan University Press, 1973); *The Fatal Environment: The Myth of the Frontier in the Age of Industrialization, 1800–1890* (New York: Atheneum, 1985); and *Gunfighter Nation: The Myth of the Frontier in Twentieth-Century America* (New York: Atheneum, 1992).

INDEX

Abolition Army, 208, 209, 210
abolitionists, 179, 180, 182–83, 207
Adams, John, 44, 60–61, 68, 153, 176
Adams, John Quincy, 158, 159, 174, 176, 190, 216
Africans: and collision of histories in America, 4–6; differences among, 4–5, 27; and knowledge of rice production, 10–11; *see also* slavery
Alabama: in aftermath of Civil War, 226–27; land issues, 77, 92, 95; Mobile, 102, 210–11; numbers of slaves in, 102, 103; steel industry in, 220
Albany, New York, 120–21
Algonquian speakers: claims to "middle ground" land, 59, 78; as forced laborers, 8; population of, 21
Alien and Sedition Laws, 152
Allen, Ethan, 80
Alley, John B., 197, 229, 230
Allston, Robert F.W., 137
America: colonial difference from England, 28, 31–32; colonial resemblance to Europe, 28, 29, 31, 40–41; coming of Europeans to, 3–6; differences among citizenry, 73–76; equality paradox, 36, 71, 72–73, 79, 150–51; law in, 164–69; naming of, 4; national economy, 68–70;

and westward expansion, 66–67, 89–91, 97, 98–99, 101, 132–35
American Colonization Society, 181
American Fur Company, 106
American Party, 191
American Revolution: aftermath, 66–67; causes of, 45–49; choice of independence vs. monarchy, 70; conduct of, 68–69; economic impact of, 68–70; and loyalists, 61, 63–65, 66; and Natives, 57–59
Amherst, Jeffrey, 57
Andover, Massachusetts, 13
Andros, Edmund, 54
Anthony, Susan B., 182, 183, 233
Arapahos, 239
Arkansas, 101, 103, 159
Articles of Confederation, 73, 77, 164
Astor, John Jacob, 106
Atlantic slave trade: cessation of, 67; numbers of slaves, 102–3; and Virginia, 8–10
Attucks, Crispus, 53

Bacon's Rebellion, 9, 15
Bank of the United States, 111
Barbados: slaves from, 10
Barnwell, Jane, 217
Bartlett, Mary, 63
Bautista de Anza, Juan, 90
Beecher, Catherine, 109, 232

283

railroads: vs. canals, 116–17; and land grants, 100, 101, 216; towns along, 123

Ramírez, Francisco, 149

Rappahannocks: as forced laborers, 8

Reconstruction era, 217–32

Reed, Esther De Berdt, 63

Reeve, Tapping, 166

Rensselaer Polytechnic Institute, 166

Republican Party, 186, 191, 196–97, 203, 207, 229–30

Revere, Paul, 38, 113

revolts: by Natives, 155–60; by slaves, 154–55, 177

Revolutionary War, see American Revolution

Rhode Island: and land grants, 101; Pawtucket, 112, 113; Providence, 120

rice crop: and slavery, 10–12, 18, 136–37; in South Carolina, 10–12, 18, 136–37

Richardson, Ebenezer, 52

Riggs, Stephen, 202

Rittenhouse, David, 56

Roach, Benjamin, 95, 96

Rochester, New York, 122; and Erie Canal, 116

Rockdale, Pennsylvania, 142, 143–44, 183

Rome, New York, 115, 116, 122

Rowlandson, Mary, 36

Rush, Benjamin, 56

Sacagawea, 89

St. Clair, Arthur, 155

St. John de Crèvecoeur, Hector, 133

salt cod, 29

San Francisco, 123, 127–28

Santa Ana, 178

Santa Fe, 90

Schenectady, New York: and Erie Canal, 116

Schiller, Johann, 206

Schuyler, Philip, 93, 94, 96

Scott, Dred, 161, 162, 192

Scott, Walter, 192

Scott, Winfield, 200

Sea Islands, 18, 209, 218

Sedition Act, 153

Seminoles: and land issues, 78, 131, 157

Seneca Falls conference, 183, 184, 197

Senecas, 19, 130; and land issues, 76

servants, white, 6–7

settlers, 94, 95; and common law, 99; vs. Henry Knox, 96–97, 98; and Native culture, 132–33; need for community, 134–35; pre-European, 23, 26; westward migration after American Revolution, 66–67, 97, 98–99

sharecropping, 221, 222, 224, 228

Shawnees, 107, 131, 132, 157

Shays's Rebellion, 75, 154

Shelton, Ann Bell, 239–40

Sherman, William Tecumseh, 212, 218

shivaree, 133, 145

Shoshonis, 89–90

sickle-cell anemia, 11

Sioux Indians, 202, 239

Sitting Bull, 239

Slater, Samuel, 111–12

slavery: abolition of, 61–62, 179, 180, 182–83, 207; in aftermath of Civil War, 217–20; case of James Somerset, 48–49; as cause of Civil War, 176–77, 205; during Civil War, 207–9; communities of slaves, 17–18, 44, 136–37, 178; conditions of slaves, 17–18; and Constitution, 83–84; and cotton, 104, 105, 137–39; defined by Southerners as positive, 189; departures after American Revolution, 66; as divisive issue, 147; and Dred Scott decision, 161–62, 164, 169; and emancipation, 205, 206; forced migration of slaves, 102–5; importation of slaves to America, 8–10, 27, 67, 102–3; in-